THE CONSTITUTION OF EUROPE

"DO THE NEW CLOTHES HAVE AN EMPEROR?"
AND OTHER ESSAYS
ON EUROPEAN INTEGRATION

In *The constitution of Europe*, J. H. H. Weiler presents a revised and supplemented collection of essays written over the last ten years on issues related to the law, the politics and the politics of the law of European integration. The book includes his widely discussed essay, *The transformation of Europe*, with a new afterword, as well as his 1997 London School of Economics Jean Monnet Lecture, *To be a European citizen: Eros and civilization*. The book is bound to provoke Europhiles and Euroskeptics alike. Weiler deals critically with both the ends and the means of European integration. Although individuals as legal consumers have been hugely empowered by Community law, he writes, there has been a corresponding disempowerment in their status as citizens. And despite its notable success in attaining its historical objectives of consolidating post-war peace and contributing to a new-found European prosperity, today's Union, bereft of its original transcendent ideals, risks becoming the perfect incarnation of bread-and-circus *fin-de-siècle* politics.

J. H. H. Weiler is Manley Hudson Professor of Law and Jean Monnet Chair at Harvard University and Co-Director of the Academy of European Law at the European University Institute, Florence.

THE
CONSTITUTION
OF EUROPE

"DO THE NEW CLOTHES HAVE
AN EMPEROR?"
AND OTHER ESSAYS
ON EUROPEAN INTEGRATION

J. H. H. WEILER

CAMBRIDGE
UNIVERSITY PRESS

PUBLISHED BY THE PRESS SYNDICATE OF THE UNIVERSITY OF CAMBRIDGE
The Pitt Building, Trumpington Street, Cambridge, United Kingdom

CAMBRIDGE UNIVERSITY PRESS
The Edinburgh Building, Cambridge CB2 2RU, UK   http://www.cup.cam.ac.uk
40 West 20th Street, New York, NY 10011–4211, USA   http://www.cup.org
10 Stamford Road, Oakleigh, Melbourne 3166, Australia
Ruiz de Alarcón 13, 28014 Madrid, Spain

First published 1999
Reprinted 1999

Printed in the United Kingdom at the University Press, Cambridge

Typeset in Bembo 10.5/12.5pt [CE]

A catalogue record for this book is available from the British Library

Library of Congress Cataloguing in Publication data
Weiler, Joseph, 1951–
The constitution of Europe: "Do the new clothes have an emperor?" and other
essays on European integration / by J. H. H. Weiler.
p.   cm.
Includes index.
ISBN 0 521 58473 6 (hb) – ISBN 0 521 58567 8 (pbk)
1. Constitutional law – European Union countries. 2. European
Union countries – Economic integration.   I. Title.
KJE5076.W45   1999
341.7′5′0614 – dc21   99–6555   CIP

ISBN 0 521 58473 6 hardback
ISBN 0 521 58567 8 paperback

CONTENTS

Contents

Contents

PREFACE

This volume is about the *constitution of Europe,* a deliciously rich phrase. Consider some of the multiple dictionary definitions of the word "constitution," all of which are relevant to our inquiry.

1. The *way in which a thing is composed or made up; makeup; composition.* The same can be asked of Europe: in what way or ways is the European Union composed? What is its makeup?

2. The *act or process of constituting; establishment.* How the Community and Union were constituted, the dynamic process of their evolution is as interesting and revealing as any static analysis of Europe in its current shape.

3. The *physical character of the body as to strength, health, etc.* In Victorian novels one would regularly read about a Prudence or a Roderick who suffered from a weak constitution, eventually dying from consumption. Does Europe enjoy a strong constitution? Will it die from consumption, or, perhaps, lack of it?

4. The *system of fundamental principles according to which a nation, state, corporation, or the like, is governed.* Europe falls under "the like" since it is neither a nation nor a State. Yet it is certainly governed in accordance with a system of fundamental principles. What are these? And, if the Union is neither a nation, nor a State nor, I would add, a normal international organization, what is it? Here, too, there is a lot of explaining to do.

5. The *document embodying these principles.* Europe has so many of these documents: the Treaties of Paris, of Rome, of Maastricht, even the exquisitely named Single European Act. And now we have yet a new text, the Treaty of Amsterdam. The European Parliament once had plans for a formal constitution for Europe; and the European Court has referred to the existing treaties as the "basic constitutional charter" of the Community! Was that some sort of judicial license or is the grand appellation justified?

For the last ten years or so I have been exploring these various meanings in a series of essays and articles published wherever my nomadic life has taken me in Europe and America. Believing, as we academics are prone to, that the whole (especially if it is our own work) can be more than the sum of its parts, these articles were to become chapters of a would-be monograph. I continue to believe that this whole is more than the sum of its parts. But instead of a monograph I decided to keep the original format of essay and article, albeit edited, revised and, where necessary, updated.

There are several reasons for my choice of which, I assure you, laziness is not one. Indeed, sometimes I wish that more of my colleagues would do the same. Think of the number of scholarly monographs in ever-increasing fields published each year. As book-review editor of the *European Journal of International Law* and the *European Law Journal*, I bear daily witness to the avalanche. How many are actually read rather than "skimmed"? And by how many readers, other than hapless doctoral students or conscientious book reviewers?

I suspect my own experience cannot be all that unique: I follow the publicity for new books. I read the book reviews with some attention. My interest is piqued. I may scribble a note to the embarrassingly generous library of Harvard Law School. If the book is moderately priced, I may even order my own copy. At that point I am always full of the best of intentions. The book arrives. I handle it: I like the feel and smell of a new book. I read the dust-jacket blurb, consult the table of contents, peruse the index (was I cited?), read the preface, as you, the reader, are doing now, and secretly hope that there is a chapter entitled "Conclusions." Of course at that very moment I am too busy to leave whatever else I am doing in order to read the new book. So I put it aside. Time passes. The shiny dust-jacket begins, visibly, to serve its purpose. All too often, that is the end. Like Pharaoh, I harden my heart and consign the book to my shelves or dispatch it back to the library. Sure, in some cases I do get to those "Conclusions" and I might even delve into one or two chapters which interest me most. Frequently that is not satisfactory since, as should be the case in a good monograph, the various chapters as well as the conclusions build on the preceding ones and presuppose that they have been read, as they should have been. It is this fate that I am trying to avoid!

Let me, then, first spell out my expectations and my hopes, and go on to explain briefly how I have arranged the book so as to realize them.

1. I expect that no one will read all the essays and articles in this book – not even my own doctoral students. But I do hope that many more will read some of its essays and articles than would be the case if this were a scholarly monograph of equal size.

2. I expect that even those who may be familiar with some of my articles

and essays will find quite a few in this collection which will be new to them. Some were published in rather obscure places. Where appropriate, I have done some editing and updating. Older essays are included only when I felt that their message was still fresh and relevant to the current concerns of European integration and disintegration.

3. I very much hope that my readers will consist not only of European public-law specialists but also of economists, political scientists, and perhaps even the "general reader" interested in European integration. Accessibility to a broad spectrum of readers was one of my principal selection criteria.

In a broad sense most of these essays and articles can be termed "legal." But if the odor of dusty law books already comes to your nose, fear not. As I explain in one of the essays at greater length, the "law and . . ." approach, be it law and economics, law and culture, law and society – that is, law in context – has become *de rigueur*, the new orthodoxy. Dutifully, I shall try to analyze the Community and Union constitutional order with particular regard to their living political matrix, and with the deliberate aim of demystifying legal discourse. Indeed, maybe we should stop speaking about the "law and . . ." approach and speak instead of a "law without . . ." approach, the conceit being that there cannot be a meaningful legal discourse which is oblivious to economics, politics, and all the rest. Still, even though I shall look at relationships of legal structure and political process, at law and power, my approach is not fully holistic – it is far more modest. In the story that these essays tell, de Gaulle and Thatcher, the economic expansion of the 1960s, the oil crisis of the 1970s, the fall of the Berlin Wall of the late 1980s, and all like elements of the political history of the epoch play modest parts.

If not that, then what? I can try and capture at least some of the flavour. The constant themes you will find treated are the classical themes of constitutionalism in a non–unitary (one has to avoid the word "federal") system: the relationship between Community (and Union) its Member States and the individual. Or should I have written the Member States, their Community and the individual? Or, perhaps, individuals, their States and their Community? There you have it; it is a lot about power but the permutations of empowerment in European integration are rarely obvious and always fascinating. Thus, to give one well-discussed example, the relationship between Community and Member States is not necessarily "zero sum." The strengthening of the Community has not always meant the weakening of the Member States. Interestingly, it has frequently meant the opposite. At least it has meant, even more interestingly, the strengthening of governments, the executive branch, at the expense of, say, national legislatures. You will read how the interaction of legal structure and political process explains this statal empowerment, thereby enriching other similar explanations offered by historians and international-relations experts, such as Milward and Hoffmann, with whom I feel an intellectual affinity. At the same time, I do not share the view that the Community and European integration can be explained as no more than a design of which the Member States remain masters and beneficiaries. That is what they may have intended, but in many respects the Community has become a *golem* which in significant ways has ensnared its creators.

Individuals, too, are said to have been empowered by Community law – a much touted and celebrated fact. They have. But, I argue in some of the essays, the individual empowerment as a legal consumer goes hand in hand with his or her disempowerment as a political citizen. These complex relationships will be looked at in general terms but also in different contexts such as human rights, the Community and Union as an actor in the international arena and others. I examine, too, the possible values and ideals which the Union structure and process may represent. In this way, each article and essay will pour light on a different dimension of these relationships. Hopefully, by reading a few, the richness and complexity of European constitutionalism will emerge in a way which no single essay could capture alone. That, perhaps, is the sense in which the whole is greater than its parts.

The essays span a period of ten years or so. Comparing the early and the late will give a sense of the ways in which the constitution of Europe (and my understanding of it) have evolved. The "new constitutionalism" as found, for example, in chapter 6, "The reformation of European constitutionalism," has several facets. It is less concerned to trace, and explain, the emergence of a constitutional relationship between Community and Member States and more concerned to explore the normative foundations of that development. Another aspect of this "new constitutionalism" is its challenges to the dualist prism of the more traditional constitutional image. The dualist approach places the relationship between Community/Union and the Member States at the centre of the discourse and puts a huge premium on questions of hierarchy as a representation of, and resolution to, constitutional conflict. In the earlier essays, which reflect this dualist sensibility, a lot of attention is given to, say, courts – European and national – with their centralizing, uniformizing ethos and function as one of the keys to understanding the supranational constitution and constitution of Europe. Later essays recognize, and at times suggest, a different, "horizontal," "polycentred," "infranational" image of the European polity and use conversation as a metaphor for constitutional ethos.

It should be clear that, not infrequently, I depart from the descriptive and analytic and the essays become prescriptive and normative. Even a pre-modernist like myself can acknowledge that it is at least at times laughable to adopt the positivist's conceit of an objective reality "out there" waiting to be observed and explained. Beauty, and ugliness, in the social sciences too are often in the eye of the beholder. What European integration stands for is dependent on what we make of it. I have strong views on how it should and should not be interpreted about which I am quite explicit. You are not, then, about to read an ode to European integration. There is plenty which, in my eyes, is admirable in the dream of European integration and in its realization. There is plenty which is silly and worse. I trust and hope that Euroskeptics and Europhiles alike will find much to chew on in these essays.

If one should not read all the essays, how many, then, and which? Some readers will, surely, consult the menu and make their own choices. But others may wish at least to consider my own brief recommendations. I am the *chef* after all.

There are three pieces which even the frugal reader should, in my view, try. The first is the brief introductory essay to the volume, "We will do and hearken" (chapter 1). In it I explain the overarching theme of the entire collection and the substantive organizing principle with which I made my selections and decided on the order of the different articles and essays; it is short, easy going, and, I hope, helpful. Second is the key article in Part 1, "The transformation of Europe" (chapter 2) to which has been added a new afterword. It is neither short nor, I fear, very easy going. But it is probably the single most important essay in the collection. The general reader should not be daunted by the footnotes. This essay was originally published in the *Yale Law Journal* and thus suffers from a common American disease which afflicts much legal academic writing: citisis. I have lightly reedited it so that the non-professional reader can simply disregard the footnotes without losing any of the article's sense or non-sense. Professionals too may wish to dispense with the footnote dressing. As a desert or *digestivo* (this is the last culinary metaphor in the entire book) I would recommend "To be a European citizen: Eros and civilization" (chapter 10).

To the extent that this book is about the means and ends of European integration, "The transformation of Europe" and "To be a European citizen" respectively capture best my approach to these issues.

As for the rest, the titles are for the most part self-explanatory.

Like European integration itself, the volume tries to maintain a balance between diversity and unity. Although this is a collection of separate essays, I have given much thought to its overall coherence. Obviously the various pieces are linked in that they all address in different ways the general themes reflected in the title of the book and explained briefly in this preface and elaborated in the introductory essay. But there are also tighter organic linkages among the various components. I want to borrow from a recent essay, "Identikit del fascista," by Umberto Eco to explain these linkages.

Imagine the content of the first article as consisting of *ABC*. The second will consist of *BCD*. The third will be *CDE*, the fourth *DEF* and so on. This format means, first, that when an essay or article in this collection builds on the foundation of another, as many do, the essential content from the foundation is imported into the new piece. It is this which obviates the need to read the entire volume in order to profit from individual chapters. Each piece can be read alone. In addition, these linkages mean that, even though, say, the fourth essay, the content of which is *DEF*, is quite different from the first, the content of which is *ABC*, they do belong organically to the same family through their relationship to the interceding chapters. This is crucial. For it means that there is not simply one unifying voice, my own, to this collection but that through these linkages the whole becomes, indirectly, part of each individual essay. The cost of this arrangement is a measure of overlap among some of the pieces which will be most noticeable to those who might, despite my warnings, attempt to read them all. I trust and hope that even those readers will not find this cost too burdensome.

ACKNOWLEDGMENTS

Chapter 2, *The transformation of Europe*, is based on an essay first published as "The Transformation of Europe," *Yale Law Journal* 100 (1991), 2,403. Chapter 3, *Fundamental rights and fundamental boundaries: on the conflict of standards and values in the protection of human rights in the European legal space*, is based on an essay first published as "Fundamental Rights and Fundamental Boundaries: On Standards and Values in the Protection of Human Rights," in N. Neuwahl and A. Rosas (eds.), *The European Union and Human Rights* (Martinus Nijhoff: The Hague, Boston, London, 1995). Chapter 4, *The external legal relations of non-unitary actors: mixity and the federal principle*, is based on an essay first published as "The External Legal Relations of Non-Unitary Actors: Mixity and the Federal Principle," in H. G. Schermers and D. O'Keeffe (eds.), *Mixed Agreements* (Kluwer: Deventer, Boston, 1983). Chapter 5, *The least-dangerous branch: a retrospective and prospective of the European Court of Justice in the arena of political integration*, is based on an essay first published as "Journey to an Unknown Destination: A Retrospective and Prospective of the European Court of Justice in the Arena of Political Integration," *Journal of Common Market Studies* 31 (1993), 418. Chapter 6, *Introduction: the reformation of European constitutionalism*, is based on an essay first published as "The First Annual Journal of Common Market Studies Lecture: The Reformation of European Constitutionalism," *Journal of Common Market Studies* 35 (1997), 97. Chapter 7, *Fin-de-siècle Europe: do the new clothes have an emperor?*, is based on an essay first published as "Europe After Maastricht Do the New Clothes Have an Emperor?" (Harvard Jean Monnet Working Paper 12/95, http://www.law.harvard.edu/Programs/JeanMonnet). Chapter 8, *European democracy and its critics: polity and system*, is based on an essay first published as "European Democracy and its Critique," *West European Politics* 18 (1995), 4 (with U. Haltern and F. Meyer). Chapter 9, *The autonomy of the Community legal order: through the looking glass*, is based on an essay first published as "The Autonomy of the Community Legal

Order Through the Looking Glass," *Harvard International Law Journal* 37 (1996), 411 (with U. Haltern). Chapter 10, *To be a European citizen: Eros and civilization*, is based on the author's 1997 Jean Monnet Lecture at the London School of Economics This chapter develops and, therefore, to some extent repeats ideas first mentioned in chapter 7.

ABBREVIATIONS

AFDI	*Annuaire française de droit imternationale*
CMLR	*Common Market Law Reports*
EC Treaty	Treaty Establishing the European Economic Community
ECHR	European Convention on Human Rights
ECJ	European Court of Justice
ECR	*European Court Reports*
ECSC Treaty	Treaty Establishing the European Coal and Steel Community
EMU	Economic and Monetary Union
Euratom	Treaty Establishing the European Atomic Energy Community
GATT	General Agreement on Tariffs and Trade
HC	House of Commons (UK)
ICJ	International Court of Justice
IGC	Intergovernmental Conference
ILC	International Labor Convention
ILO	International Labor Office
MEP	Member of the European Parliament
NGO	Non-Governmental Organization
PCIJ	Permanent Court of International Justice
SEA	Single European Act
TEU	Treaty on European Union
UNCLOS	UN Conference on the Law of the Sea
UNCTAD	UN Conference on Trade and Development
WTO	World Trade Organization

Part 1

"WE WILL DO ..."

1

INTRODUCTION:
"WE WILL DO, AND HEARKEN"

IN THE history of all polities there are memorable "constitutional moments" associated in the collective mind with important changes in the constitutional order. The change may be direct and formal, touching on the constitution itself such as a very consequential amendment or resettlement – say the abolition of the monarchy in Italy – or a very important judicial decision interpreting the constitution – a *Brown* v. *Board of Education* which forever transformed the discourse of race in the United States. The constitution of a polity may be thought of in less formal ways as well – as, say, an expression of the basic tenets of a polity's political and civic culture. In this case "constitutional moments" may be linked in the mind to non-legal yet symbolic historical events and the constitutional change they reflect may be indirect and informal – the beginning or end of a deeper process of mutation in public ethos or societal self-understanding. November 9, 1938 and November 9, 1989 – *Kristalnacht* and the fall of the Berlin Wall – constitute, arguably, such moments in the history of Germany.

What, then, are the great constitutional moments in the history of the European Union? There are some obvious candidates. The Schuman Declaration of May 1950? The entry into force of the Treaty of Rome in January 1958? The profoundly important decision of the European Court of July 1964 declaring the supremacy of Community law? Perhaps the 1965 "empty chair" crisis and the subsequent Luxembourg Accord with *its* hugely important impact on Community decision-making? Perhaps, in more recent times, the 1985 White Paper of the Commission setting the 1992 objective for completion of the single market, or, indeed, the 1986 Single European Act which endorsed that plan, restored majority voting to the Council of Ministers and set a veritable Europsychosis across the continent?

All these would be in contention. But for me it is Maastricht and its

3

aftermath which cross the line first. Not the content of the Treaty, important as, say, economic and monetary union may be. Not the symbolism (for it is no more than that) of Maastricht's pompous official name: the Treaty on European Union. Nor even the eventual ratification and entry into force of Maastricht. It is the public reaction, frequently and deliciously hostile, and the public debate which followed which almost sunk Maastricht which count in my book as the most important constitutional "moment" in the history of the European construct. For four decades European politicians were spoiled by a political class which was mostly supportive and by a general population which was conveniently indifferent. That "moment" has had a transformative impact: public opinion in all Member States is no longer willing to accept the orthodoxies of European integration, in particular the seemingly overriding political imperative which demanded acceptance, come what may, of the dynamics of Union evolution. This is both a threatening and exhilarating moment in the history of the Community and its Member States: threatening because an important patrimony is called into question; exhilarating because the debate and questioning represent a popular and national empowerment which, incidentally, can bestow on the Union an altogether deeper order of legitimacy.

How is it, one may ask, that this debate did not take place earlier, at those other defining moments in the history of the Community? Consider, in particular, that the European Court has been speaking for years about the Treaties as the "basic constitutional charter" of the Community and Union and that for decades lawyers have been speaking loosely about the "constitutionalization" of the Treaties establishing the European Community and Union. This has meant, among other things, the emergence of European law as a constitutionally "higher law" with immediate effect within the "legal space" of the Community. Supremacy, direct effect, and the protection of fundamental rights have all been accepted as part of the so-called *acquis* of the Community. There is a simpler way of putting this: within its ever increasing sphere of activities, the writ of the Union displaces any conflicting national legislation. This situation was brought about with the full collaboration of national governments, national parliaments, who again and again with each expansion of the Community to include additional Member States ratified the new order, and by national courts. It was in place long before Maastricht and Amsterdam.

How could such a veritable revolution occur without a profound debate within the European polity? We often look to antiquity to provide us with powerful metaphors which may both represent and explain the fundamentals of the human and social condition. Oedipus, Tantalus, Electra, and Antigone are a part of the Western heritage, the significance of which goes beyond their intrinsic literary content. Here, then, is an early "constitutional moment" of transcendent and enduring consequence which may help both represent and explain one part of the contemporary constitutional phase in the discussion of European Union constitutionalism:

> And Moses wrote all the words of the Eternal . . . And he took the book of the Covenant and read in the audience of the people: And they said, All that the Eternal hath spoken we will do, and hearken.[1]

Traditional commentary has noted the inversion in the act of acceptance by the people. First, we will do. Next, we will hearken, that is try and understand what it is we are doing. Normally we would expect the hearkening – a metaphor for the deliberative process of listening, debating, and understanding – to precede the commitment to do.

What, then, are the possible meanings of this inversion? What can we learn from it (and into it) for the present-day discussion of European Union constitutionalism?

1. Who, we may first ask, is foolish enough to accept a Covenant of such transformative character without hearkening first? But "who?" is a difficult question to ask here, since one of the things this Covenant did was to constitute in a new way its very subject: their peoplehood is forever changed, internally and externally (even if the nature of change was not fully apparent at that moment). This Covenant is revolutionary and radical not simply, though that too, in its substantive content, but in the very ontological underpinning of its subject. It effectively calls for its acceptance by the subject it seeks to constitute. Why so? I can think of two primary reasons.

   First, morally, acceptance by a bunch of pre-Torah slaves would be no acceptance at all. It is only an acceptance by a post-Torah free people (free in the world, since enslaved only to that which is beyond the world) which could have the moral autonomy to engage meaningfully in the act. Only by accepting do they attain the capacity to express meaningful acceptance! Acceptance is the condition for acceptance.

   Second, acceptance by the preconstituted subject, for ever privileges that subject as the original author. Now, of course, the logical conundrum, the circularity of the situation, is evident. How can you have acceptance by the subject which acceptance alone would constitute? Hence, the rather anomalous textual device – We will do, and hearken.

2. Not to be forgotten in the dizziness of exegesis is another striking fact of our biblical metaphor already encapsulated in our previous analysis. It is, I think, hard to challenge that the law was a constitution – not simply a

---

[1] Exodus 24:7.

higher law in the formal sense, but *constitutive law* (a law which constitutes something) or at least transformative in the material sense too, of the people, of their social organization, of their normative hierarchy, of their values and their destiny. But isn't the choice of form interesting? Even the Almighty, creator of heaven and earth chooses a covenant, a treaty. It is because a constitution is constitutive, involving values and controlling a destiny, that its acceptance should be covenantal, involving choice, autonomy and, like all long-lasting agreements, periodic renewal and adaptation.

The biblical narrative is a stunning combination of the pre-modern and the modern, of fate (revelation) and choice (covenant).

3. "We will do, and hearken" may be understood in another way. Peruse carefully the text leading to this moment. You have the Decalogue, rather well known. You have then, far less known, the basics of the civil law of torts, of contract, of criminal law, of labor law, and, of course, of some fundamental religious rituals. All this goes into the Covenant which Moses writes down. But this list is skeletal. It is quintessentially "constitutional" in a different way, a *traité cadre*, wildly indeterminate and open-textured language in many of its provisions, a program which will require immense effort of implementation if it is to become a matrix of life. The Covenant is surely a higher law, the acceptance of which will bind both public authorities and individuals. As such it is a *check* on power. But it also *bestows* immense power on all those who, cloaked with its authority, the authority of a higher law, will be charged with interpreting, implementing, filling the gaps. In this respect, accepting the constitutional covenant represents an immense act of faith. I do not refer only, or even primarily, to faith in the Almighty involved in this particular story. I mean faith in this aspect of the Covenant, of constitutionalism which requires a faith in one's self, in one's co-constituents, faith in one's institutions and their ability, in good faith, to "discover," to constitute the meaning of the constitution through its praxis. The Covenant is not only, even primarily, with the Almighty. It is with one another; it is, like all constitutions, a covenant with one's descendants, who are born into and are expected to live by it. But this will only happen if it is understood and accepted that the power and duty of giving and renewing meaning is also handed down. On this reading the inversion of doing and hearkening, of praxis and understanding, is a key to a great constitutional truth: the text itself, the words Moses wrote down, are hardly determinative or capable of controlling the true realization of the covenantal and constitutional promise. The most one can hope for is that the spirit of the moment be captured and cherished, but – to put it descriptively – it is only through the "doing"

that the true meaning of the covenant will be borne out. To state the same thing normatively: in the doing one must hearken to the spirit of the constitution so that its meaning is not perverted or lost in the praxis. Hence: we will do, and hearken.

4. Looking at the text in sociological and historical terms calls for a different order of interpretation. Do, and only then reason – why would anyone enter into a covenant on a basis of such blind faith, especially when the commitment is so consequential? Let us set aside the impact of revelation (which in any event was rather limited: within forty days of "seeing the thunderings" the Golden Calf was created). Is the blind faith acceptance so strange in the historical and psychological circumstances of the Hebrews? Here they are, having emerged from a traumatic experience into a new world, with all old values and institutions called into question, with new threats replacing the old ones around them. And here comes a Covenant which, on the one hand, refers to a distant idyllic past and then, with the other hand, literally conjures a real promised land of plenty and of peace and a spiritual challenge even greater than that. Would you not yourself have said, We will do, and hearken? What, after all, are the alternatives? Go elsewhere in time? That is Egypt. Go elsewhere in space? That will be the new enemies. Is this acceptance an act of folly or of unreasoned abandon? Perhaps. But also an act of existential decisiveness, of veritably taking one's destiny in one's hand, of following an intuition, an ideal, an aspiration.

The sequence is, well, history: an inevitable dynamic of doing first and thinking later.

For the generation of the Covenant itself, the revolutionary transformation and the challenge proved too much. There were even irredentist voices which called for a return to Egypt, to the pre-covenantal past. And later? That too is history. A constitutional covenant whose object and subject have survived millennia even though its evolving meaning is as hotly debated today as it was forty days from its acceptance, a sign of its vitality, but also a condition of its success. When the process of hearkening, of finding and renewing meaning, ends, so does the Covenant.

And Europe? There is a strange aspect to the current phase in the constitutional debate. It is not, surely, simply a discussion on codification, giving concise written form to the existing constitution the content of which is to be found, messily, in the Treaties and in a constitutional common law developed by the European Court and its Member State counterparts. The explanation, I would suggest, can take its cue from Exodus. Of Europe too it could be said that in response to the project of European integration, to the new constitutional order offered them, the metaphoric response was "We will do, and hearken." Let us be clear: the

"We" was the political class. The population at large was hardly committed. But they were, well, favorably indifferent (lack of commitment may be true also for the population at large at Mount Sinai who, as mentioned, were happily willing to turn to the Golden Calf on the first occasion). There was no deep-rooted debate about the Schuman Plan, about the Treaty of Paris or even the Treaty of Rome – and this despite their many radical, constitution-like features. There was no deep-rooted debate about the constitutionalization process, that remarkable judicial dialogue, or multilogue, between the European Court and its national counterparts.

That this should have happened is, in my view, no surprise. The Europe which emerges from *its* twelve-year slavery is in a traumatic situation in which old institutions and the old order are seriously called into question. The new European construct offers a vision which enables a reinterpretation of a painful past, and holds forth a promised land of prosperity and peace. Its discipline is sketchy, the full import of the new order yet to be worked out. Self-interest and a form of idealism, vision, and pragmatism combine in accepting the new order, and then in accepting the implications as worked out in jurisprudence and praxis. It was a spirit of "Lets do first and talk later," by a generation and its leadership whose personal experiences had instructed them that the alternative to the European dream was the recent European nightmare.

But the result is not, as suggested above, a European legal order of constitutionalism without a formal constitution, but the opposite: it is a constitutional legal order the constitutional theory of which has not been worked out, its long-term, transcendent values not sufficiently elaborated, its ontological elements misunderstood, its social rootedness and legitimacy highly contingent.

It is this understanding of the nature of the current constitutional moment which allows us to trace its trigger to Maastricht. At the popular level, Maastricht was a shock. Public opinion was more shocked to discover that which was already in place than that which was being proposed, and shocked the powers that be by registering defiance and skepticism. Maastricht and the subsequent debates, which, it is hoped, will endure, was the beginning of the first truly Europe-wide public constitutional "hearkening" of an act to which the peoples and Member States of Europe had already said, in one way or another, "We will do."

In many ways it is the very success of the project which explains the eruption of the debate. Europe is a transformed continent and polity. In part it is simply that the very conditions of prosperity and peace allow this debate. In part it is that the implications of the constitutional construct have been made far more visible. The constitutionalism of the Union, the sense in which the Treaties are the constitutional charter of the polity, have always been described in primarily structural terms: supremacy, direct effect, implied powers, and the like. And indeed, in these structural terms, the Community resembles much more, is much more, a constitutional legal order than an international legal order. But constitutionalism is not merely about the means of government; it is also about the ends of government. The ends underlying the structural means of European constitutionalism, ends which seemed so obvious to the generation of the framers, have been neglected.

Finally, the very success of the Community has undermined its appeal, the need, for the construct. Reconciliation between France and Germany does not speak much to a post-covenantal generation. The debate about prosperity is about redistribution of which the Union message is ambiguous and, in any event, controversial.

My point is that the current constitutional debate is not simply about explicating the theory and values underlining the existing constitutional order, but of redefining its meaning for a new generation and a new epoch.

The overall structure of this book follows the Doing–Hearkening divide. The first part of the book is about the "Doing." It contains essays and articles which explain the structure and process of the European polity and its constitutional dimensions as well as the dynamics of the emergent European constitutionalism. It is about means. Chapter 2, "The transformation of Europe," is the overall vision of European constitutionalism and its evolution. Subsequent essays focus on specific dimensions – the courts, human rights, Europe, and the world.

The second part of the book addresses the "Hearkening." It is about ends. It explores the values of European integration. It explores the debate about ideals, legitimacy, and democracy in the European Union. It traces what may be described as neo-constitutionalism. I do not pretend to have provided definitive answers. But I hope the reader will find the questions I pose of some interest.

2

THE TRANSFORMATION OF EUROPE

INTRODUCTION

IN 1951, France, Germany, Italy, and the Benelux countries concluded the Treaty of Paris establishing the European Coal and Steel Community. Lofty in its aspirations, and innovative in some of its institutional arrangements, this polity was perceived, by the actors themselves – as well as by the developers of an impressive academic theoretical apparatus, who were quick to perceive events – as an *avant garde* international organization ushering forth a new model for transnational discourse. Very quickly, however, reality dissipated the dream, and again quickly following events, the academic apparatus was abandoned.[1]

Forty years and more later, the European Community is a transformed polity. It now comprises more than double its original Member States, has a population exceeding 350 million citizens, and constitutes the largest trading bloc in the world. But the notion of "transformation" surely comes from changes deeper than its geography and demography. That Europe has been transformed in a more radical fashion is difficult to doubt. Indeed, in the face of that remarkable (and often lucrative) growth industry, 1992 commentary, doubt may be construed as subversion.

The surface manifestations of this alleged transformation are legion, ranging (in the eyes of the beholder, of course) from the trivial and

---

[1] For a review of integration theory and its demise, see, e.g., Greilsammer, "Theorizing European Integration in its Four Periods," *Jerusalem Journal of International Relations* 2 (1976), 129; Krislov, Ehlermann, and Weiler, "The Political Organs and the Decision-Making Process in the United States and the European Community," in M. Cappelletti, M. Seccombe, and J. H. H. Weiler (eds.), *Integration through Law* (Walter de Gruyter: Berlin, New York, 1985), vol. II, book 1, 3 at 6–11.

ridiculous[2] to the important and sublime. Consider the changes in the following:

1. The scope of Community action. Notice how naturally the Member States and their Western allies have turned to the Community to take the lead role in assisting the development and reconstruction of eastern Europe.[3] A mere decade or two ago, such an overt foreign policy posture for the Community would have been bitterly contested by its very own Member States.[4]

2. The mode of Community action. The European Commission now plays a central role in dictating the Community agenda and in shaping the content of its policy and norms. As recently as the late 1960s, the survival of supranationalism was a speculative matter,[5] while in the 1970s, the Commission, self-critical and demoralized, was perceived as an overblown and overpaid secretariat of the Community.[6]

---

[2] The winning song in the popular Eurovision Song Contest of 1990 was entitled "Altogether 1992," *The Times* (London) (May 7, 1990) at 6, col. 8.

[3] See "European Commission Defines a General Framework for Association Agreements ('European Agreements') between the EEC and the Countries of Eastern and Central Europe," *Europe*, Doc. No. 1,646/47 (September 7, 1990) at 1 (reprint of Commission communication to the Council and the Parliament). The evolution is limited, however. For example, the absence of a true Community apparatus for foreign policy rendered the political (not military) initiative in relation to the Iraqi crisis no more than hortatory. See, e.g., "Gulf Crisis: Positions Taken by the Twelve and the Western European Union," *Europe*, Doc. No. 1,644 (August 23, 1990) at 1 (statements of August 2, 10, and 21, 1990); "Gulf/EEC: The Foreign Ministers of the Twelve Confirm Their Position and Intend to Draft an 'Overall Concept' for their Relations with the Region's Countries," *Europe*, Doc. No. 5,413 (January 19, 1991) at 3–4. The Community has, however, taken a leading role in the Yugoslav crisis. On the evolving foreign policy posture of the Community in the wake of 1992, see generally R. Dehousse and J. Weiler, "EPC and the Single Act: From Soft Law to Hard Law" (European University Institute Working Papers of the European Policy Unit, No. 90/1).

[4] In 1973, the French Foreign Minister, M. Jobert, pressed the separateness (of the Framework for European Political co-operation which dealt with foreign policy) from the Community to a point of forcing the ministers to meet in EPC in Copenhagen in the morning, and to assemble the same afternoon in Brussels as a Community Council to deal with Community business: Stein, "Towards a European Foreign Policy? The European Foreign Affairs System from the Perspective of the United States Constitution," in Cappelletti, Seccombe, and Weiler, *Integration through Law*, vol. I, book 3 at 63.

[5] See, e.g., Heathcote, "The Crisis of European Supranationality," *Journal of Common Market Studies* 5 (1966), 140.

[6] See, e.g., B. Biesheuvel, E. Dell, and R. Marjolin, "Report on European Institutions" (1980), 10–12, 49–56 (report of the Committee of Three to the European Council, October 1979) (hereinafter "Report on European Institutions"); see also "Proposal for Reform of the Commission of the European Communities and its Services" (1979) (report made at the request of the Commission by an independent review body under the Chairmanship of Mr. Dirk Spierenburg) (report requested in part because of sense of malaise in Commission) (hereinafter "Spierenburg Report"). For a self-mocking but penetrating picture, see M. von Donat, *Europe: Qui Tire les Ficelles?* (Presses d'Europe: Paris, 1979).

11

3. The image and perception of the European Community. Changes in these are usually more telling signs than the reality they represent. In public discourse, "Europe" increasingly means the European Community in much the same way that "America" means the United States

But these surface manifestations are just that – the seismographer's telltale line reflecting deeper, below-the-surface movement in need of interpretation. Arguably, the most significant change in Europe, justifying appellations such as "transformation" and "metamorphosis," concerns the evolving relationship between the Community and its Member States.[7]

How can this transformation in the relationship between the Member States and the Community be conceptualized? In a recent case, the European Court spoke matter-of-factly of the EC Treaty[8] as "the basic constitutional charter" of the Community.[9] On this reading, the Treaties have been "constitutionalized" and the Community has become an entity whose closest structural model is no longer an international organization but a denser, yet non-unitary polity, principally the federal state. Put differently, the Community's "operating system" is no longer governed by general principles of public international law, but by a specified interstate governmental structure defined by a constitutional charter and constitutional principles.

This judicial characterization, endlessly repeated in the literature,[10] underscores the fact that not simply the content of Community–Member

---

[7] The juxtaposition of Community and Member States is problematic. The concept of the Community, analogous to the concept of the Trinity, is simultaneously both one and many. In some senses, the Community is its individual Member States: in other senses, it is distinct from them. This inevitable dilemma exists in all federal arrangements. Moreover, the notion of an individual state itself is not monolithic. When one talks of a Member State's interests, one usually sacrifices many nuances in understanding the specific position of that state: "[D]ifferent, conflicting and often contradictory interests, either objective or subjective, are frequently expressed as unified, subjective 'national' interests. Behind these articulated, subjective 'national' interests, however, lie a variety of sets of social, economic and political relations, as well as different relationships between private and public economic organisations and the state.": F. Snyder, *New Directions in European Community Law* (Wiedenfeld and Nicolson: London, 1990) at 90 (footnote omitted); see also *ibid.* at 32, 37. While the danger of sacrificing these many voices within a state cannot be avoided, I shall try to minimize it by referring to the interest of the Member States in preserving their prerogatives as such in the Community polity.

[8] EEC Treaty, as amended by the Single European Act (SEA).

[9] Case 294/83, *Parti Ecologiste, "Les Verts"* v. *European Parliament* [1986] ECR 1,339, 1,365 (hereinafter *"Les Verts"*).

[10] For fine recent analyses, see Lenaerts, "Constitutionalism and the Many Faces of Federalism," *American Journal of Comparative Law* 38 (1990), 205; Mancini, "The Making of a Constitution for Europe," *Common Market Law Review* 26 (1989), 595; and literature cited in both. The importance of the legal paradigm as a characterizing feature of the Community is recognized also in the non-legal literature. See, e.g., Keohane and Hoffmann, "Conclusions: Community Politics and Institutional Change," in W. Wallace (ed.), *The Dynamics of European Integration* (Pinter: London, New York, 1990), 276, 278–82.

State discourse has changed. The very architecture of the relationship, the group of structural rules that define the mode of discourse, has mutated. Also, the characterization gives us, as analytical tools, the main concepts developed in evaluating non-unitary (principally federal) polities. We can compare the Community to known entities within meaningful paradigms.

This characterization might, however, lead to flawed analysis. It might be read (and has been read[11]) as suggesting that the cardinal material *locus* of change has been the realm of law and that the principal actor has been the European Court. But this would be deceptive. Legal and constitutional structural change have been crucial, but only in their interaction with the Community political process.

The characterization might also suggest a principal temporal *locus* of change, a kind of "Big Bang" theory. It would almost be natural, and in any event very tempting, to locate such a temporal point in that well-known series of events that have shaken the Community since the middle of the 1980s and that are encapsulated in that larger-than-life date, 1992.[12] There is, after all, a plethora of literature which hails 1992 as the key seismic event in the Community geology.[13] But, one should resist that temptation too. This is not to deny the importance of 1992 and the changes introduced in the late 1980s to the structure and process of Community life and to the relationship between Community and Member States. But even if 1992 is a seismic mutation, explosive and visible, it is none the less in the nature of an eruption.

My claim is that the 1992 eruption was preceded by two deeper, and

---

[11] "Tucked away in the fairyland Duchy of Luxembourg and blessed, until recently, with benign neglect by the powers that be and the mass media, the Court of Justice of the European Communities has fashioned a constitutional framework for a federal-type structure in Europe.": Stein, "Lawyers, Judges and the Making of a Transnational Constitution," *American Journal of International Law* 75 (1981), 1; see also A. W. Green, *Political Integration by Jurisprudence* (Sijthoff: Leyden, 1969).

[12] 1992 actually encapsulates, in a game which resembles some new Cabala of Community life, a temporal move to an ever-increasing higher celestial sphere. The key dates in this game of numbers are: the 1984 European Parliament Draft Treaty on European Union and the 1985 Commission White Paper ("Completion of the Internal Market"), endorsed by the 1986 Single European Act (which entered into force in July 1987), and to which was added the April 1988 Commission (Delors) Plan of Economic and Monetary Union, endorsed in the 1989 Madrid Summit and strengthened by the Dublin 1990 decision to hold two Intergovernmental Conferences leading to the Maastricht Treaty, which came into force on 1 January 1993.

[13] "The Single European Act ... represents the most comprehensive and most important amendment to the EEC Treaty to date.": Ehlermann, "The '1992 Project': Stages, Structures, Results and Prospects," *Michigan Journal of International Law* 11 (1990), 1,097, 1,103 (hereinafter "1991 Project"). Although I agree with Ehlermann that the SEA is the most important formal amendment, I contend that earlier developments without formal amendment should be considered even more important. For a recent comprehensive bibliography of 1992 literature, see *Michigan Journal of International Law* 11 (1990), 571.

hence far less visible, profound mutations of the very foundational strata of the Community, each taking place in a rather distinct period in the Community's evolution. The importance of these earlier subterranean mutations is both empirical and cognitive. Empirically, the 1992 capsule was both shaped by, and is significant because of, the earlier Community mutations. Cognitively, we cannot understand the 1992 eruption and the potential of its shockwaves without a prior understanding of the deeper mutations that conditioned it.

Thus, although I accept that the Community has been transformed profoundly, I believe this transformation occurred in three distinct phases. In each of the phases a fundamental feature in the relationship of the Community to its Member States mutated; only the combination of all three can be said to have transformed the Community's "operating system" as a non-unitary polity.

These perceptions condition the methodological features of this chapter. One feature is a focus on evolution. I shall chart the principal characteristics of the new "operating system" in an historical framework. In other words, I shall tell a story of evolution over time. This approach will enable me not only to describe but also to analyze and explain. Each evolving facet of the new system will be presented as a "development" that needs systemic and historical analysis.

Second, in this analysis I shall focus on what I consider to be the two key *structural* dimensions of constitutionalism in a non-unitary polity: (1) the relationships between political power in the center and the periphery and between legal norms and policies of the center and the periphery; and (2) the principle governing the division of material competences between Community and Member States, usually alluded to as the doctrine of enumerated powers. The structure and process of the Community will thus occupy pride of place rather than substantive policy and content.

The final feature of my methodological approach relates to the position of law in the evolution of the Community. In a sharp critique of a classic study of the European Community legal order, Martin Shapiro made the following comments, which could be leveled against much of the legal literature on the Community:

> [The study] is a careful and systematic exposition of the judicial review provisions of the "constitution" of the European Economic Community, an exposition that is helpful for a newcomer to these materials. But . . . [i]t is constitutional law without politics . . . [I]t presents the Community as a juristic idea; the written constitution as a sacred text; the professional commentary as a legal truth; the case law as the inevitable working out of the correct implications of the constitutional text; and the constitutional court as the disembodied voice of right reason and constitutional theology . . . such an approach has proved fundamentally arid in

the study of [national] constitutions . . . it must reduce constitutional scholarship to something like that early stage of archeology that resembled the collection of antiquities . . . oblivious to their context or living matrix.[14]

The plea for a "law and . . ." approach is of course *de rigueur*, be it law and economics, law and culture, law and society, that is, in general, law in context. At one level, a goal of this chapter will be precisely to meet aspects of this critique of, and challenge to, European legal literature. I shall try to analyze the Community constitutional order with particular regard to its living political matrix; the interactions between norms and norm-making, constitution and institutions, principles and practice, and the Court of Justice and the political organs will lie at the core of this chapter.

And yet, even though I shall look at relationships of legal structure and political process, at law and power, my approach is hardly one of law in context – it is far more modest. In my story, de Gaulle and Thatcher, the economic expansion of the 1960s, the oil crisis of the 1970s, socialists and Christian Democrats, and all like elements of the political history of the epoch play pithy parts. It is perhaps ironic, but my synthesis and analysis are truly in the tradition of the "pure theory of law" with the riders that "law" encompasses a discourse that is much wider than doctrine and norms and that the very dichotomy of law and politics is questionable.

The shortcomings of this "purism" (not total to be sure) are self-evident: my contribution cannot be but a part of a more totalistic and comprehensive history. But, if successful, the "pure" approach has some virtues, as its ultimate claim is that much that has happened in the systemic evolution of Europe is self-referential and results from the internal dynamics of the system itself, almost as if it were insulated from those "external" aspects.[15]

---

[14] Shapiro, "Comparative Law and Comparative Politics," *Southern California Law Review* 53 (1980), 537, 538. In his comment Shapiro alludes to what in its own terms is a model analysis: Barav, "The Judicial Power of the European Economic Community," *Southern California Law Review* 53 (1980), 461. And, of course, not all constitutional scholarship of the Community falls into this trap. See, e.g., Snyder, *New Directions*; Lenaerts, "Constitutionalism"; Mancini, "The Making of a Constitution."

[15] The "insulation" cannot be total. External events are mediated through the prism of the system and do not have a reality of their own. *Cf.* Teubner, "Introduction to Autopoietic Law," in G. Teubner (ed.), *Autopoietic Law: A New Approach to Law and Society* (Walter de Gruyter: Berlin, New York, 1988) (the autopoietic approach to law, pioneered by Niklas Luhmann and elaborated by Gunther Teubner, acknowledges a much greater role to internal discourse of law in explaining its evolutionary dynamics; autopoiesis also gives a more careful explanation of the impact of external reality on legal system, a reality which will always be mediated by its legal perception).

1958 TO THE MIDDLE OF THE 1970S: THE FOUNDATIONAL PERIOD: TOWARDS A THEORY OF EQUILIBRIUM

The importance of developments in this early period cannot be overstated.[16] They transcend anything that has happened since. It is in this period that the Community assumed, in stark change from the original conception of the Treaty, its basic legal and political characteristics. But understanding the dynamics of the foundational period is of more than historical interest; the patterns of Community–Member State interaction that crystallized in this period conditioned all subsequent developments in Europe.

In order to explain the essentials of the foundational period, I would like to make recourse to an apparent paradox, the solution to which will be my device for describing and analyzing the European Community system.

A paradox and its solution: Exit and Voice

If we were to ask a lawyer during the foundational period to compare the evolution of the European Community with the American experience, the lawyer would say that the Community was becoming "more and more like a federal (or at least pre-federal) state." By contrast, if we were to ask a political scientist at the same point in time to compare the European system with, say, the American system, the political scientist would give a diametrically opposite answer: "They are growing less and less alike."

The paradox can be phrased in non-comparative terms: from a legal-normative point of view, the Community developed in that first phase with an inexorable dynamism of enhanced supranationalism. European legal integration moved powerfully ahead. From a political-decisional-procedural point of view, the very same period was characterized by a counter-development towards intergovernmentalism and away from European integration. It is not surprising, therefore, that lawyers were characterizing the Community of that epoch as a "constitutional framework for a federal-type structure,"[17] whereas political scientists were speculating about the "survival of supranationalism."[18]

---

[16] The intellectual genesis of this chapter is rooted in my earlier work on the Community. See Weiler, "The Community System: The Dual Character of Supranationalism," *Yearbook of European Law* (Clarendon Press: Oxford; Oxford University Press: New York, 1981), vol. I, 267. It was later developed in J. Weiler, *Il sistema comunitario europeo* (Il Mulino: Bologna, 1985) (an attempt to construct a general theory explaining the supranational features of the European Community). In the present work I have tried, first, to locate my construct, revised in the light of time, within a broader context of systemic understanding; and, second, to use it as a tool to illuminate the more recent phenomenon of 1992.

[17] Stein, "Towards a European Foreign Policy?" at 1.

[18] Heathcote, "The Crisis of European Supranationality."

Identifying the factual and conceptual contours of this paradox of the Community and explaining the reasons for it will be the key to explaining the significance of the foundational period in the evolution of the Community. What then are the contours of this legal-political puzzle? How can it be explained? What is its significance?

In *Exit, Voice and Loyalty*,[19] Hirschman identified the categories of Exit and Voice with the respective disciplines of economics and politics. Exit corresponded to the simplified world of the economist, whereas Voice corresponded to the messy (and supposedly more complex) world of the political scientist. Hirschman stated:

> Exit and Voice, that is, market and non-market forces, that is, economic and political mechanisms, have been introduced as two principal actors of strictly equal rank and importance. In developing my play on that basis I hope to demonstrate to political scientists the usefulness of economic concepts *and to economists the usefulness of political concepts*. This reciprocity has been lacking in recent interdisciplinary work.[20]

The same can be said about the interplay between legal and political analysis. The interdisciplinary gap there is just as wide.

The interplay of Exit and Voice is fairly clear and needs only a brief adjustment for the Community circumstance. Exit is the mechanism of organizational abandonment in the face of unsatisfactory performance. Voice is the mechanism of intra-organizational correction and recuperation. Apart from identifying these two basic types of reaction to malperformance, Hirschman's basic insight is to identify a kind of zero-sum game between the two. Crudely put, a stronger "outlet" for Voice reduces pressure on the Exit option and can lead to more sophisticated processes of self-correction. By contrast, the closure of Exit leads to demands for enhanced Voice. And although Hirschman developed his concepts to deal with the behavior of the marketplace, he explicitly suggested that the notions of Exit and Voice may be applicable to membership behavior in any organizational setting.

Naturally I shall have to give specific characterizations to Exit and Voice in the Community context. l propose first to discuss in legal categories the Exit option in the European Community. I shall then introduce Voice in political categories.

---

[19] A. Hirschman, *Exit, Voice and Loyalty – Responses to Decline in Firms, Organizations and States* (Harvard University Press: Cambridge, MA, 1970).
[20] *Ibid.* at 19 (emphasis in original).

Exit in the European Community: formal and selective

Formal (or total) Exit is of course an easy notion, signifying the withdrawal of a Member State from the European Community. Lawyers have written reams about the legality of unilateral Member State withdrawal.[21] The juridical conclusion is that unilateral withdrawal is illegal. Exit is foreclosed. But this is precisely the type of legal analysis that gives lawyers a bad name in other disciplines. It takes no particular insight to suggest that should a Member State consider withdrawing from the Community, the legal argument will not be the critical or determining consideration. If Total Exit is foreclosed, it is because of the high enmeshment of the Member States and the potential, real or perceived, for political and economic losses to the withdrawing state.

Whereas the notion of Total Exit is thus not particularly helpful, or at least it does not profit from *legal* analysis, I would introduce a different notion, that of Selective Exit: the practice of the Member States of retaining membership but seeking to avoid their obligations under the Treaty, be it by omission or commission. In the life of many international organizations, including the Community, Selective Exit is a much more common temptation than Total Exit.

A principal feature of the foundational period has been the closure, albeit incomplete, of Selective Exit with obvious consequences for the decisional behavior of the Member States

The closure of Selective Exit

The "closure of Selective Exit" signifies the process curtailing the ability of the Member States to practice a selective application of the *acquis communautaire*, the erection of restraints on their ability to violate or disregard their binding obligations under the Treaties and the laws adopted by Community institutions. In order to explain this process of "closure" I must recapitulate two dimensions of EC development: (1) the "constitutionalization" of the Community legal structure; and (2) the system of legal/judicial guarantees.

---

[21] For further discussion, see Weiler, "Alternatives to Withdrawal from an International Organization: The Case of the European Economic Community," *Israel Law Review* 20 (1985), 282, 284–8.

The foundational period: the "constitutionalization" of the Community legal structure

Starting in 1963 and continuing into the early 1970s and beyond,[22] the European Court in a series of landmark decisions established four doctrines that fixed the relationship between Community law and Member State law and rendered that relationship indistinguishable from analogous legal relationships in constitutional federal states.

The doctrine of direct effect

The judicial doctrine of direct effect, introduced in 1963 and developed subsequently,[23] provides the following presumption: Community legal norms that are clear, precise, and self-sufficient (not requiring further legislative measures by the authorities of the Community or the Member States) must be regarded as the law of the land in the sphere of application of Community law. Direct effect (a rule of construction in result) applies to all actions producing legal effects in the Community: the Treaty itself and secondary legislation. Moreover, with the exception of one type of Community legislation,[24] direct effect operates not only in creating enforceable legal obligations between the Member States and individuals, but also among individuals *inter se*. Critically, being part of the law of the land means that Community norms may be invoked by individuals before their state courts, which must provide adequate legal remedies for the EC norms just as if they were enacted by the state legislature.

The implications of this doctrine were and are far reaching. The European Court reversed the normal presumption of public international law whereby international legal obligations are result oriented and addressed to states. Public international law typically allows the internal constitutional order of a state to determine the method and extent to which international obligations may, if at all, produce effects for individuals within the legal order of the state. Under the normal canons of international law, even when the international obligation itself, such as a trade agreement or a

---

[22] The process of constitutionalization is an ongoing one. I suggest the 1970s as a point of closure since, as shall be seen, by the early 1970s all major constitutional doctrines were already in place. What followed were refinements.

[23] On the doctrine of direct effect and its evolution, see T. Hartley, *The Foundations of European Community Law* (Clarendon Press: Oxford; Oxford University Press: New York, 2nd edn., 1988), 183–218.

[24] Community directives may produce direct effects in the vertical relationship between public authority and individuals but not in the horizontal relationship of individuals *inter se*. See Case 148/78, *Pubblico Ministero* v. *Tullio Ratti* [1979] ECR 1,629; Case 152/84, *Marshall* v. *Southampton and South-West Hampshire Area Health Authority* [1986] ECR 723.

human-rights convention, is intended to bestow rights (or duties) on individuals within a state, if the state fails to bestow the rights, the individual cannot invoke the international obligation before national courts, unless internal constitutional or statutory law, to which public international law is indifferent, provides for such a remedy. The typical remedy under public international law in such a case would be an interstate claim. The main import of the Community doctrine of direct effect was not simply the conceptual change it ushered forth. In practice, direct effect meant that Member States violating their Community obligations could not shift the *locus* of the dispute to the interstate or Community plane. They would be faced with legal actions before their own courts at the suit of individuals within their own legal order.

Individuals (and their lawyers) noticed this practical implication, and the number of cases brought on the basis of this doctrine grew exponentially. Effectively, individuals in real cases and controversies (usually against state public authorities) became the principal "guardians" of the legal integrity of Community law within Europe similar to the way that individuals in the United States have been the principal actors in ensuring the vindication of the Bill of Rights and other federal law.

The doctrine of supremacy

The doctrine of direct effect might not strike all observers as that revolutionary, especially those observers coming from a monist constitutional order in which international treaties upon ratification are transposed automatically into the municipal legal order and in which some provisions of international treaties may be recognized as "self-executing." The full impact of direct effect is realized in combination with the second "constitutionalizing" doctrine, supremacy. Unlike some federal constitutions, the Treaty does not include a specific "supremacy clause." However, in a series of cases[25] starting in 1964 the Court has pronounced an uncompromising version of supremacy: in the sphere of application of Community law, any Community norm, be it an article of the Treaty (the constitutional Charter) or a minuscule administrative regulation enacted by the Commis-

---

[25] For a particularly subtle analysis of the supremacy of Community law and its evolution, see J. Usher, *European Community Law and National Law – The Irreversible Transfer* (1981), 30–8. For a more skeptical view, see De Witte, "Retour à Costa: La primauté du droit Communautaire à la lumière du droit international," *Revue trimestrielle du droit européen* 20 (1984), 425. For a survey and analysis of the most recent constitutional developments, see Jacobs, "Constitutional Developments in the European Community and the Impact of the Single European Market after 1992," *Michigan Journal of International Law* 11 (1990), 887. Recently, the final resistance to supremacy was removed with the decision of the French Conseil d'Etat in *Raoul Georges Nicolo and Others* [1990] CMLR 173.

sion, "trumps" conflicting national law whether enacted before or after the Community norm. Additionally, although this has never been stated explicitly, the Court has the *"Kompetenz-Kompetenz"* in the Community legal order, i.e., it is the body that determines which norms come within the sphere of application of Community law.[26]

In light of supremacy, the full significance of direct effect becomes transparent. Typically, in monist or quasi-monist states like the United States, although treaty provisions, including self-executing ones, may be received automatically into the municipal legal order, their normative status is *equivalent* to national legislation. Thus the normal rule of "later in time" (*lex posteriori derogat lex anteriori*) governs the relationship between the treaty provision and conflicting national legislation. A national legislature unhappy with an internalized treaty norm simply enacts a conflicting national measure and the transposition will have vanished for all internal practical effects.[27] By contrast, in the Community, because of the doctrine of supremacy, the EC norm, which by virtue of the doctrine of direct effect must be regarded as part of the law of the land, will prevail even in

[26] The principle of supremacy can be expressed, not as an absolute rule whereby Community (or federal) law trumps Member State law, but instead as a principle whereby each law is supreme within its sphere of competence. This more accurate characterization of supremacy renders crucial the question of defining the spheres of competence and in particular the concomitant institutional question of which court will have the final decision as to the definition of spheres, i.e., the question of *Kompetenz-Kompetenz*. The European Court has never addressed this issue squarely, but implicit in the case law is the clear understanding that the Court has, as a matter of Community law, the ultimate say on the reach of Community law. See, e.g., Case 66/80, *Spa International Chemical Corp.* v. *Amministrazione delle Finanze dello Strato* [1981] ECR 1,191; Case 314/85, *Firma Foto Frost* v. *Hauptzollamt Lubeck-Ost* [1987] ECR 4,199, cases in which the Court reserved to itself the prerogative of declaring Community law invalid. In principle, under the EEC Treaty, Art. 173, there are several reasons for annulling a measure of Community law: for example, infringement of an essential procedural requirement under EEC law. This issue, clearly, seems to belong in the exclusive province of the European Court. On second look, however, one of the grounds for annulment, indeed the first mentioned in Art. 173, is "lack of competence." If the issue of competence relates only to the respective competence of the various Community institutions, there is no problem in regarding this issue too as falling exclusively in the hands of the European Court of Justice. But the phrase "lack of competence" clearly applies also to the question of general competence of the Community *vis-à-vis* its Member States. The question as to what part of legislative competence was granted the Community by the Member States is, arguably, as much an issue of Member State constitutional law as it is of Community law. By claiming in the aforementioned cases exclusive jurisdiction to pronounce on these issues, the Court was implicitly, but unquestionably, asserting its *Kompetenz-Kompetenz*, its exclusive competence to determine the competence of the Community. Of course, one rationale of these decisions is to ensure the uniform application of Community law throughout its legal space. But this rationale, functionally persuasive as it may be, does not necessarily override from the perspective of a Member State the interest in the integrity of a state's constitutional order.

[27] Of course, on the international plane, a wrong, for which state responsibility would lie, would have been committed. The remedies for this wrong would be on the international plane as well.

these circumstances. The combination of the two doctrines means that Community norms that produce direct effects are not merely the law of the land but the "higher law" of the land. Parallels to this kind of constitutional architecture may, with very few exceptions, be found only in the internal constitutional order of federal states.

The doctrine of implied powers

One possible rationale underlying the Court's jurisprudence in both direct effect and supremacy has been its attempt to maximize the efficiency by which the Community performs the tasks entrusted to it by the Treaty. As part of this rationale, one must consider the question of specific powers granted to the Community to perform these tasks. Direct effect and supremacy will not serve their functions if the Community does not have the necessary instruments at its disposal. The issue in which this consideration came to the fore, in 1970, was the treaty-making power of the Community. The full realization of many EC internal policies clearly depended on the ability of the Community to negotiate and conclude international treaties with third parties. As is the case with Member States, the problems facing the Community do not respect its internal territorial and jurisdictional boundaries. The Treaty itself was rather sparing in granting the Community treaty-making power, limiting it to a few specified cases.

In its landmark decision of that period[28] (the period *circa* 1971) the European Court held that the grant of internal competence must be read as implying an external treaty-making power. The European Court added that Community international agreements would be binding not only on the Community as such, but also, as appropriate, on and within the Member States.[29] The significance of this ruling goes beyond the issue of treaty-making power. With this decision, subsequently replicated in different contexts,[30] the European Court added another rung in its constitutional ladder: powers would be implied in favor of the Community where

---

[28] Case 22/70, *Commission of the European Communities* v. *Council of the European Communities* [1971] ECR 263 (hereinafter "*ERTA*").

[29] For the evolution of the foreign-relations power of the Community, see J. Groux and P. Manin, *The European Communities in the International Order* (Commission of the European Communities: Brussels, 1985); Lachmann, "International Legal Personality of the EC: Capacity and Competence," in *Legal Issues of European Integration* 3 (1984); Weiler, "The External Legal Relations of Non-Unitary Actors: Mixity and the Federal Principle," in H. G. Schermers and D. O'Keeffe (eds.), *Mixed Agreements* (Kluwer: Deventer, Boston, 1983) at 35.

[30] The doctrine of implied powers is discussed fully in A. Tizzano, "Les compétences de la Communauté," in *Trente ans de droit Communautaire* (European Commission, Perspectives Européennes, 1982), 45, 49–52.

they were necessary to serve legitimate ends pursued by it. Beyond its enormous practical ramifications, the critical point was the willingness of the Court to sidestep the presumptive rule of interpretation typical in international law, that treaties must be interpreted in a manner that minimizes encroachment on state sovereignty. The Court favored a teleological, purposive rule drawn from the book of constitutional interpretation.

In a parallel, although much less noticed, development, the European Court began to develop its jurisprudence on the relationship between areas of Community and Member State competence. The Treaty itself is silent on this issue. It may have been presumed that all authority granted to the Community was to be shared concurrently with the Member States, subject only to the emerging principle of supremacy. Member States could adopt national policies and laws, provided these did not contradict Community law in the same sphere.

In a bifurcated line of jurisprudence laid in place in the early 1970s and continued thereafter, the European Court developed two complementary doctrines: exclusivity and preemption.[31] In a number of fields, most importantly in common commercial policy, the European Court held that the powers of the Community were exclusive. Member States were precluded from taking any action *per se*, whether or not their action conflicted with a positive measure of Community law. In other fields the exclusivity was not an *a priori* notion. Instead, only positive Community legislation in these fields triggered a preemptive effect, barring Member States from any action, whether or not in actual conflict with Community law, according to specific criteria developed by the Court.

Exclusivity and preemption not only constitute an additional constitutional layer on those already mentioned but also have had a profound effect on Community decision-making. Where a field has been preempted or is exclusive and action is needed, the Member States are pushed to act jointly.

The doctrine of human rights

The last major constitutional tremor was in the field of human rights.[32] The Treaty contains no Bill of Rights and there is no explicit provision for judicial review of an alleged violation of human rights. In a much discussed

---

[31] See Waelbroeck, "The Emergent Doctrine of Community Pre-emption – Consent and Redelegation," in T. Sandalow and E. Stein (eds.), *Courts and Free Markets* (Clarendon Press: Oxford; Oxford University Press: New York, 1982), vol. II, 548.

[32] See Weiler, "Eurocracy and Distrust: Some Questions Concerning the Role of the European Court of Justice in the Protection of Fundamental Human Rights within the Legal Order of the European Communities," *Washington Law Review* 61 (1986), 1,103.

line of cases starting in 1969, the Court asserted that it would, none the less, review Community measures for any violation of fundamental human rights, adopting for its criteria the constitutional traditions common to the Member States and the international human-rights conventions to which the Member States subscribed. This enormously complex jurisprudence will be discussed later in this chapter, but its symbolic significance in a "constitution-building" exercise deserves mention here. The principal message was that the arrogation of power to the Community implicit in the other three doctrines would not be left unchecked. Community norms, at times derived only from an implied grant of power, often directly effective, and always supreme, would be subjected to a human-rights scrutiny by the Court. This scrutiny is important given the "democracy deficit" in Community decision-making.

If nothing else, this jurisprudence was as clear an indication as any of the audacious self-perception of the European Court. The measure of creative interpretation of the Treaty was so great as to be consonant with a self-image of a constitutional court in a "constitutional" polity. It should be noted further that the human-rights jurisprudence had, paradoxically, the hallmarks of the deepest jurists' prudence. The success of the European Court's bold moves with regard to the doctrines of direct effect, supremacy, implied powers, and human rights ultimately would depend on their reception by the highest constitutional courts in the different Member States.

The most delicate issue in this context was that of supremacy. National courts were likely to accept direct effect and implied powers, but found it difficult to swallow the notion that Community law must prevail even in the face of an explicit later-in-time provision of a national legislature to whom, psychologically, if not in fact constitutionally, Member State courts owed allegiance. Accepting the supremacy of Community law without some guarantee that this supreme law would not violate rights fundamental to the legal patrimony of an individual Member State would be virtually impossible. This would be especially true in Member States like Italy and Germany where human rights enjoy constitutional protection. Thus, even if protection of human rights *per se* need not be indispensable to fashioning a federal-type constitution, it was critical to the acceptance by courts in the Member States of the other elements of constitution-building. One by one, the highest jurisdictions in the Member States accepted the new judicial architecture of Europe.[33]

---

[33] The story of the acceptance of the principle of supremacy by national courts is charted in H. Schermers and D. Waelbroeck, *Judicial Protection in the European Communities* (Kluwer: Deventer, Boston, 4th edn., 1987), 115–24. See also M. van Empel, *Leading Cases on the Law of the European Communities* (Kluwer: Deventer, Boston, 1990), 203–39.

The skeptic may, however, be justified in challenging the "new legal order" I have described incorporating these doctrines,[34] especially the sharp lines it tries to draw in differentiating the "new" Community order from the "old" public international law order. After all, a cardinal principle of international law is its supremacy over national law. The notion of direct effect, or at least self-execution, is also known to international law, and implied-powers jurisprudence has operated in the jurisprudence of the International Court of Justice as well.[35] If international law shares these notions of supremacy, direct effect, and implied powers,[36] the skeptic may be correct in challenging the characterization of Community development in the foundational period as something out of the ordinary.

One reply is that the Community phenomenon represents a quantitative change of such a magnitude that it is qualitative in nature. Direct effect may exist in international law but it is operationalized in so few instances that it must be regarded as the exception which proves the general rule of its virtual non-existence. In the Community order direct effect is presumptive.[37] The question of supremacy, however, brings the key difference between the two systems into sharp relief. International law is as uncompromising as Community law in asserting that its norms are supreme over conflicting national norms. But, international law's horizontal system of enforcement, which is typically actuated through the principles of state responsibility, reciprocity, and counter-measures, gives the notion of supremacy an exceptionally rarified quality, making it difficult to grasp and radically different from that found in the constitutional orders of states with centralized enforcement monopolies.

The constitutionalization claim regarding the Treaties establishing the European Community can only be sustained by adding one more layer of analysis: the system of judicial remedies and enforcement. It is this system, as interpreted and operationalized by the European judicial branch, that truly differentiates the Community legal order from the horizontality of classical public international law.

---

[34] See, e.g., Wyatt, "New Legal Order, or Old?" *European Law Review* 7 (1982), 147; see also De Witte, "Retour à Costa."

[35] See, e.g., *Reparations for Injuries Suffered in the Service of the United Nations* [1949] ICJ 174.

[36] One could also argue that the protection of fundamental human rights has become part of the customary law patrimony of international law. *Cf.*, *Filartiga* v. *Peña-Irala*, 630 F. 2d 876 (2d Cir. 1980) (deliberate torture under color of official authority violates universally accepted norms of international law of human rights).

[37] See Pescatore, "The Doctrine of 'Direct Effect': An Infant Disease of Community Law," *European Law Review* 8 (1983), 155.

The Community system of judicial review

As mentioned above, the hierarchy of norms within the European Community is typical of a non-unitary system. The higher law of the Community is, of course, the Treaty itself. Neither Community organs nor the Member States may violate the Treaty in their legislative and administrative actions. In addition, Member States may not violate Community regulations, directives, and decisions. Not surprisingly, then, the Community features a system of judicial review, operating on two levels. Two sets of legislative acts and administrative measures are subject to judicial review: (1) the measures of the Community itself (principally acts of the Council of Ministers, the Commission, and the European Parliament), which are reviewable for conformity with the Treaties; and (2) the acts of the Member States, which are reviewable for their conformity with Community law and policy, including the above-mentioned secondary legislation.

Needless to say, in the context of my discussion of the closure of Exit and of Member States' attempts to disregard those obligations they dislike, the effectiveness of review of the second set of measures assumes critical importance. Therefore, I focus only on that aspect of judicial review here.

Judicial review at the Community level

Either the Commission or an individual Member State may, in accordance with Articles 169–72 of the EC Treaty, bring an action against a Member State for failure to fulfill its obligations under the Treaty. Generally, this failure takes the form of either inaction in implementing a Community obligation or enactment of a national measure contrary to Community obligations. The existence of a mandatory and *exclusive* forum for adjudication of these types of disputes sets the Community apart from many international organizations.

The role of the Commission is even more special. As one commentator noted: "Under traditional international law the enforcement of treaty obligations is a matter to be settled amongst the Contracting Parties themselves. Article 169, in contrast, enables an independent Community body, the Commission, to invoke the compulsory jurisdiction of the European Court against a defaulting Member State."[38]

At the same time, the "intergovernmental" character of this procedure and the consequent limitations on its efficacy are clear. Four weaknesses are particularly glaring:

---

[38] Evans, "The Enforcement Procedure of Article 169 EEC: Commission Discretion," *European Law Review* 4 (1979), 442, 443.

1. the procedure is political in nature; the Commission may have appropriate non-legal reasons not to initiate a prosecution;
2. a centralized agency with limited human resources is unable adequately to identify, process, and monitor all possible Member State violations and infringements;
3. Article 169 may be inappropriate to apply to small violations; even if small violations are properly identified, dedicating Commission resources to infringements that do not raise an important principle or create a major economic impact is wasteful; and
4. finally, and most importantly, no real enforcement exists; proceedings conclude with a "declaratory" judgment of the European Court without enforcement sanctions.

Judicial review at the Member State level

The weaknesses of Articles 169–172 are remedied to an extent by judicial review within the judicial systems of the Member States in collaboration with the European Court. Article 177 provides, *inter alia*, that when a question concerning the interpretation of the Treaty is raised before a national court, the court may suspend the national proceedings and request a preliminary ruling from the European Court in Luxembourg on the correct interpretation of the Treaty. If the national court is the court of last resort, then it must request a European Court ruling. Once this ruling is made, it is remitted back to the national court which gives, on the basis of the ruling, the opinion in the case before it. The national courts and the European Court are thus integrated into a unitary system of judicial review.

The European Court and national courts have made good use of this procedure. On its face the purpose of Article 177 is simply to ensure uniform interpretation of Community law throughout the Member States. That, apparently, is how the framers of the Treaty understood it.[39] However, very often the factual situation in which Article 177 comes into play involves an individual litigant pleading in national court that a rule, measure, or national practice should not be applied because it violates the Community obligations of the Member State. In this manner the attempts of Member States to practice selective Community membership by disregarding their obligations have become regularly adjudicated before their

---

[39] Pescatore, "Les travaux du 'Groupe Juridique' dans la négociation des Traités de Rome," *Studia diplomatica* 34 (1981), 159, 173 ("Pour autant que je m'en souvienne, l'acceptation de cette idée dans son principe, ne fit pas de difficultes: je penche a croire que tous, peut-être, n'avaint pas conscience de l'importance de cette innovation." Translated: "As far as I can remember, the acceptance of that idea as to its principle did not face any difficulties: I am inclined to think that perhaps not everybody was aware of the importance of that innovation.").

own national courts. On submission of the case, the European Court has rendered its interpretation of Community law within the factual context of the case before it. Theoretically, the European Court may not itself rule on the *application* of Community law. But, as one scholar notes:

> [I]t is no secret . . . that in practice, when making preliminary rulings the Court has often transgressed the theoretical border line . . . [I]t provides the national judge with an answer in which questions of law and of fact are sufficiently interwoven as to leave the national judge with only little discretion and flexibility in making his final decision.[40]

The fact that the national court renders the final judgment is crucial to the procedure. The binding effect and enforcement value of such a decision, coming from a Member State's own court, may be contrasted with a similar decision handed down in declaratory fashion by the European Court under the previously discussed Article 169 procedure. A national court opinion takes care of the most dramatic weakness of the Article 169 procedure: the ability of a Member State, *in extremis*, to disregard the strictures of the European Court. Under the Article 177 procedure this disregard is impossible. A state, in our Western democracies, cannot disobey its own courts.

The other weaknesses of the Article 169 procedure are also remedied to some extent: individual litigants are usually not politically motivated in bringing their actions; small as well as big violations are adjudicated; and, in terms of monitoring, the Community citizen becomes, willy nilly, a decentralized agent for monitoring compliance by Member States with their Treaty obligations.

The Article 177 system is not complete, however. Not all violations come before national courts; the success of the system depends on the collaboration between national courts and the European Court; and Member States may, and often have, utilized the delays of the system to defer ruling.

On the other hand, the overall effect of the judicial remedies cannot be denied. The combination of the "constitutionalization" and the system of judicial remedies to a large extent *nationalized* Community obligations and introduced on the Community level the *habit of obedience* and the respect for the rule of law which traditionally is less associated with international obligations than national ones.[41]

---

[40] Rasmussen, "Why is Article 173 Interpreted against Private Plaintiffs?" *European Law Review* 5 (1980), 112, 125.

[41] See H. L. A. Hart, *The Concept of Law* (Clarendon Press: Oxford, 1961) (especially chapters 3 and 10); see also Jones, "The Legal Nature of the European Community: A Jurisprudential Analysis Using H. L. A. Hart's Model of Law and a Legal System," *Cornell International Law Journal* 17 (1984), 1.

It is at this juncture that one may speculate about the most profound difference between the Community legal order and international law generally. The combined effect of constitutionalization and the evolution of the system of remedies results, in my view, in the removal from the Community legal order of the most central legal artifact of international law: the notion (and doctrinal apparatus) of exclusive state responsibility with its concomitant principles of reciprocity and counter-measures. The Community legal order, on this view, is a truly self-contained legal regime with no recourse to the mechanism of state responsibility, at least as traditionally understood, and therefore to reciprocity and counter-measures, even in the face of actual or potential failure.[42] Without these features, so central to the classic international legal order, the Community truly becomes something "new."

At the end of the day the debate about the theoretical difference between international law and Community law may have the relevance of some long-lasting theological disputes, i.e., none at all. Whatever the differences in theory, there can be no argument that the Community legal order as it emerged from the foundational period appeared in its operation much closer to a working constitutional order, a fact which, as will shortly emerge, had a fundamental impact on the way in which it was treated by its Member States.

---

[42] The argument for treating the Community as a fully self-contained regime in which states cannot resort to counter-measures rests, briefly, on two lines of reasoning. First, the Treaty itself provides for a comprehensive system of compulsory judicial dispute resolution and remedies, akin to that in a federal state, which would exclude the apparatus of state responsibility and counter-measures, a creature of the self-help horizontality of international law. *Cf.* Submissions of the Commission cited approvingly by the Court in Joined Cases 142 and 143/80, *Amministrazione Delle Finanze Dellostato* v. *Essevi* [1981] ECR 1,413, 1,431 ("Above all, it must be pointed out that in no circumstances may the Member States rely on similar infringements by other Member States in order to escape their own obligations under the provisions of the Treaty."); Joined Cases 90 and 91/63, *EEC Commission* v. *Luxembourg* [1964] ECR 625; Case 232/78, *EEC Commission* v. *France* [1979] ECR 2,729. See also *Ministere Public* v. *Guy Blanguernon* [1990] 2 CMLR 340; [1990] I-ECR 83 at 92, recital 7 ("[A]ccording to settled case law, a Member State cannot justify failure to fulfill its obligation ... by the fact that other Member States have also failed to fulfill theirs ... Under the legal system laid down by the Treaty the implementation of Community law by Member States cannot be subject to a condition of reciprocity."). Second, even in an extreme case in which a Member State failed to execute a judgment of the European Court, the recourse to counter-measures would inevitably affect individuals removed from the dispute, militating against the very notion of a "new legal order of international law ... the subjects of which comprise not the only Member States but also their nationals." Case 26/62, *NV Algemene Transport-en Expeditie Odememing van Gend and Loos* v. *Nederlandse administratie der belastingen* [1963] ECR 1, recital 3 (hereinafter "*van Gend and Loos*"). *Contra* Simma, "Self Contained Regimes," *Netherlands Yearbook of International Law* 16 (1985), 111, 123–9 (sustains the ultimate recourse, even for the Community, to public law and classical state responsibility).

The dynamics of Voice in the foundational period

I return to the main theme of this part of the analysis: the relationship between Voice and Exit. The closure of Exit, in my perspective, means that Community obligations, Community law, and Community policies were "for real." Once adopted (the crucial phrase is "once adopted"), Member States found it difficult to avoid Community obligations. If Exit is foreclosed, the need for Voice increases. This is precisely what happened in the European Community in the foundational period. In what may almost be termed a ruthless process, Member States took control over Community decision-making.

We may divide the Community decision-making process into the following phases: (1) the political impetus for a policy; (2) the technical elaboration of policies and norms; (3) the formulation of a formal proposal; (4) the adoption of the proposal; and (5) the execution of the adopted proposal.

The Treaty's original decision-making process had strong supranational elements. The European Commission, the Community body *par excellence*, had virtually exclusive proposal-making competence (the nearly exclusive "right of initiative"), essentially enabling it to determine the agenda of the Community. The Commission was also responsible for preparing the proposals for formal adoption by the Council of Ministers (comprising the representatives of the Member States) and for acting as the secondary legislature of the Community. The adoption process was supranational, especially in relation to most operational areas, in that it foresaw, by the end of the transitional period, decision by majority voting. Finally, execution (by administrative regulation) was, again, the preserve of the Commission.

During the foundational period, in every phase of decision-making, the Member States, often at the expense of the Commission, assumed a dominant say. The cataclysmic event was the 1965 crisis brought about by France, which objected to the entry into force of the Treaty provisions that would actually introduce majority voting at the end of the transitional period. The crisis was "resolved" by the legally dubious Luxembourg Accord,[43] whereby, *de facto*, each and every Member State could veto Community proposed legislation. This signaled the rapid collapse of all other supranational features of Community decision-making.

---

[43] The text may be found in H. R. Simmonds (ed.), *Encyclopaedia of European Community Law* (Sweet & Maxwell: London; Green: Edinburgh; Bender: New York), vol. B:2, para. B10-336. Although the Accord does not as such sanction the veto power, "a convention giving each Member State, in effect, a right of veto in respect of its 'very important interests' was established by the practice of the Council after 1965": *ibid.* at para. B10-337.

The European Council of Ministers, an organ *dehors* the Treaties, assumed the role of giving impetus to the policy agenda of the Community. The Commission formally retained its exclusive power of proposal, but in reality was reduced to something akin to a secretariat. Technical elaboration became infused with Member State influence in the shape of various groups of national experts.[44] In the proposal-formulation process the Commission commenced a practice of conducting a first, unofficial round of negotiations with COREPER, the sub-organ of Council.[45] In addition, as mentioned, the Luxembourg Accord debilitated the Council's voting process, giving each Member State control over proposals and their adoption. Even in the execution of policies, the Commission and Community were "burdened" with a vast range of management and other regulatory committees composed of Member State representatives who controlled that process as well.[46]

Increased Voice is thus a code for a phenomenon of the Member States jointly and severally taking control of decision-making, leading to the process by which the original institutional structures foreseen in the Treaties broke down. It caused the so-called *lourdeur*[47] of the Community process and is believed by many to be the source of much of the Community malaise of that period and beyond.

The relationship between Exit and Voice in the foundational period

How then do we explain these conflicting developments on the legal and political planes? I suggest explanations at three overlapping levels. The combination captures the richness and significance of the Community experience in the foundational period.

First, the developments in each of the respective political and legal domains can be explained as entirely self-referential and self-contained. Thus, for example, the very advent of de Gaulle had a major negative impact in the political realm.[48] Within the realm of law there was a clear

---

[44] See, e.g., "Report On European Institutions"; A. Spinelli, *Towards the European Union* (1983).

[45] COREPER, the Committee of Permanent Representatives, is composed of permanent representatives of the Member States to the Community who fulfill the essential day-to-day role of State representatives to the Council. On the role of COREPER within the work of the Council of Ministers, see, e.g., "Report on European Institutions" at 39–41.

[46] In passing, I should note that Member State control meant governmental-executive control. One net effect of this process was the creation of the so-called democracy deficit, which I discuss at pp. 77–86 below.

[47] The heaviness of the decisional process, debilitating to the efficiency of the Council and the Community as a whole. See, e.g., "Report on European Institutions" at 27–9, 37–8.

[48] "Throughout the eleven years during which General de Gaulle [who was 'allergic' to anything supranational] remained in power, no notable progress could be made in integration, either in

internal legal logic which led the Court from, for example, the doctrine of direct effect to the doctrine of supremacy.[49]

The second explanation is that in the face of a political crisis already manifest in the 1960s, resulting from, *inter alia*, a new posture of France under de Gaulle and declining political will among the Member States to follow the decision-making processes of the Treaty and to develop a loyalty to the European venture, the European Court stepped in to hold the construct together.[50] In this second level of analysis the relationship is unidirectional. The integrating federal legal development was a response and reaction to a disintegrating confederal political development.

The most fascinating question in this regard is how to explain the responsiveness of the Member State courts to the new judicial architecture. We have already noted that absent such responsiveness – normatively in accepting the new constitutional doctrines and practically in putting them into use through the application of the preliminary reference procedure of Article 177 – the constitutional transformation ushered by the European Court would have remained with all the systemic deficiencies of general public international law. One could hardly have talked with credibility about a new legal order.

Due to its nature, a reply to the question must remain speculative. In addition, probably no one answer alone can explain this remarkable phenomenon. The following are some possible explanations in brief, all of which may have contributed to the overall enlistment of the judicial branch in Europe.

The first reply, one which holds considerable force, is the most obvious. Courts are charged with upholding the law. The constitutional interpretations given to the Treaty of Rome by the European Court carried legitimacy derived from two sources: first, from the composition of the Court, which had as members senior jurists from all Member States; and,

---

the political domain, the institutional domain, the monetary domain or in the geographical extension of the common market.": Greilsammer, "Theorizing European Integration" at 141.

[49] If one accepts, as one must, the principle of the uniform application of Community law throughout the Community, a clear link exists whereby a holding of direct effect compels a holding of supremacy. In *van Gend and Loos* [1963] ECR 1, recital 2, the Commission and the Advocate-General differed as to whether direct effect existed. The Advocate-General argued that, since the Community had no principle of supremacy, there was no direct effect. The Commission argued that direct effect would compel supremacy. Thus, although they disagreed on the result, they acknowledged the linkage between the two.

[50] The most radical challenge to the Court as an integrationist activist transcending the political will of the Member States is H. Rasmussen, *On Law and Policy in the European Court of Justice* (Martinus Nijhoff: Dordrecht, Boston, 1986), which also critiques most books on the Court that support this approach. But see Cappelletti, "Is the European Court of Justice 'Running Wild'?" *European Law Review* 12 (1987), 3; Weiler, "The Court of Justice on Trial," *Common Market Law Review* 24 (1987), 555 (review essay of Rasmussen's book).

second, from the legal reasoning of the judgments themselves. One could cavil with this or that decision,[51] but the overall construct had an undeniable coherence, which seemed truly to reflect the purposes of the Treaty to which the Member States had solemnly adhered.

Secondly, it is clear that a measure of transnational incrementalism developed. Once some of the highest courts of a few of the Member States endorsed the new constitutional construct, their counterparts in other Member States heard more arguments that those courts should do the same, and it became more difficult for national courts to resist the trend with any modicum of credibility. The fact that the idea of European integration in itself held a certain appeal could only have helped in this regard.

Last, but not least, noble ideas (such as the rule of law and European integration) aside, the legally driven constitutional revolution was a narrative of plain and simple judicial empowerment. The empowerment was not only, or even primarily, of the European Court, but of the Member State courts, of lower national courts in particular. Whereas the higher courts acted diffidently at first, the lower courts made wide and enthusiastic use of the Article 177 procedure. This is immediately understandable both on a simple individual psychological level and on a deep institutional plane. Lower courts and their judges were given the facility to engage with the highest jurisdiction in the Community and thus to have *de facto* judicial review of legislation. For many this would be heady stuff. Even in legal systems such as that of Italy, which already included judicial review, the EC system gave judges at the lowest level powers that had been reserved to the highest court in the land. Institutionally, for courts at all levels in all Member States, the constitutionalization of the Treaty of Rome, with principles of supremacy and direct effect binding on governments and parliaments, meant an overall strengthening of the judicial branch *vis-à-vis* the other branches of government. And the ingenious nature of Article 177 ensured that national courts did not feel that the empowerment of the European Court was at their expense.[52]

Finally there is a third, critical layer that explains the relationship between the contrasting legal and political developments during the foundational period. It might be true that the Court of Justice stepped in in the face of a political decline. But it would be wrong to consider the relationship in exclusively unidirectional terms. The relationship has been

---

[51] Indeed, in several of the key cases, such as *van Gend and Loos*, the Court's own Advocate-General differed from the Court. For an analysis, see Stein, "Towards a European Foreign Policy?" See also Rasmussen, *On Law and Policy*.

[52] In some areas, such as human rights, the high courts of at least some of the Member States needed some judicial persuasion. See pp. 23–5 above and pp. 45–6 below.

bi-directional and even circular. The integrating legal developments at least indirectly influenced the disintegrating political ones.

I suggest a tentative thesis, which perhaps could even be part of a general theory of international law-making. This thesis meshes neatly with Hirschman's notion of Exit and Voice and posits a relationship between "hard law" and "hard law-*making.*" The "harder" the law in terms of its binding effect both on and within states, the less willing states are to give up their prerogative to control the emergence of such law or the law's "opposability" to them. When the international law is "real," when it is "hard" in the sense of being binding not only on but also in states, and when there are effective legal remedies to enforce it, decision-making suddenly becomes important, indeed crucial.[53] This is a way of explaining what happened in the Community in that period.

What we called, in Hirschmanian terms, the closure of Selective Exit

---

[53] For example, in the United Nations, the following structure exists: in the General Assembly, resolutions (in principle, not binding) may be adopted by majority vote: in the Security Council, resolutions (binding) may be vetoed by the permanent members. The permanent members must be seen, at least partially, as representative of the major interests of the different political groupings in the General Assembly. The Council of Europe, to a certain extent, with the exception of the human-rights apparatus, has a similar construction. Year after year, the Council of Europe passes resolutions and treaties in a seemingly effortless stream. This is so because resolutions and draft treaties of the Council of Europe do not, as such, bind the Member States. Members can always "go home," think about individual proposals, and decide to accept or reject them. A similar linkage exists in relation to the conclusion of multilateral treaties and the permissible regime of reservations. Under the old regime, texts of multilateral treaties were adopted, unless otherwise provided, by unanimous vote of the contracting parties (Enhanced Voice). The corollary was that states were highly restricted in their ability to make reservations; these had to be accepted by all parties to the Treaty (Limited Exit). Under the new treaty law – ushered by the *Reservation to the Convention on Genocide Case* [1951] ICJ 15, and later by the Vienna Convention on the Law of Treaties (1969), Arts. 9(2) and 19–21 – the text of a multilateral treaty could be adopted by the vote of two-thirds of the states present and voting (Reduced Voice); but the corollary was the greater ease with which States could make reservation to such texts. In some modern conventions, such as the 1982 Law of the Sea Convention, the unanimous adoption (Enhanced Voice) was again accompanied by a prohibition on reservations (Reduced Exit). A similar development may be noted in relation to the doctrine of the persistent objector in the formation of customary law. It is clear that the modern approach to custom is more lenient towards the formation of custom with more limited participation of states in that formation (Reduced Voice), It has been predicted that this in turn will lead to a greater invocation by states of the doctrine of persistent objector (Enhanced Exit), See Stein, "The Approach of the Different Drummer: The Principle of the Persistent Objector in International Law," *Harvard International Law Journal* 26 (1985), 457. The relationship between decision-making and normative outcomes exists beyond the realm of public law and may be found in private law institutions as well. Thus Gilmore, in discussing the evolution of contract theory, contrasts the nineteenth-century model, which embraced a narrow consideration theory (whereby it was difficult to enter into a contract), but also a narrow excuse theory (difficult to get out). In our terms, this would correspond to High Voice and Restricted Exit. Twentieth-century contract theory saw a move towards "a free and easy approach to the problem of contract formation" (Reduced Voice), which "goes hand in hand with a free and

was just that: the process by which Community norms and policy hardened into binding law with effective legal remedies. The increase in Voice was the "natural reaction" to this process. The Member States realized the critical importance of taking control of a decision-making process, the outcome of which they would have to live with and abide by. By "natural reaction" I do not mean to imply a simplistic causal relationship. I do not suggest that, as a direct result of the decisions of the Court, in say, *van Gend and Loos*[54] (in 1963) or *Costa* v. *ENEL*[55] (in 1964), the French government decided (in 1965) to precipitate the crisis that led to the Luxembourg Accord. I suggest that the constitutionalization process created a normative construct in which such a precipitous political development becomes understandable. Because Community norms in terms of substance were important,[56] and because they were by then situated in a context that did not allow selective application, control of the creation of the norm itself was the only possible solution for individual states.[57]

Historically (and structurally) an equilibrium was established. On the one hand stood a strong constitutional integrative process that, in radical mutation of the Treaty, linked the legal order of the Community with that of the Member States in a federal-like relationship. This was balanced by a relentless and equally strong process, also deviating radically from the

easy approach to the problem of contract dissolution or excuse" (Easy Exit): G. Gilmore, *The Death of Contract* (Ohio State University Press: Columbus, OH, 1974), 48.

[54] [1963] ECR 1.   [55] Case 6/64, *Flaminio Costa* v. *ENEL* [1964] ECR 585.

[56] Even if the Community did not, in its initial phases, affect the lives of many citizens, it was crucial in some important economic and political sectors, for example, agriculture.

[57] It is difficult to adduce hard proof for this thesis, but the following is evocative. In the United Kingdom's White Paper presented to Parliament by the Prime Minister in July 1971 advocating the UK's accession to the Community, the linkage is rather clear. See "The United Kingdom and the European Communities" (Cmnd. 4715, 1971), paras. 29–30. In "Membership of the European Community: Report on Renegotiation" (Cmnd. 6003, 1975), the linkage is actually made. In a section entitled "The Special Nature of the Community" (para. 118), one finds first an explanation of the "direct applicability of Community law in member countries" (para. 122), corresponding to our analysis of the constitutionalization and the closure of Selective Exit. Immediately afterwards, in "Power of Member Governments" (paras. 123–5), one finds: "[T]he importance of accommodating the interests of individual member states is recognised in the Council's general practice of taking decisions by consensus, so that each member state is in a position to block agreement unless interests to which it attaches importance are met" (para. 124). The authoritative *Encyclopaedia of European Community Law*, in interpreting the Luxembourg Accord and the veto power, states: "the existence of that convention [veto power] was a significant factor in the decision by Denmark and the United Kingdom, and subsequently by Greece, to enter the Communities.": *Encyclopaedia of European Community Law*, vol. B:2 at 11, B10–337. In *ERTA*, one of the key "constitutionalizing" cases, Advocate-General Dutheillet de Lamothe seems to suggest the same type of linkage: "Finally, from the point of view of the development of common policies, are there not grounds for fearing that the Ministers would resist the adoption of regulations which would result in the loss, in cases not provided for by the Treaty, of their authority in international matters?": *ibid.* at 292.

Treaty, that transferred political and decision-making power into a confederal procedure controlled by the Member States acting jointly and severally.

The linkage between these two facets of the Community may explain and even resolve several issues regarding the process of European integration. The first issue relates to the very process of constitutionalization in the 1960s and early 1970s, a phenomenon that has been, as noted, at the center of legal discourse about the Community. Indeed, insiders refer to this period, especially in the jurisprudence of the European Court, as the "heroic period." But, as we observed, these profound constitutional mutations took place in a *political* climate that was somewhat hostile to, and suspicious of, supranationalism. How then – and this is the dilemma – could changes so profound, which would normally require something akin to a constitutional convention subject to elaborate procedures of diplomatic negotiation and democratic control, occur with a minimal measure of political (i.e., Member State) opposition?[58] Part of the answer rests, of course, in the fact that constitutionalization during the foundational period was judicially driven, thus attaching to itself that deep-seated legitimacy that derives from the mythical neutrality and religious-like authority with which we invest our supreme courts.

The explanation I suggest is derived from the hard law/hard law-making theorem, from the interplay of Exit and Voice. Instead of a simple (legal) cause and (political) effect, this subtler process was a circular one. On this reading, the deterioration of the political supranational decisional procedures, the suspension of majority voting in 1966, and the creation and domination of intergovernmental bodies such as COREPER and the European Council constituted the political conditions that allowed the Member States to digest and accept the process of constitutionalization. Had no veto power existed, had intergovernmentalism not become the order of the day, it is not clear to my mind that the Member States would have accepted with such equanimity what the European Court was doing. They could accept the constitutionalization because they took real control of the decision-making process, thus minimizing its threatening features.

Our speculation should not stop here: while this description of the legal-political equilibrium may explain how and why the Member States were willing to digest, or accept, the constitutional revolution, it does not explain their interest in doing so. A theory of state action without interest analysis is incomplete. What, then, was the interest of the Member States in

---

[58] Our confusion is enhanced if we consider that the changes introduced by the Single European Act in 1986 were *per se* less radical, and yet necessitated a tortuous political process, including a constitutional challenge in the supreme court of one of the Member States. See *Croty* v. *An Taoiseach* [1987] CMLR 666 (Irish Supreme Court).

not simply accepting the changing morphology of the Community but actually pursuing it?

The fundamental explanation is that the Member States, severally and jointly, balanced the material and political costs and benefits of the Community. Both the Community vision and its specific policy agenda were conceived as beneficial to the actors. It may, at first sight, seem reasonable when thinking about the Community and its Member States to conceive of this relationship as a zero-sum game: the strengthening of the Community must come "at the expense" of the Member States (and *vice versa*). However, the evolution of the Community in its foundational period ruptures this premise of zero-sum. The strengthening of the Community was accompanied by the strengthening of its Member States.[59] Stanley Hoffmann gave a convincing political explanation of this phenomenon.[60] But the phenomenon also derives from the unique legal-political equilibrium of the Community structure.

The interplay between the Community normative and decision-making regimes, as explained above, gave each individual Member State a position of power brokerage it never could have attained in more traditional fora of international intercourse. The constitutional infrastructure "locked" the Member States into a communal (read "Community") decision-making forum with a fairly rigorous and binding legal discipline. The ability to "go it alone" was always somewhat curtailed and, in some crucial areas, foreclosed. The political superstructure, with its individual veto power and intergovernmental discourse, gave each Member State a decisive position of influence over the normative outcome.

Finally, in at least an indirect way, these basic features of the foundational period accentuate and explain a permanent feature of the Community: its so-called democracy deficit.[61]

As already mentioned, the reference to "Member State" as a homogeneous concept or actor is misleading in several ways,[62] increasingly so in an

---

[59] It is easy to identify the interest that the small states would have in this structure: their weight in, and power over, decision-making in inherently interdependent policy areas becomes incomparably larger compared to outside arm's-length negotiations. In principle this is true also for larger Member States. *Cf.* "The United Kingdom and the European Communities" at 7–14. In addition, the larger Member States had particular interests that could be vindicated effectively through the Community. Examples are the French interest in a European-wide common agricultural policy and the German interest in relegitimation.

[60] Hoffman, "Reflection on the Nation-State in Western Europe Today," in L. Tsoukalis (ed.), *The European Community: Past, Present and Future* (Basil Blackwell: Oxford, 1983), 21, 22.

[61] See D. Marquand, *Parliament for Europe* (Jonathan Cape: London, 1979), 64–6; see also "Report Drawn up on behalf of the Committee on Institutional Affairs on the Democratic Deficit in the European Community," PE Doc. No. A 2-276/87 (February 1, 1988).

[62] See note 7, p. 12 above.

ever more complex Community.[63] In discussing the democracy deficit it is more accurate to speak instead of the "government," i.e., the executive branch, of each Member State. Admittedly, the Treaty itself laid the seeds for the democracy deficit by making the statal executive branch the ultimate legislator in the Community. The decision-making Council members are first of all members of their respective executive branches and thus directly representative of their home-state governments. The only democratic check on Council decisions is a submission to the meek control of the European Parliament. Direct democratic accountability, by design or by default, remains vested in national parliaments to whom the members of the Council are answerable.

The mutations of the legal structure and the political process in the foundational period impacted this basic deficiency in a variety of ways.

The process of constitutionalization, hardening Community measures into supreme, often directly effective laws, backed with formidable enforcement mechanisms, meant that once these laws were enacted, national parliaments could not have second thoughts or control their content at the national, implementing level. The only formal way in which accountability could be ensured would be by tight *ex ante* control by national parliaments on the activities of ministers in Community fora. This has proved largely not feasible.[64] The net result is that the executive branches of the Member States often act together as a binding legislator outside the decisive control of any parliamentary chamber.

The changes in the decision-making processes meant that it was not simply the Voice of the Member States that was enhanced, but the Voice of "governments." It is not entirely fanciful to surmise that the acceptability of the Community system in the foundational period was not simply because it vindicated the interests of Member States but also because it enhanced the power of governments (the executive branch) *per se*.

Conclusions to the foundational period

The foundational period has been characterized by legal scholars as an heroic epoch of constitution-building in Europe, as a time of laying the foundation for a federal Europe. It has been described by political scientists as a nadir in the history of European integration, as an era of crumbling supranationalism. The thrust of my argument has been that a true under-

---

[63] See Snyder, *New Directions* at 32–6.

[64] See Sasse, "The Control of the National Parliaments of the Nine over European Affairs," in A. Cassese (ed.), *Parliamentary Control over Foreign Policy* (Sijthoff and Noordhoff: Alphen aan den Rijn, Germantown, MD, 1980), 137. Denmark may be the exception: see Mendel, "The Role of Parliament in Foreign Affairs in Denmark," in *ibid.* at 53, 57.

standing of this period can only be achieved by a marriage of these two conflicting visions into a unified narrative in which the interaction of the legal and the political, and the consequent equilibrium, constitute the very fundamental feature of the Community legal structure and political process.

This very feature helps explain the uniqueness and stability of the Community for much of its life: a polity that achieved a level of integration similar to that found only in fully fledged federal states and yet that contained unthreatened and even strengthened Member States.

1973 TO THE MIDDLE OF THE 1980S: MUTATION OF JURISDICTION AND COMPETENCES

Introduction

The period from the middle of the 1970s to the middle of the 1980s is traditionally considered a stagnant epoch in European integration. The momentum created by the accession of the UK, Ireland, and Denmark did not last long. The oil crisis of late 1973 displayed a Community unable to develop a common external posture. Internally the three new Member States, two of which, the UK and Denmark, were often recalcitrant partners, burdened the decision-making process, forcing it to a grinding pace. It is not surprising that much attention was given in that period to proposals to address a seriously deteriorating institutional framework and to relaunch the Community.[65]

And yet it is in this politically stagnant period that another large-scale mutation in the constitutional architecture of the Community took place, a mutation that has received far less attention than the constitutional revolution in the foundational period. It concerned the principle of division of competences between Community and Member States.

In most federal polities the demarcation of competences between the general polity and its constituent units is the most explosive of "federal" battlegrounds. Traditionally, the relationship in non-unitary systems is conceptualized by the principle of enumerated powers. The principle has

[65] See "Report on European Institutions"; Spierenburg Report; the six Reports and Resolution of the European Parliament on Institutions of July 9, 1981 (Hänsch, Diligent Baduel, Glorioso, van Miert, Elles, Antoniozzi); "The Institutional System of the Community: Restoring the Balance," *Bulletin of the European Communities* (Supp. 3/82), 5; "French Government Memorandum on Revitalization of the Community," *Bulletin of the European Communities* 14 (11-1981), 92; "German–Italian Initiative: Draft European Act," *Bulletin of the European Communities* 14 (11-1981), 87 (Genscher–Colombo Initiative); and "Report on European Political Cooperation," *Bulletin of the European Communities* (Supp. 3/81), 14. See generally, on that epoch and these proposals, Weiler, "The Genscher–Colombo Draft European Act: The Politics of Indecision," *Journal of European Integration* 6 (1983), 129.

no fixed content and its interpretation varies from system to system; in some it has a stricter and in others a more relaxed construction. Typically, the strength by which this principle is upheld (or, at least, the shrillness of the rhetoric surrounding it) reflects the strength of the belief in the importance of preserving the original distribution of legislative powers as a defining feature of the polity. Thus, there can be little doubt about the very different ethos that underscored the evolution of, for example, the Canadian and US federalisms, in their formative periods and beyond, regarding enumeration. Nowhere is this different ethos clearer than in the judicial rhetoric of enumeration. The *dicta* of Lord Atkin[66] and Chief Justice Marshall[67] concerning powers are the theater pieces of this rhetoric. Likewise, the recurring laments over the "death of federalism"[68] in this or that federation are typically associated with a critique of a relaxed attitude towards enumeration and an inevitable shift of power to the center at the expense of the states.

The different views about the strictness or flexibility of enumeration reflects a basic understanding of federalism and integration. Returning to the Canadian–US comparison, we find the Atkin and Marshall *dicta* reconceptualized as follows. Wade, in the context of the Canadian experience, suggests that:

> The essential elements of a federal constitution are that powers are divided between the central and provincial governments and that neither has legal power to encroach upon the domain of the other, except through the proper process of constitutional amendment ... [T]he spirit ... which is inherent in the whole federal situation [is] that neither side, so to speak, should have it in its power to invade the sphere of the other.[69]

In contrast, Sandalow, reflecting on the US experience, suggests that:

> The disintegrative potential of [questions concerning the legality of governmental

---

[66] On enumeration, Lord Atkin stated: "No one can doubt that this distribution [of legislative powers between the Dominion and the Provinces] ... is one of the most essential conditions, probably the most essential condition [in the Canadian federal arrangement] ... While the ship of state now sails on larger ventures ... she still retains the watertight compartments which are an essential part of her original structure.": *A.-G. Canada* v. *A.-G. Ontario* (1937) 1 DLR 673 at 682–4 (PC).

[67] Over a century before, Chief Justice Marshall asserted: "Let the end be legitimate, let it be within the scope of the Constitution, and all means which are appropriate, which are plainly adapted to that end, which are not prohibited, but consist with the letter and spirit of the [C]onstitution, are constitutional.": *McCulloch* v. *Maryland*, 17 US (4 Wheat.) 316 (1819) at 421.

[68] E.g., van Alstyne, "The Second Death of Federalism," *Michigan Law Review* 83 (1985), 1,709.

[69] Wade, "Amendment of the Constitution of Canada: The Role of the United Kingdom Parliament," in *British North America Acts: The Role of Parliament*, 2 HC 42 (1981) at 102, 108 (memorandum and evidence submitted to the Foreign Affairs Committee of the House of Commons).

40

action] is especially great when they [challenge] the distribution of authority in a divided or federal system ... [Where] Congress determines that a national solution is appropriate for one or another economic issue, its power to fashion one is not likely to be limited by constitutional divisions of power between it and the state legislatures.[70]

These differences in approach could be explained by formal differences in the structure of the British North American Act (which predated the current Canadian Constitution) as compared to the US Constitution. But they also disclose a principled difference in the way the two systems value enumerated powers within the federal architecture, a difference between ends and means, functions and values. In the Wade conception of the Canadian system the division of powers was considered a *per se* value, an end in itself. The *form* of divided governance was considered to be on par with the other fundamental purposes of a government, such as obtaining security, order, and welfare, and was viewed as part of its democratic architecture. In the United States, the federal distribution retained its constitutional importance as the system evolved. In practice, however, it would seem that the principle of division was subjected to higher values and invoked as a useful *means* for achieving other objectives of the US union. To the extent that the division became an obstacle for the achievement of such aims it was sacrificed.[71] We may refer to this approach as a functional one. The dichotomy is, of course, not total; we find strands of both the functional and *per se* approaches in each of the systems. Nevertheless, clear differences exist in the weight given to each of the strands and in the evolution of the two federations. In addition, the legal debate about division of powers was (and remains) frequently the code for battles over raw power between different *loci* of governance, an aspect ultimately of crucial importance.

In Europe, the Treaty itself does not precisely define the material limits of Community jurisdiction.[72] But it is clear that, in a system that rejected a "melting pot" ethos and explicitly in the preamble to its constituent instrument affirms the importance of "an ever closer union among the *peoples* of Europe," that saw power being bestowed by the Member State on the Community (with residual power thus retained by the Member States) and consecrated in an international Treaty containing a clause that effectively conditions revision of the treaty on ratification by parliaments of

---

[70] Sandalow, "The Expansion of Federal Legislative Authority," in Sandalow and Stein, *Courts and Free Markets*, 49 at 49–50 (I have reversed the order of quoted sentences).

[71] These developments have had their critics: e.g., van Alstyne, "The Second Death of Federalism"; *cf.* Amar, "Of Sovereignty and Federalism," *Yale Law Journal* 96 (1987), 1,425.

[72] Arts. 2 and 3 of the EEC Treaty set out the "tasks" or "purposes" of the Community, from which its competences are derived in rather open-textured language.

all Member States,[73] the "original" understanding was that the principle of enumeration would be strict and that jurisdictional enlargement (*rationae materia*) could not be lightly undertaken. This understanding was shared not only by scholars,[74] but also by the Member States and the political organs of the Community, as evidenced by their practices,[75] as well as by the Court of Justice itself. In its most famous decision, *van Gend and Loos*, the Court affirmed that the Community constitutes "a new legal order of international law for the benefit of which the states have limited their sovereign rights, *albeit in limited fields*."[76] And earlier, in even more striking language, albeit related to the Coal and Steel Community, the Court explained that:

> The Treaty rests on a derogation of sovereignty consented by the Member States to supranational jurisdiction for an object strictly determined. The legal principle at the basis of the Treaty is a principle of limited competence. The Community is a legal person of public law and to this effect it has the necessary legal capacity to exercise its functions but only those.[77]

In light of the Member States' vigorous reaction to the constitutional mutation of the Community during the foundational period, seizing effective control of Community governance, and the fact that a lax attitude to enumeration would indeed seem to result in a strengthening of the center at the expense of the states, we would expect that this "original" understanding of strict enumeration would be tenaciously preserved.

I characterize the period of the 1970s[78] to the early 1980s as a second and fundamental phase in the transformation of Europe. In this period the Community order mutated almost as significantly as it did in the foundational period. In the 1970s and early 1980s, the principle of enumerated

---

[73] EEC Treaty, Art. 236.

[74] Judge Pescatore, who later became one of the formidable champions of an expansive and evolutive view of the Community, offered a classic endorsement of this original narrow understanding in at least some of its aspects: Pescatore, "Les relations extérieures des Communautés européenne," *Receuils des cours* (1961-II), 1.

[75] For example, in the enactment of Council Regulation No. 803/68, 1968 OJ (L 148), 6 (June 28, 1968), relating to the customs value of goods, a matter at the heart of the common market and the economic sphere of Community activity, the Council resorted to Art. 235 of the Treaty as the legal basis, not believing it had inherent authority in the customs-union provisions of the Treaty.

[76] *van Gend and Loos* [1963] ECR 1 (emphasis added).

[77] Joined Cases 7/56 and 3 to 7/57, *Dinecke Algera* v. *Common Assembly of the European Coal and Steel Community* [1957–8] ECR 39 (hereinafter "*Algera*").

[78] 1973 seems an appropriate signpost, since it followed the European Council meeting of October 1972 in which an explicit decision was made to make full (and, on my reading, expansive) use of Art. 235 as part of the general reinvigoration of the Community. This process coincided with the accession of the three new Member States. Declaration of Paris Summit, *Bulletin of the European Communities* (10-1972).

powers as a constraint on Community *material* jurisdiction (absent Treaty revision) was substantially eroded and in practice virtually disappeared.[79] Constitutionally, no core of sovereign state powers was left beyond the reach of the Community. Put differently, if the constitutional revolution was celebrated in the 1960s albeit "in limited fields," the 1970s saw the erosion of these limits. As an eminent authority assesses the Community today: "There simply is no nucleus of sovereignty that the Member States can invoke, as such, against the Community."[80]

The 1970s mutation I describe went largely unnoticed by the interpretive communities in Europe: the Member States and their governments, political organs of the Community, the European Court and, to an extent, academia.[81] This lack of attention is all the more ironic and striking when it is noted that the interaction among those interpretive communities brought about this fundamental mutation. To be sure, the expansion of Community jurisdiction in the 1970s and early 1980s was widely observed. Indeed, this growth was, as mentioned above, willed by all actors involved.

What was not understood was that, during this process of growth and as a result of its mechanics, the guarantees of jurisdictional demarcation between Community and Member States eroded to the point of collapse. This cognitive dissonance in accounts of the period is so striking that I shall attempt to explain not only the legal–political process by which strict enumeration eroded and practically disappeared, but also the reasons so fundamental a change in the Community architecture was not obvious to all.[82]

---

[79] I should emphasize that my analysis is confined to the question of material competences. Organic and institutional changes are jealously guarded. That, as shall emerge, is part of my thesis. In other words, it is the fact that organic and institutional changes are kept under tight control (essentially conserving the prerogatives of the Member States gained in the foundational period) that enables the Member States to be lax about material demarcation.

[80] Lenaerts, "Constitutionalism" at 220. Note that Lenaerts refers in this statement to what I have termed in this article "absorption."

[81] But see Tizzano, "Lo sviluppo delle competenze materiali delle comunita europee," *Rivista di diritto europeo* 139 (1981); Sasse and Yourow, "The Growth of Legislative Power of the European Communities," in Sandalow and Stein, *Courts and Free Markets*, 92.

[82] The erosion of jurisdictional limits did not mean that the Community and its Member States would never resort to Treaty amendment. Clearly changes as to the method of exercising jurisdiction such as the shift from unanimity to majority voting under Art. 100 would require such amendment. Not all Treaty amendment concerns jurisdictional limits. More interestingly, even in areas where jurisdiction was already clearly asserted, such as in the environmental field, the Member States would, for example in the Single European Act, "reinvent the wheel." And in matters concerning monetary and economic union, they are now negotiating Treaty amendments to give effect to the new monetary constructs. My claim is that this has become their choice, and if they had wished they could have introduced the new monetary regime under Art. 235, easily showing, in the light of other practice concerning 235, that it was necessary for the good functioning of the common market. There are, however, many

Naturally, because the process itself went largely unnoticed when it occurred, its far-reaching consequences and significance were not appreciated at the time. It is a general theme of this article that the first series of mutations in the foundational period conditioned those that followed in the 1970s. I additionally argue that the consequences and significance of the then-unnoticed mutations in the 1970s are becoming acutely transparent today in the final phase of Community evolution. Together with the early mutations, the mutations of the 1970s define the very significance of the Community's evolution.

A typology of jurisdiction in the European Community

In mapping the original understanding of the distribution of competences of the Community and Member States in schematic terms, the following picture emerges.

1. there are areas of activity over which the Community has no jurisdiction;
2. there are areas of activity that are autonomous to the Community (therefore beyond the reach of the Member States' jurisdiction as such); and
3. there are large areas of activity where Community and Member State competences overlap.

A very strict concept of enumeration would suggest that this jurisdictional demarcation, whatever its precise content, could and should change only in accordance with the provisions for Treaty amendment. Jurisdictional mutation in the concept of enumeration would occur where there is evidence of substantial change in this map without resort to Treaty amendment.

In fact, during the period in question, mutation thus defined occurred. Moreover, it was not occasional or limited, but happened in a multiplicity of forms, the combination of which leads to my claim of erosion of constitutional guarantees of enumeration. The picture may best be grasped

advantages to pursuing the Treaty amendment route: to mention just two, the new regime becomes entrenched and cannot be changed by simple legislation (something important for, say, the independence of the proposed central European bank), and it enjoys a higher level of political legitimacy since it calls for ratification by all Member State parliaments. It is also important to understand that I am not claiming that in this period jurisdictional expansion was *quantitatively* impressive. This would be strange in a Community that was decisionally stagnant. In fact, there were many areas of explicit Community competence, such as transport regulation, where nothing was done. The interesting tale concerns the variety of new fields into which the Community moved, each on its own of relatively little importance. In fact, it could be argued that these activities emerged as a distraction, given the Community's inability to deal with its truly pressing problems. But the cumulative effect of all these activities was significant.

by thinking of mutation as occurring in four distinct categories or proto-types.

The categories of mutation

Extension

Extension is mutation[83] in the area of autonomous Community jurisdiction. The most striking example of this change is the well-known evolution of a higher law of human rights in the Community. As already mentioned, the Treaty contains elaborate provisions for review of Community measures by the European Court.[84] It does not include a "Bill of Rights" against which to measure Community acts, nor does it mention, as such, human rights as a grounds for review. Yet, as mentioned earlier, in a process starting in 1969 but consolidated in the 1970s,[85] the Court constructed a formidable[86] apparatus for such review. Despite legal and policy rationales, such a development could not have occurred had the Court taken a strict view of permissible change in the allocation of competences and jurisdiction. Had the Court taken such a view, such a dramatic change could have taken place only by Treaty amendment.

An equally striking example from an area of autonomous Community jurisdiction concerns the standing of the European Parliament. The plain and simple language of the Treaty would seem to preclude both action against and by the European Parliament.[87] Yet the Court, in an expansive, systemic (and, in my view, wholly justified[88]) interpretation of the Treaty,

---

[83] It is important that we do not use the term "mutation" loosely. As a "Framework Document," the Treaty itself often calls for, or allows, change without Treaty amendment. I want to reserve the term "mutation" to those instances where the change is fundamental. Obviously, as shall be seen, when mutation does occur it is always justified by some reference to the Treaty and its "implicit" principles. It is important to understand that I do not make a normative or interpretative argument for some construction of a legal basis in the Treaty. The strict "legal" evaluation is of little interest in my view. My point is that the relevant interpretative communities, by choosing to opt for the wide and flexible reading of the Treaty, have transformed strict enumeration into a very flexible notion, practically emptied of material content in the Community.

[84] See pp. 26–9 above.

[85] For a comprehensive description and analysis of human-rights jurisprudence in the Community, see Clapham, "European Union – The Human Rights Challenge," in A. Clapham (ed.), *Human Rights and the European Community: A Critical Overview* (Nomos: Baden-Baden, 1991), vol. I.

[86] For a critique, see *ibid.*; and Weiler, "The External Legal Relations of Non-Unitary Actors."

[87] See EEC Treaty, Art. 173.

[88] Weiler, "Pride and Prejudice – Parliament v. Council," *European Law Review* 14 (1989), 334.

first allowed Parliament to be sued[89] and then, after some hesitation,[90] granted Parliament standing to sue other Community institutions.[91]

The category of extension requires four ancillary comments. First, it must be emphasized that the analysis of extension (and indeed the other categories of mutation) is intended, for the time being, to be value-neutral. I do not present these examples as a critique of the Court "running wild" or exceeding its own legitimate interpretative jurisdiction. Evaluating these developments, to which I shall return later, involves considerations far wider and weightier than the often arid discussion of judicial propriety. What is important, if there is any force in my argument, is the recasting of known judicial developments, usually analyzed in other legal contexts,[92] as data in the analysis of jurisdictional mutation.

Second, in the case of extension, the principal actor instigating extension was the Court itself, although, of course, at the behest of some plaintiff. Other actors played a more passive role. The action of the Court must be viewed simultaneously as reflective of a flexible, functional approach to enumeration and constitutive of such an ethos in the Community.

Third, this jurisdictional mutation, despite the radical nature of the measures themselves, was rather limited, since it was confined to changes within the autonomous sphere of the Community and did not have a direct impact on the jurisdiction of the Member States. Indeed, the human-rights jurisprudence actually curtailed the freedom of action of the Community.[93] The changes of standing concerning the Parliament were similar in potentially chilling the legislative power of Commission and Council, although in a more muted form.

Finally, and perhaps not altogether surprisingly, these developments and others like them were, with limited exceptions, both welcomed and accepted by the different interpretative communities in Europe, partly because they were seen as pertaining to the other legal categories and partly because they did not encroach directly on the Member State jurisdiction. In any event, these developments were hardly perceived as pertaining to the question of jurisdictional demarcation.

---

[89] *Parti Ecologiste "Les Vertes"* v. *European Parliament* [1986] ECR 1,339.

[90] Case 302/87, *Comitology* [1988] ECR 5615.

[91] Case 70/88, *Parliament* v. *Council* [1990] ECR 2,041.

[92] Thus the human-rights jurisprudence has been discussed essentially as part of a debate on judicial review and not seen as an issue of enumerated powers. Likewise, the issue of parliamentary standing has been seen as an issue of procedure and institutional balance but, again, not as one of enumeration ethos.

[93] Indirectly, of course, this curtails the freedom of the Member States acting *qua* Council of the Community.

Absorption

Absorption is a far deeper form of mutation. It occurs, often unintentionally, when the Community legislative authorities, in exercising substantive legislative powers bestowed on the Community, impinge on areas of Member State jurisdiction outside the Community's explicit competences.

One of many striking illustrations[94] is offered by the events in the *Casagrande* case.[95] Donato Casagrande, an Italian national, son of Italian migrant workers, lived all his life in Munich. In 1971 and 1972 he was a pupil at the German Fridtjof-Nansen-Realschule. The Bavarian law on educational grants (BayAföG) entitles children who satisfy a means test to receive a monthly educational grant from the Länder. The city of Munich refused his application for a grant relying on Article 3 of the same educational law, which excluded from entitlement all non-Germans except stateless people and aliens residing under a right of asylum.

Casagrande, in an action seeking a declaration of nullity of the educational law, relied principally on Article 12 of Council Regulation 1612/68.[96] The article provides that "the children of a national of a Member State who is or has been employed in the territory of another Member State shall be admitted to that State's general educational, apprenticeship, and vocational training courses under the same conditions as the nationals of that State, if such children are residing in its territory." Further, the Member States must encourage "all efforts to enable such children to attend these courses under the best possible conditions."[97]

The Bayerisches Verwaltungsgericht, in an exemplary understanding of the role of review of the European Court, sought a preliminary ruling on the compatibility of the Bavarian educational provision with Article 12 of the Council Regulation.

The submission of the Bavarian public prosecutor's office (Staatsanwaltschaft), which intervened in the case, illustrated the issue of powers and mutation well. It was submitted that the Council exceeded its powers under Articles 48 and 49 of the EC Treaty.[98] These Articles concern the conditions of workers. "Since individual educational grants come under the sphere of educational policy [in respect of which the Council has no jurisdiction] . . . it is to be inferred that the worker can claim the benefit of assimilation with nationals [as provided in Article 12] only as regards social

---

[94] See, e.g., Joined Cases 6 and 11/69, *EEC Commission* v. *France* [1969] ECR 523 and the discussion thereof in Lenaerts, "Constitutionalism."

[95] Case 9/74, *Casagrande* v. *Landeshauptstadt München* [1974] ECR 773 (hereinafter "*Casagrande*").

[96] 1968 OJ (L 257), 2.   [97] *Ibid.* at Art. 12.   [98] *Casagrande* [1974] ECR 773 at 776.

benefits which have a direct relation with the conditions of work itself and with the family stay."[99]

Under this view, Article 12 of the Regulation must be read as entitling children of migrants to be admitted to schools under the same conditions as children of citizens, but not to receive educational grants. If we give the Bavarian public prosecutor's assertion its strongest reading, he denied the very possibility of a conflict between Article 12 and the Bavarian BayAföG, since Article 12 simply could not apply to educational grants. Under a weaker interpretation, he was pleading for a narrow interpretation of the Article 12 provision because of the jurisdictional issue. Underlying this submission was the deeper ground that if education is outside the Community competence, then the Regulation itself transgressed the demarcation line. In any event, the interpretation sought by Casagrande could not stand.

How then did the Court deal with the question? One can detect two phases in the process of judicial consideration. The first phase consisted of an interpretation of the specific Community provision in an effort to understand its full scope. While engaging in this phase the Court acted as if it were in an empty jurisdictional space with no limitations on the reach of Community law. Not surprisingly, the Court's rendering of Regulation 12 led it to the conclusion that the article did cover the distribution of grants.[100]

In the second phase of analysis the Court addressed the jurisdictional mutation problem.[101] We must remember that the primary ground for the illegality of a measure, the infringement of the Treaty, certainly includes jurisdictional competence.[102] The Court first acknowledged that "educational and training policy is not *as such* included in the spheres that the Treaty had entrusted to the Community institutions."[103] The allusion to the Community institutions is important: the case after all deals with an issue of "secondary legislation" enacted by the political organs. But, in the key, although oblique, phrase the Court continued, "it does not follow that the exercise of powers transferred to the Community," enlarging thus the language from Community institutions to the Community as a whole and hence from secondary legislation to the entire Treaty, "*is in some way limited if it is of such a nature as to affect . . . [national] measures taken in the execution of a policy such as that of education and training.*"[104] Now we understand the importance of the two-phased judicial analysis.

In phase one the Court explained the meaning of a Community measure. The interpretation may be teleological but not to the same extent

---

[99] *Ibid.*   [100] *Ibid.* at judgment recitals 8 and 9.   [101] *Ibid.* at judgment recitals 10–15.
[102] See EEC Treaty, Art. 173.   [103] *Casagrande*, at judgment recital 12 (emphasis added).
[104] *Ibid.* (emphasis added).

as the Court's performance in the evolution of the higher law of human rights. Absorption is in this way distinguishable from extension. In the second phase, the Court stated that, to the extent that national measures, even in areas over which the Community has no competence, conflict with the Community rule, these national measures will be absorbed and subsumed by the Community measure. The Court said that it was not the Community policy that was encroaching on national educational policy; rather, it was the national educational policy that was impinging on Community free-movement policy and thus must give way.

The category of absorption also calls for some interim commentary. First, in this higher form of mutation at least two interpretative communities are playing a role in the erosion of strict enumeration: principally the legislative interpretative community, comprising in this case the Commission, Parliament, and the Council (with a decisive role for the governments of the Member States), and the judicial one.[105] This is important in relation to the question of the acceptance of the overall mutation of jurisdictional limits. As a simple examination of extension might have indicated, it cannot be seen as a judicially led development, although legal sanctioning by the Court plays an important role in encouraging this type of legislation in future cases.

Second, the limits of absorption are important. Although absorption extends the effect of Community legislation outside the Community jurisdiction, it, critically, does not give the Community original legislative jurisdiction (in, for example, the field of education). The Community could not, in light of *Casagrande,* directly promulgate its own fully fledged educational policy.

This distinction should not diminish the fundamental importance of absorption and its inclusion as an important form of mutation. This can be gauged by trying to imagine the consequences of a judicial policy that would deny this possibility of absorption. The scope of effective execution of policy over which the Community had direct jurisdiction would, in a society in which it is impossible to draw neat demarcation lines between areas of social and economic policy, be significantly curtailed. But at the same time there is a clear sacrifice and erosion of the principle of enumeration. And, of course, the absorption doctrine invokes a clear preference for Community competence over Member State competence. In a sense the language of the Court suggests a simple application of the principle of supremacy. But this is not a classical case of supremacy. After all, in relation to issues of jurisdiction, supremacy may only mean that each level of

---

[105] The case highlights the fiction of assimilating government with Member State. Bavaria is as much a part of the Federal Republic of Germany as the central German government.

government is supreme in the fields assigned to it. Here we have a case of conflicts of competences. The Court is suggesting that in such conflicts Community competence must prevail. This is the doctrinal crux of absorption.

Incorporation

The term "incorporation"[106] is borrowed from the constitutional history of the United States and denotes the process by which the federal Bill of Rights, initially perceived as applying to measures of the federal government alone, was extended to state action through the agency of the Fourteenth Amendment. The possibility of incorporation within the Community system appears at first sight improbable. We noted already the absence of a Community "Bill of Rights." Community incorporation would entail not one but two acts of high judicial activism. First, the creation of judge-made higher law for the Community, and then its application to acts of the Member States.

Looking at this issue not through the prism of human–rights discourse, but as a problem of jurisdictional allocation, suggests that incorporation may not, after all, be so inconceivable. In the field of human rights, incorporation invokes no more than a combination of extension and absorption. The frequency and regularity by which these two other forms of Community mutation are exercised suggest that incorporation is a distinct possibility.

The interplay of the actors in pushing for this form of mutation is interesting. In an early case, the Court, of its own motion, seemed to open the door to this development. In subsequent cases, the Commission pushed hard for such an outcome, but the Court's responses have been mixed. In some cases it seemed to be nodding in this direction, while in other cases it firmly rejected the possibility.[107]

I cannot therefore present incorporation as a *fait accompli* in the evolving picture of mutation of jurisdictional limits. But the concept, even in its current embryonic Community form, is important for two reasons. First, it shows again the internal interplay of the various actors in pushing the frontiers of Community jurisdiction. At times it is the Court; at other times the legislative organs in conjunction with the Court; at other times still the Commission trying, as in the *Cinéthèque* case, to enlist the Court's support

---

[106] I dealt with this issue extensively in Weiler, "The European Court at a Cross Roads: Community Human Rights and Member State Action," in F. Capotorti (ed.), *Du droit international au droit de l'intégration* (Nomos: Baden-Baden, 1987), 821 and present here merely the bare bones of the argument.

[107] For cases and analysis, see Weiler, "The European Court at a Cross Roads."

(in this case rather unsuccessfully[108]). Second, it shows the dynamics of the enumeration. That incorporation could be tried, more than once – at first causing a split between the opinions of the Court and its Advocate-General, which later developed into a somewhat bifurcated jurisprudence[109] – is only conceivable in a legal-political environment which has already moved, through the agencies of extension and incorporation, far away from a strict concept of enumeration.

Expansion and its causes

Expansion is the most radical form of jurisdictional mutation. Whereas absorption concerned Community legislation in a field in which the Community had clear original jurisdiction, and describes a mutation occurring when the effects of such legislation spill over into fields reserved to the Member States, expansion refers to the case in which the original legislation of the Community "breaks" jurisdictional limits.

I have already alluded to the expansive approach to implied powers adopted by the Court as part of the constitutionalization process in the foundational period. If expansively applied, the implied-powers doctrine may have the *de facto* consequence of permitting the Community to legislate and act in a manner not derived from clear grants of power in the Treaty itself. This would not constitute veritable expansion. The implied-powers doctrine is not veritable expansion because typically the powers implied are in an area in which the Community clearly is already permitted to act, and the powers to act would be construed precisely as "instruments" enabling effective action in a permissible field. Thus, in the leading case of implied powers,[110] there was no question that the Community could act in the field of transport policy; what the Court did was to enable it, within this field, to conclude international agreements.

Even though the implied-powers doctrine cannot be construed strictly as true expansion as defined above, it is important in this context. First, the way a court approaches the question of implied powers is in itself an indirect reflection of its attitude toward enumeration. Even if implying powers as such does not constitute a mutation, a court taking a restrictive approach to enumeration will tend to be cautious in implying powers, whereas a court taking a functional, flexible approach to enumeration will be bolder in its implied-powers jurisprudence. It is interesting that the European Court itself has changed its attitude toward implied powers and,

---

[108] See Cases 60 and 61/84, *Cinéthèque SA* v. *Federation National des Cinémas Français* [1985] ECR 2,605.

[109] For discussion, see Weiler, "The European Court at a Cross Roads" at 824–30.

[110] See *ERTA* at 273, 290.

by implication, toward enumeration. In its very early jurisprudence, it took a cautious and reserved approach to implied powers; it was really only in a second phase that it changed direction on this issue as part of the process of constitutionalization.[111]

Second, even though, strictly speaking, the implied-powers doctrine is intended to give the Community an instrument in a field within which it already has competence, these distinctions often break down in reality. When the Court in the 1970s considered and construed the powers that flowed from the common commercial policy, it did, even on a very conservative reading, extend the jurisdictional limits of the Community.[112]

It is, however, in the context of Article 235 of the Treaty that we find the *locus* of true expansion. Article 235 is the "elastic clause" of the Community – its "necessary and proper" provision. Article 235 provides that:

> if action by the Community should prove necessary to attain, in the course of the operation of the common market, one of the objectives of the Community and this Treaty has not provided the necessary powers, the Council shall, acting unanimously on a proposal from the Commission and after consulting the European Parliament, take the appropriate measures.

On its face, this is no more than a codified version of an implied-powers doctrine; clearly, Article 235 should not be used to expand the jurisdiction of the Community (which derives from its objectives and functional definition as explicitly and implicitly found elsewhere in the Treaty) by adding new objectives or amending existing ones. Since, however, the language of the article is textually ambiguous, and concepts such as "objectives" are by their nature open-textured, there has been a perennial question how far beyond the literal Treaty definition of the Community's spheres of activities and powers the use of Article 235 will permit without actually amending the Treaty.

The history of Article 235 in legislative practice, judicial consideration,

---

[111] Compare *Algera* (denying the right to set aside administrative measures) with *ERTA* (establishing the right to enter into agreements with third countries).

[112] See, e.g., Opinion 1/78, Opinion given pursuant to the second subparagraph of Art. 238(1) of the EEC Treaty [1979] ECR 2,871; [1979] 3 CMLR 639 ("*Rubber*"). The Council (and France and the UK as interveners) claimed that the conclusion of the Rubber Agreement, as an instrument of co-operation and development which also impinges on broader strategic concerns of the Member States, was outside the scope and competence of the Community's Common Commercial Policy. The Court gave an extensive reading to the limits of the exclusive (!) Common Commercial Policy and held that: "it is clear that a coherent commercial policy would no longer be practicable if the Community were not in a position to exercise its powers also in connexion with a category of agreements which are becoming, alongside traditional commercial agreements, one of the major factors in the regulation of international trade": *ibid.* at 2,912, recital 43.

and doctrine includes several changes which reflect the changes in the development of the Community itself. In the period from 1958 to 1973, Article 235 was used by Community institutions relatively infrequently[113] and, when used, was usually narrowly construed. Under the restrictive view, shared by all interpretative communities at the time,[114] the function of Article 235 was to compensate *within an area of activity explicitly granted by the Treaty* for the absence of an explicit grant of legal power to act. Two examples demonstrate the early conception of the article. One was the enactment on the basis of Article 235, in 1968, of Regulation 803/68 on customs valuation, setting out the criteria by which the value of imported goods to the Community for the purpose of imposing customs duties would be calculated. Implicit in this recourse to Article 235 was the belief that:

1. customs valuation was necessary to attain the objectives of the Treaty; but

2. since the reach of the Community spheres of activity had to be narrowly construed, one could not use the common commercial policy or Article 28 as a legal basis, as these did not explicitly cover customs valuation.

A second example is the use of Article 235 as a legal basis for extending the list of food products in Annex II to the Treaty.[115] Here it was clear that the sphere of activities did cover the measure in question, but that there was no specific grant of power in relation to new products. Recourse to Article 235 seemed necessary. The explanation for this restrictive quantitative and qualitative usage is simple. Quantitatively, in that phase of establishing the basic structures of the Community system, the Treaty was relatively explicit in defining the legislative agenda and granting legal powers. The initial legislative program simply did not call for frequent recourse to Article 235. Qualitatively, that period, especially since the middle of the 1960s, was characterized by a distinct decline in the "political will" of at least some of the Member States to promote expansion of Community activity.

Following the Paris Summit of 1972, where the Member States explicitly decided to make full use of Article 235 and to launch the Community into

---

[113] For quantitative analysis, see Weiler, *Il sistema comunitario europeo* at 195.

[114] E.g., Usher, "The Gradual Widening of European Community Policy on the Basis of Article 100 and 235 of the EEC Treaty," in J. Schwarze and H. G. Schermers (eds.), *Structure and Dimensions of European Community Policy* (Nomos: Baden-Baden, 1988), 30 ("Article 235 was obviously intended as an exceptional measure").

[115] Art. 38(3) of the EEC Treaty provides, *inter alia*, that "products subject to [the Common Agricultural Policy of the EEC] are listed in Annex II to this Treaty." It also explicitly foresees that this list should be enlarged by adding new products. And yet despite this explicit invitation the political organs did not believe that they had the power to amend the list without recourse to Art. 235.

a variety of new fields, recourse to Article 235 as an exclusive or partial legal basis rose dramatically. Therefore from 1973 until the entry into force of the Single European Act (the SEA), there was not only a very dramatic quantitative increase in the recourse to Article 235, but also a no less dramatic understanding of its qualitative scope. In a variety of fields, including, for example, conclusion of international agreements, the granting of emergency food aid to third countries, and creation of new institutions,[116] the Community made use of Article 235 in a manner that was simply not consistent with the narrow interpretation of the article as a codification of the implied-powers doctrine in its instrumental sense. Only a truly radical and "creative" reading of the article could explain and justify its usage as, for example, the legal basis for granting emergency food aid to non-associated states.[117] But this wide reading, in which all political institutions partook,[118] meant that it would become virtually impossible to find an activity which could not be brought within the "objectives of the Treaty."[119] This constituted the climax of the process of mutation and is the basis for my claim not merely that no core activity of state function could be seen any longer as still constitutionally immune from Community

[116] For fuller accounts of the wide use and wide construction, see, e.g., Usher, "The Gradual Widening" at 114; H. Smit and P. Herzog, *Law of the European Community* (Bender: New York, 1991), vol. VI, 269.

[117] The Community Framework Regulations on food-aid policy and food-aid management were initially based jointly on Art. 43 (Common Agricultural Policy) and Art. 235 of the EEC Treaty. See Council Food Aid First Framework Regulation No. 3,391/82, 1982 OJ (L 352), 1; Council Food Aid Second Framework Regulation No. 3,972/86, 1986 OJ (L 370), 1, as amended by Regulation No. 1930/90, 1990 OJ (L 174), 6, is based exclusively on Art. 235. Before the adoption of Framework Regulations, there were a few decisions on emergency operations which were based exclusively on Art. 235. See, e.g., Council Regulation No. 1,010/80, 1980 OJ (L 108), 1; Council Regulation No. 3,827/81, 1981 OJ (L 392), 1 (both concerning the supply of sugar to UNRWA as food aid for refugees); Council Regulation No. 3,723/81, 1981 OJ (L 373), 11 (concerning the supply of exceptional food aid to the least developed countries). So long as the food aid is a mechanism for the disposal of Common Agricultural Policy (CAP) surpluses there is no question of legal basis and competence based on Art. 43 of the EEC Treaty. The inclusion of Art. 235 would cover the incidence of food aid that is not so tied to CAP objectives and mechanisms. The current exclusive reliance on Art. 235 is deliberate in order to disconnect food aid from the CAP and to emphasize that it is not an instrument of the CAP. Laudable as the granting of food aid is, it is difficult to see how the functioning of the common market, a condition for the recourse to Art. 235, is served by granting humanitarian food aid to non-associated countries. But see Marenco, "Les conditions d'application de l'Article 235 du Traité CEE," *Revue du marché commun* 12 (1970), 147.

[118] Parliament has pushed for the usage of Art. 235 as well, since, *inter alia*, it is one of the provisions under which consultation with Parliament is obligatory.

[119] Elsewhere I have argued, tongue in cheek, that, on this reading defense would also be a permissible usage of Art. 235, since the common market could hardly function with the territories of the Member States under occupation: Weiler, *Il sistema comunitario europeo* at 188. For broad interpretation of the "objectives" of the Community, see Case 242/87, *Commission v. Council* [1989] ECR 1,425 (hereinafter "*Erasmus*").

action (which really goes to the issue of absorption), but also that no sphere of the material competence could be excluded from the Community acting under Article 235. It is not simply that the jurisdictional limits of the Community expanded in their content more sharply in the 1970s than they did as a result of, for example, the Single European Act. The fundamental systemic mutation of the 1970s, culminating in the process of expansion, was that any sort of constitutional limitation of this expansion seemed to have evaporated.

It is important to emphasize again that, for this inquiry, the crucial question is not the *per se* legality of the wide interpretation of Article 235.[120] In the face of a common understanding by all principal interpretative communities, that question has little if any significance and perhaps no meaning.[121] Far more intriguing and far more revealing is to explore the

---

[120] The Court tacitly sanctioned this wide usage. Broadly speaking, two principal conditions must be fulfilled to invoke Art. 235. The measure must be "necessary," in the course of the operation of the common market, to attain one of the objectives of the Treaty. In addition, Art. 235 may be used when the Treaty does not provide the "necessary" powers. The Court addressed both conditions liberally in the leading case of the early period, Case 8/73, *Hauptzollamt Bremerhaven* v. *Massey Ferguson GmbH* [1973] ECR 897 (hereinafter "*Massey Ferguson*"). Regarding the second, the Court was explicit. In an action for annulment of the regulation adopting the above-mentioned Community customs-valuation regime, the Court had to decide whether reliance on Art. 235 as an exclusive basis was justified. While acknowledging that a proper interpretation of the alternative legal bases in the EEC Treaty (Arts. 9, 27, 28, 111, and 113) would provide an adequate legal basis, and thus, under a strict construction, render Art. 235 not "necessary," the Court, departing from an earlier statement, none the less considered that the Council's use of Art. 235 would be "justified in the interest of legal certainty": *Massey Ferguson* [1973] ECR 897 at 908. Legally, this might have been an unfortunate formulation since an aura of uncertainty almost *ipso facto* attaches to a decision to make recourse to Art. 235. Politically, it may have been wise, for a more rigid interpretation could have thwarted the desire of the Member States, consonant with the Treaty objectives, to expand greatly the areas of activity of the Community, even if by the dubious use of Art. 235. Practically speaking, recourse to Art. 235 in that period made little difference in the content of measures adopted, because virtually all measures were adopted under the penumbra of *de facto* unanimity. Taking their cue from this case, Community institutions henceforth made liberal use of Art. 235 without exhaustively considering whether other legal bases existed. Regarding the first requirement that the measure be "necessary" to attain one of the objectives of the Treaty, the Court was willing to construe Community legal reach and the notion of objectives very widely, not only in a whole range of cases not directly concerned with Art. 235, but also in *Massey Ferguson* itself. Since Member States had the ability to control the usage of Art. 235, disagreements, often acrimonious, on the proper scope to be given to the first condition were resolved within the Council and not brought before the Court.

[121] The doctrinal writing continues the attempt to ascribe material limitations on the usage of Art. 235 even in the face of this overwhelming practice. *The Encyclopaedia of European Community Law* is a typical example: "Art. 235 does not open unlimited opportunity to increase the powers of the Community. In the first place, recourse to Art. 235 is limited by the objectives of the Treaty." Then comes the retreat: "Extensive interpretation as to the nature of these objectives is, of course, always possible, but the strongest guarantee against abuse is the required unanimity of the Council.": *The Encyclopaedia of European Community Law*, vol. B:2 at B10/70/19, General

explanation for and the significance of the phenomenon. One should not, after all, underestimate its enormity in comparison to other non-unitary (federal) systems. Not only did the Community see in this second phase of its systemic evolution a jurisdictional movement as profound as any that has occurred in federal states, but even more remarkable, indeed something of a double riddle, this mutation did not, on the whole, ignite major "federal" political disputes between the actors (for example, between the Member States and the Community).

No one factor can explain a process so fundamental in the architecture of the Community. I suggest the following as some of the more important factors of this change.

Incrementalism

Part of the explanation to the riddles can be found already in the very description I offered of the process of jurisdictional mutation. There is no single event, no landmark case, that could be called the focal point of the mutation. Even some of the important cases I mentioned, such as those in the field of human rights, were not seen through the prism of jurisdictional mutation. Instead, there was a slow change of climate and ethos whereby strict enumeration was progressively, relentlessly, but never dramatically, eroded. Extension, absorption, incorporation, and powers implied by the Court, all feed on each other in cog-and-wheel fashion so that no dissonances are revealed within the constitutional architecture itself as it is changing. When the Court is very activist in an area, in extension, for example, it is so toward the Community as such and not the more sensitive Member States.[122] By contrast, in the cases of absorption and expansion, areas where the mutative effect impinges on Member State jurisdiction, the

Note to Article 235 (Release 40:23-ix-86). The learned commentator implicitly admits the futility of the task and then, abandoning an analytical attempt to circumscribe the article in normative terms, resorts to an institutional guarantee, as if the Council could not itself, even if acting unanimously, abuse Art. 235. Where writers try to insist on material limits, they end up flying in the face of the legislative practice. See, e.g., "Les guillons, extension des competence de la CEE par l'Article 235 du Traité de Rome," *Annuaire Français de droit internationale* (1974), 996; Lachmann, "Some Danish Reflections on the Use of Article 235 of the Rome Treaty," *Common Market Law Review* 18 (1981), 447. For other more or less successful attempts, see Giardina, "The Rule of Law and Implied Powers in the European Communities," *Italian Yearbook* 1 (1975), 99; Marenco, "Les conditions d'application"; Olmi, "La place de l'Article 235 CEE dans le système des attribution de competence de la Communauté," in *Melanges Fernand Dehousse* (Nathan: Paris; Labor: Brussels, 1979), 279; Waelbroeck, "Article 235," in J. Megret, J.-V. Louis, D. Vignes, and M. Waelbroeck (eds.), *Le droit de la Communauté economique européenne* 15 (Presses Universitaires: Brussels, 1987), 521, 530.

[122] The exception to this institutional "coziness" is the case law concerning the "exclusive" competence of the Community. See Weiler, "The External Legal Relations" at 71–2.

role of the Court is in a kind of "active passivism," reacting to impulses coming from the political organs and opting for the flexible rather than strict notion of enumeration. In its entire history there is not one case, to my knowledge, where the Court struck down a Council or Commission measure on grounds of Community *lack of competence*.[123] The relationship between the Court and the political organs was a bit like the offense in American football.[124] The Court acted as the "pass protectors" from any constitutional challenge; the political organs and the Member States made the winning pass.

Nevertheless, incrementalism alone cannot explain a change so radical and a reaction so muted. Politically, the Community architecture at the end of the foundational period was unlike any other federal polity. Therein lies one emphatically important aspect of this development. Even if the judicial signals indicated that strict enumeration would not be enforced by the Court, these could, after all, have remained without a response by the political organs and the Member States.

---

[123] There have been many cases of annulment of Council and Commission measures, but not on grounds that the Community exceeded its competences. In Joined Cases 281, 283 to 285, and 287/85, *FRG* v. *Commission of the European Communities* [1987] ECR 3,203 (concerning the immigration of non-Community workers), the Court annulled a Commission decision as going beyond the scope of the Commission's powers under Art. 118. The parties invited the Court to consider the social sector as being the preserve of the Member States, "from which it follows that, like all the other fundamental choices made in the Treaty, that choice may only be amended by use of the procedure provided for in Article 236": *ibid*. at 3,232. The Court, however, pointedly refrained from endorsing that proposition, gave a wide reading to the scope of action of the Community in the social field, and annulled the decision on the grounds that the Commission exceeded its powers, not that the Community had no competence in the field. In recitals 23 and 24 of the judgment the Court said: "[M]igration policy is capable of falling within the social field within the meaning of Article 118 only to the extent to which it concerns the situation of workers from non-member countries as regards their impact on the Community employment market and working condition. As a result, in so far as Decision 85/381/EEC includes the promotion of cultural integration as a whole among the subjects for consultation, it goes beyond the social field in which, under Article 118, the Commission has the task of promoting co-operation between Member States." This judgment has been read as a decision implicitly excluding cultural integration from Community competence: Bradley, "The European Court and the Legal Basis of Community Legislation," *European Law Review* 13 (1988), 379, 384. I disagree with this reading. The Court specifically mentions that it is interpreting the meaning of the social field within the meaning of Art. 118, which is special in that it gives certain powers to the Commission. In the light of the broad reading given by the Court to the scope of Community objectives in the context of Art. 235 in a case such as *Erasmus* (where the Court construed the objectives of the Community to include the enhancement of the quality of teaching and information furnished by Community universities with a view to ensuring the competitiveness of the Community in world markets and also "the general objective" of creating a citizens' Europe) I submit that, had the same decision been made by the *Council* rather than the Commission on the legal basis of Arts. 118 *and* 235, the Court would have held it to be within *Community* competences.

[124] Of which, despite five years in the Midwest, I am still happily ignorant of most nuances.

Two factors, one historical and one structural, combine to explain the aggressiveness with which the political process rushed through the opening judicial door. Both factors are rooted in the heritage of the foundational period.

A strategy of revival

In a determined effort commencing in 1969,[125] the end of the de Gaulle era, and culminating in the successful negotiation of the UK, Danish, and Irish accessions in 1973, the Community sought ways to revitalize itself, to shake off the hangovers of the Luxembourg Crisis, to extricate itself from the traumas of the double UK rejection, and to launch itself afresh. The Paris Summit of 1972, in which the new Member States participated, introduced an ambitious program of substantive expansion of Community jurisdiction and a revival of the dream of European union. Article 235 was to play a key role in this revival. In retrospect this attempt was a failure, since the Community was unable to act in concert on the issues that really mattered during the 1970s, such as developing a veritable industrial policy or even tackling with sufficient vigor Member State obstacles to the creation of the common market. The momentum was directed to a range of ancillary issues, such as environmental policy, consumer protection, energy, and research, all important of course, but a side game at the time. Yet, although these were not taken very seriously in substance (and maybe because of that), each required extensive and expansive usage of Article 235 and represented part of the brick-by-brick demolition of the wall circumscribing Community competences.

Structuralism: the abiding relevance of Exit and Voice

But the structural, rather than historical, explanation of the process of expansion and its riddles is the critical one. The process of decline in the decisional supranational features of the Community during the foundational period, demonstrated by the enhanced Voice of the Member States in the Community policy-making and legislative processes, was the key factor giving the Member States the confidence to engage in such massive jurisdictional mutation and to accept it with relative equanimity.

In federal states, such a mutation would by necessity be *at the expense* of Member State government power. In the post-foundational period

---

[125] Prompted by and reflected in the "Report of the Working Party Examining the Problem of the Enlargement of the Powers of the European Parliament," *Bulletin of the European Communities* (Supp. 4/72), 1 (the "Vedel Report").

Community, in contrast, by virtue of the near total control of the Member States over the Community process, the community appeared more as an instrument in the hands of the governments rather than as a usurping power. The Member State governments, jointly and severally, were confident that their interests were served by any mutative move.[126] If the governments of the Member States could control each legislative act, from inception through adoption and then implementation, why would they fear a system in which constitutional guarantees of jurisdictional change were weakened? Indeed, they had some incentive, in transferring competences to the Community, to escape the strictures, or nuisance, of parliamentary accountability. In federal states, the classical dramas of federalism in the early formative periods presuppose two power centers: the central and the constituent parts. In the Community, in its post-foundational period architecture, the constituent units' power *was* the central power.

As we see in several cases from that period, it was hardly feasible politically, although it was permissible legally, for a Member State to approve an "expansive" Community measure and to challenge its constitutionality as *ultra vires*.[127] It is easy also to understand why the Commission (and Parliament) played the game. The Commission welcomed the desire to reinvigorate the Community and to expand its (and the Commission's own) fields of activity. Since most Community decision-making at that time was undertaken in the shadow of the veto consecrated by the dubiously legal Luxembourg Accord, the Commission found no disadvantage, and in fact many advantages, in using Article 235. Neither the Commission nor Parliament, which was to be consulted under the Article 235 procedure, were likely to challenge judicially the usage. Moreover, since Article 235 enabled the adoption of "measures," whether regulations, directives, or decisions, it provided a flexibility not always available when using other legal bases.

---

[126] To be sure, Art. 235 provides for unanimity: Member State confidence was boosted because of the knowledge that also in the implementation of any measure their interests would be guaranteed.

[127] A Member State may challenge an act even if it voted in favor of it: Case 166/78, *Government of the Italian Republic* v. *Council of the European Communities* [1979] ECR 2,575, 2,596. But it will normally not choose to challenge on the grounds of lack of competence. In Case 91/79, *Commission* v. *Italy* [1980] ECR 1,099, Italy was sued by the Commission for its failure to implement an environmental-protection directive the *vires* of which (pre-SEA) could have been challenged in defense; Italy explicitly elected not to do so.

Evaluating the mutation of jurisdictional limits and the erosion of strict enumeration in the 1970s

The process of mutation is evidence of the dynamic character of the Community and its ability to adapt itself in the face of new challenges. It is also evidence that what were perceived as negative and debilitating political events in the 1960s had unexpected pay-offs. I do not believe that the Community would have developed such a relaxed and functional approach to mutation had the political process not placed so much power in the hands of the Member States. Yet even then at least two long-term problems were taking root.

The question of constitutionality

I have argued that the *de facto* usage of Article 235, from 1973 until the Single European Act, implied a construction, shared by all principal interpretive communities, that opened up practically any realm of state activity to the Community, provided the governments of the Member States found accord among themselves. This raised two potential problems of a constitutional nature.

From the internal, autonomous legal perspective, it is clear that Article 235 could not be construed simply as a procedural device for unchecked jurisdictional expansion. Such a construction would empty Article 236 (Treaty revision) of much of its meaning and would be contrary to the very structure of Article 235. Legal doctrine was quick to find autonomous internal constructions which would not empty the article of meaning, but which would emphasize its virtually limitless substantive scope. Thus it has been suggested that Article 235 cannot be used in a way that would actually violate the Treaty.[128] Few writers (or actors) sought to check the expansive use of the article.[129] The general view had been (and in many quarters remains) that the requirement of unanimity does effectively give the necessary guarantees to the Member States. If there has been a debate over the article's meaning, it concerns the analytical construction of the article. The Community is no different from any other legal polity. Language, especially such contorted language as found in Article 235, has never been a serious constraint on a determined political power.

The constitutional problem with an expansive interpretation of Article

---

[128] As mentioned earlier, institutional and organic changes would in principle require Treaty amendment, though Usher, "The Gradual Widening" gives examples of institutional changes under Art. 235.

[129] See Lachmann, "Some Danish Reflections" (detailing strong Danish principled opposition to the wide use of Art. 235).

235, and in general with the entire erosion of strict enumeration, does not thus rest in the realm of autonomous positivist legalisms.

The constitutional danger is of a different nature. As we saw, results of the constitutional "revolution" of the Community in the 1960s and the system of judicial remedies upon which they rest depend on creating a relationship of trust, a new community of interpretation, in which the European Court and Member State courts play complementary roles.

The overture of the European Court toward the Member State courts in the original constitutionalizing decisions, such as *van Gend and Loos*, was based on a judicial-constitutional contract idea. Suggesting that the new legal order would operate "in limited fields,"[130] the European Court was not simply stating a principle of Community law, which, as the maker of that principle, it would later be free to abandon. It was inviting the supreme Member State courts to accept the new legal order with the understanding that it would, indeed, be limited in its fields.

The acceptance by the Member State legal orders was premised, often explicitly, on that understanding. Thus the Italian Constitutional Court, when it finally accepted supremacy, did so "on the basis of a *precise criterion of division of jurisdiction.*"[131]

The danger in this process is now clear. Whereas the principal political actors may have shared a common interest in the jurisdictional mutation, it was, like still water, slowly but deeply boring a creek in the most important foundation of the constitutional order, the understanding between the European Court and its national counterparts about the material limits to Community jurisdiction. The erosion of enumeration meant that the new legal order, and the judicial-legal contract which underwrote it, was to extend to all areas of activity – a change for which the Member State legal orders might not have bargained. With the addition of the SEA, what was an underground creek will become one of the more transparent points of pressure of the system.

There is another, obvious sense in which erosion of enumeration is problematic from a constitutional perspective. The general assumption that unanimity sufficiently guarantees the Member States against abusive expansion is patently erroneous. First, it is built on the false assumption that conflates the government of a state with the state. Constitutional guarantees are designed, in part, to defend against the political wishes of this or that government, which government after all, in a democratic society, is contingent in time and often of limited representativeness. Additionally, even where there is wall-to-wall political support, there will not necessarily

---

[130] *van Gend and Loos* [1963] ECR 1.
[131] *Frontini* v. *Amministrazione Delle Finanze* [1974] CMLR 372, 385 (emphasis added).

be a recognition that constitutional guarantees are intended to protect, in part, individuals against majorities, even big ones. It is quite understandable why, for example, political powers might have a stake in expansion. One of the rationales, trite yet no less persuasive, of enumeration and divided powers is to anticipate that stake to prevent concentration of power in one body and at one level. When that body and that level operate in an environment of reduced public accountability (as is the case of the Commission and the Council in the Community environment) the importance of the constitutional guarantee even increases.

Mutation and the question of the democratic character of the expansion

Treaty amendment by Article 236 satisfies the constitutional requirement all Member States have that calls for assent of national parliaments. The expansive usage of Article 235 evades that type of control. At a very formal level, the jurisdictional mutation of the nature that occurred in the 1970s accentuates the problems of democratic accountability of the Community. This deficit is not made up by the non-binding consultation of the European Parliament in the context of Article 235.

The "democratic" danger of unchecked expansion is not, however, in the formal lack of Member State parliamentary ratification: the structure of European democracies is such that it is idle to think that governments could not ram most expansive measures down willing or unwilling parliamentary throats. After all, in most European parliamentary democracies, governments enjoy a majority in their national parliaments and members of parliaments tend to be fairly compliant in following the policies of the party masters in government. The danger of expansion rests in a more realistic view of European democracies.

The major substantive areas in which expansion took place were social: consumer protection, environmental protection, and education, for example. These are typically areas of diffuse and fragmented interests. Whether we adopt a traditional democratic or a neo-corporatist model,[132] we cannot fail to note that the elaboration of the details of such legislation in the Community context had the effect of squeezing out interest groups representing varying social interests, which had been integrated to one degree or another into national policy-making processes.[133] The Commu-

---

[132] Parliament is only one of the actors in the outplay of the democratic choices. *Cf.* P. Schmitter, "Democratic Theory and Neo-Corporatist Practice" (European Union Institute Working Papers, No. 83/74).

[133] On the ambivalent position of pressure groups at the EC level, see, e.g., Loosli-Surrans, "Quelle sécurité pour les consommateurs européens?"; Micklitz, "Considerations Shaping Future Consumer Participation in European Product Safety Law," in C. Joerges, *Product*

nity decision-making process, with its lack of transparency and tendency to channel many issues into "state interests," tends to favor certain groups well placed to play the Community–Member State game and disfavor others, especially those that depend on a parliamentary chamber and the "principle of reelection" to vindicate diffuse and fragmented interests.

Expansion thus did not simply underscore the perennial democracy deficit of the Community, but actually distorted the balance of social and political forces in the decisional game at both the Member State and Community level.

Conclusion

The principal feature of the period lasting from the middle of the 1970s into the 1980s is that precisely in this period, one of political stagnation and decisional malaise, another important, if less visible, constitutional mutation – the erosion of the limits to Community competences – took place. The full importance of this mutation and some of its inherent dangers and risks come to light only now, in the 1992 epoch. And yet a final word is called for. Unlike the constitutional revolution in the foundational period, which seems irreversible and which constitutes the very foundation of the Community, the mutation of the 1970s can perhaps be checked. I shall return to this theme below.

1992 AND BEYOND

Introduction

The 1992 program and the Single European Act determine both the current agenda of the Community and its *modus operandi*.[134] Neither

---

Liability and Product Safety in the European Community (European Union Institute Working Papers, No. 89/404). See generally A. Philip, "Pressure Groups in the European Community" (University Association for Contemporary European Studies Occasional Papers, No. 2, 1985).

[134] See generally J. Deruyt, *L'acte unique européen* (1989); R. Bieber *et al.* (eds.), *1992: One European Market* (Nomos: Baden-Baden, 1988); Berman, "The Single European Act: A New Constitution for the Community?" *Columbia Journal of Transnational* Law 27 (1989), 529; Dehousse, "1992 and Beyond: The Institutional Dimension of the Internal Market Programme," *Legal Issues of European Integration* 1 (1989), 109; Ehlermann, "The Internal Market Following the Single European Act," *Common Market Law Review* 24 (1987), 361; Ehlermann, "1992 Project"; Glaesner, "The Single European Act," *Yearbook of European Law* (Clarendon Press: Oxford; Oxford University Press: New York, 1986), vol. VI, 283; Glaesner, "L'Article 100A: Un novel instrument pour la realisation du marché commun," *Cahiers de droit européen* 25 (1989), 615; Moravcsik, "Negotiating the Single European Act: National Interests and Conventional Statecraft in the European Community," *International Organization* 45 (1991), 19.

instrument is on its face functionally radical; the White Paper[135] goal of achieving a single market merely restates, with some nuances, the classical (Treaty of Rome) objective of establishing a common market. The bulk of the 1992 program is little more than a legislative timetable for achieving in seven years what the Community should have accomplished in the preceding thirty. The SEA is even less powerful.[136] Its forays into environmental policy and the like fail to break new jurisdictional ground, and its majority-voting provisions, designed to harmonize non-tariff barriers to trade, seem to utilize such restrictive language, and open such glaring new loopholes,[137] that even some of the most authoritative commentators believed the innovations caused more harm than good in the Community.[138] Clearly, the European Parliament and the Commission were far from thrilled with the new Act.[139]

---

[135] "Completing the Internal Market" (Milan, June 28–9, 1985) Com (85) 310 (White Paper from the Commission to the European Council). In this White Paper, the Commission outlined its internal-market strategy, later to be called the 1992 program.

[136] "Measured against Parliament's Draft Treaty of European Union and other recent reform proposals, as well as against the stated preferences of the Commission and certain Member States, the Single European Act is not a revolutionary product.": Berman, "The Single European Act" at 586.

[137] See, e.g., SEA, Art. 100A(4) (supplementing the EEC Treaty, Art. 100).

[138] See, e.g., Pescatore, "Some Critical Remarks on the Single European Act," *Common Market Law Review* 24 (1987), 9 (describing the SEA as a "severe setback" for the European Community); see also Pescatore, "Die 'Einheitliche Europäische Acte,' Eine ernste Gefahr für den Gemeinsamen Markt," *Europarecht* 21 (1986), 153.

[139] See Address by Commission Vice-President Frans Andriessen, Signing Ceremony for SEA (1986) *Bulletin of the European Communities* (2-1986), point 1.1.1 (giving the SEA a decidedly cool reception); see also Address by Jacques Delors, Programme of the Commission for 1986, reprinted in *Bulletin of the European Communities* (Supp. 1/86). Delors gave the Act a cool reception but put on a brave face: "You [Parliament] have your reservations, we have ours; but it would be a mistake to be *overly* pessimistic" (emphasis added). Ehlermann, in his 1987 paper, comments that: "Comparing the final text of the Single European Act with the Commission's original ideas shows that the differences are greatest in the area of the internal market. Nowhere does the end result depart so radically from the Commission's original paper.": Ehlermann, "Internal Market" at 362. This is revealing since it suggests that, at its core, the internal market, the SEA seemed at first disappointing. Ehlermann's comments are particularly authoritative since he was Director-General of the Commission's Legal Service and privy to most developments from the inside. His assessments also reflect the Commission's moods. See "Parliament Fights On for More Say," *European Parliament News* (UK edn., January 1986) at 1, col. 1 (a report on the Parliament's negative reaction to the outcome of the intergovernmental conference). See the following debates of the European Parliament: Resolution following the Debate on the Statement by the Council and the Commission after the Meeting of the European Council on December 2–3, 1985, in Luxembourg, 1985 OJ (C 352), 60; Resolution on the Position of the European Parliament on the Single Act Approved by the Intergovernmental Conference on December 16–17, 1985, 1986 OJ (C 36), 144; Resolution on European Union and the Single Act, 1986 OJ (C 120), 96; Resolution on Relations between the European Parliament and the Council, 1986 OJ (C 283), 36; Resolution on Relations between the European Parliament and the Commission in the Institutional Context of the Treaties,

And yet, with the hindsight of just three years, it has become clear that 1992 and the SEA do constitute an eruption of significant proportions.[140] Some of the evidence is very transparent. First, for the first time since the very early years of the Community, if ever, the Commission plays the political role clearly intended for it by the Treaty of Rome. In stark contrast to its nature during the foundational period and the 1970s and early 1980s, the Commission in large measure both sets the Community agenda and acts as a power broker in the legislative process.[141]

Second, the decision-making process takes much less time. Dossiers that would have languished and in some cases did languish in impotence for years in the Brussels corridors now emerge as legislation often in a matter of months.[142]

For the first time, the interdependence of the policy areas at the new-found focal point of power in Brussels creates a dynamic resembling the almost forgotten predictions of neo-functionalist spillover.[143] The ever-widening scope of the legislative and policy agenda of the Community manifests this dynamic. The agreement to convene two new intergovernmental conferences to deal with economic and monetary union just three

---

1986 OJ (C 283), 39; Resolution on the Ratification Procedure for the Single Act in National Parliaments and on the Attainment of European Union, 1986 OJ (C 29), 119; Resolution on the Single European Act, 1987 OJ (C 7), 105; Resolution on the Strategy of the European Parliament for Achieving European Union, 1987 OJ (C 190), 71; Resolution on the Results Obtained from Implementation of the Triple Act, 1988 OJ (C 309), 93; and Resolution on Relations between Parliaments and the European Parliament, 1989 OJ (C 69), 149.

[140] Again Ehlermann can serve as our barometer. Writing in 1990 he comments: "The '1992 Project' has radically changed the European Community. It has given the 'common market' new impetus and has lifted the Community out of the deep crisis in which it was bogged down in the first half of the 1980s." He adds: "[The] Single European Act ... represents the most comprehensive and most important amendment to the EEC Treaty to date ... [T]he core and the 'raison d'être' of the [SEA] are the provisions on the internal market.": Ehlermann, "1992 Project" at 1,097, 1,103. This change in nuance in assessing the SEA reflects a general shift in opinion in Community institutions. My own assessment has been that the dynamics generated by the SEA and 1992 surprised most observers and actors.

[141] This development is the expected result of "returning" to majority voting. Amendments to Commission proposals must be unanimous: EEC Treaty, Art. 149(1). But the Commission "may alter its proposal at any time during the procedures [of decision-making]": EEC Treaty, Art. 149(3). The Commission may amend its own proposal, finding a *via media* among contrasting amendments. None of the amendments on its own could gain unanimity, but a compromise version, in the form of the Commission's altered proposal, may gain a majority. This prerogative of the Commission obviously gives it considerable power it did not have under the shadow of the veto.

[142] See Ehlermann, "1992 Project" at 1,104–6.

[143] *Cf.* Keohane and Hoffmann, "Conclusions: Community Politics and Institutional Change," in W. Wallace (ed.), *The Dynamics of European Integration* (Pinter: London, New York, 1990), 276, 282*ff.* For a review of neo-functionalist spillover, see Greilsammer, "Theorizing European Integration."

years after the adoption of the SEA symbolizes the ever-widening scope of the agenda, as does the increased perception of the Community and its institutions as a necessary, legitimate, and at times effective *locus* for direct constituency appeal.

But if the instruments themselves (especially the SEA) are so meager, how can one explain the changes they have wrought? In the remainder of this chapter I shall do the following: first, I shall take a closer look at the impact of the SEA on the elements of Community structure and process analyzed in the preceding sections of this chapter. I shall try to show that the changes are greater than meet the eye. I believe that their significance, analyzed in the light of the transformation effected in the previous two periods in the Community evolution, is far reaching. Then, instead of elaborating further on the promise inherent in this last period in Community evolution, a subject on which there has been no shortage of comment and celebration, I shall attempt to point out dangers and raise critical questions.

Structural background to 1992 and the Single European Act: the tension and its resolution

The balance of constitutionalism and institutionalism, of reduced Exit and enhanced Voice, was the heritage of the foundational period and explains much of the subsequent strength and stability of the Community polity.[144] But the foundational period equilibrium was not without its costs. Those costs are the ones inherent in consensus politics: the need to reach unanimous agreement in policy-making and governance.

From the little empirical evidence available, we know that consensus politics did not significantly impede policy management during the 1960s, 1970s, and into the 1980s.[145] However, the Community became increasingly unable to respond to new challenges, that called for real policy choices. Thus, while consensus politics (the manifestation of enhanced Voice) explains the relative equanimity with which the jurisdictional limits of the Community broke down in the 1970s, this very consensus model also explains why, within the Community's expanded jurisdiction, it was unable to realize its most traditional and fundamental objectives, such as establishing a single market in the four factors of production.[146] From a structural point of view, one critical impediment to these goals was the

---

[144] See pp. 34–9 above.

[145] See Krislov, Ehlermann, and Weiler, "The Political Organs" at 30–57.

[146] For an analysis of the fragmented market despite close to three decades of a common market regime, see J. Pelkmans and A. Winters, *Europe's Domestic Market* (Royal Institute of Internatioanl Affairs: London; Routledge: New York, 1988).

growth in the number of Member States. In just over a decade the number of Member States doubled. But the new Member States entered a Community with decisional processes that were created in the foundational period and that were not changed to accommodate the increased number of participants. Achieving consensus among the original six was difficult enough. It became substantially more difficult with the first enlargement to nine and virtually debilitating when the number grew to twelve. In addition, the entry first of the UK, Ireland, and Denmark and then of Greece, Spain, and Portugal caused the Community to lose a certain homogeneity of policy perception and cultural orientation. This loss of homogeneity accentuated a problem that would exist in any event by the pure numbers game. Community decision-making fell into deep malaise. It is not surprising that almost every initiative between 1980 and the SEA recognized the need to change processes of decision-making, usually by moving to some form of majority voting.

Another structural element encouraged change. The evolving rules concerning the free movement of goods and other factors of production between the Member States created a regulatory gap in the European polity. A rigorous (and courageous[147]) jurisprudence of the Court of Justice seriously limited the ability of the Member States to adopt protectionist measures *vis-à-vis* each other.[148] Indeed, it went further. The Court held that once the Community enacted measures regulating non-tariff barriers to movement of goods, such measures would preempt any subsequently enacted Member State legislation that frustrated the design of the extant Community measures.[149] In addition, it is important to remember that this was an area in which the Treaty provided for unanimous decision-making. The Treaty rule on decision-making and the Court's jurisprudence on the preemptive effect of such decision-making combined to chill the climate in which the Community and its Member States were to make critical decisions to eliminate the numerous barriers to a true common market. Not only was it difficult to achieve consensus on one Community norm to replace the variety of Member State norms, but also there was the growing

---

[147] Unlike those of most other systems in Europe, judges on the European Court serve for renewable terms (EEC Treaty, Art. 167). This rule compromises the appearance of independence. Currently the intergovernmental conference holds a proposal to extend the terms of judges to twelve years and make them non-renewable. See "Resolution of European Parliament on the Intergovernmental Conference," PE 146.824, Art. 167.

[148] The famous line of the decision from Case 8/74, *Procureur du Roi* v. *Benoit and Gustave Dassonville* [1974] ECR 837 and its progeny. See generally L. Gormley, *Prohibiting Restrictions on Trade within the EEC* (North Holland: Amsterdam, New York, 1985).

[149] See, e.g., Case 148/78, *Pubblico Ministero* v. *Ratti* [1979] ECR 1,629, 1,643 (recital 27); Case 5/77, *Tedeschi* v. *Denkavit Commerciale* [1977] ECR 1,555, 1,576–7 (recital 35) (hereinafter "*Denkavit*").

fear that once such a norm was adopted, it would lock all Member States into a discipline from which they could not exit without again reaching unanimity. If the Community once agreed on a norm on, for example, the permissible level of lead in gasoline, no Member State could subsequently reduce the level further without the consent of all twelve Member States within the Community decision-making process. The combination of legal structure and political process militated against easy consensus even on non-protectionist policy.

The deep political subtlety of the Commission White Paper outlining the 1992 program becomes clear in this context, as does its ultimate success. Unlike all earlier attempts and proposals to revive the Community, the 1992 White Paper, although innovative in its conception of achieving a Europe without frontiers,[150] was entirely functional. It delineated the ostensibly uncontroversial goal of realizing an internal market, and, in the form of a technical list of required legislation, the uncontroversial means necessary to achieve that goal. Critically, it eschewed any grandiose institutional schemes. These were to come as an inevitable result, once 1992 was in place. Because of this technocratic approach, the White Paper apparently appealed to those with different, and often opposing, ideological conceptions of the future of Europe. To some, it represented the realization of the old dream of a true common marketplace, which, because of the inevitable connection between the social and the economic in modern political economies, would ultimately yield the much vaunted "ever closer union among the peoples of Europe." To others, it offered a vision of the European dream finally lashed down to the marketplace, and, importantly, a market unencumbered by the excessive regulation that had built up in the individual Member States. Dismantling regulation that impeded intra-Community trade would, on this reading, yield the dismantling of regulation altogether.

The key to the success of the 1992 strategy occurred when the Member States themselves agreed to majority voting. They took this step clearly not as a dramatic political step toward a higher level of European integration in the abstract, but rather as a low-key technical necessity in realizing the "non-controversial" objectives of the White Paper. This movement found expression in the single most important provision of the SEA, Article 100A.

As indicated above, this provision at face value seems minimalist and even destructive. First, the move to majority voting in Article 100A is couched as a residual measure and derogation from the principal measure, which requires unanimity, namely old Article 100.[151] Second, the exception

---

[150] Ehlermann, "1992 Project" at 1,099.
[151] See Art. 100A(1) ("By way of derogation from Article 100 . . .").

to Article 100A, Article 100A(4), was drafted in an even more restrictive form by the heads of state and government themselves.[152] The exception states that for enactments by majority voting a Member State may, despite the existence of a Community norm, adopt national safeguard measures.[153] Indeed, this exception may be seen as an ingenious attempt by the Member States to retain the equilibrium of the foundational period in the new context of majority voting.

The essence of the original equilibrium rested on the acceptance by the Member States of a comprehensive Community discipline on the condition that each would have a determinative Voice, the veto, in the establishment of new norms. In Article 100A, the Member States, by accepting a passage to majority voting, seemed to be destroying one of the two pillars of the foundational equilibrium. But, by allowing a Member State to derogate from a measure even in the face of a Community norm (adopted by a majority!) the other pillar of comprehensive Community jurisdiction seems to be equally eroded, thereby restoring the equilibrium. The exception breaks, of course, the rule of preemption established by the Court in cases where harmonization measures were adopted.[154]

Finally, as an indication of the low-key attitude toward the new voting procedure, a proposal to formally "repeal" the Luxembourg Accord was rejected by the Member States. Indeed, when presenting the SEA to their national parliaments, both the French and British ministers for foreign affairs claimed that the Single European Act left the Luxembourg Accord intact. Thus the French Foreign Minister solemnly declared in the Assemblée Nationale, responding to concerns that the SEA gave too much power to the Community at the expense of the Member States, that "en toute hypothèse, même dans les domaines où s'applique la règle de la majorité qualifiée, l'arrangement de Luxembourg de janvier 1966 demeure et conserve toute sa valeur." Likewise, in the House of Commons the British Foreign Secretary assured the House that "as a last resort, the Luxembourg compromise remains in place untouched and unaffected."[155]

---

[152] See Ehlermann, "Internal Market" at 381.

[153] Art. 100A(4): "If, after the adoption of a harmonization measure by the Council acting by a qualified majority a Member State deems it necessary to apply national provisions on grounds of major needs referred to in Article 36 . . . it shall notify the Commission of these provisions. The Commission shall confirm the provisions involved after having verified that they are not a means of arbitrary discrimination or a disguised restriction on trade between Member States. By way of derogation from the procedure laid down in Articles 169 and 170, the Commission or any Member State may bring the matter directly before the Court of Justice if it considers that another Member State is making improper use of the powers provided for in this article."

[154] See *Denkavit* [1977] ECR 1,555.

[155] On the failure of the proposal to repeal the Accord, see Ehlermann, "1992 Project" at 1,106. For declarations in the UK Parliament and the French Parliament on the continued existence

These three elements together may have given the Member States the feeling that the step they took was of limited significance and the outside observer the impression that the basic equilibrium was not shattered. It is most striking in this connection to note that even Mrs. Thatcher, the most diffident head of government among the large Member States, characterized the Single European Act on the morrow of its adoption by the European Council as a "modest step forward."[156] But shattered it was, since each of these precautions was either ill-conceived or rendered impracticable because of open-textured drafting and a teleology that traditionally presaged for construing derogations to the Treaty in the narrowest possible way.

Although the language of the provision suggests the new system was intended as a derogation, the prevailing view is that Article 100A has become the "default" procedure for most internal market legislation, and that the procedure of other articles is an exception.[157] Significantly, the connection between Article 100A and Article 8A means that majority voting should take place, except where specifically excluded,[158] for all measures needed to achieve the objective of an internal market. The internal market is defined as "an area without internal frontiers in which the free movement of goods, persons, services and capital is ensured."[159] This requirement of majority voting extends the scope of the Article 100A procedure beyond the harmonization of technical standards affecting the free movement of goods. The net result is that few cases exist that would *compel* resort to the old legal basis and its unanimity requirement. The Commission proposes the legal basis of decisions; any change of such basis would be subject itself to a unanimous Council vote, which would be difficult to achieve. In any event, even if the Council could change the legal basis, the Court, if a challenge were brought, would tend to side with the Commission on issues of legal basis.[160]

---

of the Luxembourg Accord even after the SEA, see 96 *Parliamentary Debates*, HC (5th series, 1986), 320 (debates of the House of Commons of April 23, 1986); Séance of the Assemblée Nationale (November 20, 1986), JO No. 109, 111 AN (CR), 8th Législature, 81st Séance, 6,611 (November 21, 1986).

[156] *Washington Post* (December 4, 1985) at A29, col. 1.

[157] "Article 100A thus gives the Council enormous scope for action, which is limited principally, I suspect, only by the existence of other enabling provisions": Ehlermann, "Internal Market," 134 at 384. Ehlermann argues convincingly that Art. 100A will be used in most cases, even in amending old Art. 100 legislation, a case in which Art. 235's provision for unanimity may have been used in the past. He says it will be used also for legislation of a scope that goes beyond the grounds of Art. 100, which was limited to harmonization of national measures that affected the establishment or functioning of the common market. Thus, Art. 100A will be used, in most cases, when new legislation to achieve the common market is needed: *ibid.*

[158] E.g., SEA, Art. 100A(2).   [159] SEA, Art. 8A.

[160] In a series of cases, starting with Case 45/86, *Commission of the European Communities* v. *Council*

Likewise, and contrary to some of the doomsday predictions,[161] the derogation to the principle of preemption in Article 100A(4), so carefully crafted by prime ministers and presidents, has had and must have very little impact. It allows a Member State to adopt, under strict conditions and subject to judicial review, unilateral derogations of Community harmonizing measures when the Member State seeks to uphold a higher level of protection. But that does not seem to be the real battlefield of majority voting. The real battlefield is regulation by the Community in areas in which Member States may feel that they do not want any regulation at all, let alone a higher Community standard.[162]

The sharpest impact, however, of majority voting under the SEA does not turn on these rather fine points. Earlier I explained that, although the language of the Luxembourg Accord suggested its invocation only when asserting a vital national interest, its significance rested in the fact that practically all decision-making was conducted under the shadow of the veto and resulted in general consensus politics.[163]

Likewise, the significance of Article 100A was its impact on *all* Community decision-making. Probably the most significant text is not the SEA, but the consequently changed rules of procedure of the Council of Ministers, which explain the rather simple mechanism for going to a majority vote.[164] Thus, Article 100A's impact is that practically all Community decision-making is conducted under the shadow of the vote (where

---

of the European Communities [1987] ECR 1,493 (general tariff preferences), the Commission has challenged the Council's use of Art. 235 (which provides for unanimity) rather than alternative legal bases in the Treaty. In a clear departure from its precedent, which would have allowed the Council to do so, in *Massey Ferguson*, the Court sided with the Commission. See also Case 51/87, *Commission of EC* v. *Council of EC* [1988] ECR 5,459; Case 165/87, *Commission of EC* v. *Council of EC* [1988] ECR 5,545; Case 275/87, *Commission of EC* v. *Council of EC* [1989] ECR 259; Case 288/87. But see Case 242/87, *Commission of EC* v. *Council of EC* [1989] ECR 1,425.

161 See, e.g., Pescatore, "Some Critical Remarks."

162 The UK strongly opposed, on principle, the adoption of Council Directive No. 89/662 on the approximation of the laws, regulations, and administrative provisions of the Member States concerning the labeling of tobacco products, 1989 OJ (L 359). It did not oppose the low standard of the regulation but argued that the Community did not have competence in the field of health. The derogation in Art. 100A(4) was useless in the face of this type of opposition. The UK had recourse only if it wanted a higher standard of protection against the danger of smoking.

163 The only habitual prior exception concerned decisions within the process of adopting the Community budget.

164 See amendment of the Council's Rules of Procedure adopted by the Council on July 20, 1987, 1987 OJ (L 291), 27. New Art. 5(1) provides: "The Council shall vote on the initiative of its President. The President shall, furthermore, be required to open voting proceedings on the invitation of a member of the Council or of the Commission, provided that a majority of the Council's members so decides." The new rules do not differentiate between votes under Art. 100A and any other legal basis which provides for majority voting in the Treaty.

the Treaty provides for such vote). The Luxembourg Accord, if not eliminated completely, has been rather restricted. For example, it could not be used in the areas in which Article 100A provides the legal basis for measures. In addition, to judge from the assiduousness with which the Member States argue about legal bases, which determine whether a measure is adopted by majority or unanimity,[165] it is rather clear that they do not feel free to invoke the Luxembourg Accord at whim. If the Accord persists at all, it depends on the assertion of a truly vital national interest, *accepted as such* by the other Member States, and the possibility of any Member State forcing a vote on the issue under the new rules of procedure. In other words, in accordance with the new rules, to invoke the Luxembourg Accord a Member State must persuade at least half the Member States of the "vitality" of the national interest claimed.

Under the shadow of the vote

Majority voting thus becomes a central feature of the Community in many of its activities.[166] A parallel with the opposite (Luxembourg Accord veto) practice of the past exists: today, an actual vote by the majority remains the exception. Most decisions are reached by consensus. But reaching consensus under the shadow of the vote is altogether different from reaching it under the shadow of the veto. The possibility of breaking deadlocks by voting drives the negotiators to break the deadlock without actually resorting to the vote. And, as noted above, the power of the Commission as an intermediary among the negotiating members of Council has been considerably strengthened.

This chapter has emphasized the relationships between the transformations of each of the definitional periods of the Community. In discussing each of the earlier periods, I have already pointed out the evolution of some important structural elements, such as the growth in the number of the Member States, that partially caused this "return" to majority voting.

But, of course, the crucial linkage to the past is not cause but effect. The "(re)turn" to majority voting constitutes a transformation as momentous as those that occurred earlier in the life of the Community because of those earlier changes. It is trite but worth repeating that, absent the earlier process of constitutionalization, a process that gave a real "bite" to Community norms, adoption by majority would be of far lesser significance. What puts the Community and its Member States in a new "defining" situation is the

---

[165] See Art. 235 cases listed in note 160, pp. 70–1 above.

[166] Several important Community areas remain that require unanimity. Art. 100A(2) provides for exceptions from majority voting in the field of the movement of persons, fiscal provisions, and the rights and interests of employed persons.

fact that the foundational equilibrium, despite attempts to rescue it in the actual drafting of the SEA, seems to be shattered.[167] Unlike any earlier era in the Community,[168] and unlike most of their other international and transnational experience, Member States are now in a situation of facing binding norms, adopted wholly or partially against their will, with direct effect in their national legal orders.

Likewise, the erosion of enumeration is far more significant in the environment of majority voting. There is something almost pitiful in the rude awakening of some of the Member States. For example, in 1989, the Council, in a hotly contested majority vote on the basis of Article 100A, adopted the new Community cigarette-labeling directive, which specifies a menu of mandatory warnings. Manufacturers must choose a warning to print on all cigarette packets.[169] The directive was hotly contested not because of the content of the warnings or even the principle of warnings, but because one of the Member States challenged the competence of the Council (meeting as a Council of Health Ministers) to adopt legislation pursuing the *objective* of health. Strictly speaking, to achieve a common market in tobacco products, it would be enough to pass a measure providing that cigarette packages carrying any of the warnings agreed upon could not be impeded in its intra-Community free movement. This

---

[167] If the Member States did not want to be in this situation, why did they, in practice, construe the SEA as they did? One can only speculate as to the answer. Critically, Member States differ in relation to the turn to majority voting. Some feel that the reality of interdependence is such that a blocking possibility pays less than the ability to force a recalcitrant major player in certain circumstances. In addition, it seems that, as in earlier episodes, some simply did not appreciate the significance of their constitutionalizing moves and unwittingly found themselves in the "trap" of Community discipline, where the stakes of rupture are possibly very high. It always seems difficult to root an explanation in ignorance by, or mistake of, major state actors But how else does one explain the statements made by the UK and French Foreign Ministers in their respective parliamentary assemblies? See note 155, pp. 69–70 above. Or how does one explain Thatcher's early evaluation of the SEA as a "modest" step – a step which later has come to be regarded as the "most comprehensive and most important amendment to the EEC Treaty to date"? Was she deliberately underestimating the nature of change brought about by, in particular, the shift to majority voting, or was she, as I argue in the text, not fully aware of the limits to the safeguards built into the revised Art. 100A? Failure of Member States to appreciate the full impact of their action is not new. As indicated above, it would appear that in negotiating Art. 177 the Member States were not fully aware of its far-reaching constitutional implications. See pp. 27–8 above.

[168] There were a few episodes in which the Luxembourg Accord did not "save" a Member State. The agricultural–price-increase episode in 1982 is an example. See *The Times* (London) (May 19, 1982) at 1, 5, 30 (articles on EEC override of UK veto); "A Failure for Europe," *ibid.* at 15; see also "Editorial Comments: The Vote on the Agricultural Prices: A New Departure?" *Common Market Law Review* 19 (1982), 371.

[169] See Council Directive No. 89/662 on the approximation of the laws, regulations and administrative provisions of the Member States concerning the labelling of tobacco products, 1989 OJ (L 359).

directive goes much further, however. Instead of stopping at the market rationale, its legal basis includes the European Council meeting of June 1985, which launched a European action program against cancer, and the resolution of July 1986 on a program of action of the European Communities against cancer.[170]

What, in June 1985 (prior to the SEA), may have seemed a totally banal resolution under which Member States could control any operationalization of the action program against cancer, attained an altogether different meaning in 1989, when the measures could be, and were, adopted by majority vote. However, in the light of the erosion of the principle of enumeration in the 1970s, a challenge to the constitutionality of the measure as *ultra vires* would likely fail.

Member States thus face not only the constitutional normativity of measures adopted often wholly or partially against their will, but also the operation of this normativity in a vast area of public policy,[171] unless the jurisprudence changes or new constitutional amendments are introduced.[172]

---

[170] 1986 OJ (C 184), 19.

[171] Admittedly, legislating on the outer reaches of Community jurisdiction requires resorting to Art. 235, which does provide for unanimity. But, as discussed at pp. 70–1 above, Art. 100A could be used in some instances instead of Art. 235, especially given the new Commission strategy, supported by the Court, of limiting the use of Art. 235 whenever another Treaty legal basis exists; the cigarette labeling directive illustrates this point quite forcefully.

[172] In fact, in this new decisional climate, a heightened sensitivity to demarcation of competences exists, one which hardly existed in the past. See "Resolution of Parliament of July 12, 1990, on the principle of Subsidiarity," PE 143.504: "[H]aving regard to the future development of the Community, in particular its commitment to draw up a draft constitution for European Union and the fact this process of transforming the European Community *requires a clear distinction to be made between the competences of the Union and those of the Member States* . . .": preamble to Resolution, at 13 (emphasis added); see also "27th Report of the Select Committee on the European Communities [of the UK House of Lords] on Economic and Monetary Union and Political Union of October 30, 1990" (HL Paper 88-I) at paras. 143–4, 204 ("There is also a more general fear that the Community is taking collective decisions in areas where such choices could perfectly well be left to the member States"). See generally Jacqué and Weiler, "On the Road to European Union – A New Judicial Architecture: An Agenda for the Intergovernmental Conference," *Common Market Law Review* 27 (1990), 185, 199–206; and "Editorial Comments," *Common Market Law Review* 27 (1990), 181. For a recent harsh critique of the unchecked expansion of jurisdiction, see Hailbronner, "Legal-Institutional Reforms of the EEC: What Can We Learn from Federalism Theory and Practice?" *Swiss Review of International Economic Relations* 46 (1991), special issue 3/4. In the leaked "Non-Paper" of the Luxembourg Presidency of April 15, 1991, setting out the state of negotiation of the Intergovernmental Conference, the principle of subsidiarity has been inserted as an operational part of the Treaty. The proposal is included as an amendment to EEC Treaty, Art. 3 and reads as follows: "La Communauté agit dans les limites des compétences qui lui sont conférées et des objectifs qui lui sont assignés par le present traité. Dans les domaines que ne relévent pas de sa competénce exclusive, la Communauté intervient conformément au principe de la subsidiarité, si et dans la mesure où les objectifs qui lui sont assignes peuvent être mieux réalisés au niveau

The challenge of majority voting

As indicated above, I think enough has been written about the promise of the enhanced "efficiency" of the decisional process and the internal dynamic generated and manifested, for example, in the current intergovernmental conferences.[173] In contrast, I wish to explore less visible implications of the change. Since the SEA does rupture a fundamental feature of the Community in its foundational period, the equilibrium between constitutional and institutional power, it would follow from the analysis of the foundational period that the change should have implications that go beyond simple legislative efficiency. On this reading, the SEA regime does truly constitute a defining experience for the Community. The lack of any temporal perspective suggests great caution in this part of the analysis, and I pose my points as questions and challenges rather than affirmations.

The challenge of compliance[174]

Although the problem of compliance with Community norms by the Member States is not new, the context of the SEA regime changes our evaluation. In reading the explanation earlier that the Community has developed effective mechanisms for the enforcement of Community law, one should not be misled to think that no violations, by Member States, Community institutions, or individuals, occur. They occur regularly and, as Community activities and impact expand, increasingly.[175] In this respect the Community is no different (in principle) than, for example, any state of equivalent size and complexity. Indeed, that was the critical factor in our analysis. When violation takes place it does so in a constitutional context with an ethos of domestic rather than international law. Since the Member States were able to control the elaboration of Community legislation in all its phases and were able to block any measure not to their liking, the non-

---

Communautaire qu'au niveau des états membres oeuvrant isolément, en raison des dimensions ou des effets de l'action envisagée.": "Non-paper: project d'articles de Traité, en vue de la mose en place d'une union politique" (Luxembourg. April 15, 1991) at 12. This proposal, which was ultimately adopted as Art. 3B, on my reading, provides a new criterion for judicial review by the Court under Arts. 173 and 177(b). The fact that subsidiarity, often thought of as a principle incapable of translation into an operative positive obligation, has been included is an indication of the strength of feeling concerning the question of erosion of jurisdictional limits.

[173] For the "bright side of the moon," see Ehlermann, "1992 Project."

[174] See generally Weiler, "The White Paper and the Application of Community Law," in Bieber, *1992: One European Market?* at 337.

[175] The White Paper raises the issue explicitly in section 152.

compliance reflex would tend to operate at a surface and convenience level and thus would not indicate fundamental discontent.[176]

Under the new regime non-compliance could become more of a strategy. If the equilibrium of Voice and Exit is shattered by reducing the individual power of Member State Voice, the pressure might force a shift to strategies of Exit, which, in the Community context, means selective application rather than withdrawal. There are some signs that this may be happening.[177] In any event, although the Community is impressively on course in "implementing" the 1992 legislative program, a "black hole" of knowledge exists regarding the true level of Member State implementation.[178]

This problem of compliance is merely one manifestation of the deep

---

[176] The Commission drew a bleak picture in the White Paper: "Of the total number of complaints received by the Commission, some 60 percent, i.e., on average 255 each year, relate to Articles 30–36 of the Treaty, but because of the lack of resources it can, in a given year, settle only one hundred cases. The resulting delays and backlogs benefit the infringing States, impede systematic action, proceedings, and frustrate the confidence of industry as well as that of the man in the street. Measures have to be taken to remedy the situation.": *ibid.* at section 153. One should not minimize the pragmatic nature of the problem, accentuated by the ability of Member States to disregard judgments of the Court in direct Art. 169 actions. None the less, it is interesting to note that the protectionist violation the Commission points out has been in some measure at least a response to the jurisprudence of the Court and not to consensual legislation. As far as directives are concerned, in most cases, non-incorporation is a result of objective constitutional and procedural difficulties at the national level (especially in Italy and Belgium) and not from an evasive or defiant strategy by a Member State.

[177] The problem was considered sufficiently grave to merit specific mention in the conclusions of the Dublin Summit of June 25–6, 1990, which set up the new Intergovernmental Conferences. Thus, in Annex I, mention was made of the need to give consideration to the automatic enforceability of Arts. 169 and 171 judgments of the European Court and of Member States ensuring the implementation and observance of Community law and European Court judgments: Dublin Summit, Annex I, reprinted in "Conclusions of the European Council Dublin 25 and 26 June 1990," *Europe*, Doc. No. 1,632/1,633 (June 29, 1990) at 9. The European Parliament, in its proposed Treaty amendments submitted to the Intergovernmental Conference, suggested amending Art. 171 to read: "The court may combine its judgments with financial sanctions against the Member State that has been found to be in default. The amount and method of collection of such sanctions shall be determined by a regulation adopted by the Community in accordance with the procedure laid down pursuant to Art. 188(b). The Court may also impose on recalcitrant states other sanctions such as suspension of right to participate in certain Community programs, to enjoy certain advantages or to have access to certain Community funds.": Art. 171, PE 146.824. The Select Committee of the House of Lords observed: "[T]here are Member States which seem to treat their obligation to translate Directives into national law by a certain date as little more than a vague guideline": "27th Report of the Select Committee on the European Communities [of the UK House of Lords] on Economic and Monetary Union and Political Union of October 30, 1990" (HL Paper 88-I) at para. 146: see also *ibid.* paras. 45–8, 205.

[178] On the general picture of implementation, see "Septième rapport annuel au parlement européen sur le controle de l'application du droit Communautaire," Com (90) 288 Final (May 22, 1990). See also Commission Reports on the Implementation of the White Paper.

dilemma involved in dismantling the foundational equilibrium. It is useful here, albeit in a very loose manner, to introduce Hirschman's third notion, Loyalty. Two possible readings of the future present themselves. On one reading, the dismantling of the foundational equilibrium will constitute a destabilizing act of such dimension that it threatens the acceptance not simply of a particular Community measure but of the very constitutional foundation. Alternatively, acceptance of Community discipline may have become the constitutional reflex of the Member States and their organs.[179] A Loyalty to the institution may have developed that breaks out of the need for constant equilibrium. The two decades of enhanced Voice thus constitute a learning and adaptation process resulting in socialization; at the end of this period decisional changes affecting Voice will not cause a corresponding adjustment to Exit. Time will tell, but there are signs that Loyalty with a large mixture of expediency may prevent or at least reduce the otherwise destabilizing effect of the new change.

Challenges of "democracy" and "legitimacy"[180]

1992 also puts a new hue on the question of the democracy deficit. A useful starting point could indeed be a focus on the European Parliament and its role. It is traditional to start an analysis of the role of the European Parliament in the governance structure of the Community with a recapitulation of the existing democracy deficit in EC decision-making. This deficit informs, animates, and mobilizes the drive to change the powers of the European Parliament. In addition, to the extent that the governments of the Member States have responded, weakly and grudgingly, to this drive, it is surely because even they recognized the compelling power of the democracy deficit argument.

---

[179] For suggestions that this issue may be not quite as settled as one may wish, not even among the courts of the Member States, see, e.g., Cartabia, "The Italian Constitutional Court and the Relationship between the Italian Legal System and the European Community," *Michigan Journal of International Law* 12 (1990), 173; Szyszczak, "Sovereignty: Crisis, Compliance, Confusion, Complacency?" *European Law Review* 15 (1990), 480.

[180] See Weiler, "Parlement européen, intégration européenne, démocratie et légitimité," in J.-V. Louis and D. Waelbroeck (eds.), *Le parlement européen* (Editions de Université de Bruxelles: Brussels, 1988), 325, in which I have elaborated these points more expansively. I have been considerably helped by, and have drawn in particular on, the following works: L. Brilmayer, *Justifying International Acts* (Cornell University Press: Ithaca, NY, 1989): T. Franck, *The Power of Legitimacy among Nations* (Oxford University Press: New York, 1990); J. Habermas, *Legitimation Crisis* (Beacon Press: Boston, 1975); L. Henkin, *Constitutionalism, Democracy and Foreign Affairs* (Columbia University Press: New York, 1990); Dahl, "Federalism and the Democratic Process," in J. R. Pennock and J. W. Chapman (eds.), *Liberal Democracy*, XXV Nomos (New York University Press: New York, 1983) at 95. My own synoptic presentation cannot do justice to the richness of the works cited.

The typical argument views the European Parliament as the only (or at least principal) repository of legitimacy and democracy in the Community structure. The phrase most often used in this context is "democratic legitimacy."[181] The Commission, in this view, is an appointed body of international civil servants, and the Council of Ministers represents the executive branch of each national government which, through Community structures, has legislative powers it lacks on respective national scenes.

Thus, the Council, a collectivity of ministers, on a proposal of the Commission, a collectivity of non-elected civil servants, could, and in some instances must, pass legislation which is binding and enforceable even in the face of conflicting legislation passed by national parliaments. This occurs without corresponding parliamentary scrutiny and approval. Indeed, the Council could pass the legislation in the face of the European Parliament's disapproval. This happens often enough to render the point not simply theoretical. What is more, the Council can legislate in some areas that were hitherto subject to parliamentary control at the national level. We have already seen how the constitutionalization process in the foundational period and the erosion of enumerated powers in the second period accentuated this problem.

According to this view of the Community, the powers of the European Parliament are both weak and misdirected. They are weak in that the legislative power (even post-SEA) is ultimately consultative in the face of a determined Council. Even the Parliament's budgetary powers, though more concrete, do not affect the crucial areas of budgetary policy: revenue raising and expenditure on compulsory items.[182] The power to reject the budget *in toto* is a boomerang which has not always proved effective, although in 1984 the budget ultimately was amended in a direction that took account of some of the Parliament's concerns. The possibility of denying a discharge on past expenditure lacks any real sanction power.

Those parliamentary powers that are real, the powers to dismiss the Commission, to ask questions of the Commission, and to receive answers, are illusory at best and misdirected at worst. They are illusory because the power to dismiss is collective and does not have the accompanying power

---

[181] The problem of democratic structures is addressed this way by the Dublin Summit in "Conclusions of the European Council Dublin 25 and 26 June 1990," Annex I at 8.

[182] Parliament has a final say (within limits set by the Commission) only on expenditure items which are not mandated by the Treaty itself. For the best explanation of the Parliament's powers in this field, see J. Jacqué, R. Bieber, V. Constantinesco, and D. Nickel, *Le parlement européen* (Economica: Paris, 1984), 178. See also Case 34/86, *Council* v. *Parliament* [1986] ECR 2,155 (concerning the 1986 Budget) (especially the opinion of Advocate-General Mancini). Parliament was granted real approval control as regards association agreements under Art. 238 and the accession of new Member States under Art. 237. It has no formal powers, even of consultation as regards trade agreements under Art. 113.

to appoint. They are misdirected because the Council is the "villain of the peace" in most European Parliament battles. All these well-known factors taken together constitute the elements of the democracy deficit and create the crisis of legitimacy from which the Community allegedly suffers.

Although the democracy deficit is prominent in Parliamentary rhetoric, the day-to-day complaint of Parliament especially in the pre-SEA days was not that the Community legislator (the Council) was over-vigorous and violated democratic principles, but rather that it failed to act vigorously enough. Critics argued that the Council had incapacitated itself and the entire Community by abandoning Treaty rules of majoritarian decision-making by giving a *de facto* veto to each Member State government that asserts a "vital national interest."

The veto power arrogated by the Member States produced another facet of the democracy deficit: the ability of a small number of Community citizens represented by their minister in the Council to block the collective wishes of the rest of the Community.

Parliamentarians almost uniformly claim that both facets of the malaise could be corrected by certain institutional changes, which on the one hand would "de-block" the Council by restoring majority voting, but which would also significantly increase the legislative and control powers of Parliament. Increased powers to the Parliament, directly elected by universal suffrage, would, so it is claimed, substantially reduce the democracy deficit and restore legitimacy to the Community decision-making process. It is further argued that, regarding the decisional malaise, Parliament has over the years boasted a *communautaire* spirit which would, if given effective outlet, transcend nationalistic squabbles and introduce a dynamism far more consonant with the declared objectives of the Treaties. The large majority accorded to the draft Treaty Establishing the European Union is cited as a typical example of this dynamism. Although these points seem obvious, they receive little critical analysis.

The absence of a critical approach derives in part from a loose usage of the notions of democracy and legitimacy. Very frequently in discourse about the Parliament and the Community the concepts of democracy and legitimacy have been presented interchangeably although in fact they do not necessarily coincide. To be sure, today, a non-democratic government or political system in the West could not easily attain or maintain legitimacy, but it is still possible for a democratic structure to be illegitimate – either *in toto* or in certain aspects of its operation.[183]

---

[183] A stark example may drive the point home better than an abstract explication: Germany during the Weimar period was democratic but the government enjoyed little legitimacy. Germany during National Socialism ceased to be democratic once Hitler rose to power, but the

In spite of all the conceptual difficulties of dealing with "legitimacy,"[184] even in this brief excursus it may be useful to draw one classical distinction between formal (legal) legitimacy and social (empirical) legitimacy. The notion of formal legitimacy in institutions or systems implies that all requirements of the law are observed in the creation of the institution or system. This concept is akin to the juridical concept of formal validity. In today's Europe, as in the West generally, any notion of legitimacy must rest on some democratic foundation, loosely stated as the People's consent to power structures and process. A Western institution or system satisfies formal legitimacy if its power structure was created through democratic processes.[185] Thus, in the Community context, I simply point out that the Treaties establishing the Community, which gave such a limited role to the European Parliament, were approved by the national parliaments of all founding Member States and subsequently by the parliaments of six acceding Member States. Proposals to give more power to the European Parliament have failed, for a variety of reasons, to survive the democratic processes in the Member States.[186] This definition of formal legitimacy is thus distinct from that of simple "legality." Formal legitimacy is legality understood in the sense that democratic institutions and processes created the law on which it is based (in the Community case, the Treaties).

Thus, in this formal sense, the existing structure and process rests on a formal approval by the democratically elected parliaments of the Member States; and yet, undeniably, the Community process suffers from a clear democracy deficit in the classical sense outlined above.

"Social legitimacy," on the other hand, connotes a broad, empirically determined, societal acceptance of the system. Social legitimacy may have an additional substantive component: legitimacy occurs when the government process displays a commitment to, and actively guarantees, values that are part of the general political culture, such as justice, freedom, and general welfare.[187]

---

government continued to enjoy widespread legitimacy well into the early 1940s. Cf. G. Craig, *Germany 1866–1945* (Oxford University Press: New York, 1978) at chapters 15 and 18.

[184] See generally Hyde, "The Concept of Legitimation in the Sociology of Law," *Wisconsin Law Review* (1983), 379.

[185] Franck's synthesis of "legitimacy" as it applies to the rules applicable to states is: "Legitimacy is a property of a rule or rule-making institution which itself exerts a pull toward compliance on those addressed normatively because those addressed believe that the rule or institution has come into being and operates in accordance with generally accepted principles of right process.": Franck, *The Power of Legitimacy among Nations* at 24.

[186] The SEA, which touches only slightly the so-called democracy deficit, was ratified by the parliaments of all the Member States. Likewise, with each Community enlargement, in 1973, 1981, and 1986, national parliaments had the opportunity to protest the non-democratic character of the Community, but instead reconfirmed the governance system.

[187] Franck usefully sorts legitimacy theories into three groups. The first group regards legitimacy as

An institution, system, or polity, in most, but not all, cases, must enjoy formal legitimacy to enjoy social legitimacy. This is most likely the case in Western democratic traditions, which embody the rule of law as part of their political ethos. But a system that enjoys formal legitimacy may not necessarily enjoy social legitimacy. Most popular revolutions since the French Revolution occurred in polities whose governments retained formal legitimacy but lost social legitimacy. These admittedly primitive distinctions will become relevant to our discussion with one further excursus into the notions of integration and democracy.[188]

Obviously, democracy cannot exist in a modern polity as in "the Greek polis" or "the New England town." Representative democracy replaces direct participation. None the less, democracy can be measured by the closeness, responsiveness, representativeness, and accountability of the governors to the governed. Although this formula is vague, it is sufficient for present purposes.

Imagine three independent polities, each enjoying a representative democracy. Let us further assume that each government enjoys legislative and regulatory power in the fields of education, taxation, foreign trade, and defense. In relation to each of these four functions the electors can influence directly their representatives, through elections and the like, as to the polity's education policy, level of taxation, type of foreign trade (e.g., protectionist or free), and defense-force composition and policy. Assume finally that for a variety of reasons the three polities decide to integrate and "share their sovereignty" in the fields of taxation, foreign trade and defense.

If this decision to integrate was democratically reached within each

---

process. He cites Weber: "Weber postulates the validity of an order in terms of its being regarded by the obeying public 'as in some way obligatory or exemplary' for its members because, at least, in part, it defines 'a model' which is 'binding' and to which the actions of others 'will in fact conform . . .' At least, in part, this legitimacy is perceived as adhering to the authority issuing an order, as opposed to the qualities of legitimacy that inhere in an order itself.": Franck, *The Power of Legitimacy among Nations* at 16–18, 250 note 29 (quoting from M. Weber, *Economy and Society: An Outline of Interpretive Sociology* (Bedminster Press: New York, 1968) at 31). The second group mixes process and substance. This notion "is interested not only in how a ruler and a rule were chosen, but also in whether the rules made, and commands given, were considered in the light of all relevant data, both objective and attitudinal": Franck, *ibid.* at 17. Franck quotes Habermas: "Legitimacy means that there are good arguments for a political order's claim to be recognized as right and just": *ibid.* at 248 note 27 (quoting J. Habermas, *Communication and the Evolution of Society* (Beacon Press: Boston, 1979) at 178–9). His third group, primarily neo–Marxist, focuses on outcomes: "In this view, a system seeking to validate itself . . . must be defensible in terms of the equality, fairness, justice, and freedom which are realized by those commands": *ibid.* at 18. We do not have to choose among these different conceptualizations of legitimacy, since all three support my simple proposition distinguishing social legitimacy from both democracy and legal validity *simpliciter*.

[188] See generally Dahl, "Federalism and the Democratic Process."

polity, the integrated polity certainly enjoys formal legitimacy. However, by definition, initially the new integrated polity's "responsiveness" will be less than that of the three independent polities. Prior to the integration, the majority of electors in polity A would have a controlling influence over their level of taxation, the nature of their foreign trade policy, and the size and posture of their army. In the integrated polity, even a huge majority of the electors in polity A can be outvoted by the electors of polities B and C.[189] This will be the case even if the new integrated polity has a perfectly democratically elected "federal" legislator. The integrated polity will not be undemocratic but it will be, in terms of the ability of citizens to influence policies affecting them, less democratic.[190]

This transformation occurs, in reverse form, when a centralized state devolves power to regions, as in the cases of Italy, Spain, and recently France. Regionalism, "the division of sovereignty" and granting of it to more or less autonomous regions is in some respects the opposite of integration. One of the prime motivations for regionalism is to enhance democracy in the sense of giving people more direct control of areas of public policy that affect their lives.

To suggest that in the process of integration there is a loss, at least in one sense, of democracy, does not, as such, condemn the process of integration. The electors in polities A, B, and C usually have formidable reasons for integrating despite this loss of some direct control over policy when it is made in the larger polity. Typically the main reason is size. By aggregating their resources, especially in the field of defense, total welfare may be enhanced despite the loss of the more immediate influence of their government's policies. Similar advantages may accrue in the field of foreign trade. Phenomena such as multinational corporations, which may manage to escape the control of any particular polity, may exist, and only an integrated polity can tax or regulate them effectively. In other words the independence and sovereignty of the single polities may be illusory in the real interdependent world. None the less, the ability of the citizens of polity A, B, or C directly to control and influence these areas will have diminished.

Even within each polity the minority was obliged to accept majority decisions. So why do I claim that in the enlarged, integrated polity, in

---

[189] The dilution in Voice operates on two levels: a diminution in the specific gravity of each voter's weight in the process, and a diminution in the gravity of each voter's state.

[190] Different federal options will of course have consequences also for the allocation choices of voters and substantive policy outcomes. For a sustained discussion of this issue, see Rose-Ackerman, "Does Federalism Matter? Political Choice in a Federal Republic," *Journal of Political Economy* 89 (1981), 152.

which an equally valid majoritarian rule applies, a loss of democracy occurs? This is among the toughest aspects of democratic theory.

What defines the boundary of the polity within which the majority principle should apply? No theoretical answer to this question exists. Long-term, very long-term, factors such as political continuity, social, cultural, and linguistic affinity, and a shared history determine the answer. No one factor determines the boundaries; rather they result from some or all of these factors. People accept the majoritarian principle of democracy within a polity to which they see themselves as belonging.[191]

The process of integration – even if decided upon democratically – brings about at least a short-term loss of direct democracy in its actual process of governance. What becomes crucial for the success of the integration process is the social legitimacy of the new integrated polity despite this loss of total control over the integrated policy areas by each polity.

How will such legitimacy emerge? Two answers are possible. The first is a visible and tangible demonstration that the total welfare of the citizenry is enhanced as a result of integration. The second answer is ensuring that the new integrated polity itself, within its new boundaries, has democratic structures. But more important still is giving a temporarily enhanced Voice to the separate polities. It is not an accident that some of the most successful federations which emerged from separate polities – the United States, Switzerland, Germany – enjoyed a period as a confederation prior to unification. This does not mean confederation is a prerequisite to federation. It simply suggests that in a federation created by integration, rather than by devolution, there must be an adjustment period in which the political boundaries of the new polity become socially accepted as appropriate for the larger democratic rules by which the minority will accept a new majority.[192]

From the political, but not legal, point of view the Community is in fact a confederation. The big debate is therefore whether the time is ripe for a radical change toward a more federal structure, or whether the process should continue in a more evolutionary fashion.

These answers about the possible emergence of legitimacy can be at odds

---

[191] "Thus it does not seem possible to arrive at a defensible conclusion about the proper unit of democracy by strictly theoretical reasoning: we are in the domain not of theoretical but of practical judgment.": Dahl, "Federalism and the Democratic Process" at 106; see also Brilmayer, *Justifying International Acts* at 13–27, 52–78 (chapter 1, "Political Legitimacy and Jurisdictional Boundaries" and chapter 3, "Boundary Assumptions in Domestic Political Theory").

[192] We do not have to take the formal transfer as the actual transfer. Arguably, the United States became truly federal only after the Civil War.

with each other. Giving an enhanced Voice to each polity may impede the successful attainment of the goals of integration. Denying sufficient Voice to the constituent polities (allowing the minority to be overridden by the majority) may bring about a decline in the social legitimacy of the integrated polity with consequent dysfunctions and even disintegration. In terms of democratic theory, the final objective of a unifying polity is to recoup the loss of democracy inherent in the process of integration. This "loss" is recouped when the social fabric and discourse are such that the electorate accepts the new boundary of the polity and then accepts totally the legitimacy – in its social dimension – of being subjected to majority rule in a much larger system comprised of the integrated polities.

We can now see how these notions play out in a reconstructed analysis of the democracy issue in the Community. As stated above, a premise of the traditional analysis is that the Community suffers from a legitimacy crisis. Is the absence of legitimacy formal? Surely not. The Community, including its weak Parliament, appointed Commission, and unaccountable Council, enjoys perfect formal legitimacy. The Treaties all have been approved by the Community electorate through their national parliaments in accordance with the constitutional requirement of each Member State. In addition, the Treaties have been approved several times more with the accession of each new Member State and most recently with the adoption of the Single European Act.

If there is a crisis of legitimacy, it must therefore be a crisis of social (empirical) legitimacy. What is the nature of this crisis of social legitimacy, if indeed it exists? The traditional view is that the absence of legitimacy is rooted in the democracy deficit. As stated above, the implication is that any increase in the legislative and control powers of the European Parliament at the expense of the Council contributes to an elimination of this legitimacy crisis. I challenge the premise and the conclusion. I believe that Parliament should be given enhanced powers, because I acknowledge the democracy deficit in the formal sense explained above. But I think that it is at least questionable whether this will necessarily solve the legitimacy problems of the Community. It may even enhance them.

The legitimacy problem is generated by several factors, which should be discussed separately. The primary factor is, at least arguably, that the European electorate (in most Member States) only grudgingly accepts the notion that crucial areas of public life should be governed by a decisional process in which their *national* voice becomes a minority which can be overridden by a majority of representatives from other European countries. In theoretical terms there is, arguably, still no legitimacy to the notion that the boundaries within which a minority will accept as democratically legitimate a majority decision are now European instead of national. It is interesting, and significant, that for the first time national parliaments are taking a keen interest in the structural process of European integration and are far from enamored with the idea of solving the democracy deficit by simply enhancing the powers of the European Parliament.[193]

At its starkest, this critical view claims that in terms of social legitimacy no difference exists between a decision of the Council of Ministers and a decision of the European Parliament. To the electorate, both chambers present themselves as legislative, composed of Member States' representatives. In both cases, until time and other factors resolve this dimension of legitimacy, the electorate of a minority Member State might consider it socially illegitimate that they have to abide by a majority decision of a redefined polity.

On this view, the most legitimating element (from a "social" point of view) of the Community was the Luxembourg Accord and the veto power. To be sure, a huge cost in terms of efficient decision-making and progress was paid. But this device enabled the Community to legitimate its program and its legislation. It provided the national electorates an *ex ante* "insurance policy" that nothing could pass without the electorate Voice having a controlling say. The "insurance policy" also presented an *ex post* legitimation as well: everything the Community did, no matter how unpopular, required the assent of national ministers. The legitimacy of the output of the Community decisional process was, thus, at least partially due to the public knowledge that it was controllable through the veto power. The current shift to majority voting might therefore exacerbate legitimacy problems. Even an enhanced European Parliament, which would operate on a co-decision principle, will not necessarily solve the legitimacy problem. The legitimacy crisis does not derive principally from the accountability issue at the European level, but from the very redefinition of the European polity.

Pulling all the threads together, the conclusion provides at least food for thought: in a formal sense, majority voting exacerbates the democracy deficit by weakening national parliamentary control of the Council without increasing the powers of the European Parliament. But even increasing the powers of the European Parliament (to full co-decision on the most ambitious plan) does not wholly solve the problem. It brings to the fore the intractable problem of redefining the political boundaries of the Community within which the principle of majority voting is to take place. It is an open question whether the necessary shift in public loyalty to such a

---

[193] See, e.g., "27th Report of the Select Committee on the European Communities [of the UK House of Lords] on Economic and Monetary Union and Political Union of October 30, 1990" (HL Paper 88-I) at paras. 157, 158, and 210.

redefined boundary has occurred even if we accept the formalistic notion of state parliamentary democracy.

BEYOND 1992: TWO VISIONS OF THE PROMISED LAND: THE IDEOLOGY, ETHOS, AND POLITICAL CULTURE OF EUROPEAN INTEGRATION

By way of conclusion I would like to examine, far more tentatively, another facet of the transformation of Europe: the ideology, ethos, and political culture of European integration, particularly in relation to 1992.[194]

Ideological discourse within the Community, especially in the pre-1992 period, had two peculiar features. On the one hand, despite the growing focus of Community activity on important issues of social choice, a near absence of overt debate on the left–right spectrum existed. 1992 (as a code for the overall set of changes) represents a break from this pattern. On the other hand, there was abundant discourse on the politics and choices of the integration model itself. But this discourse was fragmented. In specialized political constituencies, especially those concerned with Community governance, public discourse was typically a dichotomy between those favoring the Community (and further European integration) and those defending "national sovereignty" and the prerogatives of the Member State. The outcome of the debate was curious. In the visible realm of political power from the 1960s onwards, it seemed that the "national interest" was ascending.[195] The "high moral ground" by contrast, seemed to be occupied fairly safely by the "integrationists."

[194] In the earlier parts of this chapter I rested my interpretation, as much as possible and at least in its factual matrix, on an "objective" reality rooted in "empirical" and consequently "refutable" data. Likewise, my analytical moves were transparent enough to open them to rational critique. Obvious and inevitable limitations on the resulting "scientific objectivity" of the chapter exist. Clearly, to give the most banal example, my own prejudices, overt and less overt, shaped the selection of factual data, and, of course, their perception and analysis. Readers are always better placed than the writer to expose those prejudices and discount them in assessing the overall picture. In turning to ethos, ideology, and political culture, the screening process of the "self" (my "self") plays an even bigger role in the narrative. To try to "document" my assertions and conclusions here would be to employ the semblance of a scholarly apparatus where it is patently not merited. I do not, and cannot, claim to root this part of the chapter on the kind of painstaking research and complex tools that characterize the work of the social historian or the historical sociologist. Caveat lector! None the less, my brief narrative will, I hope, serve a function. Compared to the plethora of systemic and substantive theories and analyses of the processes of European integration, a real dearth of ideological and cultural scrutiny exists. Two recent extremely illuminating reflections on these issues are Snyder, *New Directions*; and J. Orstrom Moller *Technology and Culture in a European Context* (Nyt Nordisk Forlag: Copenhagen, 1991). By offering my perspective on these issues I hope the reader is drawn to reflect, and thereby, challenged to take position.

[195] The constitutional revolution was not immediately apparent even to relatively informed

So far as the general public was concerned, the characterizing feature of public discourse was a relatively high level of indifference, disturbed only on rare occasions when Community issues caught the public imagination. Although opinion polls always showed a broad support for the Community, as I argued earlier, it was still possible to gain political points by defending the national interest against the threat of the faceless "Brussels Eurocracy."

Here, the importance of 1992 has not been only in a modification of the political process of the Community, but also in a fascinating mobilization of wide sections of general public opinion behind the "new" Europe. The significance of this mobilization cannot be overstated. It fueled the momentum generated by the White Paper and the Single European Act, and laid the ground auspiciously for creating Community initiatives to push beyond 1992. These Community initiatives included the opening in December 1990 of two new Intergovernmental Conferences designed to fix the timetable and modalities of economic and monetary union, as well as the much more elusive task of political union. Although no one has a clear picture of "political union,"[196] with open talk about Community government, federalist solutions, and other such codes,[197] even if the actual changes to the existing structure will be disappointing, in the ideological "battle" between state and Community, the old nationalist rhetoric has become increasingly marginalized and the integrationist ethos has fully ascended. The demise of Prime Minister Thatcher symbolizes this change.

audiences. See Weiler, "Attitudes of MEPs towards the European Court," *European Law Review* 9 (1984), 169. One of the interesting conclusions of this survey of attitudes is that even those Members of the European Parliament strongly opposed to the dynamics of European integration and the increase in power of the Commission and Parliament regarded the Court with relevant equanimity.

[196] The term has no fixed meaning and is used to connote a wide variety of models from federalist to intergovernmentalist. See generally R. Mayne and J. Pinder, *Federal Union: The Pioneers* (St. Martin's Press: New York, 1990); R. Pryce (ed.), *The Dynamics of European Union* (Croom Helm: London; Methuen: New York, 1987) (usefully tracing the evolution of the concept of political union over the history of European integration up to the Single European Act): J. Lodge (ed.), *European Union: The European Community in Search of a Future* (Macmillan: London, 1986).

[197] See, e.g., President Delors' speech to the European Parliament of January 17, 1990: "Cet exécutif [of the future Community on which Delors was speculating – the Commission according to the logic of the founders] devra être responsable, bien entendu, devant les institutions démocratique de la future *féderation* ..." (Translated: "It is self-evident that this executive has to be responsible to the democratic institutions of the future *federation* ..."): "Jacques Delors presente de programme de la Commission et dessine un profit de l'Europe de demain," *Europe* Doc. No. 1,592 (January 24, 1990) at 7 (emphasis added). Likewise, when speaking approvingly of Mitterrand's idea of an "all-European confederation," Delors adds: "Mais ma conviction est qu'une telle confédération ne pourra voir le jour qu'une fois réalisé l'Union politique de la Communauté!" (Translated: "But my conviction is that such a federation cannot emerge once the political Union of the Community is realised!"): *ibid.* at 4.

The impact of 1992, however, goes well beyond these obvious facts of mobilization and "European ascendancy." Just below the surface lurk some questions, perhaps even forces, which touch the very ethos of European integration, its underlying ideology, and the emergent political culture associated with this new mobilization. Moreover, in some respects the very success of 1992 highlights some inherent (or at least potential) contradictions in the very objectives of European integration.

I shall deal first with the break from the Community's supposed ideological neutrality, and then turn to the question of the ethos of European integration in public discourse.

1992 and the "ideological neutrality" of the Community

The idea of the single market was presented in the White Paper as an ideologically neutral program around which the entire European polity could coalesce in order to achieve the goals of European integration. This idea reflected an interesting feature of the pre-1992 Community: the relative absence of ideological discourse and debate on the right–left spectrum. The chill on right–left ideological debate derived from the governance structure of the Community.[198]

Since in the Council there usually would be representatives of national governments from both right and left, the desired consensus had to be one acceptable to all major political forces in Europe. Thus, policies verged towards centrist pragmatic choices, and issues involving sharp right–left division were either shelved[199] or mediated to conceal or mitigate the choice involved. The tendency towards the lowest common denominator applied also to ideology.

Likewise, on the surface, the political structure of the European Parliament replicates the major political parties in Europe. National party lists join in Parliament to sit in European political groups. However, for a long time the politics of integration itself, especially on the issues of the European Parliament's power and the future destiny of the Community, were far more important than differences between left and right within the chamber. The clearest example was the coalescing of Parliament with a large majority behind the Independent Communist Spinelli and his draft Treaty for European Union.[200]

---

[198] Of course I do not suggest that choices with ideological implications were not made. But they were rarely perceived as such.

[199] Thus, the proposed European company statute was shelved for many years because of the inability to agree, especially on the role of labor in the governance structure of the company.

[200] Typically, right and left have differed sharply in Parliament on issues of foreign affairs and extra-Community policies.

Most interesting in this perspective is the perception of the Commission. It is an article of faith for European integration that the Commission is not meant to be a mere secretariat, but an autonomous political force shaping the agenda and brokering the decision-making of the Community. And yet at the same time, the Commission, as broker, must be ideologically neutral, not favoring Christian Democrats, Social Democrats, or others.

This neutralization of ideology has fostered the belief that an agenda could be set for the Community, and the Community could be led towards an ever closer union among its peoples, without having to face the normal political cleavages present in the Member States. In conclusion, the Community political culture which developed in the 1960s and 1970s led both the principal political actors and the political classes in Europe to an habituation of all political forces to thinking of European integration as ideologically neutral in, or ideologically transcendent over, the normal debates on the left–right spectrum. It is easy to understand how this will have served the process of integration, allowing a non–partisan coalition to emerge around its overall objectives.

1992 changes this in two ways. The first is a direct derivation from the turn to majority voting. Policies can be adopted now within the Council that run counter not simply to the perceived interests of a Member State, but more specifically to the ideology of a government in power. The debates about the European Social Charter and the shrill cries of "socialism through the back door," as well as the emerging debate about Community adherence to the European Convention on Human Rights and abortion rights are harbingers of things to come. In many respects this is a healthy development, since the real change from the past is evidenced by the ability to make difficult social choices and particularly by the increased transparency of the implications of the choice. At the same time, it represents a transformation from earlier patterns with obvious dysfunctional tensions.

The second impact of 1992 on ideological neutrality is subtler. The entire program rests on two pivots: the single market plan encapsulated in the White Paper, and its operation through the new instrumentalities of the Single European Act. Endorsing the former and adopting the latter by the Community and its Member States – and more generally by the political class in Europe – was a remarkable expression of the process of habituation alluded to above. People were successfully called to rally behind and identify with a bold new step toward a higher degree of integration. A "*single European* market" is a concept which still has the power to stir. But it is also a "single European *market*." It is not simply a technocratic program to remove the remaining obstacles to the free movement of all factors of production. It is at the same time a highly politicized choice of ethos, ideology, and political culture: the culture of "the market." It is also a philosophy, at least one version of which – the predominant version – seeks to remove barriers to the free movement of factors of production, and to remove distortion to competition as a means to maximize utility. The above is premised on the assumption of formal equality of individuals.[201] It is an ideology the contours of which have been the subject of intense debate within the Member States in terms of their own political choices. This is not the place to explicate these. Elsewhere, two slogans, "The One Dimensional Market" and "Big Market as Big Brother," have been used to emphasize the fallacy of ideological neutrality.[202] Thus, for example, open access, the cornerstone of the single market and the condition for effective non-protectionist competition, will also put pressure on local consumer products in local markets to the extent these are viewed as an expression of cultural diversity. Even more dramatic will be the case in explicit "cultural products," such as television and cinema. The advent of Euro-brands has implications, for better or for worse, which extend beyond the bottom line of national and Community economies. A successful single market requires widespread harmonization of standards of consumer protection and environmental protection, as well as the social package of employees. This need for a successful market not only accentuates the pressure for uniformity, but also manifests a social (and hence ideological) choice which prizes market efficiency and Europe-wide neutrality of competition above other competing values.

It is possible that consensus may be found on these issues, and indeed that this choice enjoys broad legitimacy. From my perspective, it is important to highlight that the consensus exudes a powerful pressure in shaping the political culture of the Community. As such, it is an important element of the transformation of Europe.

The ethos of European integration: Europe as unity and Europe as Community

As indicated above, 1992 also brings to the fore questions, choices, and contradictions in the very ethos of European integration. I shall explore these questions, choices, and contradictions by construing two competing visions of the promised land to which the Community is being led in 1992

---

[201] There is an alternative construction of the Community political ideology also present in the European debate, one which recognizes "inequalities but deploring their inequities, considers the market to be just one of several basic means of governing society.": Snyder, *New Directions* at 89.

[202] Biener, Dehousse, Pinder, and Weiler, "Back to the Future: Policy, Strategy and Tactics of the White Paper on the Creation of a Single European Market," in Bieber, *1992: One European Market?* at 18–20.

and beyond. The two visions are synthetic constructs, distilled from the discourse and praxis of European integration.

Unitarian and communitarian visions share a similar departure point. If we go back in time to the 1950 Schuman Declaration and the consequent 1951 Treaty of Paris establishing the European Coal and Steel Community, these events, despite their economic content, are best seen as a long-term and transformative strategy for peace among the states of western Europe, principally France and Germany.[203] This strategy tried to address the "mischief" embodied in the excesses of the modern nation-state and the traditional model of statal intercourse among them that was premised on full *"sovereignty," "autonomy," "independence,"* and a relentless defense and maximization of the national interest. This model was opposed not simply because, at the time, it displayed a propensity to degenerate into violent clashes, but also because it was viewed as unattractive for the task of reconstruction in times of peace.[204] The European Community was to be an antidote to the negative features of the state and statal intercourse; its establishment in 1951 was seen as the beginning of a process[205] that would bring about their elimination.

At this point, the two visions depart. According to the first vision, unity, the process that started in 1951 was to move progressively through the steps of establishing a common market and approximating economic policies[206] through ever tighter economic integration (economic and monetary union), resulting, finally, in full political union, in some version of a federal United States of Europe. If we link this vision to the governance process and constitutional structure, the ultimate model of the Community and the constitutionalized treaties stands as the equivalent, in the European localized context, of the utopian model of "world government" in classical

---

[203] See, e.g., Schuman Declaration of May 9, 1950, reprinted in *Bulletin of the European Communities* 13 (1980), 14, 15 (hereinafter "Schuman Declaration") ("The gathering of the nations of Europe requires the elimination of the age-old opposition of France and the Federal Republic of Germany."); and the preamble to 1951 Treaty of Paris, reprinted in European Community Information Service, *Treaties Establishing the European Communities* (1987) ("Considering that world peace can be safeguarded only by creative efforts commensurate with the dangers that threaten it ...").

[204] This does not mean that states and leaders were engulfed in some teary-eyed sentimentalism. Signing on to the Community idea was no doubt also a result of cool calculation of the national interest. See A. Milward, *The Reconstruction of Western Europe 1945–51* (University of California Press: Berkeley, CA; Methuen: London, 1984). But this does not diminish the utility of seeking the overall ethos of the enterprise that they were joining.

[205] On the one hand: "In taking upon [it]self for more than 20 years the role of champion of a united Europe, France has always had as [its] essential aim the service of peace." On the other hand: "Europe will not be made all at once, or according to a single ... plan." Schuman Declaration at 15.

[206] EEC Treaty, Art. 2.

international law. Tomorrow's Europe in this form would indeed constitute the final demise of Member State nationalism and, thus, the ultimate realization of the original objectives through political union in the form of a federalist system of governance.[207]

The alternative vision, community, also rejects the classical model of international law which celebrates statal sovereignty, independence, and autonomy and sees international legal regulation providing a "neutral" arena for states to prosecute their own ("national") goals premised on power and self-interest.[208] The community vision is, instead, premised on limiting, or sharing, sovereignty in a select albeit growing number of fields, on recognizing, and even celebrating, the reality of *interdependence*, and on counterpoising to the exclusivist ethos of statal autonomy a notion of a *community* of states and peoples sharing values and aspirations.

Most recently, it has been shown convincingly, not for the first time, how the classical model of international law is a replication at the international level of the liberal theory of the state.[209] The state is implicitly treated as the analogue, on the international level, to the individual within a domestic situation. In this conception, international legal notions such as self-determination, sovereignty, independence, and consent have their obvious analogy in theories of the individual within the state. The idea of community is thus posited in juxtaposition to the international version of pure liberalism and substitutes a modified communitarian vision.

Since the idea of "community" is currently in vogue and has become many things to many people, I would like to explain the meaning I attach to it in this transnational European context.[210] The importance of the EEC interstatal notion of *community* rests on the very fact that it does not involve

---

[207] Of course, even in this vision, one is not positing a centrist unified Europe but a federal structure of sorts, in which local interests and diversity would be maintained. Thus, although Delors speaks in his October 17, 1990, speech of Europe as a federation, he is – in good faith – always careful to maintain respect for "pluralism." See "Jacques Delors at the College of European in Bruges," reprinted in *Europe* Doc. No. 1,576 (October 21, 1989), 1 at 5 (hereinafter "Delors Speech of October 17, 1990").

[208] This, of course, is the classical model of international law. It is not monolithic. There are, in international law, voices, from both within and without, calling for an alternative vision expressed in such notions as the "common heritage of humankind." See, e.g., R. Sands, *Lessons Learned in Global Environmental Governance* (World Resources Institute: Washington, DC, 1990).

[209] M. Koskenniemi, *From Apology to Utopia* (Finnish Lawyers' Publishing Co.: Helsinki, 1989) at xvi, *passim*.

[210] I certainly do not find it useful to make an explicit analogy to the theories of community of domestic society, although I would not deny their influence on my thinking. See, e.g., M. Sandel, *Liberalism and the Limits of Justice* (Cambridge University Press: Cambridge, New York, 1982); M. Walzer, *Spheres of Justice* (Basic Books: New York, 1983); and the fierce debates about these, e.g., Dworkin, "To Each His Own," *New York Review of Books* (April 14, 1983); "Spheres of Justice: An Exchange," *New York Review of Books* (July 21, 1983).

a negation of the state. It is neither state nor community. The idea of community seeks to dictate a different type of intercourse among the actors belonging to it, a type of self-limitation in their self-perception, a redefined self-interest, and, hence, redefined policy goals. To the interest of the state must be added the interest of the community. But crucially, it does not extinguish the separate actors who are fated to live in an uneasy tension with two competing senses of the polity's self, the autonomous self and the self as part of a larger community, and committed to an elusive search for an optimal balance of goals and behavior between the community and its actors. I say it is crucial because the unique contribution of the European Community to the civilization of international relations – indeed its civilizing effect on intra-European statal intercourse – derives from that very tension among the state actors and between each state actor and the Community. It also derives from each state actor's need to reconcile the reflexes and ethos of the "sovereign" national state with new modes of discourse and a new discipline of solidarity.[211] Civilization is thus perceived not in the conquering of Eros but in its taming.[212]

Moreover, the idea of Europe as community not only conditions discourse among states, but it also spills over to the peoples of the states, influencing relations among individuals. For example, the Treaty provisions prohibiting discrimination on grounds of nationality, allowing the free movement of workers and their families, and generally supporting a rich network of transnational social transactions may be viewed not simply as creating the optimal conditions for the free movement of factors of production in the common market. They also serve to remove nationality and state affiliation of the individual, so divisive in the past, as the principal referent for transnational human intercourse.

The *unity* vision of the promised land sees then as its "ideal type" a European polity, finally and decisively replacing its hitherto warring Member States with a political union of federal governance. The *community* vision sees as its "ideal type" a political union in which Community and Member State continue their uneasy co-existence, although with an ever-increasing embrace. It is important also to understand that the voice of, say, Thatcher is not an expression of this community vision. Thatcherism is one

---

[211] *Cf.* EEC Treaty, Art. 5.

[212] This tension between actor and community finds evocative expression in the preamble and the opening article of the EEC Treaty, the foundation of the current Community. The preamble speaks of "an ever closer union among the *peoples* of Europe" (emphasis added); whereas Art. 2 speaks of "closer relations between the *States* belonging to it" (emphasis added). Note, too, that the preamble speaks about the peoples of Europe rejecting any notion of a melting pot and nation-building. Finally, note the "ever closer union": something which goes on for "ever" incorporates, of course, the "never." See EEC Treaty, preamble.

pole of the first vision, whereby Community membership continues to be assessed and reevaluated in terms of its costs and benefits to a Member State, in this case the UK, which remains the ultimate referent for its desirability. The Community is conceived in this way of thinking not as a redefinition of the national self but as an arrangement, elaborate and sophisticated, of achieving long-term maximization of the national interest in an interdependent world. Its value is measured ultimately and exclusively with the coin of national utility and not community solidarity.

I do not think that 1992 can be seen as representing a clear preference and choice for one vision over the other. But there are manifestations, both explicit and implicit, suggesting an unprecedented and triumphal resurgence and ascendancy of the unity vision of Europe over the competing vision of community: part and parcel of the 1992 momentum. If indeed the road to European union is to be paved on this unity vision, at the very moment of ascendancy the Community endangers something noble at its very core and, like other great empires, with the arrival of success may sow the seeds of self-destruction.

Why such foreboding? Whence the peril in the unity vision? At an abstract logical level it is easy to challenge the unity vision which sets up a fully united Europe as the pinnacle of the process of European integration. It would be more than ironic if a polity with its political process set up to counter the excesses of statism ended up coming round full circle and transforming itself into a (super)state. It would be equally ironic that an ethos that rejected the nationalism of the Member States gave birth to a new European nation and European nationalism. The problem with the unity vision is that its very realization entails its negation.

But the life of the Community (like some other things) is not logic, but experience. And experience suggests that with all the lofty talk of political union and federalism we are not about to see the demise of the Member States, at least not for a long time. The reports leaking out of the Intergovernmental Conference suggest fairly modest steps on this road.

That being the case, the unease with the unity vision none the less remains. For if the unity ethos becomes the principal mobilizing force of the polity, it may, combined with the praxis and rhetoric of the 1992 single market, compromise the deeper values inherent in the community vision, even if the Community's basic structure does not change for years to come.

I suggested above that these values operated both at the interstate level by conditioning a new type of statal discourse and self-perception and at the societal and individual level by diminishing the importance of nationality in transnational human intercourse. How then would the unity vision and the 1992 praxis and rhetoric corrode these values?

The successful elimination of internal frontiers will, of course, accentuate in a symbolic and real sense the external frontiers of the Community. The privileges of Community membership for states and of Community citizenship for individuals are becoming increasingly pronounced. This is manifest in such phenomena as the diffidence of the Community towards further enlargement (packaged in the notion of the concentric circles),[213] in the inevitable harmonization of external border controls, immigration, and asylum policies, and in policies such as local European content of television-broadcasting regulation. It assumes picaresque character with the enhanced visibility of the statal symbols already adopted by the Community: flag, anthem, Community passport. The potential corrosive effect on the values of the community vision of European integration are self-evident. Nationality as referent for interpersonal relations, and the human alienating effect of *us* and *them* are brought back again, simply transferred from their previous intra-Community context to the new inter-Community one. We have made little progress if the *us* becomes European (instead of German or French or British) and the *them* becomes those outside the Community or those inside who do not enjoy the privileges of citizenship.

There is a second, slightly more subtle, potentially negative influence in this realm. A centerpiece of the agenda for further integration is the need of Europe to develop the appropriate structures for a common foreign and defense policy.[214] It has indeed been anomalous that despite the repeated calls since the early 1970s for a Europe that will speak with one voice,[215] the Community has never successfully translated its internal economic might to commensurate outside influence. There could be much positive in Europe taking such a step to an enhanced common foreign and security policy. The potential corrosive element of this inevitable development rests in the suspicion that some of the hearkening for a common foreign policy is the appeal of strength and the vision of Europe as a new global superpower. Europe *is* a political and economic superpower and often fails to see this and discharge its responsibilities appropriately. But the ethos of strength and power, even if transferred from the Member State to the European level, is closer to the unity rather than community notion of Europe and, as such, partakes of the inherent contradiction of that vision.

All these images and the previous question marks are not intended as an indictment of 1992 and the future road of European integration. Both in its structure and process, and, in part, its ethos, the Community has been more

---

[213] See Delors Speech of October 17, 1990.

[214] *Ibid.*; see also "Proposals of European Parliament to Intergovernmental Conference," PE 146.824, new Art. 130U (proposing full-fledged apparatus for European foreign and security policy).

[215] On the history of European political co-operation and the idea of Europe speaking with one voice, see Stein, "Towards a European Foreign Policy?"

than a simple successful venture in transnational co-operation and economic integration. It has been a unique model for reshaping transnational discourse among states, peoples, and individuals who barely a generation ago emerged from the nadir of Western civilization. It is a model with acute relevance for other regions of the world with bleak histories or an even bleaker present.

Today's Community is impelled forward by the dysfunctioning of its current architecture. The transformation that is taking place has immense, widely discussed promise. If I have given some emphasis to the dangers, it is not simply to redress a lacuna in the literature. It is also in the hope that as this transformation takes place, that part, limited as it may be, of the Community that can be characterized as the modern contribution of Europe to the civilization of interstatal and intrastatal intercourse shall not be laid by the wayside.

THE TRANSFORMATION OF EUROPE: AN AFTERWORD

Infranationalism

The central thesis of the preceding essay concerned a relationship – complex at times – between Community legal structure (constitutionalism, normative supranationalism, "Exit") and Community political process (institutionalism, decisional supranationalism, "Voice"). These two poles were used simultaneously as a narrative device (that is, a way of telling the story) and as an analytical device (that is, a way of explaining it). Critically, the relationship was neither one-dimensional in its direction (from law to politics or from politics to law) or in its causality (this legal development explains this political process or *vice versa*). Instead, both description and analysis were circular – political process explaining and conditioning legal structure and legal structure conditioning and explaining political process.

One important pay-off in my view was the ability to assess the key relationship of Community and Member States in an equally complex and partially circular manner. The picture of transformation presented is at odds with two theses which have had some currency in the literature.

One thesis, finding, perhaps, its louder expression in Euroskeptic rather than Europhile circles, views the march of Community evolution as representing a continued net loss of sovereignty.[216] Implicitly, this view regards European integration as a zero-sum game between the Member

---

[216] See, e.g., Schmidt, "National Patterns of Governance under Siege: The Impact of European Integration," in B. Kohler-Koch (ed.), *The Transformation of Governance in the European Union* (Routledge: 1998).

States and the Community as power brokers in the public square. The history of most federal states, in which centralization has taken place at the expense of local power, lends credibility aplenty to this view. The analysis in "Transformation" militates against this evaluation and attempts to dispel a straightforward zero-sum analysis.

An alternative thesis argues in different guises[217] that the Member States have all along remained the central players in Community evolution and that most evolution, even in the critical field of constitutionalization, was willed and served the interest of the Member States. A more nuanced version of this thesis unpacks the concept of Member State and argues that, at a minimum, governments, the executive branch, of Member States have been empowered by the Community structure and process at the expense of, say, other branches of Member State government. The analysis in "Transformation" sustains some part of this thesis but also qualifies it substantially. Even the enhanced "Voice" of the Member States prior to the shift to majority voting took place in an institutional and constitutional environment which was quite unlike classical intergovernmental fora, even in an increasingly interdependent and "globalized" world. As to the thesis of executive branch empowerment, whilst this is largely true in general formal terms and also true in the big Newtonian events of Community life such as intergovernmental conferences (where big events take place at low speed), it has to be qualified by an Einsteinian perspective of the Community – its day-to-day atomistic management (where small events happen at large speed). There,[218] governments often find themselves as impotent as other national or even Community actors.

Further, even if there is much force to the executive branch empowerment argument, it has been over a shrinking public policy domain. Nowhere will this be as visible as in the area of economic and monetary union.

With a distance of six years or so since the publication of "Transformation," I am able to be more decisive in characterizing the third period of European integration which, in my analysis, comes after the watershed of

---

[217] See, e.g., A. Moravcsik, "Preference and Power in the European Community: A Liberal Intergovernmentalist Approach," in S. Bulmer and A. Scott (eds.), *Economic and Political Integration in Europe: Internal Dynamics and Global Context* (Blackwell: Oxford, Cambridge, MA, 1994); and A. Moravcsik, "Why the European Community Strengthens the State: Domestic Politics and International Cooperation" (Harvard University CES Working Paper Series No. 52, 1994).

[218] See, e.g., Alexander Ballmann, "Infranationalism and the Community Governing Process," Annex to J. H. H. Weiler, Alexander Ballmann, Ulrich Haltern, Herwig Hofmann, Franz Mayer and Sieglinde Schreiner-Linford, "Certain Rectangular Problems of European Integration" (Project IV/95/02, Directorate General for Research, European Parliament, http://www.iue.it/AEL/EP/fpp.html, 1996).

the SEA and the restoration of qualified majority voting in widespread areas of Community life. The foundational period was one which saw the emergence of constitutionalism and with it the basic equilibrium between legal structure and political process which, in my view, was the key to explaining that dimension of the polity for its first decades. The 1970s and the period leading up to the adoption of the SEA were times which, I argued, were not "stagnant" from a structural point of view, but saw a major constitutional quiet revolution: the collapse of an effective system of enumeration and constitutional guarantees to the limits of Community legislative and other action.

What, then, would be the hallmark of the last decade from a constitutional and institutional perspective?

It is, in my view, the emergence of *infranationalism* as a central feature of Community governance.[219] Infranationalism is explained in a couple of essays in the second part of this volume. It is based on the realization that increasingly large sectors of Community norm creation are done at a meso-level of governance. The actors involved are middle-range officials of the Community and the Member States in combination with a variety of private and semi-public bodies players. Comitology[220] and the remaining netherworld of Community committees are the arena, and the political science of networks is the current analytical tool which tries to explain the functioning of this form of governance. From a constitutional point of view, my argument is simple: infranationalism is not constitutional or unconstitutional. It is outside the constitution. The constitutional vocabulary is built around "branches" of government, around constitutional functions,[221] around concepts of delegation, separation, checks, and balances among the arms of government etc. Infranationalism is like the emergence of viruses for which antibiotics, geared towards the control of microbes and germs, were simply ill-suited. Infranationalism renders the nation and state hollow and its institutions meaningless as a vehicle for both

---

[219] See José de Areilza, "Sovereignty or Management?: The Dual Character of the EC's Supranationalism – Revisited" (Harvard Jean Monnet Working Paper No. 2/95, 1995; http://www.law.harvard.edu/Programs/JeanMonnet/); and Ballmann, "Infranationalism."

[220] See, e.g., R. H. Pedler and G. F. Schaefer (eds.), *Shaping European Law and Policy – The Role of Committees and Comitology in the Political Process* (European Centre for Public Affairs, European Institute of Public Administration Maastricht: 1996); Vos, "The Rise of Committees," *European Law Journal* 3 (1997), 210; Bradley, "The European Parliament and Comitology: On the Road to Nowhere?," *European Law Journal* 3 (1997), 230; and Joerges and Neyer, "From Intergovernmental Bargaining to Deliberative Political Processes: The Constitutionalisation of Comitology," *European Law Journal* 3 (1997), 273.

[221] E. U. Petersmann, *Constitutional Functions and Constitutional Problems of International Economic Law: Foreign Trade Law and Policy in the USA, the EC and Switzerland* (1991).

understanding and controlling government – hence my choice of this appellation.

I believe that increasingly both academia and the political process itself will turn towards the phenomena associated with infranationalism as meriting most attention in understanding and improving the quality and transparency of Union governance.

The Community equilibrium in the 1990s and beyond

"Transformation" left open the question concerning the potential consequences of the introduction of relatively widespread majority voting on the institutional and constitutional architecture of the Community with the coming into force of the SEA in the late 1980s.

If we revert to the equilibrium theorem which underlies "Transformation," the introduction of majority voting (for reasons explained in the essay itself), which in some ways limits the individual voice of individual Member States, should have resulted in challenges to the Exit pole of the equilibrium, that is, the constitutional architecture of the Community. Alternatively, one could look for evidence that the sustained period of equilibrium between Voice and Exit helped foster a loyalty to the new emergent polity in which Voice achieved through the normal channels of Community decision-making would be considered adequate.

Several essays in the second part of this volume provide what could be considered as evidence that such a loyalty, if it exists at all, is precarious and argue that it is precarious because there is a legitimacy dissonance between the constitutional claims of the polity and its social reality. They also provide some evidence that the constitutional architecture is, indeed, coming under challenge. Let me present briefly some of that evidence:

1. There are challenges from the collectivity of states. Consider first the Maastricht Treaty itself under the shadow of which we are still operating. EMU aside, in a praiseworthy and deservedly famous article reflecting on the constitutional dimensions of Maastricht, "The Constitutional Structure of the Union: A Europe of Bits and Pieces," Deidre Curtin criticized the fragmentation and constitutional incoherence of the Union structure and had, too, harsh words for a certain assault on the ECJ in the Maastricht process.[222] Amsterdam is generally even more anemic, but whilst expanding somewhat the role of the European Parliament in the decisional process, one cannot but notice a growing reticence towards the constitutional architecture on issues such as

---

[222] D. Curtin, "The Constitutional Structure of the Union: A Europe of Bits and Pieces," *Common Market Law Review* 30 (1993), 65.

majority voting, the role of the Commission, and, arguably, foreign policy.

2. There are challenges from individual Member States. In the Maastricht process it was the UK and Denmark. In the Amsterdam IGC there was the Franco-German (!) initiative which introduced such variable geometry as to make the Community pillar itself one of bits and pieces. The final version, under strenuous pressure from small Member States, emasculated much of the original initiative. But its very proposal is of some significance. In the same breath one could mention the breathtaking proposal which surfaced during the IGC to amend Article 189A which requires unanimity to modify a Commission proposal. A better targeted attack on the constitutional powers of the Commission is more difficult to imagine. This proposal was blocked – a deal-breaker for the Commission – but it is a sign of the attack on the constitutional–institutional balance.

3. There are challenges from constitutional actors within Member States. Most interesting are the challenges coming from the national judiciary and in particular the highest courts. The German Constitutional Court and its Belgian counterpart have been most explicit on the issue of jurisdiction. The Italian Court which has declared that it was under no duty to make references to the ECJ under Article 177 since it was not a "jurisdiction" in the sense of the Treaty has been more subtle but even more insidious at the same time. There are signs from others as well, challenging precisely the hegemony of the ECJ.[223] There has been an understandable reaction trying to minimize and paper over the cracks. But it is there for anyone who wishes to look. Also at lower levels of the judiciary, the *Francovich* jurisprudence, for example, is not receiving quite the same welcome as earlier constitutional advances of the ECJ.[224]

4. There are challenges from, yes, new constituencies within the ECJ. (We should not commit the error of imagining the ECJ as an homogeneous actor free of internal factions, disagreements and internal conflicting views on many issues, including the contours of constitutionalism. The oft-deep divisions on fundamental issues between Advocates-General – full members of the ECJ – and the ECJ itself surely mirror similar divisions within the College of Judges.) Consider the post-Maastricht

---

[223] For a sober account of the evolving relationship between the European Court of Justice and national courts, see generally, Slaughter, Stone and Weiler (eds.), *The European Court of Justice and National Courts* (Hart Publishing: Oxford, 1998).

[224] See Caruso, "The Missing View of the Cathedral: The Private Law Paradigm of European Legal" (Harvard Jean Monnet Working Paper 9/96, 1996; http://www.law.harvard.edu/ Programs/JeanMonnet/); and Harlow, "Francovich and the Problem of the Disobedient State," *European Law Journal* 2 (1996), 199.n Market Law Review 31 (1994), 459.

jurisprudence of the ECJ itself – for example its famous (or, to some, infamous) *Keck* decision which shifted the balance back to the Member States in the critical area of the internal market. Assailed by many champions of the single market as a heresy, Norbert Reich used that decision among those justifying his analysis of a veritable economic constitutional *revolution*.[225] But there were others such as the controversial decisions which cut the role and power of the Community in the World Trade Organization or the one which denied the Union the competence to adhere to the European Convention on Human Rights.

5. Most important, in my view, are the challenges from general public opinion in several Member States. Maastricht, refreshingly, gave the lie to years of a Eurobarometer ostrich syndrome. It is clear that Euro-skepticism is not just another English vice. At a minimum, "Europe" is no longer part of consensus, non–partisan politics in many Member States, not least the new ones. Politicians can no longer count on automatic approval of their architectural changes to Community and Union.

As in "Transformation" itself, I cannot overemphasize that my argument is not about a direct causal relationship: "Majority voting? Let's attack the constitutional foundation" is no more my point than "Supremacy and direct effect? Let's insist on a veto" was in "Transformation." What I am arguing is that there is a nexus between the two spheres of politics and law where developments in one create a climate, act as a catalyst, help sustain developments, and moves in the other.

Put differently, my argument is that the current political processes of Community governance offer a much less hospitable environment for the continued development or even the sustaining of the constitutional architecture. A new transformation is called for. What it may be like and on what basis it may be forged is part of the subtext of many of the essays in the second part of this book.

---

[225] Reich, "The 'November Revolution' of the European Court of Justice: Keck, Meng and Audi Revisited," *Common Market Law Review* 31 (1994), 459.

3

FUNDAMENTAL RIGHTS AND FUNDAMENTAL BOUNDARIES: ON THE CONFLICT OF STANDARDS AND VALUES IN THE PROTECTION OF HUMAN RIGHTS IN THE EUROPEAN LEGAL SPACE

INTRODUCTION

JUDICIAL PROTECTION of fundamental human rights by the European Court may operate as a source of both unity and disunity in the dialectical process of European integration. There is, of course, the classical vision which regards a commitment to fundamental human rights as a unifying ideal, one of the core values around which the peoples of Europe may coalesce. When the Court, in the very well-known story, held itself out as the guarantor of fundamental human rights in the field of Community law, it was, on this view, merely giving judicial expression (and teeth!) to that core value. But, judicial protection by the European Court, of both Union measures and Member State measures, can also be a source of tension.

First, and this goes to the heart of this essay, beyond a certain core, reflected in Europe by the European Convention on Human Rights (ECHR), the definition of fundamental human rights often differs from polity to polity. These differences, I shall argue, reflect fundamental societal choices and form an important part in the different identities of polities and societies. They are often that part of social identity about which people care a great deal. What menu and flavor of human rights are chosen in the Community context matters and can become a source of tension even absent direct conflict of norms. The choice of human rights is about the choice of fundamental values so the stakes are rather high. In the first part of this essay I shall explore these situations of conflict and tension and, from a distance, try and explain how the European Court has attempted to mediate the tensions and blunt the conflicts.

Second, judicial review of Community measures but especially Member State measures can be seen, and have been seen, as part of a relentless and highly problematic extension of jurisdiction into areas of social regulation which are, or ought to be, the prerogative of the

Member States. I shall deal, in some detail, with this extension of jurisdiction and its roots.

I should clarify that my focus is not on the problems which result from the fact that it is judge-made law – an issue with which I have dealt elsewhere. I am concerned with the meeting of European rights with national rights. I should also explain that in this essay I shall remain firmly within the liberal-rights paradigm leaving for another occasion the rights-critique apparatus.

Before turning to the actual jurisprudence I shall explore a little deeper the notion of human rights as societal values and their potential for conflict in the European architecture. Modern liberal States, taking their cue principally from the American rather than British democratic tradition, increasingly acknowledge a higher law – typically a constitution, and, in more recent times, international treaties – which bind even the legislature of the state. In an increasing number of modern democracies the higher law is backed up by the courts and a system of judicial review which give it, so to speak, teeth. Within this constitutional ethos the judicial protection of fundamental human rights has a central place. Constitutionalism, despite its counter-majoritarian effect, is regarded as a complementary principle to majoritarianism rather than its negation. One formulation which describes the complex relationship between the two is the notion of protection against a tyranny of the majority – seemingly an oxymoron. I think the appeal of rights has to do with two roots. The first of these two roots regards fundamental rights (and liberties) as an expression of a vision of humanity which vests the deepest values in the individual which, hence, may not be compromised by anyone. Probably one of the oldest and most influential sources of this vision is to be found in the Pentateuch: "And God created man in His own image, in the image of God created He him."[1] With this trademark, what legislator has the authority to transgress the essential humanity of the species? Naturally, there are secular, humanist parallels to this vision aplenty.

The other root for the great appeal of rights, and part of the justification even if counter-majoritarian, looks to them as an instrument for the promotion of the *per se* value of putting constraints on power. Modern democracy emerges, after all, also as a rejection of absolutism – and absolutism is not the prerogative of kings and emperors.

Similar sentiments inform the great appeal of fundamental boundaries in non-unitary systems such as federal states and the European Union. I use the term "fundamental boundaries" as a metaphor for the principle of enumerated powers or limited competences which are designed to

---

[1] Genesis 1:27.

guarantee that in certain areas communities (rather than individuals) should be free to make their own social choices without interference from above. If you wish, if fundamental rights are about the autonomy and self-determination of the individual, fundamental boundaries are about the autonomy and self-determination of communities. The appeal of fundamental boundaries rests as well on two parallel roots. First it is an expression of a vision of humanity which vests the deepest values in communities (potentially existing within larger polities) which, thus, must be protected. This community vision of humanity derives from an acknowledgment of the social nature of humankind, as a counter-balance to the atomistic view of the individual which is reflected in the concept of individual rights and liberties. It too finds a powerful biblical expression in the Pentateuch: "And the Lord God said: It is not good that man should be alone."[2] Fundamental boundaries around communities-of-value become the guarantee against existential aloneness – the protection of the *Gemeinschaft* against the *Gesellschaft*.

Its second root is a reflection at the level of social organization of that same *per se* value of non-aggregation of power. Fundamental boundaries constitute and thus ensure different realms of power.

At first blush it would seem that these two basic principles need not clash at all. There could be, it would seem, a neat and tidy way to situate fundamental rights and fundamental boundaries within the constitutional architecture of Europe. For example, one set of norms and institutions, national-constitutional and/or transnational, would take care of human rights: ensuring that no public authority at any level of governance would violate the basic autonomy and liberty of the individual. Another set of norms, national-constitutional and/or transnational, would take care of boundaries: ensuring that transnational governance would not encroach on fundamental societal choices of, principally, States.

The adoption of the ECHR by the Member States of the Council of Europe is a reflection of this tidy arrangement: the High Contracting Powers of the Convention retain their full prerogatives as sovereign states. State boundaries thus constitute *par excellence* fundamental boundaries which guarantee full autonomy of their respective national societies. The one self-limiting exception concerns the core fundamental human rights given expression in the ECHR which may not be transgressed in any of these societies. Thus, the universalism of human rights and the particularism of fundamental boundaries may rest together like the wolf and sheep.

You will note, however, that I used the term "core fundamental rights" in drawing this idyll. The neat arrangement which the ECHR may be said

---

[2] Genesis 2:18.

to represent can only work in relation to a core which gives expression to those "rights," or to those "levels of protection," which are said to be universal, transcending any legitimate cultural or political difference among different societies in, at least, the universe of Europe. The ECHR is premised on this understanding.

Critically the ECHR does not exhaust the spectrum of human rights. By its own self-understanding, whereas the ECHR provides the "minimum standard" of protection "below" which no State may fall, the High Contracting Parties are free, perhaps even encouraged, to offer "higher" standards of protection to individuals. Indeed, part of the uniqueness of States, part of what differentiates them from each other may be the very way they give protection beyond the core universal standard.

Thus, the commitment to, and the acceptance of, the ECHR as a universal, culturally transcendent core of human rights is, surely, an expression of a very important aspect of the political culture of a State which brings it together with other States and societies. When this is backed up by submission to transnational machinery of enforcement the commitment is all the more expressive.

But, I would argue, the differences in the protection of human rights in these societies within the large band which exists beyond the universal core, is no less an important aspect of the political culture and identity of societies. Human rights constitute, thus, both a source of, and index for, cross-national differentiation and not only cross-national assimilation.

Here is a banal example to illustrate the point. Freedom of expression is a fundamental right in relation to which a transcendent universal core of protected speech may be defined across national divides in the framework of, say, the ECHR. But there is, evidently, a large margin for rights discourse beyond that core of protected speech. In America, a band of neo-Nazis may march with full regalia in the neighborhood of Holocaust survivors. Any attempt by the local authorities to ban such a march will be struck down as compromising the fundamental right to freedom of expression of the marchers. In many European countries, and clearly in, say, Germany, such speech would be prohibited without that prohibition being construed in violation of core freedom of expression.

I would make three comments on the example. First, we do not capture the contrast of values inherent in this example by simply saying that in America you get a little bit more protection of freedom of expression than in, say, Germany. Often, there is much more to these differences. It is through these differences, and others like them, that societies at times define some of their core values which go to their very self-understanding – their particularized identity rooted in history and social and political culture. America is saying something very important about itself (good and/or bad) when it insists on the right of the individual to engage in such extremist, even injurious, speech. Germany says something very important about itself (good and/or bad) when it would deny the individual such a right. It may even be saying something rather profound about a different emphasis on individualism and communitarianism in the respective polities.

Secondly, there is another sense in which it would be simplifying these societal choices to articulate them as a "mere" difference between the levels of protection of human rights. Human rights are almost invariably the expression of a compromise between competing social goods in the polity. In liberal democracies, the most typical is an accommodation between, on the one hand, the various interests of the collectivity represented by governmental authority and, on the other, the interest of the individual in autonomy and individual liberty. Society may find it very important to empower the individual against government authority. That is how we normally think of human rights. But society may find it very important too to empower government authority against the individual. The fight against crime, perhaps, comes first to mind. Alternatively, in the context, say, of rights to private property and land reform, differences between capitalist-liberalism and the gamut of socialist worldviews is a good context in which the need to look at human rights as a looking-glass reflection of government or public rights is self-evident. The extent of government power (as well as the desirability) to interfere with private property rights (e.g., programs for nationalization) was for long a dividing line between governments of left or right persuasion within European liberal democracies.

Critically, when a society strikes that balance between these competing interests and characterizes that balance as a fundamental right or liberty (to property, to free speech, etc.) it is the balance which is fundamental: the fundamental right of the individual to be protected against government power, set against the fundamental right of the public through government to act in accordance with the general interest. Note that it is as injurious to the social choice involved in this balance to compromise the right of the individual as it would be to limit the rights of government. This balance is an expression, then, of core values, of basic societal choices. This is the point where the distinction between rights and boundaries collapses since fundamental rights – beyond the core – become an expression of the kind of particularized societal choice of which fundamental boundaries are an expression. Fundamental boundaries are designed, thus, to allow communities and polities to make and live by those difference balances which they deem fundamental. Beyond the agreed core, to foist a fundamental right onto a society is, arguably, to tamper with its fundamental boundaries.

Thirdly, and finally, the position of the ECHR in relation to this tension is, once more, worth defining. Imagine that the example of the neo-Nazi march were transported into Europe. Imagine further one ECHR State following the American solution. So now we would have one State prohibiting the march and one State protecting it. The jurisprudence of the ECHR would not hold the prohibition on the march as a violation of the freedom of expression protected by the Convention. But, in this type of case, it would also not interfere with the state which protected the rights of the marchers. In relation to freedom of expression the ECHR would be concerned to define a core of protected speech, a minimum level of protection. Once it was decided (for good or for bad) that the neo-Nazi hate speech did not fall within this core, States would be free to protect it or to ban it and to part define themselves and differentiate themselves in terms of the choice they make on this issue. This is part of the famous margin of appreciation which the ECHR allows. States might, as I mentioned, even constitutionalize such a choice, and make it a "fundamental" part of their self-understanding. The difference between the States would thus become fundamental. By contrast, in relation to speech found to be within the core protected by the ECHR, States would not be able to make that choice. They would be bound by a shared view, that the protection of that particular speech vindicated a right which was transcendent and to which all were bound. In this case the commonality between the States would be fundamental.

Another way of describing the play of the ECHR in this context is to say that it defines the margin within which States may opt for different fundamental balances between government and individuals. It defines the area within which fundamental boundaries may be drawn. However, certain balances, tilted too much in favor of government, are not permitted. It is against this background that I turn now to the protection of fundamental rights in the legal order of the Union.

HUMAN RIGHTS IN THE COMMUNITY LEGAL ORDER

Review of Community measures: the conundrum of "high" and "low" standards

Neither the Treaty of Paris nor the Treaty of Rome contained any allusion to the protection of fundamental human rights. And yet, once the European Court put in place its constitutional jurisprudence in cases such as *van Gend and Loos* and *Costa* v. *ENEL*, it became legally and politically imperative that a way be found to vindicate fundamental human rights at the Community level. How could one assert the direct effect and supremacy of European law – vesting huge constitutional power in the political organs of the Community – without postulating embedded legal and judicial guarantees on the exercise of such power? After all, the effect of direct effect and supremacy would be to efface the possibility of national legislative or judicial control of Community law. This imperative was all the more urgent given the notorious democratic deficiencies of European governance, in some respects more acute in the 1960s than in the 1980s and 1990s. How could one expect the constitutional and other high courts of the Member States, especially of those Member States with national constitutional orders and judicial review such as, at the time, Germany and Italy, to accept the direct effect and supremacy of Community norms without an assurance that human rights would be protected within the Community legal order and, critically, that individuals would not lose any of the protections afforded under national constitutions?

Protecting human rights became a joined legal and political imperative. The response to this imperative, the story of *Stauder*[3] and *Nold*[4] and all the rest has been told so many times as to obviate the necessity of recapitulation.[5] Likewise, of equal tedium is the investigation into the legal basis and formal constitutional legitimacy of this act of so-called judicial activism by the European Court whereby the Court put in a place, or discovered, an unwritten Bill of Rights against which to check the legality of Community measures.[6]

It is the perspective of rights-as-values that is of interest to me in this essay. The issues can be drawn out at their sharpest by imagining the European Court's jurisprudence as a dialogue with, or a monologue given to, its national counterparts.

Let us take the *Hauer*[7] case as our basic factual matrix. Imagine (following *Hauer*) a Community measure, say a Regulation, which restricts the use of agricultural land, prohibiting its exploitation as a vineyard by its owner, a German national, and, thus, arguably compromising her right to "private property." States differ in the extent to which they will protect private property against governmental authority. Imagine therefore further, merely for the sake of argument, that in Germany the constitutional norm and practice affords greater protection to private property than, say, in Italy and that both offer more protection than the core guaranteed under the

---

[3] Case 29/69, *Stauder* [1969] ECR 419.

[4] Case 4/73, *Nold, Kohlen and Baustoffgroßhandlung* v. *Commission of the European Communities* [1974] ECR 491.

[5] See, for example, A. Clapham, *Human Rights and the European Ccommunity: A Critical Overview* (Nomos: Baden-Baden, 1991).

[6] See, for example, *ibid.*

[7] Case 44/79, *Liselotte Hauer* v. *Länd Rheinland-Pfalz* [1979] ECR 3,727.

ECHR. Let us, finally, imagine that Germany affords protection of private property greater than any other Member State in the Community.

Direct effect and supremacy mean that the national legal orders must uphold the Community measure restricting the use of agricultural land and potentially compromising the fundamental human right to private property. It therefore falls to the European Court to check the Community Regulation.

The potential conflict of values emerges, classically, in response to the question: which standard of protection should the European Court adopt? Given the legal and political imperatives I suggested above, there would seem to be a ready and easy answer: the Court should adopt the high, German, standard.

Several reasons argue for this "maximalist" approach. First, it may be argued with an idealistic turn, that the Community should always seek to adopt the highest standard of human rights around. If, in the field of property rights, it is a German standard, so be it. After all, it is often asserted in the regulatory area that European political decision-making creates the danger of a "race to the bottom," of lowest-common-denominator choices. Why, then, not have in the field of human rights a "race to the top"? Idealism would, in this instance, be complemented by expediency: how would you expect the German Constitutional Court to accept less? From the German perspective, it would not be enough that the European Court undertake in principle to scrutinize Community legislation for violation of human rights. Its yardstick for scrutiny must be "up to standard" – the German standard. It is only the combination of the procedural with the material, of the institutional with the constitutional, that will give the assurances necessary to accept supremacy and all the rest.

The virtue of the maximalist approach goes even further since, it is argued, while it would satisfy the German legal order, it would not dissatisfy the other legal orders. For, if the Court were to adopt the "high" German standard in this area, what would be the reaction of, say, the Italian legal order and that of the other Member States? They, the argument goes, would not and should not object since the measure to be judged by the high German standard would be a Community measure. Their own legislation would not be touched. And, in other areas, the European Court would be looking to their standards, always choosing the highest around.

And yet, the maximalist approach does not work, cannot work and, for good reason, has been rejected by the Court. The maximalist approach would be satisfactory neither from an individual Member State perspective nor from a Community or Union perspective. In some cases it is not achievable at all.

To explain why, consider first another hypothetical. Imagine a Member

State like Ireland, with relatively little heavy industry. Imagine further that the Member State adopts a constitutional amendment which introduces a fundamental human right to clean air which was then interpreted by the domestic constitutional court as requiring a very high level of purity. To impose these standards on, say, heavy coal and steel industries would be to render them economically non-viable, but this is a matter which need not concern the Irish political and legal policy-maker since Ireland has no coal and steel industries. Imagine now that at some stage the Community adopts an industrial policy which in combination with its environmental-protection policy allows certain levels of factory emissions which exceed the strict ("high") Irish standard. If, at this point, the European policy were challenged before the European Court, would it, under the maximalist approach, be obliged to adopt the Irish standard for the entire Community and strike the policy down?

Let us now move beyond the hypothetical case and articulate in more abstract terms the high-low conundrum. If, on the one hand, the Community's constitutional architecture, which includes direct effect and supremacy, should not compromise the protection of individual rights guaranteed in the various Member States, and if the Court is to secure and maintain the loyalty of its national counterparts to the EU constitutional structure, then, it would seem, the Court would have to adopt the maximalist approach – in each case it would have to choose the highest level of human-rights protection which exists among the Member States.

No wonder that the Court in *Hauer* said the following:

> [F]undamental rights form an integral part of the general principles of the law, the observance of which it ensures; that in safeguarding those rights, the Court is bound to draw inspiration from constitutional traditions common to the Member States, *so that measures which are incompatible with the fundamental rights recognized by the constitutions of those States are unacceptable in the Community*; and that, similarly, international treaties for the protection of human rights on which the Member States have collaborated or of which they are signatories, can supply guidelines which should be followed within the framework of Community law.[8]

If, on the other hand, the Court were to adopt in each case the highest standard of protection, it would mean, as in our hypothetical Irish example, that it would be subject to the constitutional dictate of individual Member States even when these national standards of protection may be considered as entirely unsuitable for the Community as a whole. In the *Hauer* case, the Court also stated:

> [T]he question of a possible infringement of fundamental rights by a measure of the Community institutions can only be judged in the light of Community law

---

[8] Recital 15; emphasis added.

itself. *The introduction of special criteria for assessment stemming from the legislation or constitutional law of a particular Member State would, by damaging the substantive unity and efficacy of Community law, lead inevitably to the destruction of the unity of the Common Market and the jeopardizing of the Cohesion of the Community.*[9]

The problem is even more complex, calling into question the very utility of using the "high" and "low," maximal and minimal nomenclature in this context.

Consider first the situation when at issue is a fundamental human right which seeks to protect rights as between individuals *inter se*. No clearer is the case in relation to abortion as recently emerged in the *Grogan* case. *Grogan* provides a classic illustration why the maximalist approach was rejected and why it cannot both as a matter of policy and logic be accepted in this type of case. In Ireland there was a very "high" level of protection for the unborn. What if in another Member State, the "opposing" right of a woman to autonomy over her body was constitutionally guaranteed including the right to abort a foetus in certain circumstances? Which of the two rights would the Court choose to recognize as a Community right? Is there any meaning to a maximalist approach in this situation? In the case of abortion, how can the Court recognize the near absolute right of the unborn in the Irish constitution and at the same time uphold a woman's right to self-determination, which, say, in another Member State permits abortion in some situations?

It could, however, be argued that the abortion situation is special, pitting as it were one individual against another. In most situations, it could be argued, the philosophy of rights pits the individual against public authorities. In those cases, the vast majority, it still does make sense to talk about high and low standards of protection, and, consequently, the maximalist approach would be feasible and desirable. To understand the fallacy of this argument we have to recall the introductory remarks on human rights as an expression of a fundamental balance between rights of the individual and rights of public authorities. To say, as we did in our hypothetical case based on *Hauer*, that Germany has the highest level of protection of private property among the Member States is also to say that Germany, in this area, places the largest number of restrictions on public authorities to act in the general interest. The rights of the public at large have the "lowest" level of protection. Even if this is so, we could still ask why it would matter to the Italian legal order that in the area of private property rights the Court adopt the "high" German standard? After all, as we already mentioned, that choice does not interfere with the conduct of Italian socio-economic policies by Italian public authorities.

[9] Recital 14; emphasis added.

111

This very question represents a failure to grasp that what is fundamental in fundamental rights is the balance struck between individual and public interests. If this is understood, surely the answer to the question is that it could and should matter to the Italian legal order that the Court adopts the German standard simply because it is the "highest." The fallacy rests in the unstated assumption that "higher" standards are always desirable. But we know better. We know that to adopt the "higher" German standard (or that of another Member State, as the case may be) is to adopt for the Community as a whole the societal *Weltanschauung* struck in a particular Member State between the individual and the public at large. It is to adopt for the Community as a whole the fundamental values of a particular Member State.

At least two things are problematic with such an outcome. The Community is comprised of many Member States and peoples. Its basic values should be an expression of that *mélange*. The maximalist approach would always privilege the core values of one Member State, the one which happened to accord the "highest" level of protection to the individual, the "lowest" level of protection to the public and the general interest.

Further, when applied across the board, the maximalist approach could lead to an interesting result. In all Member States there would tend to be a balance among different human rights – some privileging the individual, others the public and the general interest, If the Court were to adopt a maximalist approach this would simply mean that for the Community in each and every area the balance would be most restrictive on the public and general interest. A maximalist approach to human rights would result in a minimalist approach to Community government. This, in the eyes of some, would be a fine choice of socio-economic values. It may be so, or may not. But it should not happen as the unintended consequence of a (non-workable) protecting of human rights.

How, then, can one solve, if at all, this conundrum? How can one reconcile the need to ensure that the Union constitutional architecture not be bought at the expense of compromising individual rights hitherto protected by national constitutions which points towards a maximalist standard policy with the realization that such a policy is inherently flawed, and in some instances simply not workable? How has the Court sought to square this vicious circle?

Again *Hauer* can provide the cues. Let us here move from the hypothetical to the actual decision and see how the Court attempts to resolve the conundrum. The Court first repeats its basic philosophy and methodology in this specific context:

> The right to property is guaranteed in the Community legal order in accordance with the ideas common to the constitutions of the Member States, which are also reflected in the first Protocol to the [ECHR].[10]

Earlier it said that "measures which are incompatible with the fundamental rights recognized by the constitutions of those States are unacceptable in the Community."[11] There is now a subtle change: the Court is insisting that the right to property will be guaranteed in accordance with *ideas* common to the constitutions of the Member State. I interpret that as the Court itself edging away from the vocabulary of standards.

Interestingly, the Court deals first with the protection afforded through the ECHR. The Court cites Article 1 of the first Protocol to the ECHR:

> Every ... person is entitled to the peaceful enjoyment of his possessions. No one shall be deprived of his possessions except in the public interest and subject to the conditions provided for by law and by the general principles of international law. The preceding provisions shall not, however, in any way impair the right of a State to enforce such laws as it deems necessary to control the use of property in accordance with the general interest or to secure the payment of taxes or other contributions or penalties.

The Court goes on to note simply that the Council Regulation in question would come within the right of the State "to enforce such laws as it deems necessary to control the use of property in accordance with the general interest." Further, the provisions in the Convention, in the eyes of the Court, do not enable a sufficiently precise answer to be given to the question submitted by the German Court.[12]

It is clear that for the purposes of its decision the Court regards itself as subject to the requirements of the Protocol, despite the fact that the Community as such is not a signatory. Secondly, it is in my view evident that the Court regards the Convention and its Protocols as mere starting points, as the first and not the most difficult steeplechase which the Community regulation has to pass. It is particularly important to note that, although the Court regards the Community as bound by the Convention, it does not regard the Convention as setting *the* standard of protection for the Community. Like a State, the Community may not violate the Convention but may go beyond it.

The Court then moves to define its own balance. Its starting point seems to respect the rhetoric employed earlier:

> [I]n order to be able to answer [the question], it is necessary to consider also the indications provided by the constitutional rules and practices of the nine [as there then were] Member States.[13]

---

[10] Recital 17.   [11] See note 8, p. 110 above.   [12] Recital 19.   [13] Recital 20.

In practice the Court gives only three textual examples (from the German, Italian, and Irish constitutions) but then goes on to declare that:

> In all the Member States, numerous legislative measures have given concrete expression to [the] social function of the right to property [namely] that those rules and practices permit the legislature to control the use of private property in accordance with the general interest. [I]n all the Member States there is legislation on agriculture and forestry, the water supply, the protection of the environment and town and country planning, which imposes restrictions, sometimes appreciable, on the use of real property. More particularly, all the wine-producing countries of the Community have restrictive legislation, albeit of differing severity, concerning the planting of vines [etc.] ... [which is not] considered to be incompatible in principle with the regard due to the right to property.

This, in my view, is the most critical juncture in its decision. If all the Court was doing was to *ensure that measures which are incompatible with the fundamental rights recognized by the constitutions of those States are unacceptable in the Community*, it could have reached a rapid conclusion to its decision at this point. Surely the above analysis proves beyond doubt that the Community regulation in question is not incompatible with the fundamental rights recognized by the constitutions of the Member States.

But there would have been a huge price to pay had the Court ended its decision at this point. The implication could have been that, had it discovered that a similar measure were held unconstitutional in one of the Member States, then the Community measure too would have to be struck down. At a stroke we would be back to the maximalist-standard trap. Instead, the Court reverts to the second strand in its reasoning: that the right to property is guaranteed in the Community legal order in accordance with the *ideas* common to the constitutions of the Member States. The constitutional practices of the Member States are not used by the Court as a test for the constitutionality of the Community measure but simply as a source for culling the "ideas" inherent in the right to private property. This the Court defines, not surprisingly, as a requirement that interference with private property "correspond to objectives of general interest pursued by the Community" and, in a cumulative test (though the Court uses the word "or") the measure must not "constitute a disproportionate and intolerable interference with the rights of the owner, impinging upon the very substance of the right to property."

These two tests of substantive and procedural policy *bona fide* and proportionality are of course known in virtually all systems of administrative and legislative review. It is worth noting that in substance the Court has not really developed criteria which are in any way more precise than those enumerated in the ECHR and which it had earlier dismissed rather curtly as not enabling it to give an answer.

Since we are not interested in the substance of property law in the EU, it is not necessary to go into the detailed assessment by the Court of the aims of the agricultural policy at the basis of the contested regulation nor into its assessment of the reasonableness of the measure itself save to make some general comments on the method as a whole.

First it is clear that, in assessing what is the "general interest" which the measure must serve, the Court makes reference to the *Community* general interest and not to an aggregate or cumulative Member State interest. In adducing the general interest, the Court looks at the preamble of the regulation and at the general objectives of the Common Agricultural Policy as enunciated in the Treaty.

Proportionality is also discussed in terms of the Community policy. The Court makes reference to the temporary nature of the regulation and the conjunctural situation of the Community as a whole suffering from a surplus in the vine sector. In the light of its analysis of these factors the Court concludes:

> [T]he measure criticized does not entail any undue limitation upon the exercise of the right to property. Indeed, the cultivation of new vineyards in a situation of continuous over-production would not have any effect, from the economic point of view, apart from increasing the volume of the surpluses; further, such an extension at that stage would entail the risk of making more difficult the implementation of a structural policy at the Community level in the event of such a policy resting on the application of criteria more stringent than the current provisions of national legislation concerning the selection of land accepted for wine-growing.
>
> [T]he restriction ... is justified by the objectives of general interest pursued by the Community and does not infringe the substance of the right to property in the form in which it is recognized and protected in the Community legal order.

What does this have to tell us on the way the Court addresses the issue of "high" and "low" standards? The following is my interpretation of this case and the general jurisprudence.

It is clear that the Court rejects the maximalist approach. To repeat:

> [T]he question of a possible infringement of fundamental rights by a measure of the Community institutions can only be judged in the light of Community law itself. *The introduction of special criteria for assessment stemming from the legislation or constitutional law of a particular Member State would, by damaging the substantive unity and efficacy of Community law, lead inevitably to the destruction of the unity of the Common Market and the jeopardizing of the cohesion of the Community.*

But the Court's move is even bolder. It rejects, in my view, any attempt at some mathematical-averages approach to this issue. In its dialogue with its national counterparts its claim is jurisdictional: only the European Court is in a position to make the determination on the compatibility of a Community measure with fundamental human rights.

I shall explain this in two steps. Assume first that the Court were to adopt the "German" standard (or that of any other Member State). It would still have to apply that standard to the facts of the case and to the material, geographic, social, and other matrices of the Community which are different from that of any Member State. Imagine that the German government were to pass an identical measure restricting the growth of vineyards in its territory. Imagine further that *on the German market* planting such a vineyard would make economic sense. It is conceivable that the German Constitutional Court would find that the State could not prove a sufficiently strong general interest to outweigh the interest of the individual in his or her unrestricted use of their private property. But in the Community geographic and socio–economic context it is possible that planting the vineyard in Germany could put someone out of work in Sicily. The Court's first claim is that only it, given its position, is able meaningfully to assess the claims of general interest and proportionality in the Community as a whole.

The second implicit claim in *Hauer* is even bolder. The language of the constitutional provisions it cites from the German, Italian, and Irish constitutions are as bland as the text of the ECHR Protocol. It is the respective court in each of these systems which translates the bland language into the societal choice, the fundamental balance between the individual and the general public. To the best of their ability judges will give expression to the constitutional ethos of the constitutional text and of the polity in those decisions. Why we should entrust such a fundamental choice to our judges is a different question, but that we do so entrust them with the task is beyond dispute. The care we take in choosing judges for constitutional courts is an acknowledgment of that function we give to them.

Multicultural polity and the multiple-identity individual

It is here that we reach the deepest aspect of this case for in it we can read the specific contribution of this jurisprudence to the discourse of multiculturalism and pluralism in our societies.

The deepest (implicit) claim of the European Court in this jurisprudence goes to the issue of values and the conflict among them. The claim is that in *Hauer*-like situations the Community legal order can do no better or worse than its national counterparts. It inevitably falls to a court to make that fundamental balance for the Community legal order. But clearly the European Court, when fleshing out the bland language of general interest and proportionality should try and give expression to a constitutional ethos which derives from *its* controlling texts – not the constitution of one Member State but of all of them. Just as in the geographical-political sense, the Community constitutes a polity different from its Member States with a general interest which must include Bavaria and Sicily, so too its constitutional ethos should reflect the various Member State constitutions as well as the Union's own founding Treaties. It is a new polity the constitutional ethos of which must give expression to, or at least take account of, a multiplicity of traditions.

The implicit claim of the European Court is that in the field of Community law a Community law choice will have to be struck which derives from the specificity of the Community. The Court is calling on its national counterparts to accept that it, the European Court, will do and has to do within the Community legal order what they, national courts, do, have to do, within the national realms. It is not about high or low standards. It is a call to acknowledge the Community and Union as a polity with its own separate identity and constitutional sensibilities which has to define its own fundamental balances – its own core values even if these cannot be dissociated entirely from the context in which the Community is situated. The Community *is* its Member States and their citizens. The Community is, too, an autonomous identity. If you find this multiplicity hard to grasp, turn to 2,000 years of profound Christian theological reflection on the Trinity.

This gives us an interesting final tentative thought on the broader issue of multiculturalism. The appeal of multiculturalism as an idea and movement is in its invitation to a pluralist, ever richer understanding and acceptance of human potentialities within the polity. The Tower of Babel dispersal is conceived by multiculturalism as a blessing rather than a punishment. But often embedded in the multicultural political agenda is dangerous contradiction. The call for a pluralist multicultural society in which the diversity of different groupings has to be acknowledged and celebrated is all too frequently, for obvious political reasons, associated with a stifling conformism within each group comprising the multicultural polity, a conformism which privileges one aspect of individual identity (race or ethnicity, or gender, etc.) – that aspect which is constitutive of the group claiming multicultural recognition – and which would have each individual define himself or herself in terms of that identity aspect.

With numbing regularity the translation of the multi-dimensional vision of *society* is, in the arena of political praxis, achieved at the expense of a forced, one dimensional vision of the *individual* within that society – multicultural society composed of monocultural individuals.

If we go back now to my interpretation of the human-rights issue in

Europe I would suggest that it is possible to construe it as an interesting way of addressing this problem, remembering at all times that human rights are but a small fragment of a much broader legal discourse and that law is but a fragment of a much broader human discourse. My claim is not that the legal human-rights discourse as such actually results in truly appreciable concrete results but that it is illustrative of a way of thinking, that it charts a direction for dealing with the problem.

We should first read the solution of the human-rights issue as a recognition of the cultural diversity which exists in the polity which has to be respected when making European choices. But note, critical in this construct is that it is a two-way process:

Legal production is, indeed, conscious of the multicultural soil from which this production is nourished. This soil bears fruit in the shape of the European Human Right norm (and the reconstructed multicultural societal value which it reflects) which, in the field of application of European law, now can be plucked by individuals in the Member States.

Legal consumption of the norm by individuals is a way individuals will be receiving and experiencing choices informed by a wider cultural context than the ones they are accustomed to. They may be, yes, educated in the practices and sensibilities of tolerance and intolerance each time they are confronted with a norm that is different from those they normally know. Recall, of course, that the differences can play out both to their advantage and disadvantage. Some will react favorably, with tolerance. Others unfavorably with intolerance. Some might celebrate the Brave New World. Others might yearn back to the comfort of the familiar. None can be unaware of the new context to which they belong.

In this sense, then, we have a vision of a society with multicultural sensibilities which is not only reflective but also constitutive of individuals with multicultural sensibilities.

But one can go even deeper than that. Another element that is critical in the European human-rights construct is that the European human-rights apparatus *does not replace* the national ones (in the Member States) or the transnational one (the European Convention of Human Rights). It co-exists alongside them in the sphere of application of Community law which overlaps only partially the national and European Convention transnational spheres.

Implicit in this reading of the European situation is the recognition of the multiple identity of the individual. This, of course, is trite stuff but worth repeating. The individual has simultaneous belongingness (French, European, etc.) which means that the I is not a Frenchman living in Europe, but an I which is French *and* European in the same way that someone is simultaneously male and Buddhist and a Rolling Stones lover.

Implicit in this reading is an I which has a multiple identity defined by such diverse things as gender, religion, personal history and the like, each of which brings with them not only cultural sensibilities but also their own claims for loyalty and corresponding, and oft conflicting, sets of values. That there can be conflict between the sets of values is not simply banal – it is a necessary reflection of the complexes and conflicts which exist within each individual. Choices have, from time to time, to be made between the pull of conflicting values and loyalties. And often one such element will come to dominate the sense of personal identity. Whatever the choice, how much better that it is made as a result of the internal conflict and eventual, conscious or subconscious, deliberative choice. And whatever element turns out to dominate – nationality, or religion, or gender – it is much better that it is tempered by the conflict of competing claims and values. In this way multiculturalism becomes an internalized, true part of the self.

Protection of fundamental human rights: review of Member State measures

My starting point here is the well-known development in the jurisprudence of the Court from a practice which focused on Community measures to a jurisprudence which is willing to scrutinize some Member State measures too.

Here too the general story is well known. The material landmarks are *Rutili, Cinetheque, Klensch, Wachauf,* the Advocate-General in *Grogan,* and *ERT.* I do not consider it necessary to recapitulate fully the facts of these cases or their principal holdings. Briefly stated, the Court, which regards its duty as being to ensure the protection of fundamental rights within the field of Community law, has construed that field to include Member State measures implementing Community law as well as Member State measures adopted in derogation from the prohibition on restricting the free movement of the four factors of production.

In the first part of this essay we saw how even the review of *Community* measures may create a tension with fundamental values of the various Member States. Here the "assault" is more direct since at issue are *Member State* measures normally thought to be subject to the scrutiny and control of Member State courts.

And, to return to the issue of standards, in relation to Community measures we saw the possible concern of Member State Courts was that the Community standards are not high enough, thus letting stand Community measures which, but for the doctrine of supremacy, would be struck down by the national courts. In relation to Member State measures the principal concern would be reversed: that in reviewing Member State measures, the Court strike down acts authorized by the domestic jurisdiction and possibly even sanctioned by the ECHR.

The first and most pressing issue that has to be addressed in this context is the very justification for review of Member State measures by the European Court. If, as I argued in the introduction to this essay, constitutionally protected human rights express core societal choices as to the balance between individual and community interests (and visions), an "encroachment" by the European Court would be a direct challenge to the fundamental boundaries of the Member State. There already has been some considerable protest in this regard. What then is the justification for this jurisdictional drive?

The Court has extended, so far, the exercise of its human-rights jurisdiction to Member State measures in two types of situation: first, in the agency situation, when the Member State is acting for and/or on behalf of the Community and implementing a Community policy (the *Klensch Wachauf* case); and, secondly, when the State relies on a derogation to fundamental market freedoms (the *ERT* case). How is this to be evaluated from a narrower "legal" point of view?

The rationale for "agency" review

All of us often fall into the trap of thinking of the Community as an entity wholly distinct from the Member States. But of course, like some well-known theological concepts, the Community is, in some senses, its Member States; in other senses separate from them. This, as 2,000 years of Christian theology attest, can at times be hard to grasp. But in one area of Community life it is easy. In the EC system of governance, to an extent far greater than any federal state, the Member States often act as, indeed are, the executive branch of the Community. When, to give an example, a UK customs official collects a Community-imposed tariff from an importer of non-Community goods, the official is organically part of the UK customs service, but functionally they are wearing a Community hat. If the Court's human-rights jurisdiction covers, as it clearly does, not merely the formal legislative Community normative source, but its *mise-en-œuvre*, is it not really self-evident, as Advocate-General Jacobs puts it in *Wachauf*, even on a narrow construction of the Court's human-rights jurisdiction, that it should review these "Member State" measures for violation of human rights? In this case the very nomenclature which distinguished Member State and Community acts fails to capture the reality of Community governance and the Community legal order. Not to review these acts would be legally inconsistent with the constant human-rights jurisprudence and, from the human-rights policy perspective, arbitrary: if the Commission is responsible for the *mise-en-œuvre*, review will take place; but if it is a Member State, it will not.

The rationale for ERT-type review

The development in the *ERT* case, foreshadowed by the opinion of the Advocate-General in the *Grogan* case is more delicate. The Treaty interdicts Member State measures which interfere with the fundamental free-movement provisions of the Treaty. This interdiction applies to any Member State measure, regardless of its source. The mere fact that the interference may emanate from a constitutional norm is, in and of itself, irrelevant. Likewise, the fact that the constitutional measures may be an expression of a deeply held national societal more or value is, in and of itself, irrelevant. If, say, a Member State, even under widespread popular conviction and support, were to adopt a constitutional amendment which, "in the interest of preserving national identity and the inalienable fundamental rights of our citizens" prohibited an undertaking from employing foreigners, including Community nationals, ahead of that Member State's citizens or to purchase foreign goods ahead of national products, such a constitutional provision would be in violation of Community law.

Community law itself defines two situations which may exculpate such a national measure from the Treaty interdiction. First, the national measure itself must be considered as constituting an illegal interference with the market freedom. The Treaty is very vague on this and the Court has developed a rich case law in this regard. Not every measure which on its face seems to interfere will necessarily be construed as a violation of one of the market freedoms. Second, even a national measure which on its face constitutes a violation of the interdiction may, under Community law, be exculpated if it can be shown to fall under derogation clauses to be found in the Treaty. Article 36, for example, speaks of measures "justified" on grounds of public morality, health, etc.

The crucial point is that defining what constitutes a violation of the basic market freedoms is, substantively and jurisdictionally, a matter of Community law and for the Court to decide, as is the exculpatory regime. Substantively, the Court will interpret the language of the Treaty, which is often opaque: what, for example, does (or should) "justified" or "public order," mean? Jurisdictionally, the Court (in tandem with national jurisdictions) will supervise to ensure that the Member States are in fact fulfilling their obligations under the Treaty.

One way of explaining the "extension" of human-rights jurisdiction to Member State measures in the *ERT* situation is simple enough. Once a

Member State measure is found to be in violation of the market freedoms, *but for* the derogation it would be illegal. The scope of the derogation and the conditions for its employment are all "creatures" of Community law, both Treaty and judge-made. Now, it could be argued in opposition, and I would not consider this a specious argument, that one should look at the derogations as defining the limit of Community-law reach. But I am not persuaded. Even from a formalist perspective, the very structure of, say, Articles 30–36 indicates the acceptance of the Member States that the legality or otherwise of a measure constituting a *prima facie* violation of the prohibition on measures having effect to quantitative restrictions becomes a matter for Community law. From a policy perspective it could hardly be otherwise. Imagine the state of the common market if each Member State could determine by reference to its own laws and values – without any reference to Community law – what was or was not covered by the prohibition and its derogation. Surely how wide or narrow the derogation is, should be controlled by Community law. The concomitant consequence of this is that, once it is found that a Member State measure contravenes the market-freedom interdictions such as Article 30, even if it is exculpated by a derogation clause in the Treaty, the Community's legislative competence is triggered and it may become susceptible to harmonization.

Let us illustrate this by taking the most telling instance: the rule-of-reason doctrine developed principally in the *Cassis de Dijon* case of which the *Cinéthèque*[14] case is an example. Here the Court has carved out new circumstances, not explicitly mentioned in the Treaty derogation clause, which would allow the Member States to adopt measures which otherwise would be a violation of Article 30. I do not recall any protest by Member States complaining about the Court's rather audacious construction of Articles 30–36 in this regard. But, obviously, the Member States are not given a free hand. The Court will have to be persuaded that the Member State measures seeking to benefit from the rule of reason are, for example, as a matter of Community law, in the general interest and of sufficient importance to override the interest in the free movement of goods, that they are proportionate to the objective pursued, that they are adopted in good faith and are not a disguised restriction to trade. Therefore, the ability of the Member States to move within the derogations to the free-movement provisions are subject to a series of limitations, some explicitly to be found in the Treaty, others the result of judicial construction of the Treaty.

In construing the various Community-law limitations on the Member States' ability to derogate from the Treaty and in administering these limitations in cases that come before it, should the Court insist on all these

[14] Joined Cases 60 and 61/84, *Cinéthèque* [1985] ECR 2,605.

other limitations and yet adopt a "hands-off" attitude towards violation of human rights? Is it so revolutionary to insist that when the Member States avail themselves of a Community-law-created derogation they respect too the fundamental human rights, deriving from the constitutional traditions of the Member States, even if the Community construction of this or that right differs from its construction in this or that Member State? After all, *but for* the judicially constructed rule of reason in *Cassis*, France would not be able to justify at all its videocassette policy designed to protect French cinematographic culture. To respect the Community notion of human rights in this scenario appears to us wholly consistent with the earlier case law and the policy behind it.

It could be argued that in supervising the derogation the Court should not enter into the policy merits of the Member State measure other than to check that it is proportionate and not a disguised restriction to trade. Human-rights review, on this reading, is an interference with the merits. Again, I am not persuaded. First, it must be understood that the doctrine of proportionality also involves a Community value choice imposed by the Court on a Member State. Each time the Court says, for example, that a label informing the consumer will serve a policy adequately compared to an outright prohibition, it is clear that at least some consumers will, despite the label, be misled. There are ample studies to demonstrate the limited effectiveness of labels. Thus, in the most banal proportionality test "lurks" a judicial decision by the Court as to the level of risk society may be permitted to take with its consumers.

Secondly, even if human-rights review may be more intrusive than proportionately in some cases, it need not always interfere with the actual merits of the policy pursued and could still leave considerable latitude to the State to pursue their own devices. Provided they do not violate human rights, the Court will not interfere with the content of the policy. Admittedly this may sometimes thwart their wills, but that, after all, would also be the case under the European Convention on Human Rights. That on some occasions it might give teeth to the European Convention in those countries which have after decades not yet incorporated it into national law must, we assume, be welcomed by those who profess to take rights seriously.

The double scrutiny of Member State measures: institutional considerations and the question of standards

Even if there is a doctrinal and policy justification for extending human-rights review to this category of Member State measures, would it not be overly transgressing the prerogatives of Member State courts? This very question might suggest a view which sees the relationship between the European Court and its national counterparts in the area of human rights as consisting of a zero-sum game (powers granted to one are taken away from the other) or, worse, confrontational. It suggests perhaps a view which considers a tug-of-war between a *transnational* court and a *national* court. This might be so in some instances, but the relationship is far more complex and in some cases could, and in my view should, be seen as involving a transnational *court* and a national *court*: a co-operative relationship wherein the critical sense of identity results not from one body being national and the other transnational but from their sense of both belonging to the judicial branch, not confrontational but mutually reinforcing their ability to uphold the law (as they see it). Not, then, a zero-sum game, but a positive-sum game with both parties better off.

The institutional dimension is particularly intriguing in relation to the domestic application of the ECHR especially in those states, like the UK, in which the Convention has not been incorporated into domestic law. Consider, for example, the UK. By extending its jurisdiction to Member State measures the Court may be stepping into areas which previously were reserved to a national court. But that domain may be more illusory than real. What was reserved to UK courts previously? The "power" to tell hapless individuals that, for example, since successive UK governments for their own reasons have refused to incorporate the ECHR into domestic law, courts were unable to give them relief (except, in the manner of *Wachauf*, as an aid in interpretation) even in the face of egregious violations of the Convention to which their country is a party? One can, of course, take the view that UK constitutional arrangements and the denial of power to UK courts to apply the ECHR are matters which should be left to the UK. But in anybody's book that would hardly qualify as a position which takes human rights seriously. Moreover, is not the extension of jurisdiction of the Court, at least in some respects, an *empowerment* of the UK national courts and a strengthening of the protection of human rights in the UK in that at least in those areas coming within the scope of Community law as defined by the Court, UK domestic courts would have gained the right and the power, hitherto denied them, to give human-rights relief to individuals?

What then of the issue of *standards* of review? What are the potentials here for conflict of fundamental values? My reflections in this respect are very speculative, suggesting at most a possible interpretation of the scant case law. More realistically they should be taken as a prognosis of future developments.

Let us examine first the *Wachauf* situation, the review of a Member State measure implementing or acting for the Community. This review arises only in those situations when the Community norm or policy leaves some discretion to the Member State so that national authorities are choosing from several possible executing or implementing options.

Human-right standards in the Wachauf situation

Scenario A: The measure is in violation of the ECHR. *Result*: It should be struck down either by the national court or by the European Court. There would be no conflict of values since both Community and Member State regard the ECHR as a basic core which cannot be transgressed.

Scenario B: The measure clears the ECHR hurdle but is in violation of a more stringent Member State standard though it would not be in violation of the Community standard. *Result*: The measure should be struck down by the national court. Since the Community gives the Member State discretion in execution or implementation, provided the Community norm is executed or implemented by one way or another, Community law does not require that Member State standards be violated. There is no conflict of values either.

Scenario C: The measure clears the ECHR hurdle, clears national standards of human rights but fails the Community standard. *Result*: The measure should be struck down. There is a conflict of values since the public authorities of the Member State are prohibited from exercising a power in a manner which under domestic constitutional standards would be permitted. The conflict is not acute since the Member State public authorities are, *ipso facto* and *ipso jure*, acting for and on behalf of the Community.

Human-rights standards in the ERT situation

Scenario A: The Member State measure violates the ECHR. *Result*: The measure should be struck down either by the national court or by the European Court. There is no substantive conflict of values since both legal orders accept the ECHR as a basic core which cannot be transgressed. There could, of course, be a difference in interpreting the ECHR minimal standard. The mistake will inevitably fall in favor of human rights.

Scenario B: The Member State measure clears the ECHR standard but violates the national standard though it would clear the Community standard. *Result*: I would submit that the result should be a striking down of the measure. There is no Community interest in overriding a national human-rights standard applied by a national court against a Member State *derogating from the Treaty*.

Scenario C: The Member State measure clears the ECHR, clears the Member State standard but violates the Community standard. I have come to believe that in the *ERT* situation the Community should not impose its own standard on the Member State measure but allow a wide margin of appreciation, insisting only that the Member State not violate the basic core encapsulated in the ECHR. This seems to be consistent with the opinion of Advocate-General van Gerven in *Grogan*. Unlike the *Wachauf* situation where the Member State is merely the agent of the Community and the Member State measure is in truth a Community measure, here we are dealing with a Member State measure in application of a Member State policy. The interest of the Court and the Community should be to prevent a violation of core human rights but to allow beyond that maximum leeway to national policy. This would essentially equate Scenario C with Scenario A with practical effects limited essentially to those jurisdictions, such as the UK, where national courts are not empowered to enforce under national law the ECHR. They would, as suggested above, be empowered through Community law. It would also mean that should the Community harmonize disparate Member State derogation measures to, say, Article 30, the standard of human-rights review of the harmonized measure may be higher than the standard applied by the Court to reviewing the previous Member State measures.

Finally, in the *ERT* situation and more generally, even when the standard for review imposed by the Court may be no different than that applying in the Member State, I confess to a bias, rebuttable to be sure, in favor of human-rights judicial review by courts not directly part of the polity the measures of which come under review. That is why, for example, I favor accession of the Community to the European Convention of Human Rights which would subject even the jurisprudence of the European Court to a second outside scrutiny. As I noted in the introduction, transnational protection of human rights frequently involves the painful tension between the universal and the particular. So far I have insisted on the value of the particular as encapsulating a fundamental choice of the polity. It is trite to recall, however, that regularly, States defend alleged human-rights violations on the grounds of respect for deeply held local cultural practices. Sometimes there is merit in the argument. Often, as in the case of, say, the southern states in the USA defending in the 1950s and 1960s discrimination against blacks, or some countries today defending the ghastly practice of female mutilation, or corporal punishment of adults (hand chopping) and children (whippings, canings, and the like) the

Table 1. *Principal permutations of human-rights review in the Community legal order*

Type of measure	Conformity with ECHR	Conformity with Community human-right standards	Conformity with national human-rights standards	Constitutionally correct result
Community measure	violates	(necessarily) violates	(necessarily) violates	should be struck down by ECJ
Community measure	does not violate	violates	does not violate	should be struck down by ECJ
Community measure	does not violate	does not violate	violates	should be upheld and not struck down by either ECJ or Member State court
Member State measure: agency situation where Member State has discretion	violates	(necessarily) violates	(necessarily) violates	should be struck down by ECJ or Member State court
Member State measure: agency situation where Member State has discretion	does not violate	violates	does not violate	should be struck down by ECJ or Member State court
Member State measure: agency situation where Member State has discretion	does not violate	does not violate	violates	should be struck down by Member State court and implemented another way
Member State measure: ERT situation	violates	(necessarily) violates	(necessarily) violates	should be struck down by ECJ or Member State court
Member State measure: ERT situation	does not violate	violates (i.e., Community standard when applied to Community measure goes beyond core ECHR)	does not violate	should not be struck down: ECJ should not enforce own standard beyond ECHR core
Member State measure: ERT situation	does not violate	does not violate	violates	should be struck down by Member State court and implemented another way

defense is specious, a mockery of the transcendental notion of human dignity. In our impressionistic view, local courts, close to local culture, are over-susceptible to this type of argument. We are particularly suspicious of these claims when they emanate in contexts, such as Europe, of considerable common cultural affinity among peoples and a shared concept of the State and public authority. Adjudicating these competing claims between the particular and the universal is never easy and may not ultimately have a "right" answer. On balance, from the perspective of my own human-rights sensibilities, I prefer, in this respect, the bias of the transnational forum to that of the national one, tempered as it is by the doctrine of margin of appreciation and mindful that the transnational forum is, as noted, often a second bite at the apple, the national jurisdiction having already had its say.

By way of conclusion I set out in Table 1 the principal permutations of review for violation of human rights and the relationship between the different standards of review.

FURTHER READING

General

Cassese, A., Clapham, A., and Weiler, J. H. H. (eds.), *European Union – The Human Rights Challenge* (Nomos: Baden-Baden, 3 vols., 1991)

Clapham, A., *Human Rights and the European Community: A Critical Overview* (Nomos: Baden-Baden, 1991)

Coppel and O'Neill, "The European Court of Justice: Taking Rights Seriously?" *Common Market Law Review* 29 (1992), 669

Schermers, H. G. and Waelbroeck, D., *Judicial Protection in the European Communities* (Martinus Nijhoff: Dordrecht, Boston, 5th edn., 1992)

Weiler, J. H. H., "Eurocracy and Distrust," *Washington Law Review* 61 (1986), 1,103

Weiler, J. H. H. and Lockhart, " 'Taking Rights Seriously' Seriously: The European Court of Justice and its Fundamental Rights Jurisprudence," *Common Market Law Review* 32 (1995)

Human rights as a system of values and cultural relativism

An-Na'im (ed.), *Human Rights in Cross-Cultural Perspectives* (1992)

Renteln, "The Unanswered Challenge of Relativism and the Consequences for Human Rights," *Human Rights Quarterly* 7 (1987), 514

Weiler, J. H. H., "Thou Shalt Not Oppress a Stranger," *European Journal of International Law* 3 (1992), 65

The application of European human rights by national jurisdictions

Arnull and Jacobs, "Applying the Common Rules on the Free Movement of Persons –

The Role of the National Judiciary in the Light of the Jurisprudence of the European Court of Justice," in Schermers, H. G. *et al.* (eds.), *Free Movement of Persons in Europe* (1993), 272

Bingham, " 'There is a World Elsewhere': The Changing Perspectives of English Law" *International and Comparative Law Review* 41 (1992), 513

"The European Convention on Human Rights: Time to Incorporate" *Law Quarterly Review* 109 (1993), 390

Browne-Wilkinson, "The Incorporation of a Bill of Rights," *Public Law* [1992], 397

Dremczewski, A., *The European Rights Convention in Domestic Law* (1983)

Laws, "Is the High Court of Justice the Guardian of Fundamental Constitutional Rights?" *Public Law* [1993], 59

Weiler, J. H. H., "The European Court at a Crossroads: Community Human Rights and Member State Action," in Capotorti *et al.* (eds.), *Du droit international au droit de l'intégration liiber amicorum Pierre Pescatore* (Nomos: Baden-Baden, 1987)

The relationship between human rights and integration

Frowein, Schulhofer, and Shapiro, "The Protection of Fundamental Rights as a Vehicle of Integration," in Cappelletti, M., Seccombe, M., and Weiler, J. H. H., *Integration through Law* (Walter de Gruyter: Berlin, New York, 1984), vol. I, book 3, 231

Mancini, "A Constitution for Europe," *Common Market Law Review* 16 (1989), 595 at 611

Pescatore, "The Content and Significance of Fundamental Rights in the Law of the European Communities" *Human Rights Law Journal* (1981), 295

Relation between Community protection of human rights and the echr

Cohen-Jonathan, G., "La convention européenne des droits de l'homme et la Communauté européenne," in *Mélanges Fernand Dehousse* (Nathan: Paris; Labor: Brussels, 1979)

De Salvia, "La protezione dei diritti dell'uomo nel quadro della convenzione europea e seconda il diritto communitario: interferenze e problemi di coordinamento," *Diritto comunitario e degli scambi internaionale* (1979), 489

Grief, "The Domestic Impact of the ECHR as Mediated through Community Law," *Public Law* [1991], 555

Macdonald, R. St. J., "The Margin of Appreciation in the Jurisprudence of the European Court of Human Rights" *Academy of European Law* (1990), vol. I, book 2, 95

Pipkorn, "La Communauté européenne et la convention européenne des droits de l'homme," *Revue trimestrielle des droits de l'homme* 14 (1993), 221

4

THE EXTERNAL LEGAL RELATIONS OF
NON-UNITARY ACTORS: MIXITY AND
THE FEDERAL PRINCIPLE

THE ARTICLE which forms this chapter is almost fifteen years old. It discusses what I considered the defining constitutional dimension of the Community's external legal relations: the practice of the Community and its Member States jointly to conclude international treaties with third States and international organizations. The view I took was iconoclastic. Most observers considered the practice a necessary evil, a concession to political reality. I celebrated the practice as a near-unique contribution to true federalism.

After the conclusion of the Single European Act and the Maastricht Treaty there was, for a time, a feeling that the practice would go into decline. But with the recent opinion of the Court on the WTO – effectively forcing continued mixity in that important arena – the old analysis may retain its relevance after all.

INTRODUCTION

Mixed agreements have been a feature of Community external relations from very early days[1] but it has been the multilateral context – especially the UNCTAD and UNCLOS – which has focused judicial and scholarly attention on the phenomenon.[2] What are the legal and political roots of

---

[1] See Feenstra, in H. G. Schermers and D. O'Keeffe (eds.), *Mixed Agreements* (Kluwer: Deventer, Boston, 1983), 207–48. Mixity is actually foreseen in the Euratom Treaty, Art. 102: "Agreements or contracts concluded with a third State, an international organization or a national of a third State to which, in addition to the Community, one or more Member States are parties ..."; see also Ruling 1/78 [1978] ECR 2,151.

[2] See Opinion 1/76 [1977] ECR 741; Opinion 1/78 [1979] ECR 2,871; Ruling 1/78 [1978] ECR 2,151. The issues raised by mixity have of course even in the past received academic attention, even critical. See, e.g., Costonis, "The Treaty Making Power of the EEC," *Common Market Law Review* 5 (1967–8), 421, 453; Norton, "The Treaty Making Power of the EEC – A Constitutional Crisis Facing the EEC," *International Lawyer* 7 (1973), 589.

mixed agreements? How significant are they to European integration in general and to Community external relations in particular? Are there any lessons to be learnt from the experience of other non-unitary actors and especially federal states? These will be the principal questions which I shall investigate in this chapter.

The fact that mixed agreements have virtually no parallels or precedents in international practice[3] should come as no surprise: the European Community itself has no direct parallels in the international legal order. It is an entity which comes between, and in some respects straddles, the classical intergovernmental organization and federation.[4] Mixity is but one

---

[3] There are some exceptions to this alleged uniqueness. The most clamorous was the position of the Ukrainian and Byelorussian Soviet Socialist Republics who were not only members of several international organizations alongside the USSR but were also parties to several multilateral treaties – Conventions on Genocide, Abolition of Slavery, the 1958 Geneva Convention on the High Seas, etc. Most commentators were agreed, however, that internally the USSR's treaty-making power was one of a unitary state and that the position of the Ukraine and Byelorussia had more to do with the international posture of the Soviet Union in the post-War period. Despite Art. 13 of the Soviet Constitution which purported to establish the federal character of the USSR on the "basis of a voluntary union of equal Soviet Socialist Republics" and despite a constitutional amendment dating back to 1944 which granted all Republics "the right to enter into direct relations with foreign states, to conclude agreements" (Art. 18a) under the authority of the federal government, Oliver concludes that "no independent observer has been found who would classify the Soviet Union as a functioning federalism": Oliver, "The Enforcement of Treaties by a Federal State," *Receuil des Cours* 141 (1974-I), 333, 346. In similar vein, see I. Bernier, *International Legal Aspects of Federalism* (Longman: London, 1973) at 65; R. C. Ghosh, *Treaties and Federal Constitutions: Their Mutual Impact* (World Press: Calcutta, 1961) at 80–2; Dobrin, "Soviet Federalism and the Principle of Double Subordination," *Transactions of the Grotius Society* 30 (1944), 282; L. Wildhaber, *Treaty-Making Power and Constitution* (Helbing and Lichtenhahn: Basle, Stuttgart, 1969) at 283. See also Dolan, "The Member Republics of the USSR as Subjects of the Law of Nations," *International and Comparative Law Quarterly* 4 (1955), 629. It is not proposed thus to deal with the Soviet experience. See also Schermers, "A Typology of Mixed Agreements," in Schermers and O'Keefe, *Mixed Agreements*, 23–33 at 29. Given the current "hard" position of the USA *vis-à-vis* Community mixity, it might be of interest to note that in the 1919 Commission on International Labour Legislation it was the USA which suggested very strongly participation of the member states of federations in the conference and the same rights and obligations as at least the British Dominions. The UK, France, and Italy were among those who voted against. See Sohn, "Multiple Representation in International Assemblies," *American Journal of International Law* 40 (1946), 71.

[4] Thus in a very recent contribution it is said: "The Community is neither a typical international organization based on intergovernmental co-operation, nor necessarily an emerging federation at least in the traditional sense of the term. Suppose we called it a *sui generis* association of sovereign states, which could in a sense be seen as an admission of defeat as regards the taxonomical standards of profession, or even as a sign of agnosticism.": Tsoukalis, "Looking into the Crystal Ball," in L. Tsoukalis (ed.), *The European Community: Past, Present and Future* (Basil Blackwell: Oxford, 1983) at 229. One need not deny the unique features of the Community emphasized in well-known decisions of the European Court of Justice. See, e.g., Cases 90 and 91/63, *Commission* v. *Belgium and Luxembourg* [1964] ECR 625. Its uniqueness becomes comprehensible only in the context of established juridical or political categories from which it may be distinguished. This comparative approach, one early exponent of which was P. Hay, *Federalism*

131

expression of that intermediate position. Although one must take care when defining the *sui generis* features of the EC,[5] a failure to appreciate, or accept, the special character of the Community, often strange to the non-Community observer,[6] has hampered both analysis and evaluation of mixity.

Thus, in the analysis of mixed agreements, it has not been uncommon to apply to the Community only those legal concepts which were developed and are used for traditional international organizations[7] even though the Community no longer fits that category and has assumed many statal attributes. Likewise, in evaluation, although most observers would agree that where "agreements cover matters indubitably within the competence of both Community and the Member States" mixity is justified,[8] it has been quite common to adopt a federal-state "ideal-type" and to regard mixed agreements as an obstacle and impediment to the process of European integration and thus to condemn them or, at best, to tolerate them as a necessary evil. Mixed agreements require instead an analysis and evaluation that is respectful of the Community's special character and borrows from the experience of both federal states and international organizations.

Even if mixed agreements are unique to the Community, the problem they try to solve emerged, at least historically, also in the federal state. The cardinal principle of federal governance in Wheare's classical formulation, is "that the general and regional [Member State] governments are each,

---

and Supranational Organizations (1966), is now reappearing. See, for an international-law-orientated comparison, Wyatt, "New Legal Order, or Old?" *European Law Review* 7 (1982), 147; and for a federal-oriented comparison, see T. Sandalow and E. Stein (eds.), *Courts and Free Markets* (Clarendon Press: Oxford; Oxford University Press: New York, 1982); and Wallace, "Europe as a Confederation: The Community and the Nation-State" in Tsoukalis (ed.), *The European Community: Past, Present and Future* at 57.

[5] Hay characterizes the *sui generis* approach as "an unsatisfying shrug": "Federal Jurisdiction of the Common Market Court," *American Journal of Comparative Law* 12 (1963), 39; Wyatt, in "New Legal Order, or Old?" seeks to show the practical difficulties of the inward-looking approach.

[6] Stein encapsulates this neatly: "It will come as a surprise to an American lawyer that in a variety of instances an agreement is concluded by both the Community and by member states in their individual capacities.": E. Stein, "Towards a European Foreign Policy? The European Foreign Affairs System from the Perspective of the United States Constitution" in M. Cappelletti, M. Secombbe, and J. H. H. Weiler (eds.), *Integration through Law*, 5 vols. (Walter de Gruyter: Berlin, New York, 1985), vol. I, book 1.

[7] I shall not be dealing with the position of international organizations. In general see H. G. Schermers, *International Institutional Law* (Sijthoff and Noordhoff: Alphen aan den Rijn, Rockville, MD, 2nd edn., 1980), chapter 12.

[8] Cremona, "The Doctrine of Exclusivity and the Position of Mixed Agreements in the External Relations of the European Community," *Oxford Journal of Legal Studies* (1982), 393, 411. Of course, as we shall see below, the crucial factor is to distinguish between internal competence and treaty-making power, the mutual relations of which differ from the federal state to the Community and in turn affect the question of mixity.

within a sphere, co-ordinate and independent"[9] and that, at least in theory, neither central authority nor Member State "should have it in its power to invade the sphere of the other."[10] The dilemma of the federal state, like that of the Community, appears when a proposed treaty covers a field the internal competence over which lies at least partially in the hands of the Member States. Does the central authority have international legal capacity to conclude such a treaty on its own without the participation, or at least authorization, of the Member States? Does it enjoy internal constitutional treaty-making power to make a treaty which covers matters normally reserved to the Member States? And even if the answer to these two questions is in the affirmative, will the central authority be competent to implement legislatively the provisions of the treaty?

Mixity is of course one possible solution to this dilemma and yet it has rarely been on the agenda of the federal state and the international community.[11] It does not accord with what is essentially, from the legal point of view, a world order of unitary states.[12] Instead examination of the federal-state experience reveals a paradox: when it comes to treaties and international legal relations federal states behave, at least towards the outside world, as unitary actors. It would seem that federalism and foreign policy live uneasily together.[13] Are we to learn then from federations that

---

[9] K. C. Wheare, *Federal Government* (Oxford University Press: New York, 4th edn., 1964) at 10.

[10] Wade, "Memorandum and Evidence on the Amendment of the Constitution of Canada," submitted to the Foreign Affairs Committee of the [UK] House of the Commons, reprinted in *British North American Acts: The Role of Parliament*, HC (1981), vol. 2 at 102 and 108.

[11] But see J. Lador-Lederer, *International Group Protection: Aims and Methods in Human Rights* (Sijthoff: Leyden, 1968).

[12] Elazar suggests that "[n]early 40 percent of the world's population now lives within politics that are formally federal while another third live in politics that utilize federal arrangements in some way ... Of the over 150 politically 'sovereign' states now in existence ... [o]ver one third ... 58 to be exact, are involved in formal arrangements utilizing federal principles in some way to accommodate demands for self-rule or shared rule within their boundaries or in partnership with other politics.": "Introduction" in D. Elazar (ed.), *Federalism and Political Integration* (Turtledove: Ramat Gan, Israel, 1979) at 3–4. If we take a formal legal view we may understand Oliver's contrasting comments: "The number of federal States in the world community is surprisingly small: out of some 140 entities recognised as States, not more than a dozen are federal in form; and of those that are technically federalisms (i.e., having in effect constitutional arrangements that provide for the allocation of governmental powers between a central and several state authorities) only Australia, Austria, Canada, the Federal Republic of Germany, India, Malaysia, Switzerland and the United States of America offer any substantial evidence that treaty performance issues arise or may arise.": Oliver, "The Enforcement of Treaties by a Federal State" at 346. It is this second perspective which is of interest to us and confirms the view of a unitarist world order.

[13] Wheare thus comments: "Federalism and a spirited foreign policy go ill together"; and: "It is usually assumed that the foreign relations of a federation will be controlled predominantly, if not exclusively, by the general government of the whole territory. Indeed one of the arguments for establishing a federation is usually that it will provide for a unified foreign policy.": Wheare,

in international legal relations non–unitary actors are compelled to adopt a centralist posture and to eschew the federal principle? Or could it be that in mixity we find the first authentic expression of a veritable federal foreign policy?

It will have become clear that in this inquiry three concepts will be of fundamental importance: (1) the internal implementing *competence* of the central authority and the constituent members; (2) the treaty-making *power* of the central authority and the constituent members; and (3) the international *capacity* of the central authority and the constituent members.

In the first part of this chapter, I shall first examine two of these concepts – competence and power – in the context of the Canadian, United States, Australian, German, and Swiss federal-state experiences. This survey will establish on the one hand the general trend of federal states in this field towards a granting of plenary and virtually exclusive treaty-making power to the central authority and a tendency to match this power with equally wide implementing competences. On the other hand, the exceptions to this general trend and the nuances between the different federal-state experiences will reveal that this centralist ethos is not necessitated by any compelling legal logic and instead was often conditioned by policy choices of the legislature or the judiciary. The way thus will become open to query whether in the Community, even with the objective of further integration in mind, a different relationship between power and competences, conditioned by the Community's own policy considerations, and perhaps even more respectful of the federal principle, may not be appropriate.

I shall then examine the concept of capacity trying to show that, although international law and practice have favored a world order of unitary states (or federal states which behave as unitary actors), there is no impediment for both the central authority and the constituent members of a federal state to possess international capacity. Here as well the way will become open to argue that the international legal order should not obstruct the exercise by the EC of its own double capacity – even, as in the case of mixed agreements, simultaneously – as an expression of the Community's unique blend of constitutional and international law.

In the second part of this chapter, I shall examine the evolution of the Community's external relations in the light of the earlier survey of federal-state experiences. In particular I shall show how the Court of Justice adopted, in the doctrines of parallelism and preemption, a path similar to that of federal states. This was true especially in the matching of the power

Federal Government at 186 and 169. This tension between *internal* federalism and external (legal) relations should not be confused with a contrasting trend: the tendency of states to organize themselves on "federal" lines in associations of states: federacies; common markets; regional organizations.

and competence of the Community and the restrictive attitude taken towards the Member States. Although this judicial policy served the very important function of consolidating constitutionally the international personality of the Community, the time has perhaps come for its reevaluation: strict preemption can have the effect of deterring the Member States altogether from concluding Community agreements or push them towards other devices. Strict parallelism might for ever limit the range of Community agreements to those which fall fully within Community internal competences. I shall attempt to show that this reevaluation is already under way by the European Court itself.

In the third and concluding part of this chapter, I shall evaluate the phenomenon of mixed agreements. It is clear that mixed agreements can be abused internally by the Member States and used, even in cases where the EC enjoys plenary power, to prevent the conclusion of a "pure" Community agreement. Mixity can also be abused in the international legal arena whereby the Community and the Member States could seek an advantage in representation, voting, or even in the assumption of substantive obligations and responsibility.[14]

It is with these abuses in mind that I shall propose a new type of agreement which, for want of a better term, may be called a vertical mixed agreement. Unlike the classical (horizontal) mixed agreement it will be concluded by the Community alone even though it may include matters in relation to which the Community enjoys no competence. Like the familiar mixed agreement it will be implemented jointly by Community and Member States and, crucially, conclusion of the agreement will not enlarge internal Community competences nor will it obliterate Member State treaty-making power in the area.

At the same time, despite the dangers of abuse, on many occasions mixed agreements may be regarded as beneficial to the Community process and as a faithful image of the federal/international character of the EC. I shall justify this positive evaluation not simply on the basis of a pragmatic, *realpolitik* assessment of what is feasible today in the EC, but on a specific

---

[14] In passing, and anticipating a point to which I shall return below, the possible abuses of mixity manifested themselves, in reverse, also in the federal-state situation: there the central authority, in the absence of mixity, has prevented Member States from exercising their legitimate competences and powers, and, in the practice of the so-called "federal clause" which is in a sense the reverse of the "Community clause," federations could, and on occasion did, seek to abuse their non-unitary nature to favor them *vis-à-vis* their external interlocutors. The "Community clause" takes account of the non-unitary nature of the EC by allowing the conclusion of treaties by the Community *in addition* to its Member States. The "federal clause" takes account of the non-unitary nature of the federation by "allowing" its participation in the *absence* of its Member States.

interpretation of European integration and Europe's own brand of federalism.

The federal principle after all should not be confused with its specific manifestation in the federal state.[15] As Pescatore explains:

> [T]he methods of federalism are not only a means of organizing states. It would rather seem that federalism is a political and legal philosophy which adapts itself to all political contexts on both the municipal and the international level, wherever and whenever two basic prerequisites are fulfilled: the search for unity, combined with genuine respect for the autonomy and the legitimate interests of the participant entities.[16]

By studying mixity it may be that we shall not only be learning from the experience of federations – which, with the exception of German writers,[17] is often neglected by European scholars – but also contributing to a better understanding of this political and legal philosophy, federalism, still considered by many as problematic and even ill-fitted to the sphere of foreign policy.

FEDERAL STATES AND INTERNATIONAL TREATIES

Since the mixed *agreement* is the primary focus of this chapter it may be useful to concentrate the federal-state analysis on the treaty-making issue.[18]

---

[15] D. Elazar (ed.), *Self Rule – Shared Rule* (Turtledove: Ramat Gan, Israel, 1979) at 3.

[16] Pescatore, "Foreword" in Sandalow and Stein, *Courts and Free Markets*, p. x.

[17] See, e.g., A. Bleckmann, C. W. A. Timmermans, and E. L. M. Völker (eds.), *Division of Powers between the European Communities and their Member States in the Field of External Relations* (Kluwer: Deventer, 1981) (hereinafter the "Amsterdam Colloque"), especially the contributions by Bleckmann, Seidl-Hohenveldern, *passim*.

[18] There is a vast literature on this subject in relation to every federal state. I wish to express a great intellectual debt to the following comparative works: Bernier, *International Legal Aspects of Federalism*; Ghosh, *Treaties and Federal Constitutions*; Wheare, *Federal Government*; Wildhaber, *Treaty-Making Power and Constitution*; and Oliver, "The Enforcement of Treaties by a Federal State," which are general comparative studies on which I have heavily drawn; and Stein, "Towards a European Foreign Policy?," a full-fledged comparative analysis of European Community and US doctrine and practice in this field which was also invaluable. Other general works which repay careful study are: J. Hendry, *Treaties and Federal Constitutions* (Public Affairs Press, Washington, DC, 1955); E. McWhinney, *Comparative Federalism* (University of Toronto Press: Toronto, 2nd edn., 1965); Sohn and Shafer, "Foreign Affairs," in R. R. Bowie and C. J. Friedrich (eds.), *Studies in Federalism* (Little, Brown: Boston, 1954); Halsjczuk, "Les états fédéraux face au droit international," *Osterreichische Zeitschrift für Offentliches Recht* 13 (1964), 307; Hartman, "Federalism as a Limitation on the Treaty-Making Power of the United States, Western Germany and India," *Western Reserve Law Review* 18 (1966), 134; Looper, "Limitations on the Treaty Power in Federal States," *New York University Law Review* 34 (1959), 1,045; Nettl, "The Treaty Enforcement Power in Federal Constitutions," *Canadian Bar Review* 28 (1970), 1,051; Weiser, "La conclusion d'accords internationaux par les états fédérés allemands, suisses et autrichiens," in Brossard, Patry, and Weiser, *Les pouvoirs extérieurs du Québec* (Presses de

Competence, power, and capacity

The non-unitary character of the federal state manifests itself in this context in relation to three main issues: internal legislative *competence*, treaty-making *power*, and international *capacity*.[19] We must thus inquire as to the following.

1. The extent to which the internal division of *competences* between the central authority and constituent Member States affects the ability of the federal government to secure the implementation of treaty obligations which fall outside its legislative competence. The issue will manifest itself differently in federal systems according to the manner in which treaties take internal legal effect (e.g., monist or dualist) and according to the nature of the obligations themselves (self- or non-self-executing provisions).

2. The extent to which the division of internal competences affects (i.e., limits or otherwise) the *treaty-making powers rationae materiae* of the federal government regardless of any problems which may or may not arise in subsequent implementation. Is the central authority limited to making treaties only in relation to those areas over which it has internal legislative competence? A subsidiary question would be whether the Member States could derive a treaty-making power in those areas over which they have internal competence.

3. The extent to which the non-unitary character of the federal state – as expressed in the above two problems – affects the *international capacity* of the federation or the Member States. In relation to this question our presumption would be that *qua* states federations would enjoy from the international point of view full capacity but there is a question mark over the status of constituent members. Could the federal state invoke in international law its non-unitary character to invalidate an agreement if internal powers or competences were exceeded?

l'Université de Montréal: Montreal, 1967); Sorensen, "Federal States and the International Protection of Human Rights," *American Journal of International Law* 46 (1952), 195.

[19] There is a terminological confusion as regards these terms which are often interchanged and at times confused. I shall be using them throughout in the strict sense which I explain in the text even if at the price of simplification and sacrifice of sophistication. For profound analysis, see, e.g., Bleckmann, "The Competence of the EEC," Amsterdam Colloque; V. Constantinesco, *Compétences et pouvoirs dans les Communautés européennes* (Librairie générale de droit et de jurisprudence: Paris, 1974); E. Freeman, "The Division of Powers between the European Communities and the Member States" *Current Legal Problems* [1977], 159; R. H. Lauwaars, *Lawfulness and Legal Force of Community Decisions* (Sijthoff: Leyden, 1973); Louis, "Quelques réflexions sur la répartition des compétences entre la Communauté européenne et ses états membres," *Revue d'intégration européenne* (1979), 355; Louis, "Répartition des compétences entre la Communauté et ses états membres en matière de relations extérieures," *Revue d'intégration européenne* (1983).

For an illustration of these problems and different solutions thereto I propose to take some typical examples from the practice of several federal states.

Canada

Canada affords the classic and well-known illustration of a federal jurisdiction in which the implementation problem has arisen. In some ways Canada's situation[20] under the British North America Act, her former constitution, was atypical of other federations.[21] In the first place Canada's earlier status as a British Dominion resulted in a piecemeal acquisition of power and capacity to conduct her affairs as an independent actor in the international order. Not until World War II did Canada achieve full independence as an international actor.[22] Her former constitution, a UK Act of Parliament, was perhaps less suggestive to broad teleological interpretation, and the UK Privy Council which for many years was the supreme judicial authority took a strict view of its interpretative task – especially as regards the delicate issue of the division of competences between federation and provinces.[23] Although the federal principle on one view insists on the sacrosanct character of that division, the experience of

---

[20] I will not be treating the Canadian position under its Constitution. In any event the Constitution does not seem to affect this particular issue.

[21] From the large amount of material available I have relied principally on the following: Bernier, *International Legal Aspects of Federalism*; Oliver, "The Enforcement of Treaties by a Federal State"; Wildhaber, *Treaty-Making Power and Constitution*; Wheare, *Federal Government*; and E. McWhinney, *Quebec and the Constitution 1960–1978* (University of Toronto Press: Toronto, Buffalo, 1979), especially chapter 4; "Canadian Federalism and the Foreign Affairs and Treaty Power: The Impact of Quebec's Quiet Revolution," *Canadian Yearbook of International Law* 7 (1969), 3; A. S. Abel with J. L. Laskin, *Laskin's Canadian Constitutional Law* (Carswell: Toronto, 4th edn., 1973) at 202–20; Eaton, "Canadian Judicial Review and the Federal Distribution of Power," *American Journal of Comparative Law* (1958), 47; J. D. Whyte and W. R. Lederman, *Canadian Constitutional Law* (Butterworths: Toronto, 1977) at 171–8; W. R. Lederman, *Continuing Canadian Constitutional Dilemmas* (Butterworths: Toronto, Boston, 1981) at 350–8; Bonenfant, "Les relations extérieures du Québec," *Etudes Internationales* 1 and 2 (1970), 81, 84; Grenon, "De la conclusion des traités et de leur mise en œuvre au Canada," *Canadian Bar Review* 40 (1962), 151; Morin, "La conclusion d'accords internationaux pour les provinces canadiennes à la lumière du droit comparé," *Canadian Yearbook of International Law* 3 (1965), 127; Szablowski, "Creation and Implementation of Treaties in Canada," *Canadian Bar Review* 34 (1956), 28; Fitzgerald, "Educational and Cultural Agreements and Ententes: France, Canada and Quebec," *American Journal of International Law* 60 (1966), 529; See also "Federalism and International Relations" (White Paper of Canadian Government, 1968, authored by P. Martin, the then Canadian Secretary of State for External Affairs).

[22] Cf. R. Dawson, *The Development of Dominion Status 1900–1936* (Oxford University Press: London, New York, 1936).

[23] See Eaton, "Canadian Judicial Review" for a more subtle evaluation of judicial activity. See also Whyte and Lederman, *Canadian Constitutional Law*, Part II.

Canada's southern neighbor is a good example of an erosion, even a collapse of that sanctity for overriding national reasons.[24] The linguistic diversity and separatist tendency of Quebec have accentuated, on the political level, the aforementioned juridical consideration. These factors (and the "federal size" of Canada, ten provinces) while distinguishing her from some other federations, render the Canadian case particularly pertinent for comparative reflection *vis-à-vis* Europe.

The principal federal Canadian dilemma as regards international legal relations has been the competence of the federal government to implement treaty obligations within Canada.

Whereas the federal government historically had full implementing powers of Imperial treaties (concluded by the British Crown between the Empire and foreign countries[25]) the Constitution was silent as regards Canadian "autonomous" treaties. As Canada acquired full external powers the question arose as to those non-Imperial treaties which covered matters which were outside the internal jurisdiction of the federation though inside the treaty-making power.

The situation arose at its sharpest in a case which is so well known as to obviate detailed description. In the *Labour Conventions* case[26] Canada had adhered to some of the ILO Conventions and sought to implement them by *federal* maximum- and minimum-wage legislation. Could Canada's plenary external capacity and internal treaty-making power have the effect of bestowing on the federal government a corresponding internal implementing competence even in the face of a constitutional provision which left the area in question (property and civil rights) to the provinces? As is known Lord Atkin, speaking for the Privy Council, gave a firm negative reply:

> The Dominion cannot, merely by making promises to foreign countries, clothe itself with legislative authority inconsistent with the Constitution which gave it birth.

Interestingly, in the earlier *Radio* case,[27] Viscount Dunedin seems to have given the contrary reply:

> In a question with foreign powers the persons who might infringe some of the stipulations in the Convention would not be the Dominion of Canada as a whole but would be individual persons residing in Canada. These persons must so to speak be kept in order by legislation and the only legislation that can deal with them all at once is Dominion legislation.

---

[24] *Cf.* Sandalow, "The Expansion of Federal Legislative Authority," in Sandalow and Stein, *Courts and Free Markets* at 49*ff.*

[25] British North America Act 1867, section 132.   [26] [1937] AC 326.

[27] [1932] AC 304.

Although in principle both cases have equal authority, suggesting that the question is unresolved,[28] the better view is that the *Labour Conventions* case represents the Canadian position, though this has been queried on several occasions and devices have been sought to overcome some of its harsher consequences.[29]

For us, however, the interest in the *Labour Conventions* case lies in the fact that it highlights one of the potentially inherent difficulties of the federal state in international legal relations as regards implementation.

If one were to adopt the Dunedin thesis one would compromise what some would regard as an essential feature of the federal state. As Wheare points out, the provinces would have discovered that their powers "were much smaller than they had thought, and they must submit to a regulation of their economic and social life by the Dominion Parliament, a regulation of which many of them disapproved."[30] Lederman dramatizes this situation by suggesting that if the Dunedin thesis were accepted with no more, Canadian adherence to, say, the Universal Declaration of Human Rights and Fundamental Freedoms which touches "in one way or another every part of the total legal system of a modern country . . . would simply be the end of Canadian Federalism."[31] In fact most other federal jurisdictions have adopted the Dunedin position, and federalism as a whole does not seem to have come to an end. Other devices have been found to preserve the federal character.

The Atkin thesis is no less problematic. On the one hand it has, in the language of Wheare, the advantage that:

> it guarantees completely the power of the regional governments in a federation to the exclusive control of the matters which are set out as theirs . . . it is in accordance with good federal government . . . [I]f a federation is formed of units which desire to retain the exclusive control over certain matters entirely, a desire to regulate these matters according to their own lights, then provision must be

[28] Lederman, *Continuing Canadian Constitutional Dilemmas* at 354.

[29] One subsequent decision seemed to qualify the *Labour Conventions* case: see *Reference re Ownership of Offshore Mineral Rights* 65 DLR (2d) 376 (1968) especially at 380. But see E. McWhinney, *Quebec and the Constitution 1960–1968* at 43; McWhinney also points out that despite the harsh theoretical critique of the decision, in practice "[n]ot merely has the *Labour Conventions* decision not rendered impossible the conduct of a rational Canadian foreign policy. In fact no single example has ever been cited, in the years since 1937 . . . where its rationale has presented any practical difficulties, or even mild inconvenience in the conduct of Canada's foreign relations. At the concrete, empirical level it has in fact proved easily possible for Canadians to live with the decision.": McWhinney, "Canadian Federalism and the Foreign Affairs and Treaty Power" at 4–5. But see Bernier, *International Legal Aspects of Federalism* at 152–8, who seeks to prove the contrary by several examples, and who concludes at 158: "Canada is clearly at a disadvantage when it comes to participating actively in the development of international co-operation."

[30] Wheare, *Federal Government* at 171.

[31] Lederman, *Continuing Canadian Constitutional Dilemmas* at 357.

made ... whereby the general government cannot invade these fields by legislation to implement a treaty.[32]

On the other hand, the disadvantages are equally clear and are implicit in the Dunedin judgment. Such a ruling could pose a serious impediment to the international maneuverability of Canada since, to quote Wheare once more, "the Dominion ... would be handicapped ... in forming treaty obligations ... because it would be unable to guarantee the performance of obligations so formed."[33] We should add with caution at this point that the handicap may not necessarily be in the international capacity of the federal state. International law concerns itself only to a limited extent with international constitutional arrangement – a subject to which we shall return below. But the Atkin approach might have the effect of restricting the federal willingness in the sense that the federal government would not engage itself in treaties it could not guarantee to implement, and over which it could be held in breach as against other states. This then is one aspect of the federal dilemma to which two seemingly unsatisfactory replies have been given. Are there alternative solutions? It does not seem as if Canada itself has suffered fatally in her international practice. Before examining practical solutions adopted there and in other federal states let us examine first one proposed theoretical solution. Lederman sees a possible juridical solution to the dilemma as follows.

He first suggests that "if national federalism is to continue, there must be certain fundamental matters in respect of which provincial autonomy is more important to Canada than is a national power to perform international obligations concerned with such matters."[34] This, then, would reject the pure application of the Dunedin doctrine. On the other hand he rejects the Atkin principle since it "limits too severely [Canada's] participation in the growing international community."[35] The "midway" solution (and we should note that mixity is not even contemplated), inspired by the *Temperance Act* case,[36] suggests first the notion of "fundamental" provincial matters and second the principle of concurrent competences. In fact, so far it has been implicit in my presentation of the federal dilemma that the situation revolved round a choice between *mutually exclusive* federal and member state competences.

The matter changes if we consider the possibility quite well known in federal systems (including Canada) of concurrent competences. Thus, Lederman suggests, where a matter is to be regarded as "fundamental" to

---

[32] Wheare, *Federal Government* at 176.
[33] *Ibid.* at 171; but see McWhinney, "Canadian Federalism."
[34] Lederman, *Continuing Canadian Constitutional Dilemmas* at 357.   [35] *Ibid.*
[36] [1946] AC 193.

the provinces – an issue which would have to be decided by the Supreme Court of Canada on an issue-by-issue basis (and this is possibly one weakness of this solution) – the Atkin solution would prevail. Canada should not conclude a treaty calling for implementing legislation without the prior consent of the provinces.

However, in "normal" matters (the majority of cases), the federal government could, if the treaty in question were considered important to Canada as a whole, conclude the treaty, and the federal parliament could pass legislation *implementing* it even if this legislation was in an area reserved to the provinces. Crucially the competence of the federal parliament would be *specific* and "would be strictly limited to that necessary to implement the treaty obligation, and other aspects of the subject matter concerned would remain within provincial jurisdiction."[37] Neither the conclusion of the Treaty nor the subsequent legislative implementation should bestow exclusive competence on the federation and thus preempt action by the provinces in this field (unless such action was in direct conflict with the implementing legislation). Competences would be concurrent. Moreover, the federal government would not even be able to use the concurrent competence so acquired even as regards the subject matter of the treaty in any other context. Its powers would be limited to the implementation of the international obligation.

This proposed solution by Lederman may give rise to two brief and anticipatory points concerning Community mixity. Often, especially in the context of *bilateral* mixed agreements, it is really the Community as a whole which has an interest in the agreement and not individual Member States (indeed several *mixed* financial protocols, which include e.g., joint institutional machinery, are simply tacked on to a Community non-mixed agreement).[38] These agreements are mixed ostensibly because they include matters which are, as in Canada, outside the competence of the Community as such – though of course in the Community it is claimed that this lack of competence also limits Community external power and international capacity. There may naturally be a pure political reason why Member States wish to retain mixity even in this bilateral context: perhaps they do not wish to disguise, in terms of the goodwill that the agreements may yield, their national identity. But from the juridical point of view their insistence on mixity might be prompted by the fear that Community competence in the bilateral agreement might give rise:

---

[37] Lederman, *Continuing Canadian Constitutional Dilemmas.*

[38] See, e.g., Additional Protocol to the Agreement between the EEC and the State of Israel, OJ 1978, 270.

1. to claims of general Community competence in the field covered by the agreement; and/or
2. to preemptive-exclusivity claims against the Member States as regards their own treaty-making power and competences.

The Court's jurisprudence, although moderating its early "imperialistic" language on the question of preemption in external relations,[39] is still characterized by a double trend: expanding the boundaries of Community competences – and by implication power and capacity – in the external-relations field coupled with a great emphasis on exclusivity and preemption.[40]

This is a very strong potion for the Member States to swallow, one which is at least partially instrumental in the drive for mixity. Thus, for those to whom mixity seems an evil – even if at times inevitable – the Lederman proposed solution for the Canadian problem, applied *mutatis mutandis* to the Community situation, could be a way of allaying those fears which induce the mixed solution. Since if applied to the European scenario a Community agreement even in relation to matters beyond internal Community competences (assuming that problems of power and capacity could be overcome) would not entrench such matters constantly within Community competence and would certainly not preempt the Member States from operating in the same fields.

The second reflection on the Lederman proposal touches more closely on the comparative-historical theme of this paper. What is characteristic of the proposal is that it does not even raise as an option the possibility of involving the provinces directly in the actual conclusion of the agreement. I certainly do not wish to criticize that writer on this point; there were many internal political reasons in Canada why such a radical option would seem particularly inappropriate there. But at the same time it is a reflection of contemporary federal dogma that international relations should be conducted by the *federal* government; that the question is always construed as one of *enlarging the limited internal competences of the federal government to match its external power and capacity and not one of enlarging the limited external capacities of the constituent member states to match their internal competences.*

Historically, and in terms of the evolution of national (federal) cohesion this has some justification. The full international personality of the federation matched by full external capacity can be regarded as one of the cornerstones of its stated character. This is why even modern federations, keen to establish national cohesion have adopted the Dunedin rather than

[39] See Waelbroeck, "The Emergent Doctrine of Community Pre-emption – Consent and Redelegation" in Sandalow and Stein, *Courts and Free Markets* at 567–71.

[40] See pp. 172–5 below.

the Atkin solution to the power-competence dilemma.[41] This is probably why the European Court has adopted, by and large, a similar "federal" orientation. But in principle and given the maturity of many federations this classical "federal" dogma (which is, on one reading, not federal at all) may not be necessary any longer. It could be argued that its replacement is not feasible because the member states in a federation cannot be international actors. Later I shall attempt to show that some probably still do enjoy a limited, even if wafer-thin, international personality and that the crucial question in any event is their international capacity and that this in fact depends more on internal constitutional arrangements than on strict positive public international law. Indeed this has been the second crucial issue which erupted in Canada in the 1960s. It could also be argued that the international order is incapable of dealing with the juridical and practical problems that a "new federalism" in international relations would imply. But to this one could answer that mixity as it is being explored by the Community disproves this impossibility giving thereby a further option to the Lederman proposal. We shall come back to this issue in the conclusion to this chapter.

United States

The US experience in this area is equally well known and has been treated amply in the literature.[42] In the formal legal sense the solution adopted there is very much diametrically opposite to the Canadian *Labour Conventions* rationale. The federal government (President and Senate) has exclusive jurisdiction to conclude treaties.[43] The states are precluded from any

---

[41] See India's 1950 Constitution, Art. 253; Rhodesia and Nyasaland 1953 Constitution, 2nd Schedule, Part 1; *cf.* Malaya and Nigeria situation in which a limited *Labour Conventions* rationale (over local matters) seems to apply. For fuller discussion see Wheare, *Federal Government* at 177; Ghosh, *Treaties and Federal Constitutions*, chapter 7.

[42] The leading text is L. Henkin, *Foreign Affairs and Constitution* (Foundation Press: Mineola, NY, 1972). In addition, I have relied principally on Stein, "Towards a European Foreign Policy?" and P. Hay and R. D. Rotunda, *The United States Federal System* (Oceana: New York, 1982), especially 44–71. Also repaying careful study are A. D. Sofaer, *War, Foreign Affairs and Constitutional Power: The Origins* (Ballinger: Cambridge, MA, 1976); G. Gunther, *Cases and Materials on Constitutional Law* (Foundation Press: Mineola, NY, 1975), 266–76; A. H. Kelly and W. H. Harbison, *The American Constitution* (Norton: New York, 1976), chapter 31; Potter, "Inhibitions upon the Treaty-Making Power of the United States," *American Journal of International Law* 28 (1934), 456; Rodgers, "The Capacity of States of the Union to Conclude International Agreements: The Background and Some Recent Developments," *American Journal of International Law* 61 (1967), 1,021; Richberg, "The Bricker Amendment and the Treaty Power," *Virginia Law Review* 39 (1953), 753.

[43] US Constitution, Art. II, section 2, cl. 1. On executive agreements as a growing executive means for engaging the USA internationally, see Henkin, *Foreign Affairs and Constitution* at 420.

"treaty"-making and may enter into an "agreement or compact" with another state or foreign power only with consent of the Congress.[44] Moreover, treaties do not need incorporation into domestic law; the constitution proclaims them to be the supreme law of the land and binding upon states.[45] The question arises, firstly, as to the limitations on the treaty-making power of the federal government with reference to the internal distribution of competences (a matter which as such did not pose itself in Canada where federal treaty-making *power* is regarded as plenary); and, secondly, as to the ability of Congress to pass legislation implementing a non-self-executing treaty where such legislation encroaches on competences reserved to the member states.

Sufficient for our purposes will be a brief allusion to the more important judicial decisions on the issue. As regards powers, *Geofroy* v. *Riggs*[46] establishes the principle that treaties cannot violate constitutional limitations such as the Bill of Rights and similar constitutional restraints (a change in the form of government, cession of territory without the consent of the state concerned, etc.). Likewise in *Reid* v. *Covert*[47] Justice Black's opinion is considered definitive:

> [N]o agreement with a foreign nation can confer power on the Congress, or on any other branch of government, which is free from the restraints of the constitution.[48]

But what of allocative limitations? How relevant is the internal division of competences within the American system? Can it be said that treaties cannot touch on matters which normally are reserved to the member states? And what of the subsequent problem of implementation?

Here the *locus classicus* is *Missouri* v. *Holland*.[49] While the US Supreme Court (through Holmes J) accepted that there may be qualifications to the treaty-making power itself, it rejected the allocative principle as constituting, without more, such a limitation. Perhaps one should mention one phrase in the judgment which gives the extra-constitutional integrationist rationale of this sweeping power: "It is obvious that there may be matters of the sharpest exigency for the national well being that an act of Congress could not deal with but that a treaty followed by such an act could ..."[50] In this statement lurks a possible qualification, namely whether the treaty is

---

[44] US Constitution, Art. I, section 10, cl. 3; Art. I, section 10, cl. 1.

[45] US Constitution, Art. VI, cl. 2. On the hierarchical relationship between treaty law and normal federal and state legislature, see Stein, "Towards a European Foreign Policy?"; A. Cassese (ed.), *The Impact of Foreign Affairs Committees on Foreign Policy* (Oceana: New York, 1982) at 116–19, per Y. Dinstein and R. Gardner.

[46] 133 US 258 (1890).   [47] 354 US 1 (1957) at 16.

[48] For a fuller analysis and other cases, see Hay and Rotunda, *The United States Federal System* at 47.

[49] 252 US 416 (1920).   [50] *Ibid.* at 433.

really one of such national concern; but we shall not deal with this question here.[51] The judgment then confirmed that as regards treaties Congress could bring in implementing legislation (and self-executing measures could take direct effect) even in areas which normally would be reserved to the states and not the federal government.

This apparent total matching of external power with internal legislative competence was the subject of judicial and political strife[52] but *Missouri* v. *Holland* is apparently still good law.

The US experience is instructive in qualifying and rendering more subtle (and hence complex) the very definition of the federal dilemma as outlined above. It was suggested that adoption of the *Labour Conventions* rationale and a failure to match the external power with internal implementing competence even if going beyond the internal federal demarcation could lead to a crippling effect on the international treaty activity of the federal state or to the danger of assuming obligations which the federal government could not subsequently fulfill. The USA by virtue of its explicit constitutional provisions, its monist system, and judicial interpretation in the *Missouri* v. *Holland* vein seems then to have escaped from all these dangers: external powers, subject to non-allocative constitutional limitations, seem plenary, and implementing competences unimpeded. But what then of American federalism and the division of competences between states and federation? Have these been really compromised? Have the *Missouri* v. *Holland* and Dunedin doctrine adopted in the USA really signaled the death of the federal principle?

Two points, one minor, one major, serve to illustrate the fallacy of such a dichotomous, all or nothing, consequence. In the first place, it is clear that the potential implementing difficulties of the federal constitutional structure are not unique. The same type of problem may arise by virtue of substantive unconstitutionality of a treaty – a phenomenon which may occur in unitary states as well.[53] Also, in federations such as the USA, where treaties have a status which is equal, but not higher than parliamentary law, any subsequent parliament can frustrate the domestic implementation of conventional foreign policy by enacting laws in violation of a treaty.

These considerations lead us to the major point. It is artificial to regard the federal dilemma in purely legal terms and to call for a solution in terms of some sort of juridical compromise – as the one suggested by Lederman – between the Atkin and Dunedin extremes. The compromise can be political.

---

[51] The issue of limits to treaty-making power will be discussed below in the context of the Australian experience.

[52] The famous (defunct) Bricker Amendment. See Richberg, "The Bricker Amendment."

[53] See Wildhaber, *Treaty-Making Power and Constitution*, Part III.

Every federation, by its nature, has some element of such representation of state interests and powers at federal-government level – though clearly the form, strength, and influence of the state element will manifest themselves in a variety of permutations in different systems. The executive, traditionally charged with the negotiation and signature of treaties, will depend, *inter alia*, on this representation not only in the specificity of ratification of a treaty but also for its political support and overall legitimacy. The greater the measure of this dependence, formal or informal, the less acute becomes the problem of granting the federal government a full matching of its external power with its internal legislative competence since the federal government will treat with great caution this liberty granted to it. We can go even further and say that in the USA, to the extent that a federal ethos is part of the political and cultural baggage of American politicians and law-makers, the license given by *Missouri* v. *Holland* has *not* posed a threat to federalism.

This reasoning is I believe confirmed by fact. *Missouri* v. *Holland*, and indeed its predecessor cases, did not open the floodgates of wholesale federal encroachment. Thus Bernier lists an entire array of practice where the USA refrained from signing treaties because of the federal ethos (or its fear that the Senate would not approve) despite the license of *Missouri* v. *Holland*.[54]

And in their very recent study Hay and Rotunda conclude on this point that:

> United States treaty practice, both multilateral and bilateral, continues to show reluctance to utilize the treaty power when the effect would be to displace private law shaped (often with substantial variations) by the states and when moreover the federation does not possess independent domestic law-making power.[55]

At the same time the US Supreme Court clearly preferred not to restrict on allocative grounds the international maneuverability of the federal government. Perhaps it could take this extreme solution *because* it believed that the political system of checks and balances, the primary position given to the Senate (as representative of member-state interests) and the pervasive federal ethos would be sufficient guarantee against abuse.

Perhaps, and I am no more than speculating, in Canada with the notorious problem of Quebec which might have found itself permanently

---

[54] Bernier, *International Legal Aspects of Federalism* at 161–3; see also Oliver, "The Enforcement of Treaties by a Federal State" at 387–9; Wildhaber, *Treaty-Making Power and Constitution* at 334–7.

[55] Hay and Rotunda, *The United States Federal System* at 70–1. It has been suggested that this reluctance might be due to other factors: the disinterest of the US federal government in private law international treaties: Oliver, "The Enforcement of Treaties by a Federal State." Another explanation might be the use of federalism as an excuse in international fora for not signing treaties the content of which displeases the executive.

in a minority in the federal political game[56] this confidence of the US Supreme Court in their political system would have been misplaced. In addition, one could say that any other solution would be extremely difficult to adopt or implement in the USA with its fifty states.

Later we shall see that in federally smaller states (e.g., Canada, Germany, Australia) co-operative federalism between member states and federal government is advocated as a solution to the power–competence dilemma. This is gaining ground even in the US model.[57] Another vehicle of co-operative federalism in this field applicable to the USA is the involvement of Senate members in the foreign-relations process.[58]

Finally, one is left with one perplexing reflection. The US experience tends to demonstrate how the political factor can render acceptable – in federal terms – what may, from the strict juridical point of view, seem an extreme and unacceptable solution. One may legitimately wonder why the Member States of the European Community are pressing so hard for mixed agreements on the ostensible ground of lack of Community power-capacity when, in any event, they could control so tightly, as they do, any exercise of such increased capacity and/or power at the negotiation, conclusion, and implementation level.

The answer to this question inevitably involving legal and political consideration will be attempted in the third part of this chapter.

Australia

In Australia[59] it would seem that the Constitution itself[60] gives the federal government the competence to implement any legislation if pursuant to

---

[56] *Cf.* McWhinney, *Quebec and the Constitution 1960–1978, passim.*

[57] Thus per Bernier, *International Legal Aspects of Federalism* at 197: "[I]t is not unusual for the federal government to consult various states before signing international engagements relating to their field of competence." The USA also has a Conference of Governors which meets annually to discuss relations with the federal government and since 1967 there has been an office of Special Assistant to the Secretary of State for liaison with the governors in the area of external relations.

[58] See generally Kohl, "Congressional Foreign Affairs Committees in the United States of America," in A. Cassese (ed.), *Parliamentary Foreign Affairs Committees: The National Setting* (Oceana: New York, 1982) at 285.

[59] I have relied principally on: C. Howard, *Australian Federal Constitutional Law* (Law Book Co.: Sydney, 1972) at 421–60; W. Anstey-Wynes, *Legislative, Executive and Judicial Powers in Australia* (Law Book Co.: Melbourne, 4th edn., 1970) at 89–90 and 383–409; and Rowe, "Aspects of Australian Federalism and the European Communities Compared" in M. Cappelletti, M. Secombe, and J. H. H. Weiler (eds.), *Integration through Law* (Walter de Gruyter: Berlin, New York, 1985).

[60] See Art. 51(29); see Howard, *Australian Federal Constitutional Law* for an analysis of the other constitutional provisions pertaining to the matter.

external affairs. The internal federal dilemma then turns on the meaning of this term. Thus, implementation, an issue which in Canada and the USA was solved by judicial decision, has been given in principle an explicit constitutional reply in Australia, falling on the Dunedin rather than the Atkin side of the fence.

Interestingly, Howard considers the possibility of the limitation on the implementing competences of the federal government as "inherently improbable." This is so because such a solution would limit Australian federal competence "so far as they required implementation by domestic legislation, solely by reference to its legislative competence in internal affairs." In his view such a criterion would be "an irrelevant consideration." His justification is not unconvincing and applies to all those federal states which have matched, with or without restrictions, the implementing federal competences with the plenary external powers – even if this means a compromise of an important federal principle:

> [I]nternal limitations on [federal] legislative power find their origin and justification in internal factors collectively to be described as the balance of interest between [federal] and regional considerations. By definition these have no relevance to matters affecting the standing of Australia in the international community or the advancement of its interests through its relations with that Community. That being an affair of national and not regional concern, it is wholly within the proper sphere of [Australian federal] competence, even if it finds its expression from time to time in such occurrences as commercial arrangements which in detail directly affect some parts of the country but not others.[61]

This of course is a restatement of the classical doctrine which objected to Atkin's solution. It takes perhaps too little account of the growing nexus between international and domestic affairs. Lederman's warning that some international texts might if adopted sound the death knell of federalism – at least in the strict legal sense – may not be entirely irrelevant even to the Australian position. In fairness, Howard is aware of the dangers and suggests the need for some sort of unspecified compromise – though the only formal limitation he suggests is, as in the USA, the substantive (as distinct from the allocative) principles of the Constitution itself.

In earlier court decisions,[62] the Australian High Court although sensitive to the delicacy of the issue never sought to restrict the principle that the federal government/legislature should have the competence to implement foreign treaties. Instead, to a greater extent than in Canada and the USA, the question has been whether the federal external power – or, more

---

[61] Howard, *Australian Federal Constitutional Law* at 444.
[62] *R. v. Burgess, ex parte Henry* (1936) 55 CLR 608; *Airlines of New South Wales Pty. Ltd.* v. *New South Wales (No. 2)* (1965) 113 CLR 54.

precisely, federally *enforceable* external powers – should be limited either by reference to the allocation of internal competences (to which the reply has consistently been no) or by reference to the content of an external agreement and the measure to which it could be considered an exercise of *external affairs*.

Before discussing these limitations on the federally enforceable external power, it should not be thought that the neat legal solution to the question of federal implementation could operate in a political vacuum. In the USA and Canada the primary (though not exclusive) solution was to be found in the organization of state interests within federal government (with very limited machinery for gubernatorial consultation) and even an occasional grant to states of permission to conclude agreements with a neighboring foreign member state. Australia on the one hand has adopted a strict rule which bars the member states any international power. On the other hand with only seven member states it could perhaps more easily adopt co-operative federalism solutions.

Thus, in 1977, there was an internal agreement by the Australian Premiers' Conference that member states would be consulted as regards treaties having implications for matters within the competence of the states. This was despite the fact that formally the federal government could proceed without such consultation and give internal legislative effect to such an agreement (if pursuant to external affairs). A second technique to be used was an arrangement to include member-state representatives in negotiating delegations and the final technique was an undertaking by the federal government to seek to introduce where relevant a federal clause in such agreements[63] or the insertion of a "federal reservation" in the ratification of such agreements. Thus, in ratifying the UN International Covenant on Civil and Political Rights, Australia did insert such a reservation – clearly inconsistent with Article 50 of the Convention – which provides that: "The provisions of the present Covenant shall extend to all parts of federal states without any limitation or exception." One has here the reverse-mirror situation of the Community whereby Member States seeking to ratify the Law of the Sea Convention in the absence of Community participation would – at best – be under an obligation to express a reservation as regards Community competence. In both situations the reservation would seem to fly in the face of the international instrument.

These attempted solutions to the federal dilemma of Australia have

---

[63] See Rowe, "Aspects of Australian Federalism"; and Burmester, "The Australian States and Participation in the Foreign Policy Process," *University of Florida Law Review* 9 (1978), 257.

surfaced clearly in the recent case of *Koowarta*.[64] The case concerned an action by an aboriginal Australian against Queensland concerning land rights. At issue, *inter alia*, was the validity of certain sections of the Australian Racial Discrimination Act of 1975. These sections of the Act intruded on State competences under the Constitution and one of the questions before the Australian High Court was whether the allegedly offending sections, enacted in implementation of the International Convention on the Elimination of All Forms of Racial Discrimination (1966) to which Australia was a party,[65] could be struck down since they were, by virtue of their subject matter, not concerned with external affairs. Whereas in the Canadian and American illustrations given above the federal government was challenged directly on the implementation issue, here the challenge seemed to include more directly the possible limitation of the external power itself or at least of internally enforceable federal power which crossed the demarcation between Commonwealth and States. The seventy-eight-page judgment may serve in the eyes of one writer "to introduce all the major elements of . . . Australian federalism."[66] We shall glimpse at those aspects concerning the external-relations issues. In general I think the case illustrates a growing sensitivity to the delicacy of the federal dilemma and to solutions developed so far.

Since this is probably the most recent and thus least-known decision of a supreme federal court on the question of external powers of a federation, it may be worth citing in some greater detail. In a minority opinion, Chief Justice Gibbs while acknowledging that the issue was a "great constitutional battleground"[67] confirmed in accordance with earlier case law the relatively wide interpretation given to the Australian constitutional term "external affairs," the fact that the exercise of these "external affairs" gives rise to an autonomous head of legislative competences, and finally that such competence would be limited by express and implied substantive (non-allocative) provisions of the Constitution itself.

But what of an international treaty which did not as such directly involve a *relationship* with other countries? Would federal adhesion to this type of treaty also bestow internal implementing competence even if transgressing the internal divisions of federal-member state jurisdiction? In Gibbs CJ's view this was a novel question to be decided since on his reading the International Covenant − especially sections 9 and 12 − did not concern such an international relationship.

Gibbs CJ first affirms, in accordance with practice and doctrine, that no

[64] (1982) 39 *Australian Law Reports* 417.
[65] Australia signed the Convention on October 13, 1966 and ratified it on September 30, 1975.
[66] Rowe, "Aspects of Australian Federalism."
[67] (1982) 39 *Australian Law Reports* 417 at 430.

"question arises as to the power of Australia to enter into [such treaties]" since the Governor-General, exercising the prerogative power of the Crown, can make treaties on subjects which are not within the legislative power of the general federal power. In other words the Australian federal government has a plenary treaty-making power – subject only to substantive, non-allocative, constitutional limitations. In this it is in the same position as Canada and the USA.

But "[t]he power of the [federal] parliament to carry treaties into effect is not necessarily as wide as the executive power to make them." Australia finds itself on this issue between Canada and the USA. It has not got a permissive license as in *Missouri* v. *Holland*. Neither is it restricted by a *Labour Conventions* rule. It may implement treaties even across the federal line provided the treaty-making power was exercised in pursuance of external affairs.[68]

The combination of a federal state and dualist system of treaty incorporation raises the federal dilemma at its sharpest. In the first place, the federal government's international obligations might be frustrated by the federal legislature. This problem, not unique to federal states, may be obviated by withholding ratification until legislative consent is assured. In the second place, the international obligation might be frustrated again by the federal legislature's lack of implementing competence.

Gibbs CJ rejects the view that such federal incapacity would render Australia "an international cripple unable to participate fully in the emerging world order." In fact, he relies on a passage in the *Labour Conventions* case where Lord Atkin explained that the federal state as a whole was fully equipped in its international posture since although powers were distributed between province and federal government, together they constituted the totality of legislative powers. The practical way to proceed was by "co-operation between the Dominion and the Provinces." To be sure co-operative federalism has become the hallmark or a slogan of modern practice in several federations and the techniques mentioned above are examples of its usage in the field of foreign affairs in Australia.

What is important is this crystal-clear affirmation that there is nothing objectionable in legal logic for a federal government to engage in international agreements in relation to areas over which it does not have internal competence.

Gibbs CJ, cognizant in the 1980s to an extent even greater than Lord Atkin could have been in the 1930s of the interdependence of internal and external matters, seems to be veering towards the *Labour Conventions*

---

[68] A similar restriction might be read into *Missouri* v. *Holland*. The issue has never been put to the test conclusively.

rationale. Perhaps he can do that because of his faith in the inherent cohesion of Australia whereby greater sensitivity to member-state autonomy even in the field of foreign relations would not seem threatening. Of course it is possible that he was – in what is acknowledged as a delicate case involving sensitive political and social issues other than the federal one – simply seeking a way to reach what to him would seem a desirable substantive result.

Whatever the reason may be, he expresses a clear-minded fear of the *Missouri* v. *Holland* fully fledged doctrine which could mean that "the power of the [federal] Parliament could be expanded by simple executive action and expanded in such a way as to render meaningless that limitation and division of sovereign legislative authority which is of the essence of federalism."

He then suggests that the constitutional parameters of implementing competence should only reach to the limits of federal external power and that this in turn should extend only to treaties "with respect to a matter which itself can be described as an external affair." This is "defined" (vaguely) to exclude treaties such as the UN Convention which concerned internal affairs and not international relations in the proper sense. The definitional difficulties of this view are not really our concern except as an illustration of a renewed sensibility to the issue. As mentioned above Gibbs CJ relies on co-operative federalism in general to solve the debilitating effect which his view, had it been accepted, would entail. But even he admits "if such co-operation is not forthcoming" in effect the federal parliament would be limited in its ability to implement such "non-external-affairs" treaties. It might seem a contradiction in terms to describe adherence to an international treaty as not being an exercise of external affairs. But here lies a certain value choice: the very rationale which points out the untenability in today's interdependent world of distinguishing between matters which are domestic by nature and others which concern international relations is for some the justification for condemning even more forcefully the *Labour Conventions* rationale as impeding the federal state from taking its full place in international affairs. For others it could be the justification of an even greater insistence against internal federal collapse consequent on the exercise of the external power.

Indeed the division of opinion is reflected in *Koowarta*. Whereas Gibbs CJ emphasized in his reasoning the dangers to the federal division by a full matching of an unlimited external power with internal legislative competences, Mason J (in the majority) points out the true ramifications of a fragmentation between power and competences which would be "altogether too disturbing to contemplate . . . [and would be] a certain recipe for indecision and confusion, seriously weakening Australia's stance and standing in international affairs."[69]

He is also skeptical of co-operative federalism: "It is unrealistic to suggest in the light of our knowledge and experience of [federal] state co-operation and of co-operation between the states that the discharge of Australia's international obligations by legislation can be safely and sensibly left to the states acting uniformly in co-operation."[70]

And for him the question of the disturbance of the federal balance is dismissed by three arguments of considerable persuasion:

1. The allocation of plenary external power to the federal government is part of the federal balance which is as important as the internal division of competences.
2. The actual exercise is not in practice likely to affect significantly the internal division. For him the problem is theoretical.
3. To the extent that it does so disturb the division of power this disturbance "is essential to Australia's participation in world affairs."[71]

He goes as far as legitimating federal legislative competence pursuant to issues which are the "topic of international debate, discussion and negotiation . . . [even] before Australia enters into a treaty relating to it."[72] This is the most full-blooded version of the view which would consider *ipso facto* any treaty as an exercise of external affairs and would in effect become virtually indistinguishable from the *Missouri* v. *Holland* situation. For this view there was no majority on the court though on the facts a majority construed the Convention itself as coming within a definition of external affairs.

Of interest in the judgment of Murphy J is his characterization of the member states: they "have no international personality; unlike the Commonwealth [Australia as a whole] they are not nation-states. Any purported treaty or agreement between any or all of the Australian states and a foreign power is a nullity."[73] Here then we have not only the constitutional issues of competence and power which are essentially unitarist but also a strong affirmation of the international legal issue of capacity which are equally and emphatically unitarist.

Wilson J (in the minority) also held that the treaty in question lacked an "external" aspect and thus could not be implemented by federal legislation. Interestingly Wilson J recognizes that international devices to solve the federal dilemma such as the "federal clause" are less available today: "the tide of international opinion runs strongly against such clauses leaving only resort to the practice of recording reservations to the ratification of a convention or treaty."[74] We could add that the international tide seems at

---

[69] (1982) 39 *Australian Law Reports* 417 at 460.   [70] *Ibid*. at 462.   [71] *Ibid*. at 463.
[72] *Ibid*. at 467.   [73] *Ibid*. at 469.   [74] *Ibid*. at 479.

least to begin to run contrary to reservations though one may add that the efficacy of "no-reservations" clauses in multilateral treaties is doubtful since breach is rarely attacked. But even the disappearance of such international devices which would render his restrictive view even more difficult for Australia did not convince him to take the majority view.

Wilson J realizes the implementation dilemma that this poses. His reply is instructive. On the basis of an important empirical analysis[75] he asserts that the problem is more theoretical than real. But then – of particular interest to us – he resorts to the co-operative federalism concept:

> The task of enduring the co-operation of the states may present a political challenge, although the developing practice of including state representatives in [federal] delegations to international conferences on subjects which may call for implementation by state legislatures augurs well for future co-operation in the pursuit of an effective foreign policy and the maintenance of good international relations.

This of course is in fact the nearest a federal state, denying external capacity to its member units, can come to mixity. It in fact resembles the Community (non-mixed) negotiating model.

Brennan J, while accepting possible allocative limitations based on the content of "external affairs," accepted that the UN Convention did constitute such an external affair. In this case then, by a bare majority, the federal government's implementing legislation of the UN Convention was held valid. But four out of the seven judges had shown an acute sensitivity to the federal issue and have suggested *in principle* a limitation on enforceable treaty-making power. We have also come close to making mandatory co-operative federal structures in the external affairs field. It might be that the tide of federalism is beginning to shift back even in this sensitive area. In Australia then federal treaty-making power is plenary and the member states are denied any residual power. To the extent that a treaty needs internal implementation and encroaches on member-state competences, the federal government is enabled constitutionally to bring in federal implementing legislation although this is qualified in principle to treaties concerning external affairs.

Germany and Switzerland

In Germany and Switzerland we have occasion to see variations of the solutions to the issues which we have examined above. Germany, at least in the formal sense, tends more than other federal states towards an acknowl-

---

[75] See McWhinney, *Quebec and the Constitution 1960–1978*; but see also Bernier, *International Legal Aspects of Federalism*.

edgment of her federal structure even in the foreign affairs field although unlike other aspects of German federalism the presumption here is in favor of the federation and not the Länder. In Switzerland the formal tendency is the converse, although in practice this is mitigated. Both systems have evoked methods of overcoming the difficulties inherent in these basic choices.

The German Constitution[76] grants the federation the power to conclude treaties in relation, naturally, to subjects over which the central authority has exclusive jurisdiction as well as concurrent jurisdiction. Interestingly, and we shall return to this matter below, the Länder are also granted by the Constitution power to conclude treaties within *their* sphere of competence provided there is federal-government approval. In principle this approval, at least where the area is within exclusive Länder competence, is not totally discretionary and may be withheld only for genuine overriding reasons and in any event does not affect the capacity of the Länder. An agreement would probably be valid even if consent was withheld.[77] As Wildhaber points out the ambiguity of the Constitution does not allow a conclusive reply as to the extent to which the federal treaty-making power may invade the internal exclusive competence of the Länder.[78] The matter has been not only the subject of scholarly debate but also a source of political and party differences. The problem is accentuated since in the Federal Republic to use the words of Oliver, "treaty-making and treaty-enforcing (legislative) powers are not bifurcated . . . the approval of the use of the [federal] treaty-making power by the [federal] act . . . in itself also gives the treaty whatever internal effect as law it is deemed to need to have."[79] Accordingly, where terms of the international agreements are so capable (by their wording and purpose) they may produce direct effect in municipal German courts. Is the treaty-making power of the federation federally limited? One view is that Germany goes one step further than Australia in which

---

[76] Art. 32 provides: 1. The conduct of relations with foreign states is the concern of the Federation. 2. Before the conclusion of a treaty affecting the special interests of Länd, this Länd must be consulted in sufficient time. 3. In so far as the Länder have power to legislate, they may, with the consent of the Federal Government, conclude treaties with foreign states. Translation from Wildhaber, *Treaty-Making Power and Constitution* at 302–10; Bernier, *International Legal Aspects of Federalism*, passim; Leisner, "A propos de la répartition des compétences en matière de conclusion des traités dans la République Fédérale d'Allemagne," *Annuaire Français de droit internationale* 6 (1960), 291; "The Foreign Relations of the Member States of the Federal Republic of Germany," *University of Toronto Law Journal* 16 (1966), 346; Rousseau, "Commentaires sur le concordat entre le Sanit-Siège et la Basse-Saxe," *Revue générale de droit international public* 69 (1965), 768; McWhinney, "Comment on the Concordat Case," *Canadian Bar Review* 35 (1957), 842.

[77] See *Port of Kohl* case, BVerfGE, 2 (1953), 347 and see Leisner, "A propos de la répartition"; Wildhaber, *Treaty-Making Power and Constitution* at 306.

[78] *Ibid.* at 304*ff.*   [79] Oliver, "The Enforcement of Treaties by a Federal State" at 370.

enforceable treaty-making power is limited. Here it is the power itself which is subject not only to substantive limitations but also to allocative limitations. A compromise view is that federal treaty-making power (and the discretion to prohibit Länder treaties) may extend into exclusive Länder control only if the treaty concerned is of high political sensitivity. Some consider that treaty-making power could be plenary. In relation to the treaties establishing the EC the matter received of course the well known reply in the *Internazionale Handelsgesellschaft*[80] case. The restriction set out in that case seems to be limited to constitutional issues such as human rights (as in the USA) and not probably to questions of allocation of competences.[81]

As regards internal enforcement and internal implementation of treaties (the provisions of which are not self-executing), the famous and obscure 1957 *Concordat* case[82] seems to have given a reply in line with the *Labour Conventions* rationale: although the Federal Constitutional Court accepted the validity of the treaty in question and its transformation into municipal law, it held nevertheless that the Länder could not be held bound by a concordat between the Vatican and Germany which invaded the domain reserved to the Länder in matters of education.

This tension received a political if not legal solution in the well-known 1957 *Lindau Compact* where the Länder actually delegated in relation to certain matters[83] plenary treaty-making power to the federal government although this was qualified by the requirement that the treaties should be typically and predominantly "federal." For its part, where Länder interests are concerned, the federal government agreed not only to consult but also to seek approval of the Länder before an agreement would become binding. This compact, whatever its strict constitutionality, has opened the way to smooth Germany's treaty-making practice. It is supported by a permanent commission of Länder representatives which advises the federal foreign office. This means that the Germany is unlikely even to *sign* a treaty for which subsequent Länder approval will not be forthcoming.

In addition to the *Lindau Compact*, the federal government has made use

---

[80] Case 11/70, *Internazionale Handelsgesellschaft* [1970] ECR 1,125.

[81] In Case 9/74, *Casagrande* [1974] ECR 773 at recital 15, the Court held, *inter alia*: "[S]ince Regulations, under Article 189 of the Treaty, have general application and are binding in their entirety and directly applicable in all Member States, it is irrelevant that the conditions in question are laid down by rules issued by the central power, by the authorities of a country forming part of a Federal State." Indeed, what the Community had done in that case might have been forbidden to the German Federation itself. *Cf.* Advocate-General Warner at 783.

[82] BVerGE 6 (1957), 309. See McWhinney, *Quebec and the Constitution 1960–1978*.

[83] Consular relations, commerce, navigation, residence, trade, financial transactions, immunities and privileges, and adherence to international organizations. Wildhaber, *Treaty-Making Power and Constitution* at 305.

of the device of including Länder representatives in negotiating delegations. Thus although the constitutional principle, leaning towards the *Labour Conventions* model would, in theory, suggest difficulties for the exercise of a federal foreign policy (at least in so far as treaty-making is concerned), the practice, by virtue of the political devices used, has led to other results. Wildhaber concludes by suggesting that: "The German federal government is on the whole not handicapped by the federal structure in the conduct of foreign relations."[84] Finally, by contrast with the USA, the Federal Republic has shown far less "reluctance"[85] based on federal sensibilities to conclude treaties. It could be, however, as I have hinted above, that US (and to some extent Canadian) reluctance *vis-à-vis* ILO and Human Rights Conventions which is often attributed to this federal sensibility can be given two other explanations:

1. a political unhappiness with the welfare-state orientation of these instruments which are then rejected with the federal sensibility being a convenient international excuse; and
2. a decreasing interest of the federal organs with private-law treaties evident particularly in the USA.[86]

In Switzerland, despite scholarly disagreement, both doctrine and practice suggest that in the first place the treaty-making power of the federal government *rationae materiae* is plenary and that the internal competence is matched in the sense that "self-executing" provisions of treaties even in matters normally within cantonal jurisdiction will be operational and that the federal government could enact implementing legislation even transgressing the federal allocation of competences.[87]

However, as in the USA and other federal states where this drastic legal solution has been adopted, the theoretical potential for federal obliteration is attenuated by political practice. Not only will there be consultation with the cantons, but the government in such cases will always seek in the first place implementation by the cantons or a constitutional amendment enabling the federal power explicit specific competence. Moreover, Switzerland, despite these formal legal powers which would enable it to

---

[84] *Ibid.* at 309.

[85] The term used independently by Oliver and Wildhaber is probably by now a term of art.

[86] Oliver, "The Enforcement of Treaties by a Federal State."

[87] Wildhaber, *Treaty-Making Power and Constitution* at 310–21; J. F. Aubert, *Traité de droit constitutionnel suisse* (Dalloz: Paris, 1967) at 223–5, 255–61; Looper, "The Treaty Power in Switzerland," *American Journal of Comparative Law* 7 (1958), 178; Secretan, "Swiss Constitutional Problems and the International Labour Organization," *International Labour Review* 56 (1947), 1; Rousseau, "Influence de la structure fédérale de la suisse sur la conclusion des traités internationaux élaborés par l'UNESCO," *Revue générale de droit international public* 69 (1965), 840; P. Guggenheim, *Traité de droit international public* (Georg: Geneva, 2nd edn., 1967) at 142–53, 179–80.

function as a unitary state in the international field, has operated a policy of federal self-restraint having a restrictive practice of treaty conclusion in relation to treaties encroaching on cantonal powers. This would be consonant with her traditional cautious foreign policy in general. Externally, Switzerland could be said to have no restrictions derived from her federal nature. Internally, her federal character could be said to be preserved by convention rather than legal norms.

The international dimension

In general, the non-unitary actor is an irritating nuisance from the point of view of international law and the international legal order, dominated as they are by unitary states.[88] As we noted above, if we take the federal principle at its widest the number of states with some form of federal arrangement may be great. But as for international-treaty relations only a very limited number of federal states seem to raise particular problems.[89] We have seen that in most federal states from the constitutional point of view the federal government enjoys plenary power as regards the subject matter of its external contacts (subject usually to non-allocative constitutional principles) but that the internal division of legislative competences sometimes creates a reluctance, even in those federal states where there is full matching between external powers and internal competences, to use this potential freely. From the international-law point of view the basic premise is that the federal state is an actor enjoying full capacities (and responsibilities) identical to any unitary state. The principle that municipal law cannot be pleaded as a valid justification for an international illegal act is valid as regards the internal federal arrangement with, of course, the exception encapsulated in Article 46 of the Vienna Convention to which I shall return below. Two issues are pertinent to our discussion:

1. the manner in which federal states – constrained by their internal rules or ethos – have sought to accommodate the federal principle on the international plane; and
2. the extent to which member states enjoy a capacity in international law to conclude treaties.

As regards the first problem, federal states have sometimes sought, in the negotiation of international obligations, a recognition of their specific problem. This may be by way of a federal clause in a multilateral treaty or a

---

[88] Problems arise as regards treaty succession, responsibility for international delicts, jurisdiction, territorial seas, and sovereign and diplomatic immunity. See generally, Bernier, *International Legal Aspects of Federalism*, *passim*; D. P. O'Connell, *International Law* (Stevens: London, 2nd edn., 1970) at 295*ff.*
[89] See note 12 at p. 133 above.

federal reservation if the treaty so permits. The issue of federalism emerged in bilateral relations[90] (like the first "Community clauses" in bilateral mixed agreements) but received most attention in the multilateral context of the ILO. The original ILO clause although badly drafted[91] could clearly favor those federal states who claimed to be affected by it by allowing them to avoid ratification of obligations imposed on other ILO members.

The ILO federal clause was amended in 1946.[92] It would seem that under the new formulation whereas federal states availing themselves of the clause would face certain obligations as regards promotion of the ILO Convention within their respective member states, the criterion for the actual application of the clause was no longer the formal legal ability of a federal state to make or implement a convention but rather the "appropriateness" as decided by the federal government itself. Other treaties include similar lax provisions.[93] This "laxity" towards the federal states may be contrasted with some modern treaties and in particular the UN Human Rights Conventions of 1966 where a federal clause was accepted in name but rejected in substance.[94] Our examination of internal federal constitutional law reveals that from the strict legal point of view federal clauses are no longer justified since in the overwhelming majority of federal states the federal government may implement treaty obligations even if these are within the area reserved to the member states. Moreover, the evolution of co-operative federal structures and processes (consultation with member states and participation of member states in negotiating delegations) seems to diffuse the wider internal political problem.

Whatever form a federal clause takes, it abolishes strict reciprocity between the contracting parties to an international agreement. The ILO "appropriateness" formulation with its inherent subjectivity seems to give the federal government too wide a discretion. Federations might evoke the

---

[90] The main treatment is Looper, "Federal State Clauses in Multilateral Instruments," *British Yearbook of International Law* 32 (1955–6), 162. All citations are from Looper.

[91] "In the case of a Federal State, the power of which to enter into conventions on labour matters is subject to limitations, it shall be in the discretion of the Government of such a state to treat a draft convention to which limitations apply as a recommendation only." On the one hand, this clause introduces an objectively determinable element as to the limitation on the federal state which could eliminate abuse of the clause. But, as we have seen, with the possible exception of Germany (the situation was the same or even sharper between the wars), federal states enjoy plenary power to enter into treaties and the real problem was internal competence for implementation of the Treaty.

[92] It reads, *inter alia*: "In respect of Conventions . . . which the federal Government regards as appropriate under its constitutional system for federal action, the obligations of the federal state shall be the same as those members which are not federal states."

[93] For a list see Bernier, *International Legal Aspects of Federalism* at 178–9.

[94] Art. 50 of the Civil and Political Rights Convention; Art. 28 of the Social and Economic Rights Convention.

federal clause as an excuse for escaping substantive provisions the content of which are onerous. By contrast the UN Human Rights Conventions' "federal clause" ("The provisions of this [Treaty] shall extend to all parts of federal states without any limitations or exceptions") may even be construed as an interference with the internal choice of state organization and in any event may deter certain federal states from adherence to such treaties. The earlier ILO clause which exempted federal states in which there was really no legal possibility of federal implementation – some sort of objective middle way – was highly impracticable and raised the question as to which instance, national or international, would determine the issue.

Underlying these difficulties is the inherent conflict between, on the one hand, international law which is based on a fundamental principle of equality of states and effectiveness and which, thus, is cautious to accept arrangements which would favor one actor in a multilateral context. The no-reservations principle in the UNCLOS is the boldest assertion of this principle. On the other hand, there is the internal autonomy of peoples and states to choose their own form of internal government of which the federal arrangement is one such legitimate choice. To date the dilemma seems not to have found a constant and workable solution.

Oliver, who has examined this problem recently, concludes that it does not seem as if:

> federal-state clauses have proved to be a useful route to the resolution of the basic dilemma of federalism and the enforcement of treaties in a world of mainly unitary states; mutuality of obligations versus self-determination of peoples (as to form of government) in the context of seeking accommodations that will yield as much universality in the community of the treaty as [is] possible to achieve. The challenge of devising and negotiating an effective and generally acceptable federal-state clause is still outstanding, but there is not much response to it – probably because international practice shows that the federal-state clause is an idea whose time has passed.[95]

The alternative method to the federal clause is the reservation which may occur in the multilateral or bilateral context.[96] It is acknowledged that federal reservations particularly in multilateral contexts breed uncertainty and even perhaps inequality of obligation. Some writers[97] seek to justify them by reason that they are a lesser evil than complete exclusion of federal states from conventional law and that by virtue of the federal reservation at least those obligations in a treaty which correspond to a federal government's legislative competence will be fulfilled: something is better than

---

[95] Oliver, "The Enforcement of Treaties by a Federal State" at 407.
[96] For practice, see Bernier, *International Legal Aspects of Federalism* at 183–5.
[97] Sorensen, "Federal States and the International Protection of Human Rights," *American Journal of International Law* 46 (1952), 195.

nothing. Arguably, as regards this last point, mixity is a more perfect solution since it would bring about a complete fulfillment of the treaty. To be sure, mixity would raise other problems such as responsibility for breach. These problems have not been fully ventilated in international law since mixity has been virtually excluded by the very negative attitude which has developed to the notion of member state capacity to conclude treaties independently (or jointly) with the federation.

As regards the extent to which member states enjoy a capacity in international law to conclude treaties, although several federal states allow the constituent member states direct contact with foreign actors these are always under strict control. Nevertheless, the practice is not theoretically insignificant. The status of these agreements, the responsibility in case of breach, and the implications for the international personality of the member states are at best controversial, at worst obscure.

The issue of the status in international law of member states of a federation is both complex and simple. Its complexity rests in any discussion which is based on concepts of international personality and sovereignty which has been a fertile ground for theoreticians. It is my view that it is possible to cut through the complexity by:

1. insisting on the issue of treaty-making capacity; and
2. casting the argument in inductive methodology based on state practice and not as a derivation from the general doctrinal positions regarding the nature of a state, sovereignty, or independence in international law.[98]

A useful starting point may be the legislative history of the Vienna Convention on the Law of Treaties. The issue emerges in the context of Article 6.[99] In his first report,[100] Sir Humphrey Waldock considered that:

> in principle . . . international capacity to be a party to treaties is . . . possessed exclusively by the federal state . . . Accordingly, if the constitution of a federation . . . confers upon its constituent states power to enter into agreements directly with foreign states, the constituent state normally exercises this power in the capacity only of an organ of the federal state.

This probably represents the general tendency of international law:

---

[98] The theoretical debate on the international personality of member states is traced extensively in Bernier, *International Legal Aspects of Federalism*, chapter 2. His conclusion, at 82, is: "As for member states, their claim to international personality as sovereign entities fails entirely. But it does not follow that they cannot enjoy international personality. If the federal constitution grants them the right to deal separately with foreign states and such states agree to deal with them, then they are subjects of international law."

[99] Art. 6 provides that every state possesses the capacity to conclude treaties. I have relied on the legislative history as traced in S. Rosenne, *The Law of Treaties* (Sijthoff: Leyden; Oceana: Dobbs Ferry, NY, 1970) at 126–35; R. G. Wetzel and D. Rauschning, *The Vienna Convention on the Law of Treaties* (Metzher: Frankfurt, 1978) at 93–7.

[100] *Yearbook of the International Law Commission* (United Nations: New York, 1962), vol. II, 27–83.

unqualified recognition of the full international capacity of the federation and a subsidiary status allocated to the constituent members (though the organ theory has been doubted).[101] Waldock, stipulated, however, certain conditions under which a member state of a federation may enjoy international capacity in its own right:

1. if it is a member of the United Nations; or
2. if it is recognized by the federal state and by the other contracting state or states to possess an international personality of its own.

These are, in theoretical *a priori* terms, unsatisfactory and circular criteria since they tend to beg the question as to when constituent members should be admitted to the UN and when and under what conditions international personality (in itself an elusive term) should be accorded. Indeed, if the practice of autonomous treaty-making is not constitutive of international personality (and Sir Humphrey Waldock himself agrees in his principal submission that this may be regarded as a derivation–organ relationship) what criteria will establish international personality? International responsibility could be such a criterion but it suffers from the same defect of having a circular relationship to international personality with one being a condition of the other.

It is not surprising that we encounter these difficulties since Waldock's text is an obvious compromise of the position of his two predecessors. In Lauterpacht's 1953 Report, treaties by member states are deemed full treaties in international law (with all international consequences). In Fitzmaurice's 1958 Report the "agency" theory is put forward.[102]

Be this doctrinal difficulty as it may, the ILC adopted in 1962 the following formulation in Article 3(2):

> In a federal state the capacity of the member states of a federal union to conclude treaties depends on the federal constitution.

One will note that this is a more liberal view since it does not favor any doctrine but it seems, strangely, to remove any international legal criterion from the determination of the international capacity not only of the constituent member states but also of the federation itself.

Article 3(2) of the ILC 1965 draft read:

---

[101] See, e.g., Wildhaber, *Treaty-Making Power and Constitution* at 261, and cases cited therein. We have noted above that in certain cases German Länder may enter into treaties even against the wishes of the federal government. One consequence would be that no responsibility would rest on the federal government in case of breach. It would thus be difficult to square this position with a comprehensive "organ" theory. The ILC Draft on state responsibility is the best source for a full ventilation of these issues. See note 142, p. 179 below.

[102] *Yearbook of the International Law Commission* (United Nations: New York, 1953); and *Yearbook of the International Law Commission* (United Nations: New York, 1958).

States members of a federal union may possess a capacity to conclude treaties if such capacity is admitted by the federal constitution and within the limits there laid down.

This was also the final ILC draft which went before the UN Conference as Article 5(2).

Not surprisingly, these formulations which modified only slightly the earlier Waldock proposal were criticized both within the ILC[103] and later at the Vienna Conference.[104] The criticism concentrated on the need for and ability of states to interpret the internal constitutions of other states and on the negation of a decisive role for public international law in determining the issue. Although the article survived the 1968 session it was finally deleted in the 1969 session. Capotorti acknowledges the legal objections to the draft Article but he also recognizes the *political* forces by federal states which were behind the move to delete any reference to member-state capacity:

> A questi argomenti formali si è aggiunta poi una considerazione politica: cioè il timore di alcuni Stati federali che potesse essere incoraggiata l'aspirazione degli Stati membri ad una più larga, ed eccessiva, autonomia.[105]

We have thus a neat example of the international community and federal governments "closing ranks"[106] to "unitarize" international legal relations. There was a price to be paid for the failure to deal conclusively with the problem. As Capotorti points out:

> [L]a mancata soluzione del problema getta l'ombra del dubbio sui termini "ogni stato" [in the final Article 6] vi sono inclusi o no gli Stati dipendenti i quali godono di una sfera di autonomia esterna? La risposta sembra dover essere affermativa, tenuto conto della pratica internazionale e delle stesse opinioni manifestate in seno alla Conferenza.[107]

Capotorti seems to give the elements for the reply: one must look at the internal constitutional position – which would seem, for example, to exclude any capacity to the Australian member states – and at state practice

---

[103] *Yearbook of the International Law Commission* (United Nations: New York, 1966), vol. II, *passim*.

[104] Vienna Conference (1968), 1st session.

[105] "To these formal arguments was added then a political consideration, i.e., the fear by several federal states that the aspirations of member states for a larger and excessive autonomy could be encouraged": F. Capotorti, *Convenzione di Vienna sul diritto dei trattati* (Cedain: Padova, 1977) at 22–3.

[106] The vote to delete the clause was 66 for, 28 against, and 13 abstentions.

[107] Capotorti, *Convenzione di Vienna* at 23: "The absence of a solution to this problem throws a shade of doubt on the terms 'every state.' Are dependent states which enjoy a sphere of external autonomy included or not in these terms? The answer it would seem must be affirmative taking account of international practice and of the very opinions manifested within the Conference."

as regards international contacts of member states which do enjoy some international status. It should immediately be admitted that such practice as there is is sparse and declining. But Swiss cantons, German Länder, Canadian provinces and even American states have signed international agreements of one kind or another. In some cases the practice lends itself to organic theory; in other cases to a view consistent with authentic capacity of member states.[108] It is sufficient to establish two contrasting conclusions:

---

[108] The comparative literature cited in note 3 (p. 131 above), note 18 (pp. 136–7 above), note 21 (p. 138 above), note 41 (p. 144 above), note 42 (p. 144 above), note 59 (p. 148 above), note 76 (p. 156 above), and note 87 (p. 158 above) indicates the following member-state external-relations practice.

Canada: agreements between provinces except Quebec for reciprocal enforcement of judgments with the UK; these have been construed as "non-binding gentleman's agreement": *A.-G. for Ontario* v. *Scott* [1956] SCR 137. "Understandings" between New Brunswick and Maine and between Ontario and Minnesota as regards the construction of bridges over boundary rivers. British Columbia has an annual agreement with Washington state. There are numerous agreements with American states concerning vehicle registration. The most famous practice has, however, been the cultural "ententes" between Quebec and France. Quebec claimed that these were an exercise of autonomous treaty-making power and capacity vested in her by virtue of her internal competence. The central authority insisted that this "treaty"-making power would be dependent on federal approval. The matter was "solved" by an *accord cadre* signed between France and Canada under which these "ententes" can be concluded. This, however, does not solve the question of the international validity of such agreements which cannot depend solely on the federal government if other states are willing to regard the agreements with Quebec as treaties. For a full treatment, see Bernier, *International Legal Aspects of Federalism*. There have also been agreements between Quebec and Gabon and extensive Quebec or Canadian-Quebecois participation in educational conferences of French-speaking states. D. P. O'Connell reports on the *Robert Fulton Cutting* case (Hackworth, Green Hayward, *Digest of International Law* (US Government Printer's Office: Washington, DC, 1940–4), vol. V, 561) where the Canadian federal government refused to admit responsibility *vis-à-vis* the USA for the liabilities (succession duties of Quebec respecting New York stock of the Bank of Montreal) of the Province of Quebec: D. P. O'Connell, *International Law* at 966.

USA: The federal government refused proposed agreements for the promotion of trade between Florida and Cuba (in 1937) and between California and Mexico (in 1936). But no objection was raised in 1970 by accord with the Canadian government to an agreement with Canadian provinces in relation to the Northeastern Interstate Forest Fire Protection Compact. There has also been a Quebec–Louisiana Agreement on Cultural Co-operation. See Rodgers, *American Journal of International Law* 64 (1970), 380. In the case of the USA, there can be little doubt that the states are acting at best as organs of the federation and could not assert autonomous capacity. But see *McHenry County* v. *Brady* (1917) 163 *Northwestern Reporter* 540. The subject-matter of state external agreements is limited to local issues, usually of frontier character and can never override the principle of supremacy of federal law or the political external power of the USA.

Germany: Practice has declined since the Lindau compact. The Rhineland-Palatinate has agreements with Luxembourg concerning river management and recreational parks. Baden-Württemberg likewise has similar agreements with Switzerland and Austria. Bavaria has the most extensive network of treaties on similar issues. Constitutionally, the Länder are probably the strongest constituent units of a federal state. As noted in the text a Länd may conclude a valid treaty even in the face of federal opposition (if that is incorrectly imposed) and also bear alone international liability for breach.

in law there is no *per se* international rule which prevents member states from enjoying capacity and even responsibility. States will determine their willingness to engage with a member state of a federation on the basis of the latter's internal constitutional position,[109] its ability to perform, the position of the federal government, etc. In reality federations have either suppressed completely or reduced substantially the range of such agreements.

Of lesser interest in this context is Article 46 of the Convention which limits the possibility of invalidating consent to be bound by a treaty based on the fact that consent had been expressed in violation of a provision of internal law, to those situations where the violation was manifest (which would have to be obvious to any other State acting according to normal practice and in good faith) and if it concerned an internal law of fundamental importance.[110]

It is to be noted that the Convention speaks here of "competence to conclude" as against international capacity dealt with by Article 6. This corresponds to the term "power" used in this chapter, having reserved the term "competence" to internal legislative implementation.

The article is primarily concerned with alleged unauthorized conclusion by state representatives. As regards the federal situation, as Elias points out, in this context "we must ... distinguish between the invalidity of a treaty concluded by a state in its external relations and the incapacity to implement it under internal law after its conclusion."[111] It would appear that Article 46 applies to the first but not to the second of these situations. Hence, implementation problems in a federal state resulting from the division of competence cannot be a justification for invalidity on the international plane.

What could possibly be invoked is a breach of the power to conclude treaties by the federal government. But, as we saw, in most federations this power is plenary and does not depend on the allocation of legislative competences. Whereas in Germany some doubts exist as to the scope of this power, a breach could not be said to be manifest to a foreign power when scholars and judges cannot agree on the precise limitations of such

---

Switzerland: Cantonal agreement-making power is enshrined in the Constitution (Art. 9). But these agreements are limited in subject-matter and will be preempted by any federal treaty. According to Wildhaber, *Treaty-Making Power and Constitution* at 317, cantonal practice was fairly extensive until the First World War. But since then the practice has declined dramatically and concerns now double taxation, seat agreements and the sharing of electrical distribution.

[109] Contact with a member state which is precluded constitutionally could be an interference with the internal affairs of a state.

[110] For the legislative history of this provision, see Rosenne, *The Law of Treaties* at 266–9; Wetzel and Rauschning, *The Vienna Convention on the Law of Treaties* at 330–9.

[111] T. O. Elias, *The Modern Law of Treaties* (Oceana: Dobbs Ferry, NY, 1974) at 143.

power. In short, also for the purpose of Article 46 of the Convention, the non-unitary character of the federal state seems to matter little.[112]

The federal experience: conclusions

We may sum up the federal experience in the following propositions.

1. As regards international capacity, international law (and constitutional law) accord the federation full treaty-making capacity. By way of exception, in several federations, capacity is also accorded, under different conditions and with different rationales, to the member states though in practice it is not frequently exercised.

2. In all federations, federal treaty-making power, even if smaller than international capacity (by virtue of allocative or substantive constitutional limitations), is wider than the *normal* federal internal legislative competence.

3. In most federations, the principal juridical trend has been to eliminate the federal (as against the substantive constitutional) element as an impediment either to full treaty-making power or to the specific implementation of treaties. Canada, and to some extent Germany, are more the exception than the rule – though an interesting exception for the Community.

4. Despite this legal license federal states have not deliberately used their external capacity and wide treaty-making power to change the internal division of competences and in several cases have been reluctant (or resorted to federal clauses or reservations) to conclude treaties implementation of which would obliterate internal demarcations.

5. Most federations have been and are experimenting with various co-operative federalism devices in an attempt to attenuate the potential tension which the unitary external posture of the federal state implies.

We may add here that the federal bestowal of plenary and usually exclusive external power on the federal government highlights a tension inherent in the concept of a *federal state*. On the one hand such entities are committed to a division of competences *rationae materiae*. On the other hand in their very organization as a "state" is implicit a unitary ethos. Indeed, historically the external environment has been one of the cardinal factors which can explain federal *statal* evolution. So much so that it could be argued that this ability to face the outside world as *one* with the

---

[112] A more delicate question would be the possibility of a member state denying validity to a treaty on the basis of absence of power. There can be no hard and fast rule but since in most federal states which allow member state treaty conclusion federal consent is necessary, in this case it would be difficult to maintain, should it later transpire that even the federal consent was unconstitutional, that the breach was manifest.

concomitant suppression *de jure* or *de facto* of the member states' international personality or capacity is a constituent and perhaps even definitional element which at least historically distinguished the federal state from other federal entities.

Whether or not it is still necessary for federal states today to insist so rigorously on this unitary external voice is a matter which for the time being must be left open.

MIXED AGREEMENTS AND THE EVOLUTION OF COMMUNITY EXTERNAL RELATIONS

It may be useful to recall the departure point of this study: in the words of Jacobs "[i]n any system where powers [pertinent to the exercise of external relations] are shared between a central authority and State authorities, difficulties are likely to arise."[113] Federal state practice suggests on the whole "the extreme solution that only the central authority . . . should have an exclusive and all-embracing competence."[114] Mixed agreements thus represent a departure from this solution – a departure that entails many inconveniences. Barav neatly encapsulates a widely, though not universally,[115] shared evaluation: "[M]ixed agreements are probably a necessary evil, part of the integration process, but nobody would like to see any more of them."[116]

In this last part of this chapter, I shall attempt to trace certain elements in the evolution of the Community's external relations which might shed some light on the rationale for the choice of mixity, in contrast with federal-state practice, as one Community method for "solving" the problems deriving from its non-unitary character in the international environment. I shall also inquire whether it is possible to construe a model which would obviate in some cases the alleged legal and political necessity of mixed agreements whilst maintaining the EC as a *community of states*. A solution which simply stipulated or hoped for a *de jure* or *de facto* abdication by the Member States of their competence, power, and capacity in the

---

[113] Jacobs, Amsterdam Colloque at 123.   [114] *Ibid.*

[115] Burrows welcomes mixity as a device to attenuate what he considers unacceptable jurisprudence: Amsterdam Colloque, 111 at 120.

[116] Barav, Amsterdam Colloque, at 144. See also Costonis, "The Treaty Making Power of the EEC"; and Norton, "The Treaty Making Power of the EEC." *Cf.* R. J. Dupuy, "L'application des règles du droit international général des traités aux accords conclus par les organisations internationales," *Annuaire de l'institut de droit international* (1973), 263; O. Jacot-Guillarmod, *Droit Communautaire et droit international public* (1979) at, e.g., 165; van Houtte, "International Law and Community Treaty-Making Power," *Northwestern Journal of International Law and Business* 3 (1981), 621, 633–6. See also the Court itself in Case 1/76 [1977] ECR 741 at recital 14 on a particular manifestation of mixity.

external field in favor of the Community would not only be entirely unrealistic but perhaps even undesirable. Finally, I shall try to draw some general evaluative conclusions in the light of both Community and federal-state practice in the field.

Community external relations: doctrine

Although the Community in the legal constitutional sphere (as distinct from its decision-making structures and processes) has developed certain federal features[117] which classically characterize the transformation from a confederation to a federation,[118] it seemed clear, at least at its inception, that treaty-making powers – a hallmark of federal-*state* government – were to be limited to those explicitly granted to the EC. Like other international organizations the international capacity of the Community would similarly be so limited.[119] The early practice of mixed agreements may be explained by this rigid and narrow understanding of Community power and capacity: only Article 113, it was claimed, was capable of bestowing agreement-making power and capacity *vis-à-vis* other states. Association agreements under Article 238 would have to be mixed since, in respect of any provision in those agreements which went beyond a strict reading of the Common Commercial Policy, the Community would have neither treaty-making power nor capacity.[120] The largely bilateral nature of the early practice can probably explain why the internal Community and external international complex ramifications of mixity did not surface with acuteness. Examining then the Community *starting point* from the mature federal-state perspective may evoke a reaction not unlike that of Alice when peering into the Looking-Glass House: "that's just the same ... only the things go the other way."

---

[117] See Stein, "Lawyers, Judges and the Making of a Transnational Constitution," *American Journal of International Law* 75 (1981), 1.

[118] Dinstein observes that the confederation, in the legal sense, exists today more in theory than in practice. In the case of the three most well-known confederations (USA, Germany, and Switzerland) there was an evolution to a federal state. As a result of these precedents, which tend to associate confederalism with an automatic evolution to federalism (statal version), Dinstein concludes that the old objectives of confederations (retention of statehood by member units) are now achieved in international organizations. Had the EEC been established in the last century, he suggests, it probably would have been called a confederation. Y. Dinstein, *International Law* (Shoken ve-Universitat Tel Aviv: Tel Aviv, 1979), vol. V, section 754 (Hebrew).

[119] The clearest exposition of the early doctrine is Pescatore, "Les relations extérieures des Communautés européennes," *Receuil des Cours* 103 (1961-II), 1. *Cf.* C. Flaesch-Mougin, *Les accords externes de la Communauté economique européenne* (Editions de Universitaire de Bruxelles: Brussels, 1979) at 129*ff*.

[120] *Cf.* Cremona, "The Doctrine of Exclusivity" at 411.

Table 2. *Treaty-making features in federal states and in the European Community*

Central capacity	In federations the central authority enjoys full international treaty-making capacity regardless of internal treaty-making power or legislative competence. The capacity of the Member States is limited, infrequently used and often based on a delegation from the central authority.	In the Community the international capacity of the central authority was, in line with other international organizations, strictly functional and derivative. The capacity of Member States, from the international view point, remained plenary.
Central power	In federations the central authority has extensive, often plenary treaty-making power. The power is wider than the internal legislative competences of the central authority.	In the Community (pre-ERTA) treaty-making power was enumerated. It appeared that the power was narrower than internal legislative competences.
Positions of constituent units	In the classical federations Member States had effectively conceded their external capacity and power as a hallmark of their collective statehood.	In the Community Member States retain their capacity and power as a sign of their individual and autonomous statehood.
Content and subject matter of treaties	In the federal state it is readily conceded that external "high politics" should be conducted by the central authority. Any claims – Länder, provinces, cantons – for external capacity and power concern "low politics" issues.	In the Community it is easier conceded that the central authority should have treaty-making power over "low politics," and "high politics" have traditionally been seen as the *domaine réservé* of the Member States.
Political process	In the federal state, the decision-making structures enable the central authority to dominate foreign-policy-making and to contain pressures from Member States.	In the Community, the decision-making structures enabled Member States to dominate the external relations process and to contain central authority pressures.
Mixity	In federations, Member States have been unable to claim mixity.	In the Community the central authority has been unable to avoid mixity.

A comparison between the treaty-making features of federal states and the European Community is set out in Table 2.

It is against these divergent starting points that we may now examine the doctrinal and practical evolution of the Community's external legal posture.

Evolutionary trends: parallelism

Both in federal states and in the Community there has been a great pressure to link internal competences and treaty-making power and capacity. But in federal states the main line of evolution has been a movement *from* power (and capacity) *to* internal competences. Federal-government specific implementation competences have been extended (with the qualifications we have seen) by virtue of the treaty-making power. In the Community by contrast the reverse process had to happen: treaty-making power was to extend by virtue of expanding competences.

The Community story is well known and has been analyzed extensively,[121] and sufficient for present purposes will be a tracing of its salient points. In the well-known line of cases commencing with *ERTA*, the Court consecrated the doctrine of parallelism whereby treaty-making power would be co-extensive with the exercise of internal competences in any given field even without an explicit treaty-making authority in the Treaties. In the no less famous Opinion 1/76, the Court explained that parallelism could operate, when necessary (an uneasy term[122]) in advance of

---

[121] Leading comprehensive texts are J.-V. Louis and P. Brückner, *Relations extérieures*, in Waelbroeck, "Article 235," in J. Megret, J.-V. Louis, D. Vignes, and M. Waelbroeck (eds), *Le droit de la Communauté economique européenne* 15 (Presses Universitaires: Brussels, 1987), vol. XII; O. Jacot-Guillarmod, *Droit Communautaire et droit international public*; C. Flaesch-Mougin, *Les accords externes*; Boulouis, "La jurisprudence de la cour de justice des Communautés européennes relative aux relations extérieures des Communautés," *Recueil des Cours* 160 (1978-II), 339–92; Pescatore's influential "External Relations in the Case-Law of the Court of Justice of the European Communities," *Common Market Law Review* 16 (1979), 615; and Schermers, "Les relations de droit international public de la Communauté" in *Trente ans de droit Communautaire* (European Commission, Perspectives Européennes, 1982), all of which contain extensive bibliographical references. Other texts are referred to in the body of this chapter

[122] "Whenever Community law has created for the institutions of the Community powers within its internal system for the purpose of attaining a specific objective, the Community has authority to enter into the international commitments *necessary* for the attainment of that objective even in the absence of an express provision in that connexion.": [1977] ECR 741 at recital 3 (emphasis added). The language is evocative of Art. 235. It is difficult to establish whether "necessary" is a political concept leaving absolute discretion to the institutions (effectively the Council) or whether it can be given a binding juridical content. In *ERTA* [1971] ECR 263, referring to the totality of Art. 235 the Court said that it "does not create an obligation, but confers on the Council an option" (at recital 85). But see Schwartz, "Article 235 and Law Making Powers in the European Community," *International and Comparative Law*

an internal exercise of Community competence by virtue of the mere creation and existence of the competence. In this sense the external agreement could be deemed as an exercise of the internal competence.

These well-known affirmations are perhaps, through what may be called the "*ERTA* effect," of limited direct practical importance since the Community (or rather the Council) has been reluctant to conclude agreements on the basis of *ERTA* and Opinion 1/76.[123] What is of interest for our discussion is that the *ERTA* line of cases may seem to establish a *two-way* strict legal connection between competences and treaty-making power. The two are inextricably linked and we cannot have one without the other. This aspect of parallelism, although reminiscent of a similar linkage in the practice of many federal states in moving from plenary treaty-making power to matching internal implementing competences, must also be recognized as not being, in general terms, really logically necessary.

Evolutionary trends: exclusivity and preemption

The second most important juridical development in this field has been the application of the doctrine of preemption-exclusivity. Traditionally a distinction is made between preemption-exclusivity in relation to areas (essentially the Common Commercial Policy) where treaty-making power is explicitly granted by the Treaty itself and areas where the power would be implied under *ERTA* and/or Opinion 1/76. Recently, there have been signs of convergence between the two. It should be noted that in relation to both areas, preemption-exclusivity has been imposed by judicial pronouncement.

As regards the Common Commercial Policy, the Court has imposed a strict application of the doctrine. The *locus classicus* is Opinion 1/75 in which the Court affirmed that "the exercise of concurrent powers by the Member States and the Community ... is impossible."[124] In *Donckerwolcke*,[125] the Court had to grapple with a clash of legal principle – exclusivity – and political reality, the political exigencies which inevitably entail gaps in a full Community regulatory regime in this field. Its solution is consistent with the severity of its legal principle yet displaying the flexibility of the Treaty regime: "As full responsibility in the matter of commercial policy was transferred to the Community by means of Article 113(1), measures of commercial policy of a national character [necessitated

---

Quarterly 27 (1978), 614; Barav, Amsterdam Colloque; and note on Case 1/76 by Hardy, *Common Market Law Review* 14 (1977), 561 at 594.
[123] See van Houtte, "International Law and Community Treaty-Making Power" at 630.
[124] Opinion 1/75 [1975] ECR 1,355.   [125] Case 41/76 [1976] ECR 1921.

by the "fact that at the expiry of the transitional period the Community commercial policy was not fully achieved"] are only permissible after the end of the transitional period by virtue of specific authorization of the Community."[126]

As regards *ERTA* agreements, the Court's initial statements were no less severe. In *ERTA* itself the Court affirmed that: "Community authority excludes the possibility of a concurrent authority on the part of the Member States, since any initiative taken outside of the common institutions would be incompatible with the unity of the Common Market and the uniform application of Community law."[127]

However, even in *ERTA* itself[128] there is language which suggests that preemption-exclusivity in relation to *implied* treaty-making power could not be equated with equivalent statements under Article 113. First, there is already the fact that Community rules would have to be "promulgated." Secondly, it would seem that the theoretical basis for exclusivity moves in a gray area between supremacy and preemption. If the Court were to apply a simple principle of supremacy the consequence would be that the Member States would be precluded from making only those international agreements which were in direct conflict with the Community obligation. If the Court were to apply fully fledged preemption the consequence would be that Member States would be precluded from any international agreement in the area in question. Instead, the Court stands midway between these two concepts, prohibiting those international obligations which might *affect those rules or alter their scope*. This is more than supremacy but less than preemption.[129]

These hints were indeed consolidated in subsequent jurisprudence.[130] As regards the Common Commercial Policy, in the *Rubber Agreement* Opinion[131] the Court seemed to be retreating from its severe preemptory approach to the Common Commercial Policy in allowing mixed participation on the grounds that financing of the Rubber Agreement's buffer stocks would be effected by the Member States and not by the Community as such. It is possible to criticize the Court not only for being inconsistent

---

[126] *Ibid.*, recitals 27 and 32 of judgment.

[127] *ERTA* [1971] ECR 263, recital 31 of judgment.

[128] "If these two provisions [Article 3(e) and Article 5] are read in conjunction, it follows that to the extent to which Community rules are promulgated for the attainment of the objectives of the Treaty, the Member States cannot, outside the framework of the Community institutions, assume obligations which might affect those rules or alter their scope": *ibid.*, recital 22 of judgment.

[129] See Bourgeois, Amsterdam Colloque, at 101.

[130] See, e.g., Joined Cases 3, 4 and 6/76, *Kramer* [1976] ECR 1,279; Case 61/77, *Commission* v. *Ireland* [1978] ECR 417.

[131] Opinion 1/78 [1979] ECR 2,871.

with its previous ruling on a similar, though not identical issue, in Opinion 1/75, but of having put the cart before the horse: instead of allowing finance to determine exclusivity, exclusivity should have determined finance. Be that as it may, as Barav has pointed out the Court has conditioned non-exclusivity in this case on the fact (itself open to judicial determination) that the financial provisions must occupy a *central* position in the structure of the agreement.[132]

The situation as regards preemption-exclusivity would thus seem as follows. Matters falling within the Common Commercial Policy undoubtedly come under exclusive Community control with the *Rubber ratio* constituting one possible qualification. As regards *ERTA* there would be qualified exclusivity dependent on the extent to which internal competences have been exercised and Member State practice will "affect or alter the scope" of the Community measures. This should be read as meaning not only material impact but anything which might foreclose future Community activity in the field. As regards Opinion 1/76, if agreements are actually concluded on this basis the same preemptive effect as in *ERTA* would apply; otherwise Community powers would naturally be potential awaiting activation and, until such time, Member States may do as they wish. When an agreement is concluded under *ERTA* or Opinion 1/76 and probably also under Article 235, the preemptive effect operates as against conclusion of international agreements by the Member States. Internally, exclusivity will depend on the particular rules governing the subject matter within the Common Market. These may shift from field to field.[133]

Evolutionary trends: expansion

The final trend to be discussed is the material expansion of Community competences and through them treaty-making power and capacity. In relation to the Common Commercial Policy, the Opinion of the Court in *Rubber* gave a very wide reading to the scope of the Common Commercial Policy so as to encompass within it matters which go well beyond a narrow reading of the language of Article 113. In general, the Community has seen a significant widening of EC competences in fields such as, say, the protection of the environment and an increased use of Article 235.[134] The

---

[132] Recital 55 of judgment. *Cf.* White, *European Law Review* (1980), 315; Barav, Amsterdam Colloque, at 144.

[133] See Waelbroeck, "The Emergent Doctrine."

[134] For a comprehensive survey and analysis of this expansion, see Tizzano, "Lo sviluppo delle competenze materiali delle communità europee," *Rivista di diritto europeo* 21 (1981), 139; "Recenti sviluppi in tema di accordi internazionali della CEE," *Diritto comunitario e degli scambi internazionali* 20 (1981), 19.

expansion of the Common Commercial Policy would of course mean that *ipso jure* more and more areas of unilateral Member State actions would become preempted. The general material expansion of Community law could likewise have preemptory consequences also under *ERTA* and Opinion 1/76.[135]

The evolutionary trends: interim conclusions

It is really the combination of parallelism, preemption, and material expansion which characterizes the Community's external legal treaty-making posture. If we return to the federal context we could say that as a matter of *judicial policy*[136] there has been a convergence of Community legal doctrine with the general trend of federal-state evolution: Community treaty-making powers and capacity, whether express or implied, have been construed at their widest; Community internal competences, *ex hypothesi*, have been held to match power and capacity (not surprisingly since the power is frequently derived from the competence) and by virtue of preemption, the autonomous role of the Member States has been squeezed. So far as Community non-mixed agreements are concerned one could say that in principle the Community has evolved a most sophisticated structure and process for conducting international legal relations which strikes what may be considered as an ideal federal balance: the Community operates as a unitary actor *vis-à-vis* the international legal order in line with modern practice. Internally, the complications of divided implementation competences, as in the *Labour Conventions* case, are similarly avoided. And yet the internal decision-making processes, even at the level of negotiating teams – annoying and burdensome as these may be – ensure that Member State interests are fully vindicated. The key legal difference rests of course on the fact that Community treaty-making powers and capacity are not plenary, a difference which leads to important consequences.

At the same time it was only to be expected that the legal doctrine which, after all, evolved in an extremely brief period would meet with Member State opposition. For logical and neat as the solution may be, it could at the same time entail that formally (and perhaps formerly) sovereign actors would be pushed to accept not only an expansion in Community competence–power–capacity but also to see their own autonomous competence–power–capacity threatened.

---

[135] But see pp. 171–2 above. Even if agreements under *ERTA* and 1/76 could not automatically preempt internal competences, they could, by enlarging the scope of Community activity, indirectly have a similar effect. See Usher, *European Law Review* (1979), 300.

[136] With which the Commission has largely accorded. *Cf.* Stein, "Lawyers, Judges and the Making of a Transnational Constitution."

Community external relations: practice[137]

Despite the sensitivity of external relations, touching as they do on matters dear to the heart of the Member States, the number of external agreements whether mixed or not has increased dramatically and external relations have been for a long time a growth area of Community law and policy. It is worth remembering once again that the decision-making processes of the Community mean that even where an agreement is concluded by the Community alone, the Member States do not really lose any significant control over the making of such an agreement. At the same time it has become clear that the Council has been reluctant to conclude agreements under *ERTA* and Opinion 1/76. If legal reasons must be found for this reluctance (though it is clear that part of the reasons are vague political considerations of prestige and national pride), one would of course have to mention in the first place the preemptive effect of such conclusion. As regards *ERTA*, the Member States may fear their replacement on the international level; as regards Opinion 1/76, they may fear their replacement on the internal level. There has been a growing practice of using Article 235 either as a joint or as an exclusive treaty basis for international agreements. It could be, however, that Article 235 is also considered as a device to avoid the *ERTA* effect. It should be noted that, where an internal measure has been introduced on the basis of Article 235 and then an international agreement is concluded pursuant thereto, the reference to Article 235 in the agreement should not, strictly speaking, remove the preemptive effects of *ERTA*. As regards Article 113, in some instances the Council accepted the implications of the *Rubber* Opinion with equanimity; thus, in the GATT context, the Council has begun to rely largely on Article 113[138] rather than other Treaty articles. But in many other instances, of which PROBA 20[139] is just one clamorous example, the Member States have opted for mixity.

Mixity represents the greatest departure of the Community from federal-state practice. A detailed analysis of its rationale, typology, and legal and political ramifications are not necessary here. We shall confine our examination to some of the factors which have played a part in conditioning

---

[137] Useful recent accounts of practice are Wellenstein, "Twenty-Five Years of European Community External Relations," *Common Market Law Review* 16 (1979), 407; Close, "Self-Restraint by the EEC in the Exercise of its External Powers," *Yearbook of European Law* (Clarendon Press: Oxford; Oxford University Press: New York, 1981), vol. I, 45; Bourgeois, Amsterdam Colloque.

[138] Bourgeois, *ibid.* at 99.

[139] The text of PROBA 20 has not been officially published. Its existence is public knowledge: *Bulletin of the European Communities* 3 (1981) at 2.2.17.

mixed agreements and to an evaluation of the significance of mixity to European integration.

Firstly, mixity can be regarded as a *political* device whereby the Member States might seek to avoid the consequences of parallelism, preemption, and expansion. Mixed agreements, especially when they do not specify the demarcation line between Community and Member States, diffuse at a stroke the explosive issues of the scope of Community competences (and treaty-making power) and the parameters of the preemptive effect. It may thus be employed, illegally, as perceived in PROBA 20, even in those cases where the Community should act alone. It is not easy to assess the practice. From the legal point of view this particular practice must be condemned since it is a breach of the principle of preemption-exclusivity. It also prevents, naturally, the consolidation by virtue of parallelism of wider Community treaty-making power. But preemption does not operate in a legal vacuum. One purpose of the doctrine of preemption in general[140] is to induce, even force, the Member States to act in a Community framework. Preemption is designed for situations where there is an objective necessity for action. By precluding unilateral Member State activity (or joint non-Community action), it is hoped that the objective necessity will force the Member States into joint *Community* action. In some cases the reluctance of the Member States to allow exclusive Community action might be so great – especially if this could mean, say, a *de facto* confirmation of the ever-growing scope of the Common Commercial Policy – that they would prefer not to act at all. It may be that mixity is the best compromise between Community exclusivity and no action at all. Since most mixed agreements do not specify the demarcation between Community and Member State competences, this issue is left murky though it can surface again in the implementation of the mixed agreement, its amendment, termination, and/or breach. Mixity may also have advantages, even in this "false" situation, from the international point of view in terms of voting or other rights in multilateral contexts. In conclusion, one can say that this type of mixity is a symptom of the cleavage between legal doctrine and political power which at present seems unavoidable.

Secondly, probably the strongest and perhaps only *legal* justification for "genuine" mixity occurs in a situation where the subject matter of the agreement covers areas which go beyond or are concurrent with the internal competence of the Community.[141] As we noted above, this would seem to be one effect of the doctrine of parallelism. It is said that the

---

[140] See Weiler, "Community, Member States and European Integration: Is the Law Relevant?" *Journal of Common Market Studies* 21 (1982), 39, 47–50.

[141] This is implicit in Ruling 1/78 [1978] ECR 2,151.

Community could not have a treaty-making power (and capacity) for which it has not got internal competences. This accords also with the doctrine of functional personality which is now generally accepted as the basis for analyzing international organizations.

This seems politically unavoidable and legally sound. Those who wish to see the disappearance of mixed agreements would simply count on the continued substantive expansion of Community competence, and through a (strict) application of parallelism and preemption a gradual replacement of the Member States.

In federal states neither "false" nor "genuine" mixity are likely to occur. "False" mixity will not occur since even in such states as Canada where the member states retain at times exclusive implementing competence, they lack either the treaty-making power and capacity or the political strength to convince the federal government of the desirability of their co-participation. The best they achieve is involvement in pre-negotiation policy-making and background representation at the negotiating arena. "Genuine" mixity simply does not pose itself as such since the federation is considered as having full power and capacity although in, say, the cultural field in Germany, it may act for a Länd and in Canada it may allow a province autonomous *ententes*.

Thirdly, can there be, at least *de lege ferenda*, a midway construction whereby, even in the situation of an agreement going beyond Community competence, mixity could be avoided without compromising the notion of a *community of states*? I am suggesting, as a possible future construction, a situation whereby the Community alone could, on an *ad hoc* basis and in specific instances, conclude an agreement going beyond her internal competences, implementation of which would be left jointly to the EC institutions and the Member States. Such an agreement should not have the internal effect of expanding Community competences beyond those already vested in her and would not preempt the Member States from exercising their international capacity in the same field so long as they did not actually violate the Community agreement. In theoretical terms, I am suggesting the possibility of extending Community treaty-making powers beyond internal competences (as in some federal states) and (unlike some federal states) without this denying or restricting generally Member State treaty-making power or capacity. In certain circumstances this might avoid some of the complexities of mixity and not be totally unacceptable to Member States since the effect of *ERTA* and Opinion 1/76 would not come into operation.

Let us consider an agreement a large part of which falls within Community competence and where perhaps there might even be a benefit in negotiating as one bloc with the political ramifications and pragmatic advantages which such a unitary external stance might yield. The objections to a Community agreement would be legal-political: in certain cases the Community simply does not or *could not* even under Article 235 attain power without Treaty amendment under Article 236. In other cases, and the elasticity of Article 235 coupled with Articles 2 and 3 is pertinent here, the Community could attain such power from the Council, but the Member States would have to bestow on the Community internal competence also as regards those parts of the agreement which hitherto were within their own domain. This they might not wish to do. This all derives from the current doctrine which tells us that the Community cannot have capacity where it does not have treaty power and it cannot have treaty power where it does not have competence.

But as our examination of federal legal doctrine and *some* federal practice has shown, there is no general legal rule or even logic which requires a strict parallelism between an international actor's capacity, power, and competence. In fact, as we saw, federal states are recognized as having, *qua* states, full international capacity. Their treaty-making power may be narrower than their capacity (limited by substantive constitutional constraints) and their internal competence may be narrower still. As Gibbs CJ has recently affirmed in *Koowarta*, the federal government can on its own "make treaties on subjects which are not within [its] legislative power." Arguably this possibility is available only to states. The international community would not recognize in an international organization treaty-making power and capacity which goes beyond either its internal competences or its stated objectives. But this international "rule" is a consequence of state practice as are all other such rules of international law and it is not unthinkable that for this purpose third states would be willing to accept the Community as being closer to a federal state (in the Canadian mold) rather than an international organization.[142] I think that at least in some situations

---

[142] In principle the international capacity of the Community is determined by public international law, not by Community law. But, it would seem that there is a *renvoi* to Community law in the sense that public international law rules that the capacity of an international organization to conclude treaties is governed by the relevant rules of that organization (*Cf.* Art. 6 of the ILC 1979 Draft Convention, *Yearbook of the International Law Commission* (United Nations: New York, 1979), vol. I, 137). This capacity from the Community point of view would seem to depend on the treaty-making power. At present the treaty-making power (in accordance with the doctrine of parallelism) is confined to areas in which there is actual or potential competence. This is in line with the common view that an international organization can only have treaty-making power to realize its specific tasks. See van Houtte, "International Law and Community Treaty-Making Power" at 625. At the same time the ILC Draft itself, in Art. 2, recognizes that treaty-making power may be determined not only by reference to the constituent documents (which would include the judicial interpretation thereof) but also to "relevant decisions and resolutions," etc. In principle, from the international law point of view, there could not be an objection to a resolution of the competent Community authorities to

such as the one I described above, this possibility, which would obviate mixity, even where current doctrine suggests that it is legally mandatory, is worth discussing.

Would this be legally (and politically) feasible in the Community? To be sure, the initial strict understanding of enumerated powers in the Community rendered both sage and perhaps inevitable that the Court, keen on furthering the process of integration in general and extending the treaty-making power in particular, should use a severe linkage between competences and power. Moreover, this accorded with the functional model by which international organizations may attain treaty-making capacity. One could even argue that on one level the strict connection stipulated by the Court made sense not only from the point of view of Community law but also from the more general point of view of international legal relations: it prevented the *Labour Conventions* situation from ever arising in relation to those agreements for which the Community alone was responsible. Certain factors indicate that the possibility of the Community negotiating and concluding, in appropriate cases, agreements parts of which extend beyond internal powers, thus rupturing the strictness of parallelism, is not entirely fanciful.

In *Rubber* the Court took the view:

> that the fact that the agreement may cover subjects such as technological assistance, research programmes, labour conditions ... consultations relating to national tax policies ... cannot modify the description of the agreement which must be assessed having regard to its essential objective rather than in terms of individual clauses of an altogether subsidiary or ancillary nature.[143]

In effect the Court was stipulating a conclusion of a Community agreement (mixity was admitted only because of the financial regime which, as noted above, occupied a *central position* in the agreement) certain aspects of which, albeit ancillary and subsidiary, did not spring directly from Community competences, not even by the wide reading in the same Opinion of the Common Commercial Policy. The Court was willing to extend the treaty-making power beyond internal competence, actual or

---

approve a Community agreement over a matter which went beyond Community competence, it being clear that in such a decision it was implicit that the Community would be given the necessary means to face its responsibility in case of breach. If anything the problem would be one of internal Community law: such extended treaty-making power might be contrary to the Treaty. But I would submit that, if the bulk of an agreement did come within the competences of the Community, Art. 235 would be an ideal tool to give it precisely that: the extra power to conclude the Treaty as a whole especially as this would, under my construction, not invoke the extension of competences by the Community. In this way objections based on Art. 228 (section 1, para. 2) would be obviated.

[143] Recital 56.

potential, if the agreement in its essentials did fall within the (widened) notion of the Common Commercial Policy. Inevitably the Court insisted that even those aspects of the agreement would then have to be not only negotiated but also concluded by the Community regime. But it is doubtful whether the Court would later permit direct Community intervention in Member States' fiscal policies even if implementation of the agreement would so require.

A second indication of international capacity which is wider than internal competences may come from the practice of mixity itself. In mixed agreements which do not specify the internal demarcation line between Member States and the Community, breach by a Member State may engage the Community internationally, at least to the extent that a third country might evoke reciprocity against the offending Member State *and* the Community.[144]

This point can be developed further by investigating the extent to which the Community "is a party" to a mixed agreement and bound by it. One view is that the Community is bound only by those parts of the mixed agreement in relation to which it has competences and that consequently it "is a party" to the agreement only to that extent. This might seem a logical conclusion from mixity. It may create difficulties in relation to those agreements which do not specify the demarcation line between Community and Member States. In Ruling 1/78 the Court specifically said that:

> [I]t is further important to state ... that it is not necessary to set out and determine, as regards other parties to the [mixed agreement], the division of powers ... between the Community and the Member States, particularly as it may change in the course of time. It is sufficient to state to the other contracting parties that the matter gives rise to a division of powers within the Community, it being understood that the exact nature of that division is a domestic question in which third parties have no need to intervene. In the present instance the important thing is that the implementation of the [mixed agreement] should not be incomplete.[145]

This is a wise concept since otherwise the conclusion of an *external* mixed agreement could have the effect of freezing *internally* the evolution of competences within the Community. It follows from this reasoning of the Court that every time there is a shift of internal competence nothing changes internationally: as long as implementation of the agreement is complete it matters not who is implementing internally. Clearly, *under this view of the Court*, the mixed agreement does not have to be renegotiated

---

[144] See Gaja, "The European Community's Rights and Obligations under Mixed Agreements," in Schermers and O'Keeffe, *Mixed Agreements*, 133–40 at 139.
[145] Recital 35 of judgment.

each time there is an internal shift of competences. But that in turn means that the Community is already party to *the entire agreement* and, indeed, every time it gains internal competence (and replaces the Member States) it is also *bound* by the relevant provisions of the agreement to which it is already a party.[146]

This judicial rationale is very close to that of Lord Atkin over forty-five years ago in the *Labour Conventions* case where he said: "In totality of legislative power powers, Dominion and Provincial together, [Canada] is fully equipped."[147]

Likewise in the eyes of the European Court, so long as, in its totality, the Community and Member States are fully equipped, it matters not who has the internal charge of implementation.

Does this not mean, however, that in the conclusion of mixed agreements in which competences are not specified, the Community is *already* exercising a treaty-making power and an international capacity which is larger than its internal competences? And that this "extra" power does not have the effect of bestowing internal competences on the Community in the internal field until such time as these may accrue to the Community by internal and not international processes? Or, in other words, that what I am suggesting as a possible strategy for certain types of agreements, hitherto deemed to *necessitate* mixity, is already in part reality?

There can be two principal objections to this construction. First, it is possible to construe the process by which the Community becomes bound, with the *internal* shift of competences, to ever larger parts of a mixed agreement not on the basis of *ab initio* Community full (albeit potential) partnership, but on the doctrine of substitution. This would be, however, less consonant with the language of the Court in Ruling 1/78. Second, whereas it may be, in line with federal practice, that "the exact nature of ... division is a domestic question in which third parties have no need to intervene" is correct so long as the agreement is being implemented, these third parties may well wish to intervene if they contemplate the eventuality of breach. For unlike the federal state where the third parties can indeed overlook internal divisions since they have one internationally recognized actor to whom they may turn for redress in case of breach, the matter is not so clear in the Community.

The Court did not address its mind directly to this point but it is implicit in the above *dictum* that overall international responsibility, at least *vis-à-vis* third parties, could vest in the Community itself. The Community decision-making process, in which the Member States have a central position, should ensure that the Member States would not obstruct

---

[146] *Cf.* Cremona, "The Doctrine of Exclusivity" at 426–7.   [147] [1937] AC 326, 354.

responsibility for an agreement to which they will have *ipso facto* given their consent. Finally there is the very delicate case where the Community may wish to accede to an international agreement which partly affects Community competences. The Member States may not *wish* to enter a mixed agreement since they might not want to be bound by the non-Community provisions of this agreement. The Community would have to accede alone to the agreement, possibly inserting a "federal reservation." But even with a reservation, the Community would be a full partner to the international agreement. The basis for conclusion could be either the internal measure on which competence is based or Article 235. But it would in this case be difficult to argue that by virtue of its sole conclusion of the agreement the Community acquired internal competence over the whole gamut of the agreement. In this case we would have an example of Community capacity and treaty-making power extending beyond internal competence.

All these examples are perhaps very thin indications of an already existing breach in parallelism on the one hand, and functional personality on the other hand. Apart from the legal difficulties of suggesting Community agreements going beyond internal competences, there could be policy objections: one objection to this alternative construction could be that it would recreate all the problems of the *Labour Conventions* case. However, as noted above, in reality Canada has not suffered critically from that decision. Moreover, the stronger the elements of co-operative federalism, the more acceptable does the *Labour Conventions* rationale (with its respect for the internal principle of division of competences) become. The Community, by virtue of its decision-making structure and process, manifests *ipso jure* and *ipso facto* a very powerful model of co-operative federalism – with all its strengths (acceptability) and weakness (*lourdeur*). Any decision by the Council to conclude such an agreement would inevitably imply an acceptance by the Member States to implement those parts of the agreement in respect of which the Community's treaty-making power exceeded its internal competences. It is also possible that third states would find this option more convenient than the current practice of mixity; they have after all faced it with relative equanimity in their contacts with some federal states. Even as regards responsibility for breach it is already inherent in this situation that internationally the Community as such would be liable *vis-à-vis* third states and that failure by one Member State to implement its part of the agreement would thus involve the Community in an international delict for which it would be liable. But a decision by the Member States to "allow" the Community to exercise a treaty-making power wider than internal competence would automatically vest the parallel powers to face any burden of international responsibility.

CONCLUDING EVALUATION: MIXITY IN THE LIGHT OF
FEDERAL-STATE EXPERIENCE

Seven conclusions can be drawn from our discussion. Firstly, our analysis so far has revealed two possible constructions for the application of the federal principle to the international legal relations of non-unitary actors. According to one view external relations in general and treaty-making in particular are *instruments* and as such must be subordinate to the internal division of competences between the central authority and the constituent members.

A second view is that external capacity and power have a *substantive* quality and are themselves not mere instruments to further other policies. In earlier times it could perhaps be maintained that the issues of foreign policy and external legal relations fell naturally within the central-authority domain. But when it became clear that matters which were reserved to the constituent units rather than the central authority could have international implications, this second view was reconstructed. Now it is suggested that, as regards any matter with an international dimension, even in non-unitary states, the exercise of international legal relations by the central authority maximizes in the international environment the power of the federal entity as a whole which is consequently also beneficial to the constituent member states. Under this view the concentration of external power and capacity in the central authority is in itself part of the federal allocation of competences within the non-unitary entity, and the interests of the constituent units could at best be vindicated by the internal processes of foreign policy formation.

It is this second view which has characterized the constitutional doctrine and practice of federal states. The other instrumental view, if taken to its logical conclusion, seemed an unacceptable option to the federations. It raised the specter not only of a multiplicity of different foreign policies but also of a multiplicity of international legal relations which would, because of their internal effects, over-accentuate diversity rather than unity within the body politic and call into question the very *raison d'être* of the federal state in which the one and the many, the uniform and the diverse, must find a workable equilibrium. In one sense the federal-state experience might allay fears regarding respect for the internal autonomy of member states. All writers speak of a federal reluctance to exploit the wide external capacity, power, and implementing competence to the detriment of the authority of constituent units. The respect for the member state is manifested either by refraining from treaty conclusion or by developing structures for co-operative federalism. It is clearly, however, a *centralist model* and one which historically has seen the effective elimination of member states as serious international actors.

184

Secondly, the Community commenced with the strict instrumental approach. In its early restrictive manifestation this genuinely prohibited the attainment of Community objectives. At a second phase, on the constitutional level we saw the judicially inspired transformation of Community treaty-making powers enshrined in the doctrine of parallelism. However, the Court went beyond a mere extension of treaty-making powers. In the accompanying jurisprudence of preemption and expansion was implicit a clear enough option for the second federal-state model. The attempt was not only to enlarge Community treaty-making powers but to delimit correspondingly the powers of the Member States and to guard jealously the Community as a single external *alter ego* of the Member States. One could argue, on the basis of federal-state experience, that, given the internal domination by Member States of the Community decision-making process, this judicial vision which foresaw on the one hand the continued growth of external relations and on the other hand the elimination of mixity and which by virtue of the doctrines of parallelism and preemption would see a steady reduction in the role of Member States as external actors, would still be consonant with Pescatore's articulation of the principle of federalism – the search for unity combined with genuine respect for the autonomy and legitimate interests of the participant entities.[148] This is the classical federal-state model: unity in the external posture; autonomy and vindication of state interests in the internal processes. There can, however, be a different view.

Thirdly, mixity as pioneered by the Community offers a real alternative to this working out of the federal principle. Since it is the Community *together* with its Member States which concludes agreements, we do not necessarily face a multiplicity of external relations and a weakening of the strength inherent in united action. Mixity offers instead a different way in the search for unity and the respect for state interests and autonomy. It is a way which is particularly sensitive to one interest which is difficult to square with the alternative federal-*state* approach: the preservation, so far as possible, of the international personality and capacity of the Member States.

Fourthly, to be sure, the pressure for mixity has been increasing by the Member States, partly perhaps in reaction to the implicit federal-state model of the earlier jurisprudence. The Court of Justice has been showing signs that it was responding to this pressure: by, for example, modifying its absolutist preemptive principle for treaty-making power and capacity under *ERTA*, and by accepting mixity in the field of the supposedly exclusive commercial policy. Also, as I have suggested, the Court might even be tinkering with the principle of parallelism but not in order to allow a denial

---

[148] See the quote at p. 136 above.

of Community treaty-making power where it has internal competence but perhaps to allow an existence of (non-exclusive) Community treaty-making power where it *does not* have internal legislative competence – the latter being left in the hands of the Member States.

Fifthly, whereas this last development is still very speculative, it may be one way of eliminating some of the abuses of mixity. But to many mixity is considered as a retrogression in terms of European integration and the Court is on occasion being accused of, or perhaps excused for, caving in to unacceptable pressure by Member States. Both mixity and these chinks in the earlier uncompromising attitude of the Court could, however, be fitted into a different framework for evaluating European integration.

I think it is safe to assume that underlying much of the present discussion both of those favoring more "European integration" (mixity an evil) and those who think the limit has already been reached[149] is the common notion that "every political system has a centre and a periphery . . . that what happens in the centre is what is really significant politically . . . [and that] under these terms; political [and legal] integration becomes a matter of building a strong centre and tying the periphery closer to it."[150]

It is at this point that modern federal theory and integration may unite in offering a different option. As Elazar points out:

> Federalism . . . offers an alternative to the centre–periphery model . . . The essence of the federal matrix is conveyed . . . in the original meaning of the term: a womb which frames and embraces in contrast with a focal point, or centre, which concentrates . . . [I]ntegration on [this] model is potentially quite different from integration around a common centre . . . *the measure of . . . integration is not the strength of the centre as opposed to the peripheries; rather the strength of the framework.* Thus both the whole and the parts can gain in strength simultaneously and, indeed, must do so on an interdependent basis.[151]

Mixity, despite the dangers of abuse and the complex internal and external legal ramifications and difficulties, expands the pluralistic posture of the Community's external relations. It enables the Community to bridge a difficult gap which both classic international legal doctrine and internal Community law would seem to impose: either Community agreements or Member State agreements. Mixity, alongside pure Community agreements and pure Member State agreements, establishes an additional option for the conduct of external legal relations by non-unitary entities whether statal or otherwise.

Sixthly, a future scenario of Community external relations which

---

[149] E.g., Burrows, Amsterdam Colloque, at 120: "[The] Council and the Commission [should] show greater willingness to accept [mixity]."
[150] Elazar, *Federalism and Political Integration* at 1.   [151] *Ibid.* (emphasis supplied).

rejected as an ideal type the centralist and unitarist model of federal states and which substituted in its stead a new pluralistic federal model could thus include the following elements: a dwindling yet always important number of pure Member State agreements and possibly a dwindling but equally significant number of pure Community agreements. One new additional option which I propose here would be the *vertical mixed agreement* whereby the Community would be the single external party but this would not necessarily give it internal legislative implementing competences, which would remain in the hands of Member States. But surely of primary and growing importance will be the by now classical *horizontal mixed agreement* of Member States and Community. It is one more unique contribution of the European Community to the practice and doctrine of federalism as a political arrangement.

Finally, mixed agreements offend the purist but they do after all bring and tie together the main actors of European integration – Community and Member States. In my view, mixed agreements though not resulting in a further exclusive building of the *centre* may – by virtue of their capacity to eliminate tensions and by constituting a growing network whereby Community and Member States gain in international strength simultaneously and become among themselves even further inextricably linked – be regarded as a contribution to a strengthening of the overall *framework* of European integration.

5

THE LEAST-DANGEROUS BRANCH:
A RETROSPECTIVE AND PROSPECTIVE OF
THE EUROPEAN COURT OF JUSTICE IN THE
ARENA OF POLITICAL INTEGRATION

RETROSPECTIVE

Introduction

IN 1982, in the anniversary issue of the *Journal of Common Market Studies*, posturing as the legal Daniel in the den of political-science lions, I made a plea to a skeptical audience to acknowledge the importance, if not centrality, of the legal paradigm in general and of the European Court in particular, to the evolution of the constitutional and institutional architecture of the European Community.[1] I tried to situate a political analysis in a legal context.

In the essay which forms this chapter, written ten years after the anniversary issue, I shall engage in something of a reverse exercise. The importance of the Court as an actor and of law as a context in which to situate political analysis of the Community has become widely accepted.[2] Here, then, a lion in the den of Daniels, I shall try to situate legal analysis in its political context.

---

[1] Weiler, "The Community, Member States and European Integration: Is the Law Relevant?" responding to Hoffmann, "Reflections on the Nation-State in Western Europe Today," *Journal of Common Market Studies* 21 (1982), 39 (special anniversary issue). This special issue was also produced as a book, L. Tsoukalis (ed.), *The European Community: Past, Present and Future* (Basil Blackwell: Oxford, 1983).

[2] *Cf.* Keohane and Hoffmann, "Institutional Change in Europe in the 1980s" in R. O. Keohane and S. Hoffmann, *The New European Community: Decisionmaking and Institutional Change* (Westview Press: Boulder, CO, San Francisco, Oxford, 1991). Another distinction of the European Community is its legal status: no other international organization enjoys such reliably effective supremacy of its law over the laws of member governments, with a recognized Court of Justice to adjudicate disputes (at 11). Indeed, of all Community institutions, the Court has gone farthest in limiting national autonomy, by asserting the principles of superiority of Community law and of the obligation of Member States to implement it (at 11 and 12).

The Court and its interlocutors: defining a perspective for inquiry

There is more than one way towards an appreciation of the role of the Court of Justice and of the judicial process in the evolution of the Community and of European integration. The classical way relates to what lawyers call doctrine, and especially constitutional doctrine. It may be structural doctrine: laying down, in the language of binding rules, a normative framework which purports to govern fundamental issues such as the structure of relationships between Community and Member States. It may be material doctrine, doing the same in relation to, say, the economic and social content of that relationship.

But, of course, from what the Court says (constitutionally) we can learn a lot about what the Court is, or more accurately, what the Court believes itself to be, or, at least, claims to be. In the "laying down" of binding constitutional doctrine there is, inevitably, an element of constitutional (self-)positioning of the Court itself. When the Court makes those determinations it is implicitly or explicitly placing itself in a power situation as the Community institution with the ultimate authority to make such structural and material determinations.[3]

The content of its constitutional structural and material doctrines – what the Court has said over the years – is so well known a tale (at least in its broad outlines) as to obviate the necessity of elaborate description. There is really no need for me to repeat, yet again, the story of supremacy, direct effect, human rights, implied powers, preemption, and other such well-known buzz-words capturing the history of so-called constitution-making by the Court. In structural constitutionalism *van Gend and Loos*, *Costa* v. *ENEL*, *ERTA*, and others are cases whose names have transgressed disciplinary boundaries even in Europe and are no longer the reserved domain of the lawyers. And then there is *Cassis de Dijon*, whose fame has spread even further, a case emblematic of the internal-market philosophy of the Court and which may, or may not, have had a role in shaping the new approach to harmonization and the principle of mutual recognition but is certainly representative of the material content of the Court's constitution-making.

So, no reiteration of the constitutional doctrine is required, nor even an elaborate explication of the Court's self-perception implicit in that doctrine. The underlying premise of the doctrinal perspective is fairly evident: self-referential, legal, internal to a possible logic of the Treaty itself; its

---

[3] The Court roots this authority in the Treaty; but it has, of course, considerable power in interpreting the Treaty and being the ultimate arbiter of its meaning. In its recent Opinion 1/91 of 14 December 1991 [1991] I-ECR 6079; [1992] 1 CMLR 245, it even seemed to construe legal principles which even Treaty amendment could not violate.

legitimacy, in the eyes of the Court itself (and of others) indirect – mediated, as is often the case with institutional religious doctrine, through the concept of interpretation.

What, instead, I do want to write about is the *reception* of the doctrine, and especially the reception of the self-positioning of the Court implicit in the doctrine, by other actors in the Community system. I am adopting a perspective in which courts are but one actor – more or less privileged – in a broad interpretative community (and maybe even a series of interpretative communities) and in which the Court's role is understood not simply by what it says but by how (and why) it is received by others.

Under the doctrinal perspective the political institutions of the Community (Commission, Council, and Parliament) the governments of the Member States (and other actors within Member States), and transnational interests and organizations constitute each, and together, objects of the Court's jurisprudence. Under the alternative, actor approach, they are subjects, interlocutors, partners to a dialogue or "multilogue."

The position of the Court on this view is not, then, a matter of legal determination and then logical deduction from the doctrine but a matter of empirical observation and social and political explanation. Here one must go beyond the self-referential legal universe – though this universe will in itself often be of political importance even if, critically, only as one factor among many in explaining the power or otherwise of the Court. The question of doctrinal content – the interpretative claim made by the Court – is only part of the picture. It must be followed by an inquiry into the "persuasion pull" and "compliance pull" which such doctrinal claims can evoke.

In the first part of this chapter, I shall, therefore, focus on the relationships and its possible causes in that first period. In the second part of this chapter, I shall try and show how and why, in my view, the future of the relationship of the Court to its interlocutors will unfold in quite a different way.

This is the point to inject, in good lawyerly fashion, a methodological disclaimer. When I speak of "my narrative" I use the term advisedly. I am offering no "theory" (at least not explicitly), or "conceptualization," or any other grand design. The fact is that, whereas the first doctrinal dimension has been explored endlessly, there is a veritable dearth of systematic social-science empirical studies which examine the many facets of the Court as a political actor in the Community and on which one can draw. The questions that have been raised in the literature have been haphazard, as have been the answers.[4]

---

[4] There is, none the less, a growing political-science literature on the European Court. Among the

This methodological deficiency is not going to be redressed by me in this essay. I shall make some factual claims, form some hypotheses, offer some causal explanations. But, factual claims and hypotheses will be based on my own experience and observation (hardly systematic) and causal explanation will be no more than personal speculation. *Caveat lector.*

The Court and its interlocutors: "benign neglect"

Historically, the European Court achieved a remarkable relational feat. The opening line of one of the most celebrated articles in the field, Eric Stein's *Lawyers, Judges, and the Making of a Transnational Constitution*, captures this feat superbly:

> Tucked away in the fairyland Duchy of Luxembourg and blessed, until recently, with benign neglect by the powers that be and the mass media, the Court of Justice of the European Communities has fashioned a constitutional framework for a federal-type Europe.[5]

Making a federal-type constitutional framework involved an aggressive and radical doctrinal jurisprudence, a veritable "revolution" often in the face of flailing "political will" of other Community actors. At times it seemed even at the expense of the power of other actors. The content of this jurisprudence can be summed up, perhaps, in the concept of a "Commu-

---

more important contributions, earlier and more recent, from which I have profited are: A.-M. Burley and W. Mattli, "Europe Before the Court: A Political Theory of Legal Integration," *International Organization* 47 (1993), 1; G. Garrett, "International Cooperation and Institutional Choice: The European Community's Internal Market," *International Organization* (1992); Keohane and Hoffmann, "Institutional Change in Europe" at 91: Gibson and Caldeira, "Compliance, Diffuse Support, and the European Court of Justice: An Analysis of the Legitimacy of a Transnational Legal Institution" (paper delivered at the 1993 Annual Law and Society Association Meeting, Chicago, May 27–30, 1993); Gibson and Caldeira, "The Legitimacy of the Court of Justice in the European Community: Models of Institutional Support" (paper delivered at the Annual Meeting of the Midwest Political Science Association, Chicago, April 15–17, 1993); Keohane and Hoffmann, "Institutional Change in Europe in the 1980s," in Keohane and Hoffmann, *The New European Community: Decisionmaking and Institutional Change* (Westview Press: Boulder, CO, San Francisco, Oxford, 1991); Lenaerts, "Some Thoughts about the Interaction between Judges and Politicians," in *The University of Chicago Legal Forum*, vol. 1992 at 93; H. Rasmussen, *On Law and Policy in the European Court of Justice* (Martinus Nijhoff: Dordrecht, Boston, 1986); M. Shapiro, "Comparative Law and Comparative Politics," *Southern California Law Review* 53 (1980), 537, 538; Shapiro, "The European Court of Justice," in A. M. Sbragia (ed.), *Euro-Politics: Institutions and Policymaking in the "New" European Community* (Brookings Institution: Washington, DC, 1992); F. Snyder, *New Directions in European Community Law* (Wiedenfeld and Nicolson: London, 1990); M. L. Volcansek, *Judicial Politics in Europe* (Peter Lang: New York, Berne, Frankfurt 1986); A. W. Green, *Political Integration by Jurisprudence* (Sijthoff: Leyden, 1969).

[5] *American Journal of International Law* 75 (1981), 1.

nity discipline": a set of norms governing many of the relations between Community and Member State legal (and political) orders.

And yet, despite the integrative radicalness of its doctrinal construct, with few exceptions, the Court managed to hegemonize the EC interpretative community, and to persuade, co-opt, and cajole most, if not all, of the other principal actors to accept the fundamentals of its doctrine and of its position in making the constitutional determinations for the Community.

It did not happen at once; it did not happen uniformly; there have been "pockets of resistance"; but, by and large, it has happened.[6] Both political and economic discussion of, say Community reform *à la* Maastricht, are always set, usually unthinkingly and naturally, against the constitutional structure set in place by the Court. It is not simply the fact of hegemony which is fascinating (and calls for some explanation) but the fact that this has indeed been a relatively "*quiet* revolution" and that the Court has, in fact, enjoyed such a lengthy period of "benign neglect" and not suffered serious challenges to its legitimacy.

In exploring this issue I shall focus on three sets of interlocutors – the national (Member State) judiciary; Member State governments and legislatures; and academia – as the three communities of which one might have expected a less-hospitable reception towards the European Court.

The European Court of Justice and the national judicial branch

The most interesting and, in my view, consequential interlocutors of the European Court have been national courts at all levels. This is a story of a double acceptance of Community discipline by the national judiciary. One part of the story concerns doctrine: the manner in which, moving and halting, two steps forward and one backwards, the national judiciary, in a process which still continues, has come to accept the constitutional doctrines, structural and material, of the European Court.[7]

But no less important has been the equally growing involvement of the national judiciary in the administration of Community law, transforming doctrinal acceptance into processual reality. The two dimensions are equally important: for, after all, what point is there in, say, accepting the principle of the supremacy of Community law, if no process exists for its vindication in time of conflict? *Ibi jus ubi remedium!*

The largest number of cases which reach the European Court do so by

---

[6] For a comprehensive description of the reception of the constitutional doctrines in the various legal orders of the Member States, see, e.g., the excellent H. G. Schermers and D. Waelbroeck, *Judicial Protection in the European Communities* (Kluwer: Deventer and Boston, 5th edn., 1992).

[7] See Schermers and Waelbroeck, *Judicial Protection in the European Communities.*

way of a preliminary reference from Member State courts under Article 177 to which the Court responds by issuing a preliminary ruling. The importance of this well-known procedure cannot be overestimated. It has become the principal vehicle for the imposition of a judicially driven Community discipline.[8] The overwhelming number of preliminary references arise in the context of litigation before national courts in which individuals seek to enforce, to their benefit, Community obligations against their own governments or other national public authorities.

Although the pattern of usage differs from Member State to Member State and even within Member States,[9] it would be a reasonable generalization to suggest that on the whole, since the early 1960, cases which established the utility of the preliminary procedure in this context, national courts, typically lower courts, have been willing partners in this use of Article 177 "against" national public authorities. It is precisely that partnership which is, in my view, so consequential for the overall positioning of the Court even beyond its relationship with national courts. This is so for several reasons.

Firstly, viewed from the perspective of compliance it makes all the difference that it is a national court, even a "lower" (or "lowly" one), and not the European Court itself which seeks the preliminary reference, awaits the preliminary ruling and then uses it in *its* domestic final decision.

When a national court *seeks* the reference it is, with few exceptions, acknowledging that, at least at face value, Community norms are necessary and govern the dispute. This very issue may be of huge political significance and the subject of controversy among governments or between the Member States as a whole and, say, the Commission.[10] But, by fact of "their own" national courts making a preliminary reference to the European Court, governments are forced to "juridify" their argument and shift to the judicial arena in which the Court of Justice is preeminent (so long as it can carry with it the national judiciary).[11]

---

[8] For analysis and description, see chapter 2, pp. 27–9 above.

[9] See J. Weiler, R. Dehousse, and G. Bebr, "Primus Inter Pares, The European Court and National Courts: Thirty Years of Cooperation" (the Florence 177 Project, Interim Report, 1988) (mimeograph, on file with the European University Institute).

[10] In the *Demirel* decision concerning the treatment of Turkish migrant workers in Germany that was one of the main issues: the very applicability of EEC law and the jurisdiction of the European Court to adjudicate the case. If the matter were in the hands of the governments of the Member States, there is no doubt in my mind that they would never have risked taking it before the European Court. Indeed, in the Maastricht Treaty, they have attempted to excluded such issues from the jurisdiction of the Court. See TEU, Art. L. But the Art. 177 procedure takes it out of their hands.

[11] "Juridifying" a dispute means that a Member State may have to defend itself before the Court. This implies an interstatal discourse with its own discipline, language, and constraints which can be quite different to the discourse of, say, diplomacy.

When a national court *accepts* the ruling the compliance pull of Community law becomes formidable. It is an empirical political fact, the reasons for which need not concern us here, that governments find it much harder to disobey their own courts compared to international tribunals. When European Community law is spoken through the mouths of the national judiciary it will also have the teeth that can be found in such a mouth and will usually enjoy whatever enforcement value that national law will have on that occasion.

Secondly, it would be wrong, however, to locate the significance of the partnership between national courts and the European Court solely, or even principally, in the pathological context of non-compliance and enforcement. As a systemic parameter physiognomy usually trumps pathology. A country's health is probably better measured by indicators such as infant mortality and days lost through sickness than by a review of the latest hospital technologies for dealing with rare diseases and acute medicine. In this context, the relatively high involvement of the national judiciary in the administration of Community law may be said to have a prophylactic effect, to act somewhat like preventive medicine. This involvement helps more than any doctrinal statement of the European Court to render Community law not as a *counter-system* to national law, but as *part* of the national legal order to which attaches the "Habit of Obedience" and the general respect, at least of public authorities, to "The Law." To the extent that national authorities feel constrained by "The Law" in the formulation and execution of policy and in the process of governance (and this will, surely, differ from one Member State to another) the higher the involvement of national courts in the administration and application of Community law, the higher will be the chances that Community norms will be regarded as part of that "Law" to which will attach the Habit of Obedience[12] associated with domestic rather than international norms. In this respect it may be considered an advantage of the European system that "everyday" national courts rather than special "federal courts" administer so much of Community law – in co-operation with the European Court.

Last but not least, the willingness of national courts to play their role in the partnership, especially of lower courts, will widen the circle of actors, individuals, corporations, pressure groups, and others who may build a stake and gain an interest in the effectiveness of Community norms. In this respect we should think, on the one hand, of the relative remoteness of individuals to much of classical international law and, on the other hand, of the huge stake built into federal law in federations when that became accessible to individuals. Without overstating the point, courts are an

---

[12] *Cf.* H. L. A. Hart, *The Concept of Law* (Clarendon Press: Oxford, 1961).

important vehicle for popular engagement by individual and group interests with and against government. The American reader may wish to contemplate the American polity with a judicial system without any lower federal courts, with state courts indifferent to federal law, and with a Supreme Court with extremely limited individual access. That would be Europe without Article 177 and the willing partnership of national courts. Some in America (and Europe) might like the idea, but none would deny that it would certainly be a very different polity.

If, then, the overall picture, with all the important exceptions, is one in which the national judiciary accepted both the constitutional reconstruction put forward by the European Court and also played a willing and keen role in giving that reconstruction reality as measured by the coin of judicial co-operation in the administration of Community law through Article 177, the obvious question is to speculate about the reasons for this willingness of national courts.[13]

Formalism

The first possibility, one which might seem the most formal and hence the most naive, but which, in my view, has considerable force, relies on the *per se* compliance pull of a dialogue conducted between courts in "legalese." Courts are charged with upholding the law. The constitutional interpretations given to the Treaty of Rome by the European Court carried a legitimacy deriving from two sources: first from the composition of the European Court which had as members senior jurists from all Member States; and, second, from the legal language itself, the language of reasoned interpretation, "logical deduction," systemic and temporal coherence, the artifacts which national courts would partly rely upon to enlist obedience within *their own* national orders. This is not the place to enter into the vexed issue of legal indeterminacy and its compatibility with "principled" and "neutral" adjudication. As an empirical observation, legal formalism retains a very substantial power in European jurisprudence and the overall content of the European Court jurisprudence seemed (or must have seemed) to reflect a plausible reading of the purposes of the Treaty to which the Member States had solemnly adhered.

My claim about the importance of formalism as one explanation for the compliance pull of the Court is reinforced by the negative reaction of national judiciaries in the face of the Court's interpretations which seemed to do too much violence to formalistic conventions such as the initial

---

[13] I am drawing here on my own speculation in chapter 2, pp. 32–8 above; and on Burley and Mattli's fascinating theorizing in "Europe Before the Court."

holding on direct effect of directives which met national judicial hostility until a better rationale was found.[14]

Actor-interest analysis

Another explanation expands the definition of the actors involved. As Burley and Mattli have remarkably shown, it is not the national judiciary alone which is responsible for the double acceptance, but a whole community of interests, by individuals, lawyers, and courts which developed a stake — professional, financial, and social — in the successful administration of Community law by and through the national judiciary and have thus acted as an agency for its successful reception.[15]

Reciprocity and transnational "judicial cross-fertilization"

There might be, too, an explanation rooted in the transnational horizontal nature of the process. Apparently it does sometimes matter to courts in one Member States what "the brethren" in other Member States are doing.[16] One reason why national courts, especially higher courts, but also lower courts, may have been tempted to resist the double acceptance could perhaps be in the fear that they would be disadvantaging their national system and their governments in their dealings with other Member States. Accepting Community discipline does, after all, restrict national autonomy. Courts have been sensitive to this issue in the international-law field. Thus, when national courts are satisfied that they are part of a trend their own acceptance is facilitated. Additionally, holding out against accepting a new doctrine when other similarly positioned courts have committed themselves might be seen to compromise the professional pride and prestige of the recalcitrant court.

The rhetoric of judicial argument and decision provide ample evidence for both lines of reasoning. We see that transnational reciprocity is employed as a device of both persuasion and justification. National courts have referred to decisions of their counterparts in other countries in a number of critical junctures.[17]

---

[14] *Cf.* the reaction to the initial *van Duyn* decision and the subsequent change of direction in the *Ratti*, *Becker* and *Marshall* cases. For discussion and citation, see chapter 2, pp. 18–19 above.

[15] See Burley and Mattli, "Europe Before the Court."

[16] For an analysis of interstatal court watching in the international law setting, see Burley, "Law Among Liberal States: Liberal Internationalism and the Act of State Doctrine," *Columbia Law Review* 92 (1992), 1,907; and Benvenisti, "Judicial Misgivings Regarding the Application of International Norms: An Analysis of Attitudes of National Courts," *European Journal of International Law* 4 (1993).

[17] Complete citations from decisions of the various national courts illustrating this point may be

Judicial empowerment

Last but not least, normative acceptance of the Court's constitutional construct and practical utilization through the Article 177 process by national courts may be rooted in plain and simple judicial empowerment. Whereas the higher courts acted diffidently at first, the lower courts made wide and enthusiastic use of the Article 177 procedure in many Member States. This is understandable both on a commonsense psychological level and on an institutional plane as well. Lower courts and their judges were given the facility to engage with the highest jurisdiction in the Community and, even more remarkable, to gain the power of judicial review over the executive and legislative branches even in those jurisdictions where such judicial power was weak or non-existent. Has not power been the most intoxicating potion in human affairs? Even in countries which knew fully fledged judicial review, such as Italy and Germany, the EC system gave judges at the lowest level powers that had been reserved within the national system only to the highest courts in the land. Institutionally, for courts at all levels in all member States, the constitutional architecture with the Court's signature meant an overall strengthening of the judicial branch *vis-à-vis* the other branches of government. The ingenious nature of Article 177 ensured that national courts did not feel that the empowerment of the Court was at their expense. After all, it is they who held the valve. Without the co-operation of the national judiciary the Court's power was illusory.

The European Court of Justice and the national executive and legislative branches

The symbiosis between the European Court and its national counterparts may have been influenced by the similarity of the species. It is far more difficult to explain the relatively low direct level of resistance to the constitutional transformation of Europe by the governments and legislatures of the Member States.

Whereas I hope to have demonstrated that accepting the new constitutional discipline by national courts could be seen for the most part as a means for judicial empowerment, the effect on the Member States' political branches of government could not but be seen, at least at face value, as a weakening. The traditional license which governments and parliaments enjoy (and often celebrate in the name of national interest and sovereignty) to bend or break their international obligations was seriously limited by the

found in Weiler, "A Quiet Revolution: The European Court of Justice and its Interlocutors," *Comparative Politics* 26 (1994), 510.

constitutionalization. Keohane and Hoffmann note in their study that "of all Community institutions, the Court has gone farthest in *limiting national autonomy*, by asserting the principles of superiority of Community law and of the obligation of Member States to implement [it]."[18]

To be sure, there were "pockets" of resistance: in the French Parliament, and during the 1975 referendum campaign in the UK. But these must be seen as exceptions to the general rule of equanimity. A survey of the attitudes of MEPs to the European construct is evocative in this respect. The survey demonstrated a high approval rate for the Court. What, however, is most telling for our purposes is to note that many of those MEPs who expressed great skepticism towards, and were critical of, say, the Commission and the European Parliament (on the grounds of enjoying too much power and being too pro-supranational Europe), did not transfer the same discontent to the Court.[19] I think the same would be true for national parliamentarians – an anti-marketeer in the European Parliament is not, I think, a different political actor from his or her counterpart in a national chamber.

Judicial appointments by the governments of the Member States to the Court in the 1970s and 1980s confirm the same conclusions. This is a period when any misconceptions about the "least dangerous branch" would have already been dispelled. By this time, governments would have been fully aware of the huge significance of the Court. And yet, most appointees came to the Court with a past reputation of a general accord with the constitutional and material construct of the Court. In the process of judicial appointments, the Member States, so far as one can tell in relation to a procedure which is far from transparent, eschewed any possible temptation at obvious "court-packing" or "jurisdiction-stripping."

The burden of the evidence available for the period leading up to the SEA and Maastricht, is that the Court's structural and material constitutional construct and the Court's hegemonic role in defining that construct, unpalatable as they may have been in individual decisions and contested rather strongly by individual Member States on an *ad hoc* basis, were eventually accepted by both the executive and legislative branches of the Member States.

That this should have been so is not self-evident. To be sure, we have already seen the impact on the perception of Court resulting from the integration of the national judiciary into the administration of Community law. But the limits of this impact on national actors – especially govern-

---

[18] Keohane and Hoffmann, *Institutional Change in Europe in the 1980s.*

[19] Weiler, "Attitude of MEPs towards the European Court – Some Interim Results," *European Law Review* 9 (1984), 169.

ments – must be carefully drawn. The involvement of the national judiciary may explain a basic, if grudging, compliance pull of Community law and its inclusion under the domestic canopy of respect for the "rule of law." But forced respect for the rule of law cannot explain why governments will not have acted vigorously to change and even neutralize an uncomfortable or dangerous actor – by reducing the powers of the Court, trimming its jurisdiction and, if necessary, controlling its personnel. After all, in the same period, the Member States objected to the most fundamental decisional rules of the Treaty and unceremoniously overturned them with the 1966 Luxembourg Accord.

What, then, can explain the relative deference accorded the Court and its output by the political branches of Member State governments? I would suggest the following possible mutually reinforcing lines of explanation.

Formalism

The pull of formalism has a role in this arena too. In this context the formalistic claim is that the judicial process rests "above" or "outside" politics, a "neutral" arena in which courts "scientifically" interpret the meaning of policy decided by others. As noted above the European tradition tends to overemphasize somewhat the formal nature of law and its alleged neutrality. The point about formalism is that its extra-legal impact is conditioned as much, or even more, by perception as by reality. The belief in the apolitical and neutral nature of the judicial process is, in fact, the reality that counts.

"Non-partisanship"

Beyond the pull of formalism, even when the judicial process was perceived as being, in larger or smaller part, integrationist, "political," policy driven, with varying degrees of indeterminacy of result and concomitant judicial discretion, *it was not interstate politics.* The Court has been scrupulously non-partisan and non-favoratist towards this or that specific Member State or group of Member States. To that extent the Court was, and was perceived to be, neutral. This perception was helped by the composition of the Bench with its virtually even national distribution, by the nature of the judicial process and mostly by the even spread of judicial deserts in which *there were no permanent and fixed Member State winners and losers.* The Court may have been perceived as a wild card or an unruly horse but not as partisan to the interests of this or that Member State.

Interest analysis

One could object, however, that even if the Court was not partisan to any individual Member State, its structural and material jurisprudence affected dramatically, and arguably adversely, the position of all the Member States *qua* Member States and that neither the pull of formalism nor the interstatal neutrality can explain the relative equanimity and overall acceptance of the constitutional jurisprudence.

In the first place, it is overstating the case to say that there was no reaction. In certain areas of jurisprudence, such as external economic relations, the States did react to countermand the potential consequences of judicial decision-making.[20] But this reaction tended to be local and never reached the stage of a more general drive to delegitimate the Court and/or substantially recast its role through, say, Treaty amendment. Could it be that the Member States developed an interest in the new judicial *status quo* and that a stake was created in maintaining rather than challenging judicial authority? Whence this interest?

There are two ways to narrate the structural and material jurisprudence of the European Court. The classical way has been "confrontational" and "pathological." It presents such emerging structural doctrines as direct effect, supremacy and implied-powers or material doctrines in the area of free movement in a conflictual setting which pits the interest of this or that Member State against that of the Community and then demonstrates how these doctrines "compel," "constrain," "bend," and "subject" the Member State to a Community discipline. To use the medical metaphor again, the context is an illness – a Member State attempting to escape its Community obligations (that is the confrontational pathology) – and the structural and material doctrine is the medicine, the remedy. It is this narrative which can explain not only the localized resistance of this or that Member State to this or that judicial outcome, but also explain our expectation of a more generalized political resistance to the Court. The United States government, for example, is known to exclude or seriously limit the jurisdictional reach of its own judicial system and courts in relation to some of its trade agreements. The reasons for this US practice are complex, but clearly one aspect is the US government's wish not to have its hands tied by its own courts.

But it is possible to analyze the same structural and material constitutional jurisprudence in a political-dialectical fashion. On the whole, in the pre-

---

[20] See Weiler, "The Evolution of Mechanisms and Institutions for a European Foreign Policy: Reflections on the Interaction of Law and Politics" (European Union Institute Working Paper, No. 85/202).

SEA/Maastricht period, the Court interfered little in the decisional process of the Community, except for a great insistence on respect for institutional arrangements – leaving a relatively free hand to the political organs to strike their bargains.[21] By contrast it intervened, through its structural and material jurisprudence rather boldly in the post-decisional phase – creating a legal apparatus which would make these bargains stick. The judicial message was: you are free to bargain, but agreements reached (through legislation) must be respected. This analysis would suggest a strong interest on the part of the Member States to uphold the judicial construct, given their obvious interest in making bargains stick. As I have endlessly argued, the fact that the Member States, in the period under discussion, had jointly and severally virtual control over decision-making, would not only make the constitutional revolution digestible but would actually create an interest of the Member States in this construct since, arguably, delicate bargains would be disrupted if Member States could disregard and violate them at will, and the Community as a whole would be disrupted if the way of responding to such violation would be classical international-law devices such as reprisals, counter-measures, trade wars and the like to which we have become accustomed in other arenas such as EC–USA trade disputes.[22]

These two narratives can, thus, be recast as follows:

1. *Narrative 1*: structural jurisprudence as a constraint on the freedom of action of individual Member States, the imposition of a Community discipline *vis-à-vis* the Member States creating a common Member State interest in resisting the judicial move and an expectation of Member State dissatisfaction and counteraction.

2. *Narrative 2*: structural jurisprudence ensures that bargains struck in the decisional process will stick, thereby creating a common interest in upholding the judicial doctrinal moves and a expectation of support for the Court.

To say that both narratives have their truth is to undermine their falsifiability: resistant Member State behavior could be attributed to the first narrative; supportive behavior to the second. Still, both narratives do have their truth.

There is one important line of cases which cannot be explained by the second narrative: the jurisprudence of the Court concerning the internal market which derives from a direct interpretation of the relevant Treaty articles and of which the *Cassis de Dijon* case law is the most well-known trademark, though clearly not the only line of cases. In that line of cases the

---

[21] In some areas it allows Community institutions a freer hand than Member States acting unilaterally. It did intervene, however, quite aggressively to make sure that bargains were not struck outside the Community framework.

[22] For the most recent formulation of my theses in this respect see chapter 2, p. 29 above.

Court "decimated" classical mechanisms of State protectionism by non-tariff barriers and other forms of protectionism and national discrimination. It cannot be said that in the *Cassis* line of cases, and others like it, the Court was simply making a bargain, struck in 1957, stick. But what could be said is that the *Cassis* line of cases actually accorded and accords with Member State and Community interests. Although annoying to this or that Member State in a concrete situation, the internal-market jurisprudence, on this reading, advanced their collective agenda.

One should be careful not to exaggerate any extrapolation of this argument. It is clearly true that in the long run, a court's jurisprudence cannot consistently stray too far from the overall political *Weltanschauung* of the polity. It is worth remembering that, in the Community, the governments of the Member States do not hold a monopoly over the definition of that *Weltanschauung*, and that the Court's jurisprudence itself has a role in defining it. It is clearly false that a court can never, even in critical areas and on sensitive issues, depart from that *Weltanschauung*. The single-market jurisprudence of the Court should be read as charting a *via media* between these too poles.

Transparency[23]

There is one additional possible explanation for the equanimity of reception by Member State political actors. At the moment in which the constitutional foundations were put in place the material province of Community law was rather narrow and socially and politically non-controversial. *Van Gend and Loos*, the case which ushered forth the new legal order, concerned tariff reclassification of imported chemicals – not an issue which would excite public sensibilities. There is, I believe, much truth in this proposition, but it has to be taken with caution. In the first place, even some of the early cases, such as *Costa* v. *ENEL* which introduced supremacy in 1964, were socially sensitive. *Costa* concerned the ability of the Italian state to nationalize public utilities, hardly a side issue. Even more so, by all accounts the Common Agricultural Policy – of huge importance to internal French and German politics – was a centrepiece of the Community legal order. It does not strike me as plausible that the French government would not assess the implications of direct effect and supremacy in such a politically sensitive area. Elsewhere I have argued for a different variant to the perception paradigm. The Member States felt less threatened by constitutionalization because they took control of the decisional process through

---

[23] I am indebted to Ms. Karen Alter for her illuminating comments on an earlier draft in relation to this point.

the *de facto* veto of the Luxembourg Accord. As I shall argue below, it is the (re)introduction of majority voting in the post-SEA era which drove home the radicalness of the constitutionalization and which may, among other reasons, explain why attitudes to the Court may be changing. None the less, what is clearly true of the first period is that the jurisprudence of the Court "enjoyed" a low visibility in terms of general public opinion and that the character of its case law was typically not the stuff to hit the front pages of the popular press. This, too, as we shall see, is something that is changing.

The European Court of Justice and academia

Finally, though of more limited political significance, the place of the European Court among academics is of some interest. In the first place academia is, at times, a barometer to wider currents of elite public opinion. The process of European integration has from its inception been an elite-driven phenomenon. Given the importance of the judicially driven federalization, one could have expected the development in academia of a classical "counter-majoritarian"-type critique of the Court which tends to emerge in the face of judicial activism. Although the Community has had many critics over the years, the absence of a focus on legal and judicial Europe is conspicuous by its very absence. This is true for political science, economics, and law.

Academia is important in another way. In continental Europe, at least the law professorate has an influential place in legal discourse. "La Doctrine," the synthetic view of legal norms, is a quasi-source of law and has an importance far greater than in, say, the USA. Academic legal writing is elemental in shaping it: as a collectivity the legal professorate is the custodian of La Doctrine. Non-critical integration of European constitutionalism into La Doctrine could help its legitimation within the profession.

The overall response, of academia – political science, economics, and law – to the judicially driven constitutional revolution has ranged from indifference and equanimity to celebration. Among scholars working on European integration, very few critical voices emerged in the period under consideration. It is a phenomenon which merits some analysis.

The lacuna among non-legal academics was not an outcome of reflection by political scientists and economists on the role of law and of the Court and a dismissal of them as irrelevant. There is simply no indication of this reflection and conclusion in the literature. I do not think either that an explanation can be summarized on the premise of the "primacy of politics" or the "primacy of economics." After all, a turn to law and the Court by political scientists and economists was common in examining national polities.

The reason for the scarce politological literature about the Court should be looked for in the intellectual background and formation of those who turned to examination of the European integration phenomenon as a whole. Two intellectual traditions served as background to Community observers and theorists: international relations and federalism.

The most common background was in international relations, and by the 1950s whatever school of international relations one belonged to, the function, power and importance of *international law* and, say, the International Court of Justice, were – not altogether without reason – dismissed as marginal and irrelevant. Is it possible that this baggage "prejudiced" observers from even looking at the legal paradigm and at the European Court as potentially important? As for the federalists, comparative federal experience suggests that there is some mutuality in the strengthening of central institutions in federal polities. All branches, executive, legislative, and judicial, tend to strengthen (not necessarily at exactly the same pace) at the expense of their counterparts at constituent unit level. The story of European integration from the late 1950s to the middle of the 1970s – the period in which European integration received the greatest academic attention – defied the comparative federal experience. The political institutional and decision-making processes were undergoing their deepest crisis and moving in a typically non-"federal" direction, whereas this was the "heroic" and most "federal" period for the law and courts. Perhaps the non-legal academic profession assumed that the political disintegration of that period would have been coupled with a reduced role for law and the Court – as was the experience with other transnational integration experiences – and just abandoned the field as not worthy of serious attention. It is a common feature of politological writing of the period to analyze the decline of the political institutions of the Community without even mentioning the Court.

If we turn to the legal academy the picture is interestingly different. Among those who turned to Community law and legal integration as a subject of research, the role of law and the Court has, if anything, been overemphasized. This is reflected by titles such as *Political Integration by Jurisprudence*[24] and *Integration through Law*.[25] It has been overemphasized in overstated claims about the importance of law in the overall process of

---

[24] A. W. Green, *Political Integration by Jurisprudence* (Sijthoff: Leyden, 1969).

[25] M. Cappelletti, M. Secombbe, and J. H. H. Weiler (eds.), *Integration through Law*, 5 vols. (Walter de Gruyter: Berlin, New York, 1985).

European integration and the simplicity of the integration models explicitly or implicitly relied upon.

Even more interesting was the almost unanimous non-critical approach and tradition developed by Community-law scholars towards the Court of Justice. Studies of the Court tended to be, as Shapiro scathingly but aptly put it in relation to one typical example:

> Constitutional law without politics ... [presenting] the European Community as a juristic idea; the written constitution as a sacred text; the professional commentary as a legal truth; the case law as the inevitable working out of the correct implications of the constitutional text and the [European Court] as the disembodied voice of right reason and constitutional theology.[26]

Criticism of the Court, when it appeared in the legal literature, was usually of two kinds: either constitutional-law or administrative-law professors fulminating at the encroachment of their turf by the newcomers and arguing, typically from a crude "national sovereignty" basis, against the EC usurper;[27] or critics from within European-law fraternity which, to continue the Shapiro theological metaphor, were in the Lefevre or Satmar corner, castigating the Court for any deviation from the strictest integration orthodoxy. The few exceptions can be regarded as the proverbial exception that proves the general rule and their work was generally received with skepticism in Europe.[28]

The reasons for the non-critical legal approach are also rooted in the background and formation of the legal professorate who, like their colleagues in other disciplines, turned to European integration. A great many of the first generation of professors came to Community law from international law. The international legal order was, from the 1950s through to the 1980s, in deep crisis, prompted by the Cold War, which induced failure of the United Nations and most other major institutions. Academic international law suffered from a particularly acute spell of its perennial deep-seated insecurity (when compared to its domestic counterpart) and its practice was more than usually uncomfortable with the twin medicines of apology and rationalization. In some ways, Community law and the European Court were everything an international lawyer could dream about: the Court was creating a new order of international law in which norms were norms, sanctions were

---

[26] Shapiro, "Comparative Law and Comparative Politics," *Southern California Law Review* 53 (1980), 537, 538.

[27] E.g. Sorrentino, *Corte constituzionale e corte di giustizia delle comunita europee* (Guiffre: Milan, 1970) and "La tutela dei diritti fondamentali nell'ordinamento comunitario ed in quello italiano," in M. Cappelletti and A. Pizzorusso (eds.), *L'Influenza del diritto europeo sul diritto italiano* (Guiffre: Milan, 1982).

[28] *Cf.* H. Rasmussen, *On Law and Policy in the European Court of Justice* (Martinus Nijhoff: Dordrecht, Boston, 1986).

sanctions, courts were central and frequently used, and lawyers were important. Community law as transformed by the European Court was an antidote to the international legal malaise.

Secondly, with only a few exceptions, even in the national Member State public- and private-law traditions, from which other professors were drifting into Community law in the 1960s and 1970s with its expansion into new fields such as environmental protection and the like, there was no powerful critical tradition either on the continent or in the UK and Ireland. The critics from without became more or less silenced, simply swamped by the general acceptance of the integration construct around them, and also unable to keep up with the increased technical proficiency in Community law which was necessary to make one's critique effective.

Additionally, in a period in which the Community was shown to be suffering from a "democracy deficit" rooted principally in the non-accountability of the Council of Ministers directly to a parliamentary chamber and to the empowerment of the executive branch of the Member States through their reincarnation as the principal legislator when wearing their Community hat, it was easy to defend the Court as a "bulwark" against excessive power in the hands of the Council and the Commission.

Finally, no critical symbiosis developed with sister disciplines. There was no helping hand from the economic and political-science flank since, as mentioned above, they simply neglected the legal phenomenon of European integration. Even in the best political-science and economic works of the time, including those with considerable critical bite, when law and the Court were mentioned at all, the treatment was descriptive, very often by a lawyer brought in to graft a legal chapter onto a political-science volume.[29]

Conclusions to the retrospective

The relationship of the European Court, an actor with a powerful vision and remarkable influence in shaping key dimensions of the evolving Community, to its principal interlocutors may be described as an extended honeymoon:

1. With its all important national judicial counterparts, it has been, on the whole, a story of courting and eventual consummation of a mutually empowering relationship.
2. With national political organs it has been an even more remarkable story of power made acceptable to these organs by, at times, the politeness of convivial indifference, at times, the legal masks of judicial neutrality and the rule of law and, at times, the seductiveness of calculated self-interest.

[29] *Cf.* S. Henig, *Power and Decision in Europe* (Europotential Press: London, 1980).

3. With academia it has been either love scorned or rapture based on conquest and domination rendered felicitous by ignorance.

PROSPECTIVE

Introduction

That, then, concludes the narrative of the reception and acceptance of the Court by its three interlocutors. The honeymoon is, I think, at an end, and, though no divorce is predicted, it will be the ups and downs of a mature marriage which henceforth will characterize the relationship.

There is not a year in the history of the Community where some enterprising academic could not, with credibility, convene a conference or write a paper round the theme of "The Community in Change – Future Perspectives." The changes I shall focus on in the post-SEA and Maastricht period are those which in my view are likely to rock the boat in the relationship between the European Court and the three sets of interlocutors we have dealt with.

My thesis is simple enough: it is not the Court which is or has changed in a way which will affect its perception. If anything, the Court has become somewhat more "prudent" in its jurisprudence.[30] Instead, it is the environment, political and social, and the conditions in which the Court operates, which will become consequential. The Court will, I shall argue, be called upon to adjudicate disputes which will, inevitably, subject it to public debate of a breadth and depth it is unaccustomed to. For reasons I shall explain, its overall visibility is bound to grow and it will be judged by a media and public opinion far more informed than before. The adoration and adulation by academia is also, thankfully, likely to weaken.

In relation to many of these elements there is nothing the Court will be able to do, since, I shall argue, the new environment will often place it in a "no win" situation.

The following are, then, the principal considerations affecting and constituting the new environment for judicial activity.

Limits to competences of the Community

The most fundamental change in the interaction of judicial decision-making in the new political environment relates to the issue of competences, the dividing line between Community and Member State sphere of

---

[30] *Cf.* Koopmans, "The Role of Law in the Next Stage of European Integration," *International and Comparative Law Quarterly* 34 (1986), 925.

activities.[31] The student of comparative federalism discovers a constant feature in practically all federative experiences: a tendency, which differs only in degree, towards controversial concentration of legislative and executive power in the centre/general power at the expense of constituent units. This is apparently so independently of the mechanism for the allocation of jurisdiction/competences/powers between the centre and the "periphery." Differences, where they occur, are dependent more on the ethos and political culture of polities than on mechanical devices.

The Community has both shared and differed from this general experience. It has shared it in that the Community, especially in the 1970s, had seen a weakening of any workable and enforceable mechanism for allocation of jurisdiction/competences/powers between Community and its Member States.[32] This occurred by a combination of two factors.

1. profligate legislative practices especially in, for example, the usage of Article 235;[33] and

2. a bifurcated jurisprudence of the Court which on the one hand extensively interpreted the reach of the jurisdiction/competences/ powers granted the Community and on the other hand has taken a self-limiting approach towards the expansion of Community jurisdiction/ competence/powers when exercised by the political organs.

To make the above statement is not tantamount to criticizing the Community, its political organs and the Court. This is a question of values. It is a sustainable thesis that this process was overall beneficial, in its historical context, to the evolution and well being of the Community, its Member States, and their citizens and residents.

The interesting thing about the Community experience, and this is where it does not share the experience of other federative polities, is that despite the massive legislative expansion of Community jurisdiction/competences/powers and the collapse of constitutional guarantees against that expansion, there had not been any political challenge or crisis on this issue from the Member States other than on an *ad hoc* basis.

This was so mostly for the simple and obvious fact of consensus decision-making in the pre-SEA era. Unlike federal states, the governments of the Member States themselves (jointly and severally) could control absolutely the legislative expansion of jurisdiction/competences/powers. Nothing that was done could be done without the assent of all national capitals. This

---

[31] I am drawing here on Jacqué and Weiler, "On the Road to European Union – A New Judicial Architecture," *Common Market Law Review* 27 (1990), 185.

[32] For a full analysis of this Community phenomenon, see chapter 2, pp. 39–59 above.

[33] For analysis and empirical data, see Weiler, *Il sistema communitario europeo* (Il Mulino: Bologna, 1985), Part 2.

fact diffused any sense of threat and loss of power on the part of governments.

This era has now passed with the shift to majority voting in the post-SEA period. Governments of the Member States no longer have the "veto guarantee" and thus have taken a new, very hard look at the question. Limiting the competences of the Community has become one of the most sensitive issues of the Maastricht construct. The TEU introduced formally not only the principle of subsidiarity into the Community legal regime,[34] but also set severe limits on Community legislative action in some of the new fields such as culture, public health and the like.[35] Public opinion in the Member States has also become far more sensitive to this issue.

In this new climate the Court's earlier "hands-off" attitude to expansive Community competences will no longer work. Whether it likes it or not, it will be called upon, with increasing frequency, to adjudicate competence issues. And here the Court will be put into a "no-win" situation: whatever decision it will take in this vexed field, it is likely to earn the displeasure of one or more powerful constituencies.

I shall draw now, by way of hypothetical examples, four typical "competence"-related scenarios which will illustrate the new political environment.

Scenario 1: the outer reaches of Community jurisdiction

The Commission has now before the Council a controversial draft Directive proposing an almost total ban on all advertising in the Member States of tobacco products.[36] The proposal has evoked considerable controversy as evidenced by the heated debate in the European Parliament, the constant revisions by the Commission and the postponement by the Council. The Commission, which proposed Article 100A as the basis for its proposal, justifies it as a measure necessary to ensure the elimination of barriers to trade in media carrying tobacco advertisements and as a means to eliminate distortion to competition in the market. Its opposes claims that it is a health measure (for which the Community has no competence) masquerading as a single-market provision. There is discord among the Member States about the substantive merits of the total ban and about the competence of the Community to enact such a ban. This example illustrates perfectly how the issue of competences is almost always intricately involved with the substantive content of any proposal. Often,

---

[34] TEU, Art. 3B.   [35] See, e.g., TEU, Arts. 128, 129.

[36] Commission's Amended Proposal for a Council Directive on the approximation of Member States' laws, regulations and administrative provisions on advertising for tobacco products 1992 OJ (C 129/5) (May 21, 1992).

substantive opposition will be masked as opposition to the principle of Community jurisdiction and *vice versa*. Critically, in the pre–SEA period, consensus among the Member States would be necessary for adoption. Once such consensus were achieved, the issue of competences would be diffused.

Imagine then that the proposal is adopted by majority vote and reaches the Court with a challenge claiming that the Community exceeded its jurisdiction, a claim supported by some Member States and powerful economic actors (the tobacco lobby), opposed by other Member States and the equally powerful anti-tobacco public forces.

The intricacies of jurisdictional and substantive issues are daunting. To approve the measure would represent an expansive reading of Article 100A in an era when the political climate opposes, in principle, such expansive readings. The Court might draw considerable "flak" and its credibility as an effective guarantor against profligate Community legislation might be damaged. By contrast, to strike down the measure, even in part, will give rise to vocal complaints of the Court succumbing to the interests of big business and being insensitive to social issues.

There is no need to conceptualize the example – it speaks for itself. If I am right in my prediction that this type of issue is likely to rise with increasing frequency, it will become apparent that the Court will increasingly find itself in visible controversy.

Scenario 2: subsidiarity

I do not wish here to go beyond what is necessary to achieve the objectives of this chapter, by adding more waste to that growth industry, academic subsidiarity commentary. Adjudication of subsidiarity issues is likely to put the Court in the same "no-win" situation outlined above.

Article 3B of the TEU provides:

> The Community shall act within the limits of the powers conferred upon it by this Treaty and of the objectives assigned to it therein. In areas which do not fall within its exclusive competence, the Community shall take action, in accordance with the principle of subsidiarity, only if and in so far as the objectives of the proposed action cannot be sufficiently achieved by the Member States and can therefore, by reason of the scale or effects of the proposed action, be better achieved by the Community. Any action by the Community shall not go beyond what is necessary to achieve the objectives of this Treaty.

Whereas the prevailing view, influenced in part by German constitutional theory, was that subsidiarity was not a justiciable concept, in the conclusions to the Edinburgh Summit the European Council pronounced that:

[t]he principle of subsidiarity cannot be regarded as having direct effect; however, interpretation of this principle, as well as review of compliance with it by the Community institutions are subject to control by the Court of Justice, as far as matters falling within the Treaty establishing the European Community are concerned.

Issues of subsidiarity are likely to reach the Court, if at all, when there is disagreement between a majority and minority of Member States. As regards the first paragraph of Article 3B, the issue before the Court would present itself in precisely the manner of the draft tobacco directive given above and with the same political consequences. The second paragraph – subsidiarity in the strict sense – is, in my view, justiciable and should be so.[37] Given, however, the open-textured nature of the provision, the appropriate criteria for judicial review would be reasonableness and excess of jurisdiction. The Court should not simply substitute its view of the matter for that of the majority in Council, but decide whether, in the circumstances, the Council decision could reasonably be considered to accord with subsidiarity. In most cases the answer is likely to be positive.

But it is likely that, here too, substance and constitutional limits will be intricately connected, in a sensitive political context. Each time the Court affirms a measure, it will be charged as weak on constitutional limits. When it annuls, it will be accused of being political, ideological, and worse. My own view is that if the Court avoids subsidiarity issues put before it on the grounds that they are "political," it will not only lose credibility as a guarantor against Community jurisdictional excesses, but this task will be taken on by national supreme courts at huge cost to the constitutional architecture of the Community. But this does not mean that in deciding subsidiarity issues the Court will not pay a political cost as well.

Scenario 3: legal bases

The question of the legal bases for Community legislation is a sub-species of the general competences issue. Here the issue is not simply whether or not the Community may act, but what is the appropriate legal basis. In the pre-SEA period this mattered little. When in doubt there was a regular usage of the catch-all Article 235. By contrast, since 1987, under renewed Community majority voting, the legal basis means a lot: it will determine the decisional process with the intricacies of majority voting and parliamentary involvement. The intricacies of the decisional process will, in turn, determine substantive outcome. Once more, the mixture of constitutional principle and substantive content will render these controversies, of which

[37] See Jacqué and Weiler, "On the Road to European Union."

there have been quite a few already, increasingly explosive. A decision on the legal basis will often determine whether and with what content a decision will emerge. If, say, the Court in our hypothetical tobacco Directive example were to decide that Article 100A is an inappropriate legal basis and that, instead, the Community may only act on the basis of, say, Article 235, the measure in its current form will be doomed with the same political outcome.[38]

Scenario 4: competences and the national courts

The fundamental constitutional architecture of the Community as elaborated by the European Court was based, I would argue, on a subtle unstated "socio-legal contract" between the European Court and its national counterparts. The heightened sensitivity to competence issues is not likely to stop at the door of national courts. Sooner or later, "supreme" courts in the Member States would realize that the "socio-legal contract" announced by the Court in its major constitutionalizing decisions, namely that "the Community constitutes a new legal order . . . for the benefit of which the states have limited their sovereign rights, *albeit within limited fields*"[39] is at stake, and that although they (the "supreme" courts) accepted the principles of the new legal order – supremacy and direct effect – the question of who adjudicates the limits to the field is one on which a battle may be fought. The position of the European Court has been emphatic: it alone can strike down a Community measure for whatever reason, including lack of competences. But whereas national supreme courts have all accepted explicitly the basic constitutional principles of supremacy and direct effect, there has not yet been a full ventilation of the *"Kompetenz-Kompetenz"* issue and it is not clear whether at least Courts such as the German, Italian, or Irish highest courts will cede that power so easily.

Visibility

Implicit in the analysis of the competence issue is another consideration – the growing visibility of the European Court beyond the circle of practitioners and *cognoscenti*. The increased visibility is another sign of the maturing of the system and derives, in my view, from two causes.

First, a general new awareness of the Community resulting from the Maastricht debate, the first veritable Community-wide debate on the Community in its history. A recent pioneering public-opinion survey

---

[38] See, e.g., Case 45/86 *Commission* v. *Council* [1987] ECR 1,493 for a playout of this issue.
[39] Emphasis added.

conducted through the Eurobarometer is instructive in this regard.[40] In a Community-wide survey in 1992, 34.5 percent[41] of Eurobarometer respondents had some cognizance of the European Court (the highest was 63.4 percent in Denmark; the lowest was 22.7 percent in the Netherlands) though of a non-profound nature. The learned authors of the survey conclude that: "[t]hese data suggest that the Court has become more of a public institution, one that no longer works in virtual anonymity and obscurity."[42] Excluding "inattentive respondents" (those who registered no awareness of the Court) the results become even more remarkable. The authors of the survey, apparently using standard social-science techniques in this field, developed a measurement of diffuse public support or otherwise for the Court.[43] This is not the place to reproduce the intricate techniques and the prudent analysis of the survey. One of the general conclusions of its authors is "that the European Court of Justice has substantial but still very limited legitimacy" in the general public. "Overall," they add, "the European Court of Justice seems to have more enemies than friends within the mass publics of the European Community."[44]

These pioneering studies will, in time, be scrutinized, hopefully repeated, and the interpretation subjected to critical review. Much of the current diffuse public attitude towards the Court is possibly conditioned by general attitudes to the Community rather than by the specificity of Court decision-making. The timing of that particular survey, in the height of the Maastricht debate will have had its impact too. By citing some of their more dramatic conclusions I take no position except to indicate that, as public visibility grows, so will public awareness, and with it, the Court will, willy nilly, be thrown into public debate and also used by politicians in their own arenas. The results demonstrate too another lesson of Maastricht: support by elites and public and statal institutions is not necessarily an indication of the mood in the street.

Secondly, the visibility of the Court has not grown simply as a result of

---

[40] See Gibson and Caldeira, "Compliance, Diffuse Support, and the European Court of Justice: An Analysis of the Legitimacy of a Transnational Legal Institution"; and Gibson and Caldeira, "The Legitimacy of the Court of Justice in the European Community: Models of Institutional Support." Eurobarometer is a public-opinion survey of the EU Commission conducted on a regular basis.

[41] The comparable average figure for each Member State's national high court was 58 percent. For the Commission, 51.2 percent. For the Community as a whole, 81.4 percent.

[42] Gibson and Caldeira, "The Legitimacy of the Court" at 13.

[43] Thus, to give but a couple of examples, one question read: "If the European Court of Justice started making a lot of decisions that most people disagree with, it might be better to do away with the Court altogether." Another read: "The political independence of the European Court of Justice is essential. Therefore, no other European Institution should be able to override court opinions even if it thinks they are harmful to the European Community."

[44] Gibson and Caldeira, "The Legitimacy of the Court" at 15.

the Maastricht-related generally higher visibility of the Community but also because of the growth in the number of cases before the Court which are of a character to capture media and public attention. The logic of the single market *strictu sensu* has brought before the Court cases such as the British Sunday trading and the Irish abortion cases. This is the stuff of headlines even in the popular press. Delors' famous prophecy of the elevated percentage of social legislation which will emanate from Brussels is also likely to contribute to the number of such high-visibility cases.

Case load and judicial burden

In the first part of this essay I retold the success story of the Court *vis-à-vis*, *inter alia*, national courts. This success has had a cost, the principal one of which has been a dramatic rise in the workload of the European Court, a growth which has not peaked and is likely to grow with the entry of new Member States. In 1988, 373 cases were brought before the Court; in 1989, 401 (385 for the ECJ, 16 for the Court of First Instance); in 1990, 443 (384 for the ECJ, 59 for the Court of First Instance); and, in 1991, 440 (345 for the ECJ, 95 for the Court of First Instance). There are more cases today pending before the European Court of Justice than there were when the Court of First Instance was created and so many cases transferred to it. The average waiting time for a case is now 24 months which is longer than the average waiting time when the Court of First Instance was established.

This increase in the workload of the Court has had, in turn, three adverse effects:[45]

1. The time lag for Court decisions, both under Article 177 and also under all other heads of jurisdiction, is, in my view, unacceptable. Given that in Article 177 proceedings the preliminary reference and ruling are only a stage in the principal judicial proceedings before a national court, the conclusion is that the invocation of Article 177 becomes a serious time drain on the litigants, undermining in a pragmatic sense the principle of effective remedies.

2. But it is not only the time delay in itself which is problematic in relation to this increase. Even if a rearrangement of the working procedures of the Court would bring about a reduction in the time delay, the very fact of a large number of decisions, even if given in timely fashion, is, beyond a certain point, harmful. The corpus of decisions of the European Court constitutes a remarkable chapter of judicial excellence and creativity. None the less, judges are human. There can be no question that, at a certain point, the number of cases will affect

---

[45] See Jacqué and Weiler, "On the Road to European Union," which I am using here.

negatively the ability of the Court to address cases with sufficient deliberation. The quality of decisions is bound to suffer.

3. Finally, it is not only the Court that is likely to suffer from the increase in the case load. The European Court of Justice is the highest judicial organ of the Community. It plays thus, like all other "supreme" courts, a dual role. On the one hand it is of course the ultimate guardian of the administration of justice in the sphere of application of Community law. But, on the other hand, it is also responsible for overseeing and directing the judicial evolution of Community law. As such its judgments are designed to be read, interpreted, discussed, and ultimately internalized by all legal actors within the Community who have a contact with the Community legal order. Such is the case with the jurisprudence of courts like the Supreme Constitutional Courts of Germany, Italy, the House of Lords, the Supreme Court of the United States and all similar courts. However, as the experience of other supreme courts clearly demonstrates,[46] at a certain point when the quantity of cases surpasses a certain level, the ability of a supreme court to play this double role is called into question. Beyond a certain number of cases (and it is neither possible nor necessary to give a precise figure) the ability of the legal community to follow and digest appropriately the jurisprudence of its high courts begins to diminish. The specific gravity of each decision is diluted and the supreme courts' status at the apex of the judicial pyramid self-destructs. There are some signs that the European Court might already be facing this dilemma.

The only long-term solution to this problem is, in my view, the creation of regional circuit courts which will take the principal burden away from the Court of Justice, a radical redefinition of the role of the Court of First Instance and the transformation of the Court of Justice into the Constitutional Court of the European Community.[47] Until this or some other solution is found, a negative effect that these practical aspects may have on the quality of dialogue between the European Court and its national interlocutors cannot be excluded. A significant and rising delay in the administration of justice, a possible decline in the quality of judgments,[48] and a dilution of the specific gravity of decisions are all counter-indications to a continued healthy relationship between the European and national jurisdictions.

---

[46] See A. Tunc, *La cour judiciaire supreme – une enquête comparative* (Recherches Pantheon-Sorbonne, Université de Paris I, 1978).

[47] *Cf.* Jacqué and Weiler, "The Legitimacy of the Court."

[48] One cannot but note the far greater degree of legal craftsmanship which characterizes some of the decisions of the Court of First Instance compared to some recent decisions of the European Court of Justice. The time factor must be of some importance in this regard.

The cost of effectiveness

Another development which is likely to have an impact on the relationship between the Court and its national counterparts as well as the political organs within the Member States derives from the new strategies for ensuring the effectiveness of Community law. Maastricht itself provides for financial penalties for Member States who fail to comply with European Court decisions to be determined by the Court itself in an action brought by the Commission. Additionally, the Court itself, in cases such as the *Francovich, Emmott* v. *Minister for Social Welfare, Marleasing*, and *Factortame* as well as others going in the same direction,[49] has developed a new strategy for rendering it more difficult for Member States to evade their obligations under the Treaty.

This jurisprudence illustrates perfectly the dilemma of the Court. There is little doubt that a high priority must be given to ensuring uniform compliance with Community law in the different Member States and that the judicial strategy adds an important dimension in this direction. But the recent line of cases represents a potential encroachment of Community law and the authority of the European Court into procedural matters which hitherto were within the almost exclusive province of national courts. In the past the European Court was always careful to present itself as *primus inter pares* and to maintain a zone of autonomy of national jurisdiction even at the price of non-uniformity of application of Community law. If the new line of cases represent a nuanced departure from that earlier ethos, the prize may be increased effectiveness, but the cost may be a potential tension in the critical relationship between the European Court and national courts.

A changing academic environment

Several changes in academic practices and processes are also contributing to a more critical environment for Court studies. There is, on the one hand, both in Europe and the USA, a renewed and growing interest by political scientists in the Court of Justice; and, on the other hand, a growing number of Community-law lawyers, even sitting judges, whose writings situate the Court in its political, social, and economic contexts.[50] A new legal journal, *European Law In Context*, dedicated to a non-doctrinal approach to EC legal research, appeared in 1994. These new directions are

[49] See Snyder, "The Effectiveness of European Community Law: Institutions, Processes, Tools and Techniques," *Modern Law Review* 56 (1993) 19–54.
[50] See, e.g., Lenaerts, "Some Thoughts about the Interaction between Judges and Politicians," *The University of Chicago Legal Forum* (1992), 93. Lenaerts is a judge on the Court of First Instance.

broadening the scope of judicial studies; the Court is being subjected to empirical investigation, to critical theorizing, to public-attitude surveys, and to a general demystification of the Community judicial function. In other words, the Court is finally receiving the attention from social scientists which its importance in the European structure merits.

The growth of Community law and its heightened profile resulting from the 1992 psychosis and the Maastricht debate has removed it from the province of the closed circle of Community-law experts – a category which no longer exists – and extended it into the circles of national-substantive-law experts. One cannot be an "expert" in, say, Member State labor law or environmental law, without gaining proficiency in the concomitant Community law. One effect of this transformation of the field has been the importation of a far more critical apparatus to the treatment of Community law and its Court. It is critical because the Community-law importation will be judged against preexisting substantive standards and also because these national fields have often developed their own critical tradition and the practitioners do not bring to the study of the EC and its court the exuberance of the first generation of Community lawyers.

Conclusions to the prospective

I have identified five areas in which recent developments would suggest a different, politically more volatile, environment for the Court. There are signs that the effects of this volatile environment are already showing.

1. In the political arena, in the context of the delicate competence issue, one merely has to consider, by way of example, the fierce attack by Chancellor Kohl on the Court in October 1992: "If one takes the Court of Justice . . . it does not only exert its competencies in legal matters, but goes far further. We have an example of something that was not wanted in the beginning. This should be discussed so that the necessary measures may be taken later."[51] Far more ominous and dangerous was a suggestion, attempted to be tabled by a Member State at the Edinburgh Summit which suggested curtailing the powers of national courts to make references to the European Court. It is, of course, more significant that the proposal did not gain support; but as a possible harbinger of things to come it is illustrative. The express attempt at judicial exclusion from the two Maastricht non-Community "pillars"[52] should be read as a illustration of the same type of reticence *vis-à-vis* the Court.

---

[51] *Europe*, Doc. No. 5,835 (October 14, 1992). See also "Die leise Übermacht," *Der Spiegel* (49/1992) at 102.
[52] TEU, Art. L.

2. In the sphere of general public opinion one may recall the tentative conclusions of the Eurobarometer study alluded to above.[53]

3. In the academic literature, there is a growing number of hard-hitting, irreverent, "bottom-line"-oriented, legal writing about the Court.[54]

More examples could be given and should be treated, in my view, as a sign of things to come. To be sure, the general authority and support the Court enjoys is not about be overturned. But, across a broad range, its decisions are likely to be subjected to a far greater measure of critical political, popular and academic scrutiny than in the past.

All of this should not be read as a prophecy of doom, or a programmatic warning. On the contrary, these are developments which should, in great part, be welcomed as natural and healthy. Natural, since, if anything, it is really the early period which was anomalous in allowing the Court, even if tucked away in the fairyland Duchy of Luxembourg, to be blessed with benign neglect by the powers that be and the mass media, in the face of its critical centrality to the European construct. Healthy, since it is far better that institutions such as the Court, which exercise considerable power, should be subjected to the scrutiny of other institutions, academia, the media, and general public opinion.

Interesting days ahead.

---

[53] See pp. 212–13 above.

[54] See, e.g., Coppel and O'Neill, "The European Court of Justice, Taking Rights Seriously?" *Common Market Law Review* 29 (1992), 669. For critique see Weiler and Lockhart, " 'Taking Rights Seriously' Seriously: The European Court and its Fundamental Rights Jurisprudence" in *Common Market Law Review* 32 (1995), 51 (Part I) and 579 (Part II).

Part 2

"WE WILL HEARKEN ..."

6

INTRODUCTION: THE REFORMATION OF EUROPEAN CONSTITUTIONALISM

BOOTING UP

CONSTITUTIONALISM IS the DOS or Windows of the European Community. Constitutionalism came into being as a result of a process and went through "different versions." Alec Stone offers as good a characterization of constitutionalization as any:

> [T]he process by which the EC treaties evolved from a set of legal arrangements binding upon sovereign states, into a vertically integrated legal regime conferring judicially enforceable rights and obligations on all legal persons and entities, public and private, within [the sphere of application of EC law].[1]

Here is my own, more vulgar, way of giving expression to the same concept. The Community was conceived as a legal order founded by international treaties negotiated by the governments of States under international law and giving birth to an international organization. The constitutionalism thesis claims that in critical aspects the Community has evolved and behaves as if its founding instrument were not a treaty governed by international law but, to use the language of the European Court, a constitutional charter governed by a form of constitutional law.

Constitutionalism, more than anything else, is what differentiates the Community from other transnational systems and, within the Union, from the other "pillars."

The impact of constitutionalism is inevitable and profound. It is the operating system conditioning the process of governance itself and within which all Community programs – economic, social, and political – function and malfunction. These Community programs have, of course, their specific content, but they are "written in," and "written for" a

---

[1] A. Stone, "Constitutional Dialogues in the European Community" (European University Institute Working Paper RSC No. 95/38), 1.

221

constitutional setting. Even the most superficial comparison between, say, a Council of Europe and European Community policy with similar objectives and even similar material content will illustrate the differences. The former will look very much like a traditional international treaty; the latter will often be indistinguishable from national legislation in the same field in any federal state.

Because constitutionalism captures, more than anything else, what is special about the process of European integration, it becomes the focal point of both content and contempt of those involved in the process. Consider carefully the position of, say, the Commission, Champion of integration, in the ongoing saga of Treaty revision from the SEA, through Maastricht to the 1996/97 Intergovernmental Conference. The holiest cow of all has been the preservation of the *acquis communautaire*, and within the *acquis*, the holy of holies is the constitutional framework of the Community. A measure of the Commission's past success, or, perhaps, a remarkable measure of the hold of European integration itself, is that the constitutional operating system became axiomatic, beyond discussion, above the debate, like the rules of democratic discourse, or even the very rules of rationality themselves, which (until challenged by post-modern normative and epistemological precepts) seemed to condition debate but not to be part of it.

The controversies about weighted majorities, blocking minorities and other sensitive issues of voting power within the Council illustrate well this point. The debate is as fierce and consequential as it is only because it takes place within a constitutional framework. The UK government, Champion of State Rights in the Community process, had to toil so valiantly, so few against so many with tears and sweat aplenty, to preserve the voting prerogatives of the large Member States because it tacitly accepts, or puts up with, the constitutional rules of the game.

In the countless narratives of European constitutionalization, one of the high moments, possibly the single most important one in the process that transformed the EC Treaties from a set of legal arrangements binding *only* upon sovereign States, was the rendering of individuals too, no longer only States, "subjects of the law"; or so at least argue the legal purists. Whether individuals were rendered true subject is something to which I shall turn later. The international-relations realist masquerading as a legal realist, however, would argue that the true achievement of constitutionalism, and the reason the UK felt it so necessary to defend its beaches against ever-increasing majoritarian decision-making, was not in the rendering of the individual a subject of the law but in rendering *States and governments* "subjects of the law." For whatever their formal status, in relation to "normal" (unconstitutionalized) treaties, States often give the impression, under traditional "non-constitutionalized" treaties of being able to act as subjects above the law.

The constitutional operating system often hums silently in the background and it is not necessary for the actors fully to perceive or articulate its impact. Sir James Goldsmith (to give a somewhat comic example), who founded a party in the UK with a strong Euroskeptical platform, focused his campaign on the alleged evils of the Maastricht Treaty and its potential sequel. But if you scrutinize his manifesto with care you will see that, like many avowed Euroskeptics, it is the constitutional framework, already in place long before Maastricht, which is at the source of his rage.

We academics are often no less comical than the Sir James's of this world. Sometimes we would like to think, and write as if, there is "out there" a constitutional landscape offering itself to various interpretations. Yet, constitutionalism is, too (some would say is only), but a prism through which one can observe a landscape in a certain way, an academic artifact with which one can organize the milestones and landmarks within the landscape (indeed, determine what is a landmark or milestone), an intellectual construct by which one can assign meaning to, or even constitute, that which is observed.

Here, too, constitutionalism often hums silently in the background. There is increasingly a welcome, substantial, and growing literature on the various policies of the Community, be it environmental policy, consumer protection, transport, or social policy, which focuses on objectives, content, and impact but, as with the comparable literature within a national context, takes the constitutional operating system for granted. Even studies specifically dealing with the European system of governance will frequently not bother with, or not bother any longer with, the constitutional premise. For example, constitutionalism is often not part of that rusty but trusty old discussion of the Community democracy deficit (and how to solve it) but is inevitably premised on its presence. Absent constitutionalization, the same set of issues would emerge as the even rustier discussion of *Member State* democratic control of foreign policy. Likewise, new institutionalism does not, rightly, expend too much energy on the constitutional setting of the Community. But try to consider its illuminating insights outside that setting. They just do not make sense.

Trite then as it is to recall, the discourse and history of constitutionalism are not only a political-legal discourse and history in which the players are actors such as governments and courts and the script is made of cases, and treaties, and resolutions and debates and social, political, and legal praxis. They are, too, an intellectual history and discourse of conceptualization and imagination.

The political-legal history, the accounts of how "the EC treaties evolved from a set of legal arrangements binding upon sovereign states, into a vertically integrated legal regime conferring judicially enforceable rights and obligations on all legal persons and entities, public and private, within EC territory" are very well known and do not need repeating. Though constitutionalization narratives vary and despite very different interpretative optics employed, most accounts share very similar images of the key political and legal milestones and landmarks which make up the constitutional landscape. There is no need, then, to map that landscape again.

But it is my intention to discuss briefly, to map if you wish, the intellectual history of European constitutionalism and constitutionalization. Map, note, not chronicle. Whereas, as mentioned, accounts of the "out there" view of constitutionalism and constitutionalization exist aplenty, I am unaware of any systematic "discussion of the discussion" of constitutionalism and constitutionalization.

Such a discussion, even if brief, is of importance: more than any other concept of European integration, constitutionalism has been the meeting ground of the various disciplines, principally political science, international relations, political economy, law, and, more recently sociology, which engage, conceptualize, and theorize about, European integration. To understand the intellectual history of constitutionalism is to understand a goodly chunk of integration studies as a cross-disciplinary endeavour.

There is another reason for trying to map this intellectual history. For the thesis of this chapter is that European constitutionalism is undergoing a reformation – the nature of which I shall be exploring. If there is any merit, other than trendiness, to my inelegant use of DOS and Windows as a metaphor for European constitutionalism then a reformation would have the same kind of underlying and far-reaching – yet often invisible – consequences as the change in a computer operating system.

What is meant by reformation will emerge in time, but inevitably the elements of that reformation are both new data "out there" in the shape of, say, new positions adopted by key political actors and even public opinion but also by a new kind of intellectual observation and conceptualization. The reformation has to be located in both histories of European constitutionalism.

THE GEOLOGY OF EUROPEAN CONSTITUTIONALISM

Doctrine

In the beginning there was doctrine: the disparate legal doctrines of the Court grappling to interpret the Treaties, to solve concrete legal conundrums before it. Schuman, in the famous Schuman Declaration, said:

224

> Europe will not be made all at once, or according to a single, general plan. It will be built through concrete achievements, which first create a *de facto* solidarity.

To my delight this prediction – or prescription – certainly fits the first stages in constitutionalization. The first steps were just that – concrete steps. Momentous, certainly; but hardly part of a general plan and certainly not all at once. There is even truth to the *de facto* solidarity part of the Schuman declaration which fits constitutionalization. The success of the constitutional construct would depend not only, or even primarily, on the utterances of the European Court but on their acceptance by national actors, mainly courts, and principally national constitutional courts. That solidarity of national legal actors was achieved through concrete achievements, as the neo–neo-functionalists were to argue convincingly, and has remained to this day in many cases more *de facto* than *de jure*.

For its part, the first *intellectual* stratum, was the more traditional analysis of the judicial developments *qua* "doctrine": working out their contours, examining their reach, trying to understand their rationale and their legal significance. Some might dismiss this kind of work as intellectually empty, without systemic significance, etc. And yet, this doctrinal work is the foundation for all that came after. Clever archeologists may, through flights of creative imagination, construct rich interpretative narratives from fragments of pottery, debris of buildings, and remnants of documents. But someone must have dug the fragments up, exposed the debris, and salvaged the remnants. The original doctrinal work is truly foundational in this sense. It has another enviable trait – more than any other aspect of the academic discussion of constitutionalism, it has a vital and constant link to the "out there" – it is a project which retains its professional rationale and relevance. In this respect Doctrine is not a foundational stratum at all – it is more like a gold seam that runs from deep down to the very surface and still yields its riches.

The house that Eric built

> Tucked away in the fairyland Duchy of Luxembourg and blessed, until recently, with benign neglect by the powers that be and the mass media, the Court of Justice of the European Communities has fashioned a constitutional framework for a federal-type structure in Europe.

This is the famous opening line of an article by Eric Stein in the *American Journal of International Law*.[2] It is a prime example of the second stratum in academic constitutional discourse about Europe. What this type of remark-

---

[2] *American Journal of International Law* 75 (1981), 1.

able work did (and it, and some others like it, did a lot more besides) was to take disparate legal doctrines, to baptize them as "constitutional," and to put them together with the bold assertion that the whole was greater than the parts – that a constitutional framework had come into being long before the Court was willing to use that vocabulary or, arguably, even to think in those terms.

The intellectual feat here was not simply one of conceptualization. There was already in that early work an interesting working out of relationships which involved legal and other actors. Today, with hindsight, we can quibble or even quarrel with the early description and analysis. We have, say, come to appreciate, through the work of a new generation of scholars revisiting this story, that, for example, the fashioning of the constitutional framework was the result of a far broader interaction than Stein emphasized. Not only, as he perceptively explained, between Commission, governments, Advocates-General and the Court but national courts and other statal actors too. We would have written the opening sentence as something like: "The European Court with its national brethren, with [add in your favorite actors]." But all the new and transformative renovations take place in the house that Eric and his colleagues, to whom we are all indebted, built.

Eureka! Social science discovers constitutionalism

And constitutional lawyers discover social science. The Archimedes of this part of the story, arguably the single most influential contributors to general European integration theory remain Haas, Schmitter, Lindberg and Scheingold, with their neo-functionalist theorem. Even someone like myself, with a profound skepticism towards the view of humanity which underlies neo-functionalism and which provides it with its explanatory power, will readily acknowledge the impressive intellectual construct created by its architects. Interestingly, the original neo-functionalist work both understood and integrated what we have called constitutionalism even if using a different vocabulary. But, like Greek and Roman classicism, this integration was somehow forgotten, and needed a Renaissance to bring it back. The mutual "rediscovery" of social science and constitutionalism is this renaissance and it adds several strata to the geology of constitutionalism.

Social science discovered constitutionalism in more than one way. I shall consider international relations, political science, and sociology. International relations has had a fickle relationship with European integration – for many years not quite being able to decide whether the Community constituted a consort of sufficient importance worthy of its attentions. The SEA and the 1992 program facelift had, at least, one positive result: enticing international relations back. Just as lawyers have an in-built bias towards constitutionalism, so international relations has an in-built bias against it. Constitutionalism, after all, is in some ways the antithesis of internationalism. The advent of constitutionalism is to international-relations experts in the field what *perestroika* was to Sovietologists. For the practitioners of *inter*-national relations, the continued centrality of the national and the state is ontologically necessary. Like all of us, they have come to love the object of their study and would hate to see its demise. The only reason to wish the full triumph (God forbid) of constitutionalism would be to witness the comic effects of its disappearance on the EC as an object of study for international relations. The revival of international-relations interest in European integration has been, thus, accompanied with a deep ambivalence towards constitutionalism. Today (unlike, say, ten years ago) it has become uncommon to find international-relations studies which do not perceive constitutionalism as an important, unique feature of the system. The ambivalence manifests itself, however, in three principal ways. Some studies acknowledge the importance of constitutionalism (or of the phenomena which have been conceptualized by others as constitutionalism) in their descriptive matrix of the Community but then it disappears in their analytical apparatus. It apparently requires no explanation. It is just there, as a datum. Other studies take battle, overt or covert: the intergovernmental paradigm of European integration – the paradigm which most plays down supranationalism versus constitutionalism – has seen its most brilliant articulation in the immediate post-SEA period, arguably the crest of constitutionalism. But, then, aren't our finest hours frequently when under siege? We all look for the lost key, not where it is, but under our own lamp-post. The intergovernmental lamp-post of Andrew Moravcsik (a powerful proponent of the state paradigm) has, admirably, been a veritable searchlight. This approach is not without its power. By employing the concepts of delegation and principal–agent relations and by problematizing informational and institutional constraints, Moravcsik convincingly accounts for some of the reasons for the European Court's success relative to other supranational institutions, notably the Commission. At this broad level, such theories are convincing, yet such approaches, even with "two-level" extensions, remain, in political-science terms, underspecified, and, from a legal perspective, fall short of a true appreciation of the subtle, multi-level dynamics of representation and discourse that have powered the EU legal system forward. Finally, there are those, taking the wise counsel of Machiavelli, who have sought to hegemonize. If you cannot squash them, hug them, the astute Florentine instructed. So, the elements of constitutionalism are incorporated into the description – courts, law, and all. But the explanation is the familiar orthodoxy of international relations: interest, consent, or compulsion. States accept it because it is in their interest.

Political science has taken two interesting tacks towards constitutionalism. One has been to observe its constitutive systemic role and seek, within this new framework, to explore the classic concerns of political science which developed in statal contexts. There is nothing *deja vu* in the work of the likes of Majone, Sbragia, Schmitter, Fligstein, and political economists like Pelkmans, Jacquemin, and Adams. For classical as the concerns of the regulatory state, of federalism and the aggregation of power, of the distributive choices in modern society may be, they receive in the work represented by these well-known scholars and others like them a new sheen since they are explored in the context of a polity – the uniqueness and peculiarity of which are not only stipulated but are often the *raison d'être* of the inquiry. In this strand, constitutionalism is not the object of inquiry but conditions it.

A second and more direct engagement of political science with constitutionalism has been its positioning as an object in and of itself worthy of analysis – and certainly not left to lawyers alone either to describe or to articulate. In this case it was not constitutionalism as a factor or parameter in the operation of the system that needed explanation. The European Court, its doctrines and its interactions with other actors – Community institutions, national courts, the lawyers, etc. – became a central concern to political science with extraordinarily rewarding results. Of course it was possible to bring to this inquiry the conceptual and methodological insights developed in Court studies in national contexts. The work of, say, Martin Shapiro became an inspiring model – a basis from which to rethink just about all major components of the elements of constitutionalism and, in particular, trying to give explanation to judicial activity which was not rooted in hermeneutics or doctrine. Both the causal questions asked – as to the success and failure of the spread of constitutionalism – the methodology employed in trying to respond to these questions, and the implications from them broadened and deepened the discourse of constitutionalism beyond recognition – at times forcing a rethinking of certain doctrinal positions – so that even the most doctrinal of lawyers would have to take note. It is Burley and Mattli who revitalized the debate by offering the first theoretically coherent neo-functionalist account of the development of the Court, one that has spawned much research and withstood considerable criticism.[3] The work of Alter, Stone and Wincott are superb examples. On a parallel track, Dehousse has explored similar issues. And I do not want to

---

[3] For this article, and other books and articles mentioned in passing in this essay, see "Further reading," pp. 234–7 below.

give the impression that this intellectual phenomenon was a simple grafting onto Community constitutionalism disciplinary and methodological insights culled from other national contexts. One of the achievements of this work and these scholars has been in reshaping the way we think about the phenomenon of constitutionalism and its elements given its transnational experience. It is most evident to see the migration of the insights gained here to, say, the WTO and even the United Nations.

But it was not only political science which discovered constitutionalism as an important parameter in the system or as an object of inquiry in itself. Law also discovered political social science. Hjalte's Rasmussen's widely discussed study[4] of the Court is an interesting milestone. Strictly speaking his famous critique is rooted in a doctrinal approach to constitutionalism: the Court "got it wrong," meaning that it departed from acceptable (normative) and accepted (empirical) interpretative standards. But to say, from within European law, that the Court got it wrong in its most important constitutional decisions, and to say it with such fresh rudeness, was a major development. But Rasmussen's book does more than that: by making it meaningful to ask whether the Court's rulings were accepted rather than acceptable, by treating the Court as a political actor and introducing openly the question of judicial politics, by making it relevant who the actual judges were (rather than treating it as a disembodied institutional voice) by highlighting in print the existence of a critical discourse among academics who were not, however, ready to go to print, he was breaking a whole series of taboos. His own treatment of all these issues fell dramatically short of the display of sensibility in raising them but this could not detract from the achievement.

My favorite, in English, for an insightful and expanded European legal discourse of constitutionalism is Francis Snyder's admirable *New Directions in European Community Law*,[5] the first chapter of which is both manifesto, agenda, and methodology. The new directions are not only in the areas he discusses but in the way they are discussed. There are now, embryonically, a European-law sociology and a sociology of European law. There is also doctrinal discourse which is fully attuned to the socio-political context in which it is situated and which often conditions its contours and is increasingly attuned to its own position. A group of young Turks in the UK exemplified by the Shaw and More volume on the *New Legal Dynamics of the Union* is testimony to a changing legal landscape.

There is even a new journal, the *European Law Journal*, the subtitle of

---

[4] *On European Law and Policy in the European Court of Justice: A Comparative Study of Judicial Policy-Making* (Martinus Nijhoff: Dordrecht, Boston).

[5] Wiedenfeld and Nicolson: London, 1990.

which, *Review of European Law in Context*, is indication of the maturity of discourse within the law. When there is a new journal – and a very successful one at that – you know that the field has arrived.

REFORMATION: MANIFESTATIONS AND RATIONALE

The Church of Constitutionalism is under challenge. Except for a small fringe, the challenge is not revolutionary, is not a claim to overturn the *ancien régime*, but is more in the nature of "What kind of European order do we want?" Reformation, with its historical religious connotation, is not about breaking faith; it is about affirming faith. And yet, at one and the same time reformation introduces a challenge to core articles of faith and foundations. Reformation is, thus, far more radical than evolution, far more grounded than revolution. No serious political force wants totally to turn away from European integration as an essential part of the political and legal matrix in Europe. But unlike the past, the challenge is not only about the content of certain policies, nor about the future development of the Union – fast or slow, wide or deep. A central part of this reformation concerns constitutionalism itself, the systemic underpinning of the system itself.

What are the signs of the challenge to classical constitutionalism which justify talking of reformation? They are, like the early elements from which we constructed the constitutional image, varied and disparate. They take place in both views of constitutionalism and in all the gradations which take place between these two views: the view that regards constitutionalism as happening "out there" and rooted in "real" events in the "real world" and in the view which views constitutionalism as an artifact, a prism, created by observers to give meaning, indeed, constitute the "out there." In this chapter, I shall eventually focus on the challenge to, and possible reformulation of, some of the key legal doctrines which were always considered as foundational to the very constitutional construct. But before I turn to these I would like to mention other elements which, in my view, can legitimately be considered as part of the challenge. The following is a non-exhaustive list.

1. There are challenges from the collectivity of states. Consider first the Maastricht Treaty itself. In a praiseworthy and deservedly famous article reflecting on the constitutional dimensions of Maastricht, "The Constitutional Structure of the Union: A Europe of Bits and Pieces," Diedre Curtin criticizes the fragmentation and constitutional incoherence of the Union structure and has, too, harsh words for a certain assault on the Court in the Maastricht process.
2. There are challenges from individual Member States. In the Maastricht

process it was the UK and Denmark. In the current Intergovernmental Conference there is a Franco-German draft which contemplates such variable geometry as to make the Community pillar itself one of bits and pieces. Whether it will be accepted is neither here nor there – it is evidence of the challenge to what was considered a veritable orthodoxy. In the same breath one can mention the breathtaking proposal to amend Article 189A which requires unanimity to modify a Commission proposal. A better targeted attack on the constitutional powers of the Commission is more difficult to imagine. This proposal is sure not to pass – but it is a sign of the attack on the *acquis*.

3. There are challenges from constitutional actors within Member States. Most interestingly to the theme of constitutionalism are the challenges coming from the national judiciary and in particular the highest courts. The German Constitutional Court and its Belgian counterpart have been most explicit. But there are signs from others as well, challenging precisely the hegemony of the European Court. There has been an understandable reaction trying to minimize and paper over the cracks. But it is there for anyone who wishes to look.

4. There are challenges from, yes, new constituencies within the Court of Justice. We should not commit the error of imagining the Court as an homogeneous actor free of internal factions, disagreements, and internally conflicting views on many issues, including the contours of constitutionalism. The oft-deep divisions on fundamental issues between Advocates-General – full members of the Court – and the Court itself surely mirror similar divisions within the College of Judges. Consider the post-Maastricht jurisprudence of that Court itself – for example its famous (or, to some, infamous) *Keck* decision or other controversial decisions such as Opinion 1/96. Assailed by many champions of the single market as a heresy, Norbert Reich used that decision among those justifying his analysis of a veritable economic constitutional *revolution*.[6]

5. There are challenges from general public opinion in several Member States. Maastricht, refreshingly, gave the lie to years of a Eurobarometer ostrich syndrome. It is clear that Euroskepticism is not just another English vice. At a minimum, Europe is no longer part of consensus, non-partisan politics in many Member States, not least the new ones. I have already suggested that though the discontent is in many instances non-specific, it goes often to what one would consider as the constitutional *acquis*.

It is hard to gauge the depth behind these challenges and it is even harder

---

[6] Reich, "The 'November Revolution' of the European Court of Justice: Keck, Meng and Audi Revisited," *Common Market Law Review* 31 (1994), 459.

to explain the reasons for it. I would like to offer some speculations on what may account for this change of mood.

First, as regards governments and states, I believe that one explanation must rest with the hugely expanded role of majority voting which came into effect with the Single European Act. How and why the governments accepted this sea change is a story for another day. Clearly majority voting has been fundamental in the ability of the Community to move ahead with the creation of a single market (of sorts) and has generally transformed the climate of decision-making. But it also removed one of the key political artifacts which had facilitated the acceptability of constitutionalism. Constitutionalism with a veto and without a veto are two very different games and what we are seeing in the challenges of Member States – individual and collective – is an adjustment to that reality.

Secondly, I do not wish to dwell here much on courts which must be the subject of another essay. The dialogue between the European Court and national courts has become more complex, nuanced and, at times, terse. In part courts are part of their national context and reflect the changing mood of public opinion – both elite and popular. In part certain strands of the European jurisprudence and certain failures of the European Court (as perceived by its interlocutors) in such areas as competences, have become more visible and less acceptable. In part the national challenges are a paradoxical sign of an acknowledgment by national courts of the constitutional nature of the European Court's posture: it is, strangely, easier to deal with the doctrinal elements of constitutionalism (which after all constitutes the official vocabulary of the inter-court dialogues) when they can be pigeonholed as international law. A constitutional-constitutional dialogue has its inbuilt conflictual elements. Likewise, whilst reserving chapter and verse for another occasion, all of the "strange" decisions of the European Court should be seen as part of *its* response both to the general European context in which *it* finds itself and as part of its dialogue with a much more difficult national interlocutor.

Thirdly, the change in general public opinion is most interesting and, in my view, conditions much of the other responses. There is, first, what one could term the paradox of success. In its foundational period, the European construct was perceived as part of a moral imperative in dealing with the heritage of World War II. Governments and States may have been happily pursuing their national interest but the European construct could be cloaked with a noble mantle of a new-found idealism. Within Europe war may be possible but it is certainly unthinkable and with that huge success of its principal objective what Europe now is presented as delivering is bread and circus. Remove the moral imperative, remove the mantle of ideals, and it is politics as usual with the frustrating twist that in Europe you cannot

232

throw the scoundrels out at election time. So you try and throw the whole construct out.

Finally, last and least, there is also a change in the academic discourse of constitutionalism. Recall those two remarkable articles by Curtin and Reich. Their critique is as telling as the phenomena criticized. On my reading, the implicit view from which it is made is the classical European constitutional vision which privileges an image of a mono-centered, vertically integrated, polity; of a single "single market" as a constitutional value, part of the economic constitution of the Union; of an authoritative Court which enjoys and deserves deference both from national courts and all other political actors; and of a respect for Member State diversity which, however, has to be subject to a Community discipline in the sphere of application of Community law. In short, exactly the Stein vision of European constitutionalism as a "framework for a federal-type structure in Europe."

Maastricht does represent a "rebellion" against that image of constitutionalism. It is clear that the principal *raison d'être* of the "pillar" structure, with the meticulous and explicit attempt to exclude the Court, was the wish of the Member States to operate outside a constitutional structure. And if one finds a certain emotional edge in the articles dealing with decisions of the European Court in cases such as *Keck* and others like it, this is understandable. These decisions are painful since they seem like a betrayal from within the Vatican itself.

The *Weltanschauung* from which the critique is made is also totally understandable. It is entirely consistent with the repeated vocabulary of classical European constitutionalism. Consider the legal underpinnings of constitutionalism in, say, Article 177 – with its explicit rationale of a uniform interpretation (and application) of Community law. This view has a compelling pragmatic rationale to it, as well as embodying a certain vision of equality before the law. But is it not too the *par excellence* mono-centric view of the polity? Or consider the potent idea of the rule of law which, in the rhetoric of the European Court, meant that any legal act is to be subject to judicial scrutiny. This is noble and in many ways persuasive. But it has, too, far-reaching consequences to the primordial self-positioning of the Court. And to anyone who grew up on *Dassonville* as an article of faith, affirming not only the substantive unity of the market, but also the subjection of any fragmentation to Euro-scrutiny, the notion of exclusion from such scrutiny *à la Keck* is sacrilege.

We have witnessed in recent years the emergence of a new academic discourse which attempts to rethink the very way in which classical constitutionalism was conceptualized. For me, the most powerful and influential voice is that of MacCormick in his trilogy, "Beyond the Sovereign State";

"Sovereignty, Democracy and Subsidiarity"; and "Liberalism, Nationalism and the Post-Sovereign State". Here is a discourse which understands the impossibilities of the old constitutional discourse, in a polity and a society in which the key social and political concepts on which classical constitutionalism was premised have lost their meaning. I would mention in particular two of the hallmarks of this new reformed discussion: the first is a more explicitly normative and critical discussion of constitutionalism; the second is its challenges to the dualist prism of the traditional con-stitutional image. The dualist approach places the relationship between Community/Union and the Member States at the center of the discourse and, likewise, places a huge premium on a hierarchy of norms – centrist and uniform – as a representation of, and resolution to, constitutional conflict. The new reformed discussion – in MacCormick, Dehousse, and Joerges[7] – recognizes and at times suggests a different, "horizontal," "poly centered," "infranational" image of the European polity and its constitutional framework.

The chapters in this part of the volume will give expression to this new, reformed, discussion.

FURTHER READING

What follows is not an exhaustive bibliography but more of a personal recommendation for further reading on some of the themes touched upon in this essay.

Classical approaches to European constitutionalism and democratic governance

Curtin, D., "The Constitutional Structure of the European Union: A Europe of Bits and Pieces," *Common Market Law Review* 30 (1993), 65

Green A. W., *Political Integration by Jurisprudence* (Sijthoff: Leyden, 1969)

Lenaerts, K., "Constitutionalism and the Many Faces of Federalism," *American Journal of Comparative Law* 38 (1990), 205

Lodge, J., "Transparency and Democratic Legitimacy," *Journal of Common Market Studies* 32 (1994), 343

Mancini, F., "The Making of a Constitution for Europe," *Common Market Law Review* 26 (1989), 595

Neunreither, "The Democracy Deficit of the European Union," *Government and Opposition* 29 (1994), 299

Reich, N., "The 'November Revolution' of the European Court of Justice: Keck, Meng and Audi Revisited," *Common Market Law Review* 31 (1994), 459

Schermers, H. G. and Waelbroeck, D., *Judicial Protection in the European Communities* (Martinus Nijhoff: Dordrecht, Boston, 5th edn., 1992)

---

[7] See p. 236 below.

Stein, E., "Lawyers, Judges and the Making of a Transnational Constitution," *American Journal of International Law* 75 (1981), 1

Political and social science discovers European constitutionalism and constitutionalism discovers political and social sciences

General

Adams, W. J., "Economic Analysis of European Integration," *Academy of European Law* (1995), vol. IV, book 1

Fligstein, N. and Mara-Drita, I., "How to Make a Market: Reflections on the Attempt to Create a Single Market in the European Union," *American Journal of Sociology* 102 (1996), 1

Haas, E., *The Uniting of Europe* (Stanford University Press: London, 1958)

Haas, E. and Schmitter, P., "Economics and Differential Patterns of Political Integration," *International Organization* 18 (1964), 7,070

Jacquemin, A., "Imperfect Market Structure and International Trade," *Kyklos* 35 (1982) 1

Keohane, R. O. and Hoffmann, S., "Institutional Change in Europe in the 1980s," in Keohane, R. O. and Hoffmann, S., *The New European Community: Decisionmaking and Institutional Change* (Westview Press: Boulder, CO, San Francisco, Oxford, 1991)

Lindberg, L. N. and Scheingold, S. A., *Europe's Would Be Polity* (Prentice Hall: Englewood Cliffs, NJ, 1970)

Pelkmans, J. and Robson, P., "The Aspirations of the White Paper" *Journal of Common Market Studies* 25 (1987), 181

Sbragia, M. (ed.), *Euro-Politics: Institutions and Policymaking in the "New" European Community* (Brookings Institution: Washington, DC, 1992)

Scharpf, F. W., "The Joint-Decision Trap: Lessons from German Federalism and European Integration," *Public Administration* 66 (1988), 239

Snyder, F., *New Directions in European Community Law* (Wiedenfeld and Nicolson: London, 1990)

Intergovernmentalism

Moravcsik, A., "Preference and Power in the European Community: A Liberal Intergovernmentalist Approach," in Bulmer, S. and Scott, A. (eds.), *Economic and Political Integration in Europe: Internal Dynamics and Global Context* (Blackwell: Oxford, Cambridge, MA, 1994)

"Why the European Community Strengthens the State: Domestic Politics and International Cooperation" (Harvard University CES Working Paper Series No. 52, 1994)

On new institutional thinking of the Union

Bulmer, S. J., "The Governance of the European Union: A New Institutionalist Approach," *Journal of Public Policy* 13 (1994), 351

"Institutions and Policy Change in the European Communities: The Case of Merger Control," *Public Administration* 72 (1994), 423

The Court

Alter, K., "Explaining National Court Acceptance of the European Court Jurisprudence: A Critical Evaluation of Theories of Legal Integration" (European University Institute Working Paper RSC, 1995)

Burley, A. M. and Mattli, W., "Europe Before the Court: A Political Theory of Legal Integration," *International Organization* 47 (1993), 41

Rasmussen, H., *On Law and Policy in the European Court of Justice* (Martinus Nijhoff: Dordrecht, Lancaster, Boston, 1986)

Stone Sweet, A., "Constitutional Dialogue in the European Community" (European University Institute Working Paper RSC, 1995)

"From Free Trade to Supranational Polity: The European Court and Integration" (Center for German and European Studies Working Paper No. 2.45, University of California, Berkeley, CA)

Wincott, D., "Political Theory, Law, and European Union," in Shaw, J. and More, G. (eds.), *New Legal Dynamics of European Union* (Clarendon Press: Oxford, 1995)

The new constitutionalism: horizontal, fragmented, infranational approaches to European constitutionalism and governance

De Witte, B., "Droit communautaire et valeurs constitutionelles nationales," *Droit* 14 (1991) 87

Dehousse, R., "Intégration ou disintégration: cinq thèses sur l'incidence de l'intégration européenne sur les structures étatiques" (European University Institute Working Paper RSC 96/4, 1996)

Joerges, C. and Neyer, "Multi-Level Governance, Deliberative Politics and the Role of Law" (European University Institute Working Paper RSC, 1997)

MacCormick, N., "Sovereignty, Democracy and Subsidiarity," in Bellamy R., Bufacchi V., and Castiglione, D. (eds.), *Democracy and Constitutional Culture in the Union of Europe* (Lothian Foundation: London, 1995)

"Beyond the Sovereign State," *Modern Law Review* 56 (1990), 1

Majone, G., "Regulating Europe: Problems and Prospects," in Ellwein, T. *et al.* (eds.), *Jahrbuch zur Staats- und Verwaltungswissenschaft* (1989), 159

Shaw, J. and More, G. (eds.), *New Legal Dynamics of European Union* (Clarendon Press: Oxford, 1995)

Slaughter, A. M., "International Law in a World of Liberal States," *European Journal of International Law* 6 (1995) 503

The new constitutionalism: the debate about identity, demos and democracy

Boeckenfoerde, E. W., "Die Nation: Identitaet in Differenz," *Politische Wissenschaft* (1995), 974

Habermas, J., "Staatsbhrgerschaft und Nationale Identitat (1990)," in *Faktizitat und*

Geltung: Beitrage zur Diskurstheorie des Rechts und des demokratischen Rechtsstaats (Frankfurt/Main, 1992)

Meehan, E., *Citizenship and the European Community* (London, 1993)

Oldfield, A., *Citizenship and Community* (London: Routledge, 1990)

Preuss, U. K., "Constitutional Powermaking for the New Polity: Some Deliberations on the Relation Between Constituent Power and the Constitution," *Cardozo Law Review* 14 (1993), 639

"Citizenship and Identity: Aspects of a Political Theory of Citizenship," in Bellamy, R., Bufacchi, V., and Castiglione, D. (eds.), *Democracy and Constitutional Culture in the Union of Europe* (Lothian Foundation: London, 1995)

Soledad, G. (ed.), *European Identity and the Search for Legitimacy* (London, 1993)

Telo, M. (ed.), *Démocratie et construction européenne* (Brussels, 1995)

von Bogdandy, A. (ed.), *Die Europische Option* (Nomos: Baden-Baden, 1993)

Other authors mentioned in the text

Fitzgerald, B., "The Future of Belief," *First Things* 63 (1996), 23

Nolte, E., *The Three Faces of Fascism* (Wiedenfeld and Nicolson: London, 1965)

7

FIN-DE-SIÈCLE EUROPE: DO THE NEW
CLOTHES HAVE AN EMPEROR?

I

IT STARTED with a bang: the signing of the Treaty on European Union at Maastricht in February 1992. It ended in a whimper: its entry into force in November 1993: a low, anti-climatic moment in the history of contemporary European integration, not its crowning achievement; a would-be triumph turned sour.

There is a distinct mood among Community mandarins. Brecht's wicked quip may well describe the bitter, vindictive sentiment: *The People* have disappointed; Maastricht, justly hailed as a remarkable diplomatic achievement, was met in many a European street with a sentiment ranging from hostility to indifference. One cannot even derive comfort from those segments of public opinion which have rallied behind "Europe" such as the agricultural lobby in Ireland, the political establishment in France, the German partitocracy. Narrow self-interest, a formidable stake in the *status quo*, and a growing cleavage with the constituents are the respective hallmarks of this support. Maybe *The People* should, indeed, be changed.

It is not my intention in this chapter to try and explain, with the tools of social science, "what went wrong with Maastricht." My intuitive impression is that the attitude to Maastricht is, perhaps, an indication of a disillusionment which extends far deeper than any objection to the specific content of the Treaty itself. To be sure, the never-ending recession will have had its impact too, creating a general climate of uncertainty and insecurity. But could it be that "Europe" has a captivating pull only when the going is good, a Golden Calf of plenty to be rejected as matters economic turn sour? Dare one say it? The Europe of Maastricht suffers from a crisis of ideals. The Member States of the European Community are being swept by an electorate which is increasingly frustrated, alienated, and angry with politics as usual. And "Europe," once *avant garde*, has, it seems, become just that: politics as usual.

A subtle change has occurred in the positioning of the idea of European integration in public discourse. The political scientists of the realist school never tire of telling us that the evolution of European integration was driven by national self-interest and cold calculations of cost and benefit to its participating Member States. But in its formative years, and for a considerable while after that, the very idea of the Community was associated with a set of values which, it seems to me, could captivate the imagination, mobilize broadly based political forces, counteract the powerful, even captivating, but often abused, pull of nationalism. To support the Community was to "Do the Right Thing." It was a happy state in which one could believe that long-term self-interest coincided with higher values. The reception by the public of the Maastricht Treaty is the writing on the wall; could it be that the "Europe" of Maastricht is an ideal which has lost its mobilizing force? A force which has lost its mobilizing ideals?

We are obliged therefore to face squarely the ends of European integration, often neglected in what seems to be the more urgent debate of means – the instruments and mechanisms, political and economic, for achieving the specific objectives of the Treaties. This chapter is an attempt to (re)introduce a discourse on ideals into the current debate on European integration. This attempt, it is hoped, will be of some value regardless of its utility or otherwise in explaining the behavior of the various actors in the European polity.

II

A disquisition focusing explicitly on ideals is not an easy task, and this for two reasons. First, much of the social science of European integration has been dominated by the realist and neo-realist schools of international relations. Notions of ideals, ethics, and the like have a very limited place in their explanatory and normative apparatus of state behavior and transnational behavior. In non-international relations theories of integration, such as critical social theory, ideals are often there to be exposed as sham, as a mask to be lifted and debunked. All in all, ideals, like religion and spirituality are almost embarrassing topics, to be reconceptualized as ideology and treated with the reductive methodologies of psychology, sociology, and the like.

Second, a twentieth-century phenomenology of ideals is hard to construct. We should not confuse ideals with ideology or morality. Ideals are usually part of an ideology. Morality is usually part of ideals. But the terms do not conflate. Ideologies, in relation to which theories abound, often include or are premised on some ideals. But they are much more than that. Ideology is part an epistemology, a way of knowing and understanding reality; and in part a program for changing that reality to achieve certain goals. Ideals, in and of themselves, constitute neither an epistemology nor a program for realization, and are often the least explained elements of any given ideology. Morality, practical reason, the good life, will inform ideals, but ideals have a social reality which practical reason necessarily does not – though it can be an ideal to live the good life. It is not surprising that, for example, the *Macmillan Encyclopedia of Philosophy* has no separate entry for ideals.

It is surprising, however, that there appears to be no systematic analysis of the ideals – as distinct from the objectives – of European integration and the European Community. If this, indeed, is the case, one may wonder if there is no good reason for this absence. Could it be that a low "pay-off" is the explanation? I think not. I think the pay-off could be high and that the reason for the absence lies rather with the disciplinary "misfit" of ideals as an object for inquiry.

What then would be the interest, the intellectual pay-off, in exploring the ideals of European integration and the European Community? I propose to answer this question after describing first one of the Community's foundational ideals, which, in turn, will serve as a means for a general phenomenological reflection and as a tool to explain the utility of exploring the ideals of European integration.

Peace, in the immediate wake of World War II, was the most explicit and evocative of ideals for which the would-be polity was to be an instrument. Nowhere is this captured better than in the oft-repeated phraseology of the Schuman Declaration of May 9, 1950:

> World peace cannot be safeguarded without the making of constructive efforts proportionate to the dangers which threaten it ... The gathering of the nations of Europe requires the elimination of the age-old opposition of France and the Federal Republic of Germany. The first concern in any action undertaken must be these two countries ... [This] solidarity ... will make it plain that any war between France and the Federal Republic of Germany becomes, not merely unthinkable, but materially impossible.

Peace, at all times an attractive *desideratum*, would have had its appeal in purely utilitarian terms. But it is readily apparent that in the historical context in which the Schuman Plan was put forward the notion of peace as an ideal probes a far deeper stratum than simple swords into ploughshares, sitting under ones' vines and fig trees, and lambs and wolves, the classic biblical metaphors for peace. The dilemma posed was an acute example of the alleged tension between grace and justice which has taxed philosophers and theologians through the ages – from William of Ockham (pre-modern), Friedrich Nietzsche (modernist), and the repugnant but profound Martin Heidegger (post-modern).

These were, after all, the early 1950s with the horrors of war still fresh in the mind and, in particular, the memory of the unspeakable savagery of German occupation. It would take many years for the hatred in countries such as the Netherlands, Denmark, or France to subside fully. The idea, then, in 1950, of a community of equals as providing the structural underpinning for long-term peace among yesteryear's enemies, represented more than the wise counsel of experienced statesmen.

It was also a call for forgiveness, a challenge to overcome an understandable hatred. In that particular historical context the Schumanian notion of peace resonates with and is evocative of the distinct discourse, imagery, and values of Christian love, of grace – not, I think, a particularly astonishing evocation given the personal backgrounds of the founding fathers – Adenauer, de Gaspari, Schuman, and Monnet himself.

III

I shall use peace as a springboard for a more general reflection of ideals. I would like to develop four principal considerations which inform ideals as a concept and as a social construct: the idyllic, the demonic, the virtuous, and the idolatrous. If my understanding of peace as an ideal is valid and typical it would enable me to illustrate all four considerations.

The idyllic

In upholding or subscribing to an ideal, one is in part putting forward a desired state of affairs (material or spiritual) in which one would like to exist. It can be peace; it can be justice; it can be power or grandeur. It is usually, but not necessarily, futuristic. It is usually a state of affairs the desirability or appeal of which are self-evident in both an essentialist worldview and/or because they correspond to deep-seated social constructs.

The altruistic

A simple desirable state of affairs – an idyllic state: "If I were a rich man" – does not in and of itself qualify as an ideal. Often it can be almost a counter-ideal. What prevents us from making all our fantasies of desired – idyllic – states *ideals*, is that so often they are selfish and self-serving. We perceive these *desiderata*, in fact, as an expression of desire, greed, jealousy, of our Hobbesian side. In the words of Genesis: "for the imagination of man's heart is evil from his youth."[1]

Ideals then involve not simply putting forward a desired state of affairs – material or spiritual – but a recognition of our demonic tendencies. Ideals must represent a challenge to the demonic in us, a call to our better halves. Ideals, and this is a central part of their allure, contain an altruistic component.

In my view this challenge accounts for the huge appeal of the great ideals. First, there is the *per se* attractiveness and satisfaction of sacrifice: things that demand sacrifice are cherished more than things that come easily. Sacrifice invests things with value. Additionally, the combination of the idyllic and the altruistic in ideals explains their abiding centrality to all human culture: the call to overcome the demonic ennobles our self-interest; it legitimates our desires.

The desire for peace is frequently not an ideal. Like riches it is a very comfortable state of affairs – for the sake of peace I shall not fight my battles, not stand up for my values, turn my gaze, avert my eyes. What brings the message of peace in the formation of the Community into the realm of ideals, what connects it to so deep a fountain as Christian love, is the historical context of justified hatred and fear. The infamous "Peace in our Time" approach of the 1930s which saw the sacrifice of Czechoslovakia was a counter-ideal: the idyllic, the comfortable, without the altruistic. In the EC of the early 1950s and somewhat beyond, there is a context where peace has both the idyllic and the altruistic – we have to overcome our feelings of revenge, which were given full vent after World War I, but at the same time the comfort of peace is being offered. It was not then the fear of war (between say, France and Germany) which rendered peace an idealistic *desideratum* in 1950. It was the psychological and spiritual demand which it made which so rendered it.

The virtuous

The idyllic and the demonic elements have been explained in linguistic and behavioristic terms: they correspond to what we normally mean when we use the word, or think of, ideals; they imply a certain understanding of human psyche and what appeals and motivates us. They are also value-free and ahistorical. They do not differentiate between the "ideals" of Adolf Hitler or Mother Theresa. One can, after all, desire evil or mistake it for virtue, and make great sacrifices to achieve it.

---

[1] Genesis 8:21.

I would add, therefore, a third consideration: the grounding of ideals in ethics. I can justify this consideration in two ways. First, as a reflection of social reality: when ideals have been put forward as a social phenomenon, as part of a program of action, they have always been presented as being so grounded. But, I would also add this consideration as an unashamedly normative layer to ideals discourse: a refusal on my part to discuss ideals in purely behavioristic terms, even if I am mindful of the fashionability of moral relativism, and the manipulability of ethics. Even peace can pose considerable ethical dilemmas. Few of us, after all, are total pacifists.

I shall explain the fourth and final consideration later in this essay.

IV

Before we turn to examine the other ideals of European integration in its formative years I shall reflect now more deliberately on the interest in exploring ideals in general and European integration ideals in particular. I see three distinct interests

First, a large, the largest, part of EC studies is instrumentalist, rooting all explanation in actors, interests, structures and processes, and trying to explain why things are the way they are. The disciplines – political science, economics, and law – will shift the "thing" which is being explained, and will privilege one kind of explanation over another; or, alternatively, try to be interdisciplinary or even challenge the disciplinary divide altogether and adopt an holistic approach.

From this instrumental perspective, the value of looking at ideals is evident: ideals can be part of the matrix which explains socialization, mobilization, and legitimacy. In an analysis as to why certain elites or masses support or tolerate or oppose European integration in general or this or that policy in particular, ideals should clearly have a place. To deny the mobilizing force of ideals is folly.

Secondly, there can be interest in ideals (and the ideals of European integration) from a perspective which is more indifferent to the specific story of European integration but acknowledges it, and its rhetoric, as part (important or otherwise) of social intercourse. This perspective has as its focus the individual as such and "society" (national society, regional society, transnational society). The interest here then is in the "social." In particular I have in mind our "modern" understandings of constitution of the self – individual and collective, the shift from fate to choice in self-understanding and self-positioning.

Ideals are a principal vehicle through which individuals and groups interpret reality, give meaning to their life, and define their identity – positively and negatively. The idyllic in ideals refers in this context to social space, the demonic to individual self. The questions of what kind of society do I live in, and what does our society "stand for," can only be given an answer by reference, at least partially, to ideals. Similarly, the question of what kind of person I am, can only be given an answer by reference to ideals. What kind of society should I live in, aspire to; and what kind of person I should be is similarly premised on the existence of ideals. Even the rejection of ideals (a pseudo-Machiavellian approach to life) is just that: a rejection of ideals. You cannot do without them as a referent for value and meaning.

If we are, then, interested in the European persona, in a European polity, we will profit by understanding the world of ideals which is part of the polity. Can there be a psychological understanding of the individual without a reference to one's conflict with ideals? Can there be an appreciation of the political culture of a polity without reference to its values and ideals? In the tension between Eros and civilization, our discourse of civilization is in substantial part a discourse of values and ideals.

Where one might have strong disagreements is the importance that European integration ideals have had in society. Some would argue that until recently their importance was marginal. Others will disagree.

Finally, there is a third interest in ideals – an interest in ideals as a locator in the history of ideas. They are part (and with the passage of time an important part) of the cultural history and the cultural identity of an epoch. They are, sometimes, the deepest residue – or at least the most visible – which history leaves. Even educated women and men will probably be more fluent with the values of antiquity (notably the "declared values" rather than their realization!) or of the age of Enlightenment than with their respective political or social histories.

It appears to me that, even to a body of social scientists, it is a totally serious, and possibly longer-lasting enterprise, to try and define European integration in terms of its ideals and not only in terms of its structural, processual, and material components. It is an enterprise which will help locate the idea of the Community in the flow of European intellectual history.

V

We may return now to the history of the Community. In its foundational period, alongside peace, I would identify two other principal ideals: prosperity and supranationalism.

Prosperity is the second value for which the Community was to be instrumental. Max Kohnstamm used to say that the twin dilemmas for Monnet were what do we do with Germany – I translated the answer given as the peace ideal in the European construct – and how to rebuild Europe – and I translate that as the ideal of prosperity. This is captured in, among other places, Article 2 of the Treaty of Rome.

> The Community shall have as its task . . . to promote throughout the Community a harmonious development of economic activities, a continuous and balanced expansion, an increase in stability, an accelerated raising of the standard of living . . .

The focus on prosperity should not come as a surprise. After all, the economic reconstruction of the devastated continent was intimately connected with the notion of peace. Each was the means for the other. Indeed in the biblical passage, frequent in the book of Judges, peace and prosperity are linked: the vineyard and the fig tree being a symbol for both.

The idyllic, the desired state of affairs is self-evident. But at first blush it is hard to capture the altruistic, non-hedonistic dimension of the quest for prosperity. Are we not here in the presence of pure self-interest, something to be almost ashamed of – the very antithesis of altruism, challenge, and sacrifice which are essential parts of idealistic narrative? Where is the virtuous and where is the challenge to the demonic which, I argued, were essential components of ideals discourse?

There was an idealistic dimension, nuanced to be sure, to the quest for prosperity which mediated its utilitarian aspects. Its virtue appears when set against a backdrop of destruction and poverty. In these conditions (individual and social) prosperity assumed an altogether different meaning: dignity, both personal and collective. In an Enlightenment-bound vision of the individual, poverty resonates with the embarrassment of dependence on others, with the humiliation bred by helplessness, and with the degradation of a lack of autonomy. There is, thus, nothing shameful in aspiring for prosperity when it comes to mean dignity. There, then, is its virtue.

Second, the Community's quest for prosperity in its formative years took place in a period which inextricably linked it with widespread (re)construction, with visible (re)generation, with palpable effort and toil. Bread gained with the sweat of one's brow is a matter for pride rather than embarrassment, shame, and degradation.

Last but not least, linking prosperity to a co-operative enterprise inevitably blunted the sharp edges of avidity feelings. The Community in its reconstructive effort was about collective responsibility: it was a regime which attempted to constrain the unchecked search for economic prosperity by one Member State at the expense of others. To be sure, there was an economic theory of open markets, level playing fields, and all the rest which informed the Common Market. But the elements of transnational economic solidarity are an undeniable part of the discourse at the time and of the Treaty itself. This solidarity is the element which appeals to the better self. It is the control of the demonic at the statal economic level.

Put in this way, we also detect here, as with the peace ideal, the deeper roots of the Community notion of prosperity as an ideal: it links up with and is evocative of a different but no less central strand of European idealism since the middle of the nineteenth century, be it socialism, Fabianism, Communism, welfare statism, all sharing an underlying ethos of collective societal responsibility for the welfare of individuals and the community as a whole.

VI

The third ideal, is that of *supranationalism* – for want of a better word. A word of caution would be necessary here. There is no fixed meaning to the term supranationalism. Indeed, from its inception there seems to have been two competing visions of its realization through the Community: a unity vision – encapsulated in those who favored a United States of Europe – and a more attenuated Community vision. The two strands (which, of course, overlap) have continued to co-exist. But it is my reading of the historical map – the rejection of the European Defence Community and the European Political Community in the 1950s and the articulation of supranationalism in, especially, the Treaty of Rome – that the Community vision prevailed in the formative years of the EC. But clearly, even more than everything else in this chapter, the construction of supranationalism and its virtues follows my understanding with no pretense to a commonly "received knowledge."

In trying to explain the ways in which the Community is, or has become, supranational, most discussion over the years has tended, interestingly, to focus on its relation to the "state" rather than the "nation." This conflation of nation and state is not always helpful. Supranationalism relates in specific and discrete ways to nationhood and to statehood. Indeed, in my understanding and construction of supranationalism its value system is actually wrapped up with the value system of European ethno-national liberalism of the nineteenth century. In that respect supranationalism will be seen to have the same, Janus-like, quality as peace and prosperity: looking to the future whilst affirming the past – a radical conservatism.

To see the relationship between supranationalism, nationhood, and statehood, I propose to focus in turn on nationhood and statehood and try and explore their promise and their dangers. This will be then related to the ends of supranationalism. Naturally, in discussing nation and state, I shall only give a few pointers and headlines of what would otherwise have to be an extremely elaborate analysis.

Nationhood

It seems to me that, at least in its nineteenth-century liberal conception, two deep human values are said to find expression in nationhood: belongingness and originality. It should immediately be stated that nationhood is not the only social form in which these values may find expression.

Belongingness is inherent in nationhood: nationhood is a form of belonging. Nationhood is not an instrument to obtain belongingness, it *is* it. Form and substance here conflate, the way they do, say, in a love sonnet by Shakespeare: the value of the sonnet does not lie in, say, its message of love; we do not think of the sonnet as an instrument for the conveyance of the idea. Take away the form and the message is banal. What gives the sonnet its timeless value is the inextricable way in which the substance and the form were woven together by Shakespeare.

What are the values embedded in belonging, in national belonging, beyond the widely shared view that belonging is pleasant, is good? We can readily understand a certain basic appeal to our human species which is, arguably, inherently social: the appeal that family and tribe have too. Part of the appeal is, simply, the provision of a framework for social interaction. But surely one has to go beyond that: after all, much looser social constructs than nationhood, let alone tribe and family, could provide that framework. Belonging means, of course, more than that. It means a place, a social home.

The belonging of nationhood is both like and unlike the bonds of blood in family and tribe and in both this likeness and unlikeness we may find a clue to some of its underlying values. It is like the bonds of blood in family and tribe in that those who are of the nation have their place, are accepted, belong, independently of their achievements, by just being – and herein lies the powerful appeal (and terrible danger) of belonging of this type: it is a shield against existential aloneness. In, for example, the tradition of the Jewish nation, a tradition worthy of some consideration given the continuity of Jewish national survival for over three millennia, we find a normative expression to this form of belonging: "Even though he has sinned, he remains Israel."[2] The power of this belongingness may be understood by the drama and awesomeness of its opposites: isolation, seclusion, excommunication.

But nationhood transcends the family and tribe and maybe here lurks an even more tantalizing value: nationhood not only offers a place to the familyless, to the tribeless, but in transcending family and tribe it calls for loyalty – the largest coin in the realm of national feeling – towards others

---

[2] *Talmud Sanhedrin*, 44:2.

which go beyond the immediate "natural" (blood) or self-interested social unit.

And, indeed, belongingness of this type is a two-way street. It is not only a passive value: to be accepted. It is also active: to accept. Loyalty is one of those virtues which, if not abused, benefits those on both the giving and receiving ends.

The other core value of nationhood, in some ways also an instrument for national demarcation, is the claim about originality. On this reading, the Tower of Babel was not a sin against God but a sin against human potentiality; and the dispersal that came in its aftermath, not punishment, but divine blessing. The nation, with its endlessly rich specificities, co-existing alongside other nations, is, in this view, the vehicle for realizing human potentialities in original ways, ways which humanity as a whole would be the poorer for not cultivating.[3]

It is here that one may turn from the nation to the modern state. It is worth remembering at the outset that national existence and even national vibrancy do not in and of themselves require statehood, though statehood can offer the nation advantages, both intrinsic as well as resulting from the current organization of international life, which gives such huge benefits to statehood.

I would argue that in the modern notion of the European ethno-national nation-state, the state is to be seen principally as an instrument, the organizational framework within which the nation is to realize its potentialities. It is within the statal framework that governance, with its most important functions of securing welfare and security, is situated. The well being and integrity of the state must, thus, be secured so that these functions may be attained. That is not a meager value in itself. But to the extent that the state may claim, say, a loyalty which is more than pragmatic, it is because it is at the service of the nation with its values of belongingness and originality. (This conceptualization underscores, perhaps exaggerates, the difference with the American truly radical alternative liberal project of the non-ethno-national polity, and of a state, the republic, the organization of which, and the norms of citizenship behavior within which, were central to its value system.)

It is evident, however, that, in the European project, boundaries become a very central feature of the nation-state. There are, obviously, boundaries in the legal-geographical sense of separating one nation-state from another. But there are also internal, cognitive boundaries by which society (the nation) and individuals come to think of themselves in the world.

---

[3] How one decides the self which qualifies as a nation is a tantalizing issue which it is not necessary to explore here.

At a societal level, nationhood involves the drawing of boundaries by which the nation will be defined and separated from others. The categories of boundary drawing are myriad: linguistic, ethnic, geographic, religious, etc. The *drawing* of the boundaries is exactly that: a constitutive act, which decides that certain boundaries are meaningful both for the sense of belonging and for the original contribution of the nation. This constitutive element is particularly apparent at the moment of "nation building" when histories are rewritten, languages revived, etc. Of course, with time, the boundaries, especially the non-geographical ones, write themselves on the collective and individual consciousness with such intensity that they appear as natural: consider the virtual interchangeability of the word "international" with "universal" and "global": it is hard not to think, in the social sphere, of the world as a whole without the category of nation (as in "international").

Finally, at an individual level, belonging implies a boundary: you belong because others do not. As evident as the notion of boundaries is to the nation-state enterprise, so is the high potential for abuse of boundaries. The abuse may take place in relation to the three principal boundaries: the external boundary of the state; the boundary between nation and state; and the internal consciousness boundary of those making up the nation.

The most egregious form of abuse of the external boundary of the State would be physical or other forms of aggression towards other states.

There abuse of the boundary between nation and state is most egregious when the state comes to be seen not as instrumental for individuals and society to realize their potentials but as an end in itself. Less egregiously, the State might induce a "laziness" in the nation – banal statal symbols and instrumentalities becoming a substitute for truly original national expression. This may also have consequences for the sense of belongingness whereby the apparatus of the State becomes a substitute for a meaningful sense of belonging. An allegiance to the State can replace human affinity, empathy, loyalty, and a sense of shared fate with the people of the State.

There can be, too, an abuse of the internal boundary which defines belongingness. The most typical abuse here is to move from a boundary which defines a sense of belonging to one which induces a sense of superiority and a concomitant sense of condescension or contempt for the other. A sense of collective national identity implies an other. It should not imply an inferior other.

The manifestations of these abuses are a living part of the history of the European nation-state which are so well known as to obviate discussion.

VII

A central plank of the project of European integration may be seen, then, as an attempt to control the excesses of the modern nation-state in Europe, especially, but not only, its propensity to violent conflict and the inability of the international system to constrain that propensity. The European Community was to be an antidote to the negative features of the state and statal intercourse; its establishment in 1951 was seen as the beginning of a process that would bring about the elimination of these excesses.

Historically there have, as mentioned above, always been those two competing visions of European integration. Whilst no one has seriously envisioned a Jacobin-type centralized Europe, it is clear that one vision, to which I have referred as the unity vision, the United States of Europe vision, has really posited as its ideal type, as its aspiration, a statal Europe, albeit of a federal kind. Tomorrow's Europe in this form would indeed constitute the final demise of Member State nationalism replacing or placing the hitherto-warring Member States within a political union of federal governance.

It is easy to see some of the faults of this vision: it would be more than ironic if a polity set up as a means to counter the excesses of statism ended up coming round full circle and transforming itself into a (super)state. It would be equally ironic if the ethos which rejected the boundary abuse of the nation-state gave birth to a polity with the same potential for abuse. The problem with this unity vision is that its very realization entails its negation.

The alternative vision, the one that historically has prevailed, is the supranational vision, the community vision. At one level aspirations here are both modest compared to the Union model and reactionary: supranationalism, the notion of community rather than unity, is about affirming the values of the liberal nation-state by policing the boundaries against abuse. Another way of saying this would be that supranationalism aspires to keep the values of the nation-state pure and uncorrupted by the abuses I described above.

At another level the supranational community project is far more ambitious than the unity one and far more radical. It is more ambitious since, unlike the unity project which simply wishes to redraw the actual political boundaries of the polity within the existing nation-state conceptual framework, albeit federal, the supranational project seeks to redefine the very notion of boundaries of the state, between the nation and the state, and within the nation itself. It is more radical since, as I shall seek to show, it involves more complex demands and greater constraints on the actors.

How, then, does supranationalism, expressed in the community project of European integration, affect the excesses of the nation–state, the abuse of boundaries discussed above?

At the pure statal level supranationalism replaces the "liberal" premise of international society with a community one. The classical model of international law is a replication at the international level of a liberal theory of the state. The state is implicitly treated as the analogue, on the international level, to the individual within a domestic situation. In this conception, international legal notions such as self-determination, sovereignty, independence, and consent have their obvious analogy in theories of the individual within the state. In the supranational vision, the community as a transnational regime will not simply be a neutral arena in which states will seek to maximize their benefits but will create a tension between the state and the community of states. Crucially, the community idea is not meant to eliminate the national state but to create a regime which seeks to tame the national interest with a new discipline. The idyllic is a state of affairs which eliminates the excesses of narrow statal "national interest." The challenge is to control at the societal level the uncontrolled reflexes of national interest in the international sphere.

Turning to the boundary between nation and state, supranationalism is meant to prevent abuses here too. The supranational project recognizes that at an intergroup level nationalism is an expression of cultural (political and/ or other) specificity underscoring differentiation, the uniqueness of a group as positioned *vis-à-vis* other groups, calling for respect and justifying the maintenance of inter-group boundaries.

At an intragroup level nationalism is an expression of cultural (political and/or other) specificity underscoring commonality, the "sharedness" of the group *vis-à-vis* itself, calling for loyalty and justifying the elimination of intra-group boundaries.

But, crucially, nationality is not the thing itself – it is its expression, an artifact. It is a highly stylized artifact, with an entire apparatus of norms and habits; above all it is not a spontaneous expression of that which it signifies but a code of what it is meant to give expression to, frequently even translated into legal constructs. Nationality is inextricably linked to citizenship, citizenship not simply as the code for group identity, but also as a package of legal rights and duties, and of social attitudes.

Supranationalism does not seek to negate as such the interplay of differentiation and commonality, of inclusion and exclusion and their potential value. It is a challenge to the codified expressions in nationality. Since, in the supranational construct with its free-movement provisions which do not allow exclusion through statal means of other national cultural influences and with its strict prohibition on nationality- or citizenship-based discrimination, national differentiation cannot rest so easily on the artificial boundaries provided by the state. At intergroup level then it pushes for cultural differences to express themselves in their authentic, spontaneous form, rather than the codified statal legal forms. At the intra-group level it attempts to strip the false consciousness which nationalism may create instead of belongingness derived from a non-formal sense of sharedness.

Supranationalism at the societal and individual, rather than the statal, level embodies, then, an ideal which diminishes the importance of the statal aspects of nationality – probably the most powerful contemporary expression of groupness – as the principal referent for transnational human intercourse. That is the value side of non-discrimination on grounds of nationality, of free movement provisions and the like. It is precisely the absence, in the pre-Maastricht conceptualization of the Community, of a European citizenship, which is symbolically important: essential relationships are to be defined despite citizenship. In its intra-Community manifestation the ideal is the relative irrelevance of the formal category of citizenship.

It is not difficult to identify the idyllic and the demonic and the deep idealistic wellspring with which this ideal resonates. Hermann Cohen, the great neo-Kantian, in his *Religion der Vernunft aus den Quellen des Judentums*, tries to explain the meaning of the Mosaic law which call for non-oppression of the stranger. In his vision, the alien is to be protected, not because he was a member of one's family, clan religious community or people, but because he was a human being. In the alien, therefore, man discovered the idea of humanity.

We see through this exquisite exegesis that in the curtailment of the totalistic claim of the nation-state and the reduction of nationality as the principal referent for human intercourse, the Community ideal of supranationalism is evocative of, and resonates with, Enlightenment ideas, with the privileging of the individual, with a different aspect of liberalism which has as its progeny today liberal notions of human rights. In this respect the Community ideal is heir to Enlightenment liberalism.

VIII

The ideals of peace, prosperity, supranationalism which animate the Community in its foundational period are, on my reading, a new expression to the three principal strands of European idealism which the twentieth century inherits. They tap into core values of Christianity, social responsibility and the Enlightenment.

At this point a critical proviso would be in order. My claim is not, decidedly not, that the Community in its foundational period actually lived these ideals, realized their virtues (whatever these may be) or vindicated their promise. I am agnostic on this issue. To explain the ideals of the French Revolution, of the American Revolution or of the October Revolution is not to claim that post-monarchist France, republican America, or the Soviet Union lived up to the aspirations which animated these social revolutions. We are all familiar with analyses which tell a very different story of the ensuing reality of the Community.

But the reality of the ideals themselves works, none the less, at all three levels I explained before. First, mobilization, socialization, and legitimacy. European integration, it has often been claimed, was elite-driven. Ideals discourse may be part of the explanation of the mobilization of these elites. It was a construct which was safe, appealing to values inculcated deeply in a generation which grew up in this century.

The idea of Europe and the ideals of Europe may also be a part explanation for mobilization at mass level, through national party structures. All principal political forces and parties in post-World War II continental Europe regarded themselves as the true inheritors of the European idealism outlined above. The socialists and social democrats, the lay parties, decidedly do not turn their back to the Church. Christian democrats embrace the welfare state.

The vision of European integration as explicated above, may explain, in part, how it was that the Community only rarely becomes the focus of party politics in continental Europe. All parties can embrace it, because of, if you want, the appeal, or the blandness (take your pick) of its idealistic superstructure. The Community, like other political forces in post-war Europe, embraces both liberalism and social democracy so as to avoid – at the level of rhetoric – the actual choices which exist between these programs. Historically, one cannot speak of mass mobilization for Europe. But as years of Eurobarometer surveys show, it was an acceptable idea always easy to support.

At a second level we may turn to ideals as a vehicle for constitution of the self – individual and social. Consider first the generation of the so-called founding fathers who saw their world fall apart in the horrors of World War II – a negation of the very values of Christian love, of solidarity, of the Enlightenment project. European integration presents itself on my analysis as very alluring: it is not only a new political and economic architecture for post-war Europe which radically supplants the old Versailles model of post-World War I. It is a vision which, whilst being innovative and radical, is also deeply conservative, since it reaffirms their old *Weltanschauung*; indeed, it gives a new lease of life to ideals for which there are no available (meaning acceptable) substitutes at the time. It was a *par excellence* way of affirming one's identity on well known terrain and avoiding the deep dislocations which the breakdown of civility in World War II may have created.

It provided, for individuals and societies, a comfortable way of dealing with the recent past: this past need not call into question fundamental values and ideals, only the political structure and technology for their realization. Europe could (re)define itself as Christian and socially responsible, a worthy successor of the Enlightenment.

It is interesting here to consider the perception and self-perception of bureaucracies. Already in the early 1950s the renewed Frankfurt School, back from exile, develops its profound insight of the state as administration, governance as management. The personification of the New Frankfurt School's conceptualization is, I would think, the state functionary − in Germany, in France, in Italy (each with a specificity of pathology which is altogether original in the different states). To become a Beamte (a state official) is desirable, since it gives power and security, and it is also the *par excellence* expression of blind state loyalty internally, of a vindication of the national interest externally. But service in the public administration is hardly conceived in the language of ideals for these very same reasons, neither by its practitioners nor by the public. The pursuit of power and security are understandable to all, but hardly put on a pedestal.

Service in the Community administration, in its earlier period, was instead conceived as living the Community ideals − it too provided security and some power (increasing) but its "supranational" dimension, formally defying loyalty to the State and countering the national interest in favor of the community (and Community) interest, redefined it in idealistic terms. The meeting of a Community official and a Member State official of the same nationality was at some level a meeting of a "superior" supranational idealist with an "inferior" State realist. The Community official may have been earning a lot more than his or her national counterpart and enjoying working conditions and a social package which was the envy of all national administrations, but he or she was also occupying the high moral ground: a true public servant.

What I am talking about, of course, is perception, not reality. In reality there may not have been any difference between the two public servants. But if there is any truth in my claim of differing perceptions, this truth will have been rooted in an image of the Commission and a self-image of its officials, as seen through the mirror of the Community ideals.

Thirdly, as for the history of ideas, we can evaluate European integration in that epoch as being at the cusp, the very end brink of modernism. The Community idea on this reading is quintessentially European, embracing the core of European classical idealism. It was not simply a reflection of these ideals, but, as explained above, it became a vehicle for their rejuvenation, lending them a new, perhaps temporary, credibility and outlet, a mask, in some eyes, to their vacuity, a rearguard action before their final collapse. Be that as it may, importantly, indeed crucially, as pretender to the inheritance of classical idealism, Europe of the Community was placed not as an end in itself, but as a means for the realization of higher ennobling values.

IX

There is a final element to my discussion of the formative ideals which tries to pull all three ideals together. Let us first consider another set of ideals. It is, for example, certainly a great ideal for an individual to seek, say, to live a life of internal and external truth and integrity. Likewise, to give another example, we consider noble, and rightly so, those academics who pursue the life of scholarship for its own sake, unswayed by consideration of prestige, or advancement, or career. But one feels, surely, an intuitive difference of kind between these ideals and those of the European Community.

Whence the difference? What is special about the type of ideals which the European Community encapsulated is in fact their *community* nature: they are the type of ideals which depend for their realization on being shared by a group of persons; definitionally they are beyond the reach of a lone individual. Further, it is not only that they cannot be achieved by any one individual, that they require a community for their practice, in fact they are constitutive of a Community – they create the community on whose existence they depend.

That this is so in relation to peace is self-evident: it takes, as the saying goes, two to tango. It is only slightly less self-evident in relation to the supranationalism cluster. The invitation to pierce the veil of nationality is at one level to celebrate the individual as an autonomous being, a universe unto himself or herself, an end not a mere instrumentality. But it is also, at the same time, with all the richness of paradox, evocative of the two-sidedness of Enlightenment liberalism, a cry for community which transcends the artificial barriers of nationality and emphasizes the commonality of shared humanity.

It is least evident in relation to Common Market, the Community vehicle for prosperity. There is a powerful strand in the political theory of markets which idealizes them as a neutral arena in which by giving freedom to individuals to pursue vigorously individual economic self-betterment aggregate prosperity will be enhanced. The caricature of this view is the "invisible hand"; its modern hallmarks are the passivity of government, unshackling the individual from pervasive regulation, and vigorous individual competition. Arguably, it was a variant of this idea which informed and explained government mobilization behind the Single European Act. There is much power to this idea and it is certainly dominant in current discussions. It is also, just as certainly, at odds with the community notion I have been discussing. But there is a complementary view of the marketplace, with no less an impressive pedigree – Thomas Paine in his *Rights of Man* would be a good place to start – which emphasizes the social dimension of the market. Under this view, when government sets out actively to create or expand a market, against the backdrop of, say, historical agrarian autarchy and feudalism or, closer to us, national protectionism, it is not only economic goals which can be achieved. The market on this view is a forum for personal intercourse, for social interaction, for the widening of horizons, for learning about and learning to respect others and their habits. It is community too and, I believe, this view was as strong in the formation of the Community as the purely economic one.

In this light we may, indeed, return briefly to the 1992 program and the Single European Act. As mentioned above, like Maastricht, here too there was a discrepancy between the reaction of government, Community, and Member States, and of the population at large: coolness by the former, enthusiasm by the latter. Could it be, perhaps, that whereas government conceived the single market in pure economic terms, in the street that same single market was perceived not simply, or even primarily as a vehicle for economic betterment but as a metaphor for the creation of a European society encapsulated in the slogan of a Europe without frontiers?

X

What has become of ideals discourse in the Europe of Maastricht? What values, as opposed to interests, can be associated with European Union in 1993?

It is decidedly not my intention to join in that favorite game of Euro-bashing. But this does not mean that we cannot engage in a sober assessment of the ideal structure. The narrative here is short: Maastricht, emblematic of the current stage of European integration, can no longer serve as a vehicle for the foundational ideals; and not much has been offered in replacement. But to say that the European Union can no longer serve as a vehicle for the foundational ideals is not necessarily condemnation: in some measure, as I shall try to show, this is so because of the very success of the Community.

Peace, reconciliation between France and Germany, "and all that" has been achieved, thanks perhaps to the Community. To continue to posit *intra-Community* peace as a Maastricht ideal does not have much conviction. That this is so is, paradoxically then, a sign of a remarkable success of the

Community. It is also, perhaps, part of the very phenomenology of peace itself: it is an ideal during, and in the immediate aftermath, of war, for then it demands the triumph of grace. After a long period of peace, it becomes a comfort, an excuse for inaction even in the face of moral imperatives. It can, thus, be an extremely potent mobilizing force. The electorate may well prefer a platform which guarantees peace at any cost. But it is often far from an ideal.

If peace has any place in European discourse today, it is the peace of Munich, of Chamberlain, of peace in our time, which saw fifty years ago the dismemberment of Czechoslovakia and sees today the destruction of Bosnia. Again, it is not that peace within the Community has become a less attractive notion; that it should not be pursued and safeguarded. That it cannot even be an element of mobilization. But for peace to reemerge as an ideal it has to be a challenge, a demand on the self and on society. The kind of demand that the threats in eastern Europe and the former Soviet Union so clearly pose. Instead, the way peace is presented now is the opposite: passive, the *status quo*, preserving the existing comforts, looking after ourselves whilst watching, largely scared and detached, the horrors so close to our borders. How has Europe responded, not for the first time, to the "ethnic cleansing" of a religious minority so close to its historical centre? With words and palliatives. And the Maastricht provisions on a Common Security and Defence Policy have been shown up for what they are. Peace can mobilize: who in Europe wants war? But one can hardly evoke the current peace discourse as a mobilizing *ideal*.

In a more serene manner, it is not then that peace itself has lost its relevance. My argument is that if this particular ideal is to remain part of the ethos of the European Union, the way it is construed requires considerable retooling.

Prosperity too has lost its idealistic bite, thanks perhaps to the Community: in large measure, as with peace, intra-Community prosperity has been achieved. It was the move from poverty to prosperity which was virtuous. Today, even during a recession, the move is from prosperity to even more prosperity. This too can capture votes and support – pocket-book politics always has. But there is no pretense even at casting this discourse in the language of ideals.

The obsolescence of the Community as a vehicle for the foundational ideals is personified in the figures of two leading European politicians waging their Maastricht battles.

There is something altogether pathetic in the aging figure of Mr. Mitterrand preaching Franco–German peace to an incredulous electorate in 1992. And there is something equally pathetic in Mr. Major's technocratic "what's in it for us" approach as his justification for Maastricht.

What then of supranationalism? Is not Maastricht, at least in its aspirations and rhetoric, a definite clarion cry for further supranationalism? To believe that is to misunderstand supranationalism. From this perspective Maastricht is a deception. It may or may not advance the structure and processes of European integration. One has learnt to be cautious and non-dismissive of these steps in Community evolution. But its symbolism is very clear. In its rhetoric Maastricht appropriates the deepest symbols of statehood: European citizenship, defense, foreign policy – the rhetoric of a superstate. We all know that these are the emptiest and weakest provisions of the Treaty, but they undermine the ethics of supranationalism. In its statal aspect supranationalism was a move away from statism to a new uneasy relationship between Community and its Member State. Community was a fine word to capture that value. Now the operational rhetoric is Union, not Community. We have come full circle. The deep irony is that the full circle has come on the ideological level, since, in practice, Maastricht probably is an empowerment of the Member States and in at least some significant aspects (such as the legislative gags imposed on the Community in some of its new policies) a weakening of the Community.

In its individual aspect supranationalism was about the diminution of nationality as a referent for transnational intercourse. Under the rhetoric of Maastricht, the *us* is no longer Germans or French or Italians and the *them* is no longer British or Dutch or Irish. The *us* has become European and the *them*, non-European. If Europe embraces so earnestly at the symbolic level European citizenship, on what moral ground can one turn against French national fronts, German republicans, and their brethren elsewhere who embrace Member State nationalism. On the ground that they chose the wrong nationalism to embrace? The irony, if it needs spelling out, is that, whilst the idealistic moral ground has been shattered, perhaps even lost, in reality in these areas Maastricht offers very little by way of tangible prospects. On this reading, Maastricht has thrown out the supranational water without waiting for the baby to get in the bath.

XI

The Europe of Maastricht no longer serves, as its grandparents the Europe of Paris and Rome, as a vehicle for the original foundational values. This, if my analysis is correct, represents too a rupture with an earlier pre-modern and modern historical continuity of ideas.

The explanation for rupture may not, however, lie simply at the feet of the Community, and at the changed historical conditions which have rendered the Community an obsolescent vehicle for the foundational ideals. It may, too, be a reflection of a rupture in European society as such.

On this reading Maastricht becomes the mirror of the society which it is supposed to serve, a reflection of *fin-de-siècle* Europe, in which those classical ideals have lost in and of themselves their pull.

Consider afresh the Maastricht Treaty and its double structure: economic and monetary union and political union. There is a symbolism in this double structure and the relative weight given to each. It is a common-place that economic and monetary union constitute the heart of the Treaty; that the political union Intergovernmental Conference was more rhetorical than substantive, lip-service paid to the need to increase accountability and strengthen the powers of the European Parliament. The symbolism is that of the Roman circus: a scale of values which privileges economic wealth and prosperity and de-privileges control, autonomy, and responsibility.

The language of symbols is just that – symbolic. And thus not too much should be read into it. But the notion that the problem of Maastricht is in the drafting, in its prolix style, in its incomprehensibility, should perhaps be questioned. Maybe its message is all too apparent. And, to the extent that Maastricht is a reflection, a mirror of its polity, the interesting datum is not in the size of the opposition, but in the impressive support the Treaty has evoked. In this respect Maastricht is simply a creature of its time.

The personification of this symbolism is to be found in the Commission no longer occupying that high moral ground, more likely in search for a plausible justification for privilege. It is almost, but only almost, as if the tables have turned in that meeting between the Community official and his or her national counterpart. It is no secret that there is a deep crisis of morale in the Commission emblematic of the fortunes of Europe. To be sure, the cool reception of Maastricht is part of the explanation. But the low morale may have an additional explanation in keeping with the theme of this essay, namely the loss of the deeper *raison d'être* of the enterprise, the disconcerting realization that Europe has become an end in itself – no longer a means for higher human ends. No measure of information, explanation, or structural tinkering can remedy this.

XII

Assuming that there is some merit to my analysis, there could be a tendency to take it as an indication of a bleak future for Europe. That tendency should be resisted. Europe may or may not have a bleak future, but a causal nexus to the theme of this essay is tenuous. Pragmatic and utilitarian politics can be highly successful, in both mobilization and result. Providing welfare and security may be all we wish from public authority in the post-modernist age. Indeed, this is the place to mention the fourth and last element – ideals as idolatry. An unstated premise of this narrative was that ideals give meaning, ennoble existence, refine materialism. But, as Simone Weil in her anorexic state warned already in the 1940s, and as our own experience will often indicate, ideals are not only a promise but always, at the same time, a danger. For the move from, the change of, ideals to idolatry – a blinding enslavement to supposedly higher values in the name of which all manner of barbarism is committed – is almost pre-determined. European history is replete with such examples: the savagery of the Crusaders was committed in the name of Christian love; collective responsibility was the justification for the ghastliness of the gulags; and the brutality of European colonialism was committed under the flag of the Enlightenment. *Fin-de-siècle* Europe may, thus, be not a reflection of emptiness, but the sign of a healthy suspicion of ideals as idolatry.

There is, however, an alternative and more sobering consideration in this regard, whereby the European Union may be seen not simply as having suffered a loss of its earlier spiritual values, but as an actual source of social *ressentiment*.

Consider the turn to fascism in Italy, France, and Germany at the beginning of the century. In a most profound comparative analysis of the cultural-political roots of the phenomenon the common source is identified as a reaction to some of the manifestations of modernism. At a pragmatic level the principal manifestations of modernism were the increased bureaucratization of life, public and private; the depersonalization of the market (through, e.g., mass consumerism and brand names), and the commodifaction of values; the "abstractism" of social life, especially through the competitive structures of mobility; and the rapid urbanization and the centralization of power. At an epistemological level modernism was premised on, and experienced in, an attempt to group the world into intelligible concepts making up a totality which had to be understood through reason and science – abstract and universal categories. On this reading, fascism was a response to, and an exploitation of, the angst generated by these practical and cognitive challenges.

Eerily, at the end of the century, the European Union can be seen as replicating, in reality or in the subjective perception of individuals and societies, some of these very same features: it has come to symbolize, unjustly perhaps, the epitome of bureaucratization and, likewise, the epitome of centralization. One of its most visible policies, the Common Agricultural Policy, has had historically the purpose of "rationalizing" farm holdings which, in effect, meant urbanization. The single market, with its emphasis on competitiveness and the transnational movement of goods can be perceived as a latter-day thrust at the increased commodification of values (consider how the logic of the Community forces a topic such as abortion to be treated as a "service") and depersonalization of, this time, the national market. The very transnationalism of the Community, which earlier on was celebrated as a reinvention of the Enlightenment idealism is just that: universal, rational, transcendent: wholly modernist.

That the Union has ceased to be a vehicle for its foundational ideals and has thus become a contingent being and experience removed from a normative framework just gives a fashionable "post-modernist" twist to modernist anxiety.

I am not suggesting that Europe is about to see a return to fascism, nor most certainly should this analysis, if it has any merit, give joy to *fin-de-siècle* chauvinists, whose wares today are as odious as they were at the start of the century. But I am suggesting that the crisis of ends might be worse than simply a rupture with the past. It might be an unwelcome connection to another worrisome past, and, in this light, the possible turn away from community to unity in the Maastricht project is simply sad.

XIII

Even with this danger in mind, there may be an unease at a conclusion which left such stark choices with which to think about the future of Europe. This essay need not have a policy-oriented tilt at all. But it is inevitable that it will be read by some for its policy implications. For what it is worth, I would like to offer three alternative perspectives and a final conclusory thought as a brief input into the policy debates shaping the post-Maastricht era.

One approach, which would insist on a dichotomy between technology and culture, repositions, indeed reconceptualizes, the Community not as a new polity for European citizens, but as a technological instrument, an agency, for the resolution of post-industrial problems such as environmental protection, transnational trade, transport, and the like which transcend national boundaries. According to this vision, one should not look for meaning and value at all in the Community, but regard it as a device which liberates people to develop a myriad of cultural communities expressing values at the level of localities and workplace. A huge pay-off, according to this vision, is the undermining of national boundaries as the prime delimitation of political culture and the nation-state as the prime vehicle for political and social expression.

There is much that is alluring in this reconceptualization. I do not propose to explore it in detail, but one should note its weak points: to regard the Community as a technological instrument is, in the first place, to underestimate the profound political choice and cultural impact which the single market could involve – a politics of efficiency, a culture of neutral and asocial markets. Historically we know the flattening impact which markets can have on local cultural diversity. Consequently, it underestimates the critical value-choices involved in technocratic regulatory regimes.

A second approach, deeply historical, would find a new political message for the Community in its putative responsibility towards the east. We could take western Europe in 1951 and impose it without change to eastern Europe in 1991. Does eastern Europe, awakened like a sleeping beauty into the nationalist ethos of pre-1939 Europe, not need, above all, new structures for peace, prosperity, and a supranational ethos which would blunt the excesses of nationalism run amok? Could not this be the prime historical mission of the Community? It could; but it will not, if the new mean-spirited arrangements offered by the Community to eastern Europe are a sign of things to come.

A third and final approach would be one which would explore the communitarian, as opposed to the liberal, strand in the European Community ethos. This, of course, is not the place to expound the communitarian, republican, political theory and ethos, which emphasizes at all levels of social organization not only rights and liberties but civic responsibility and solidarity. This would not be an artificial graft: it is not difficult to find communitarian strands in much of Community discourse. One place to look would be in the very turn to a European citizenship. It could, after all, be reconceived as a bold challenge to the ethno-national state, as a reconceptualization of the Union as a polity belonging to its citizens rather than nationals and from there to an exploration of civic virtues at the core of Community ideals. By espousing this ethos as the guiding principle for its ever-expanding socio-economic legislative agenda, the European Community could become a vehicle for this type of politics of meaning. But, even if communitarianism is there, it is in strong opposition to the deeply rooted liberal ethic. It is not difficult to find – but would be hugely difficult to realize.

The Community is not doomed nor even fatally wounded. And its ability to rebound from crisis is part of its history. Crisis, after all, has always been the sign of its vitality, its relevance. Europe would, however, be better served if the current debate about its future addressed not only means but ends too.

FURTHER READING

On the historical origins of the community

Lipgens, W. (ed.), *Documents on the History of European Integration* (Walter de Gruyter: Berlin, 1985)

Milward, A. S., *The Reconstruction of Western Europe 1945–51* (University of California Press: Berkeley, CA, 1984)

Monnet, J. and Schumman, R., *Correspondence 1947–1953* (Fondation J. Monnet pour l'Europe: Lausanne, 1986)

On the phenomenology of ideals and on the sociology of ideals

Böcker, M., *The Social Psychological Analysis of Attitudes towards the European Community* (Peter Lang: Frankfurt, 1992)

Durkheim, E., *The Division of Labor in Society* (The Free Press: New York, 1964)

Halbertal M. and Margalit, A., *Idolatry* (Harvard University Press: Cambridge, MA, 1992)

Lynd, S., *Intellectual Origins of American Radicalism* (Harvard University Press: Cambridge, MA, 1982)

Manheim, K., *Ideology and Utopia* (Routledge and Kegan Paul: London, 1936)

Schmitt, C., *The Concept of the Political* (Rutgers University Press: New Brunswick, NJ, 1976)

Thompson, J. B., *Studies in the Theory of Ideology* (Polity Press: Cambridge, MA, 1984)

Weil, S., *Notebooks* (Putnam's Sons: New York, 1956)

Williams, B., *Ethics and the Limits of Philosophy* (Harvard University Press: Cambridge, MA, 1985)

On theories of constitution of the self

Berger, P., Berger, B., and Kellner, H., *The Homeless Mind – Modernization and Consciousness* (Vintage Books: New York, 1974)

Goffman, E., *The Presentation of Self in Everyday Life* (University of Edinburgh: Edinburgh, 1958)

Stigma (Prentice Hall: Englewood Cliffs, NJ, 1963)

On the ideology of the market

Hirschman, A. O., *Rival Views of Market Society and other Recent Essays* (Viking: New York, 1986)

On the cultural-political background to fascism

Nolte, E., *The Three Faces of Fascism* (Wiedenfeld and Nicolson, London, 1965)

On new conceptualizations of the European Community

Ostrom Moller, J., *Technology and Culture in a European Context* (Nyt Nordisk Forlag: Copenhagen, 1991)

Snyder, F., *New Directions in European Community Law* (Wiedenfeld and Nicolson, London, 1990)

8

EUROPEAN DEMOCRACY AND ITS CRITICS: POLITY AND SYSTEM

POLITY, PEOPLEHOOD, AND THEORY: PROBLEMS OF TRANSLATION

CONSIDER THE many and considerable flaws in the following description, my own,[1] of the democratic deficiencies of the European Union.

European integration has seen many, and increasingly important, government functions transferred to "Brussels," brought within the exclusive or concurrent responsibility of the Community and Union. This is problematic in a variety of ways.

Though the formal political boundaries of the State have remained intact, in the areas of transfer of responsibility to the Union the functional political boundaries of the polity have been effectively redrawn. If critical public policy choices about, say, international trade, or environmental protection, or consumer protection, or immigration come exclusively or predominantly within Community responsibility, for those matters the *locus* of decision-making is no longer the State but the Union. Even if the Union were to replicate in its system of governance the very same institutional set-up found in its constituent states, there would be a diminution in the specific gravity, in the political weight, in the level of control of each individual within the redrawn political boundaries. That is, arguendo, an inevitable result from enlarging the membership of the functional polity (when a company issues new voting shares, the value of each share is reduced) and from adding a tier of government thereby distancing it further from its ultimate subjects in whose name and for whom democratic government is supposed to operate. If you want a label,

---

[1] Weiler, Haltern and Mayer, "European Democracy and its Critique," *West European Politics* 18 (1995), 4. In parts of this essay I have relied on this previous essay though significantly revised in several crucial points.

call this "inverted regionalism." All the real and supposed virtues of regionalism are here inverted.

Inverted regionalism does not simply diminish democracy in the sense of individual disempowerment, it also fuels the separate and distinct phenomenon of de-legitimation. Democracy and legitimacy are not coterminous. One knows from the past of polities with arguably democratic structure and process which enjoyed shaky political legitimacy and were replaced, democratically, with dictatorships. One knows from the past and present of polities with egregiously undemocratic governmental structure and process which, none the less, enjoyed or enjoy high levels of legitimacy. Inverted regionalism, to the extent that it diminishes democracy in the sense outlined above or to the extent that it is thought to have that effect, will tend to undermine the legitimacy of the Union.

The perceived perniciousness of inverted regionalism and its delegitimation effect will be/are enhanced by three factors:

1. The reach of the Community or Union into areas which are, or are thought to be, classical symbolic "State" functions in relation to which "Foreigners" should not be telling "Us" (French, or Danes, or Irish, etc.) how to run our lives. These areas, socially constructed and culturally bound, are not fixed. They range from the ridiculous (the British Pint) to the sublime (the right-to-life of the Irish abortion saga).
2. The reach of the Community or Union into areas which are, or are thought to be, matters left to individuals or local communities and in relation to which "government" should not be telling "Us" (the people) how to run their lives.
3. The perception, whether or not rooted in reality, that there is no effective limit and/or check on the ability of the Community or Union to reach into areas previously thought to be the preserve of the state or of the individual.

Inverted regionalism is only one, inbuilt and inevitable, feature of the alleged democratic malaise of European integration. I wrote above: "Even if the Union were to replicate in its system of governance the very same institutional set-up found in its constituent states, there would be a diminution in the specific gravity, in the political weight, in the level of control of each individual within the redrawn political boundaries." But, of course, the Union does not replicate domestic democratic arrangements.

A feature of the democratic process within the Member States, with many variations of course, is that government, the executive branch, is, at least formally, subject to parliamentary accountability. In particular, when policy requires legislation, parliamentary approval is needed. National parliaments, apart from exercising these "power functions," also fulfill a "public forum" function described variously as information, communication, legitimation, etc. The argument is that Community and Union governance and Community institutions have a perverse effect on these principal democratic processes within the Member States and within the Union itself.

Community and Union governance pervert the balance between executive and legislative organs of government of the State. The Member State executive branch, government Ministers, are reconstituted in the Community as the principal legislative organ with, as noted above, an ever widening jurisdiction over increasing areas of public policy. The volume, complexity and timing of the Community decisional process makes national parliamentary control, especially in large Member States, more an illusion than a reality. In a majority decision environment, the power of national parliaments to affect outcomes in the Council of Ministers is further reduced. The European Parliament does not offer an effective substitution. Even after Maastricht the powers of the European Parliament in the legislative process leave formal and formidable gaps in parliamentary control. On this reading, Union governance results in a net empowerment of the executive branch of the States.

The European Parliament is debilitated not only by its formal absence of certain powers but also by its structural remoteness. The technical ability of MEPs to link and represent actual constituents to the Community process is seriously compromised in the larger Member States by simple reasons of size. Its abstract representation function of "the people" – its public forum function – is also compromised, by a combination of its ineffective powers (the real decisions do not happen there), by its mode of operation (time and place), by its language "problem," by the difficulty (and disinterest) of media coverage. It is evocative that over the years one has seen a gradual increase in the formal powers of the European Parliament and a decrease in the turn-out to European elections. And when they turn out, these elections are dominated by a national political agenda, a mid-term signal to the national party in power. This is, an evocative fact too, the opposite of American politics where State elections are frequently a mid-term signal to the central federal government. The non-emergence of true trans-European political parties is another expression of the phenomenon. Critically, there is no real sense in which the European political process allows the electorate "to throw the scoundrels out," to take what is often the only ultimate power left to the people which is to replace one set of "governors" by another. In its present state, no one who votes in the European elections has a strong sense at all of affecting critical policy choices at the European level and certainly not of confirming or rejecting European governance.

Community governance might have a distorting effect also if one takes a neo-corporatist view of the European polity. Under this view, government

266

– both executive and legislative branches – do not monopolize policy-making and are but actors, important actors, in a broader arena involving public and private parties. The importance of parliament under this model is to give voice and power to diffuse and fragmented interests whose principal political clout derives from a combination of their electoral power and the reelection drive of politicians. Other actors, such as, say, big industry or organized labor, whose "membership" is far less diffuse and fragmented, exercise influence through different channels and by different means such as political contributions, control of party organization, and direct lobbying of the administration. When policy areas are transferred to Europe there will be a *per se* weakening effect on diffuse and fragmented national interests deriving from the greater difficulty they will experience in organizing themselves at the transnational level compared to, say, a more compact body of large manufacturers (e.g., the tobacco industry). In addition, the structural weakness of the European Parliament has a corresponding effect on these interests even if organized. Electoral power simply carries less weight in Euro-politics.

Since the outcome of the Community legislative process becomes the supreme law of the land, national judicial control of primary legislation – in those systems which have such control (e.g., Italy, Germany, Ireland) – is compromised, too. The European Court, like the European Parliament, does not, arguendo, offer an effective substitution since, inevitably it is informed by different judicial sensibilities in particular in relation to interpreting the limits of Community competences. Since the governments of the Member States are not only the most decisive legislative organ of the Community, but also fulfill the most important executive function (they, much more than the Commission, are responsible for the implementation and execution of Community law and policy) they escape, too, national parliamentary (typically weak) and national judicial (typically stronger) control of large chunks of their administrative functions.

Domestic preferences are, arguably, perverted in a substantive sense, too. A Member State may elect a center–right government and yet might be subject to center–left policies if a majority of, say, center–left governments dominate the Council. Conversely, there might even be a majority of, say, center–right governments in the Council, but they might find themselves thwarted by a minority of center–right governments or even by a single such government where Community decisional rules provide for unanimity. Both in Council and in the European Parliament the principle of proportional representation is compromised whereby enhanced voice is accorded citizens of small states, notably Luxembourg, and, arguably, inadequate voice accorded citizens of the larger states, notably Germany.

Lastly, a feature which is said to pervade all Community governance, and negatively affect the democratic process, is its overall lack of transparency. This is not just a result of the added layer of governance and its increased remoteness. The process itself is notoriously prolix, extremely divergent when one moves from one policy area to another and in part kept secret. "Comitology" is an apt neologism – a phenomenon which requires its very own science which no single person has mastered.

It is easy to list many flaws in this democratic critique of the Union which derive, in part, from its overly schematic nature which, arguably, pays too much attention to the mechanics of democratic governance and not enough to an examination of its vitality in the actual governance of the Union. Here is a mere sample of such flaws. As would emerge from, say, Curtin's recent and remarkable inaugural lecture at the University of Utrecht, not enough attention is paid to the quality, deliberative or otherwise, of the political intercourse within the structures described.[2] Dehousse's work would underscore the need to attend more to the "political deficit" of Union discourse as an integral part of any analysis of its internal democratic habits.[3] Underestimating the significance of the absence of a truly European party system is another important flaw.[4] At a different level, the critique does not attend to the inherent problems of democratic discourse. Underlying the analysis of deficiencies is, at least in part, an optimistic assumption in the very possibility of meaningful democratic conversation which would improve significantly if only the deficiencies were better understood and remedied by some structural change in the European mechanism of democracy.

I do not think it would be too difficult to rewrite the critique of democracy taking into account these and similar flaws. There is, however, a more fundamental flaw which the above critique shares with a great deal of the sprawling DemDefLit ("democracy deficit" literature) which is more resistant to remedy. The origin of this more fundamental flaw is prosaic and can be described as a problem of translation: the very language of modern democracy, its grammar, syntax and vocabulary, revolve around the state, the nation and the people – its *demos*. The Union, it is generally accepted, is not a state. The result is a description of oranges with a botanical vocabulary developed for apples.

There are, in my view, several manifestations to the problem of translation. Though affirming that the Community and Union are a *not* a state

---

[2] D. M. Curtin, *Postnational Democracy* (Universiteit Utrecht, 1997).

[3] E.g. R. Dehousse, "Constitutional Reform in the European Community: Are There Alternatives to the Majority Avenue?" in J. Hayward (ed.), *The Crisis of Representation in Europe* (1995).

[4] See the critical contributions of Mair, "Political Parties, Popular Legitimacy and Public Privilege"; Andeweg, "The Reshaping of National Party Systems"; and Judge, "The Failure of the National Parliaments," in Hayward, *The Crisis of Representation*.

and similarly affirming that the famous '*peoples*' of Europe seeking an ever closer union are indeed that – peoples and not *a people* let alone a nation – DemDefLit is left with two unpalatable options: one is to insist on the intergovernmental or "confederal" nature of the European polity so that questions of democracy can be presented as a case of the domestic democratic control of foreign policy which is not, after all, unique to the European Union experience. This will not do. It is wishful ideological thinking (with which one can sympathize) to imagine the Community as no more than an association of states such as, say, the WTO. This approach masks serious problems of social control and accountability and also lulls one into a certain complacency as regards the assault on democracy which the Union often represents. The Community may have been once a mere association of states; one may wish it remained such; in some exceptional Carl-Schmittian sense of "ultimate" decisional power it may still be such. But in its day-to-day operation, in its normalcy, in its prevailing political physiognomy, it is has long ceased to be understood in those terms. That toothpaste has long been squeezed out of the tube and it makes little analytical sense to try and squeeze it back in again.

The other unpalatable option is to acknowledge that the degree of integration and enmeshment makes a nonsense for the purpose of democratic discourse of the "association of states" model in any of its variants, but then to resort inevitably, explicitly or implicitly, to a discussion of democracy as if the Community and Union were a state.

DemDefLit frequently deals differently with two other issues central to democratic discourse – peoplehood (or nationhood or *demos*) and democratic theory itself. With a number of notable exceptions[5] it is still common in the literature simply to ignore these issues. It is not surprising. Democratic theory itself, because of its statal orientation, typically presumes the existence of a *demos*. By contrast, the exponentially growing literature on new definitions of nationality and citizenship within so-called multicultural societies are concerned to a large degree with identity and access to citizenship rights. To the extent that this literature engages at all in

---

[5] See, e.g., the recent and exceptional treatment of peoplehood, citizenship and nationality by Shaw, "Citizenship of the Union: Towards Post-National Membership?" (Harvard Jean Monnet Paper Series, 1997, http://www.law.harvard.edu/Programs/JeanMonnet). See, too, Rainer Bauböck, "Citizenship and National Identities in the European Union" (Harvard Jean Monnet Paper Series, 1997, http://www.law.harvard.edu/Programs/JeanMonnet); and Preuss, "Citizenship and Identity: Aspects of a Political theory of Citizenship," in R. Bellamy, V. Bufacchi, and D. Castiglione (eds.), *Democracy and Constitutional Culture in the Union of Europe* (Lothian Foundation: London, 1995). For a sustained discussion of democratic theory in the context of European integration, see, e.g., Craig, "Democracy and Rulemaking within the EC: An Empirical and Normative Assessment" (Harvard Jean Monnet Working Paper 2/97, http://www.law.harvard.edu/Programs/JeanMonnet, 1997).

democratic discourse, it typically presumes the existence of basic statal democratic structures which may, however, need adjustment (in respect of, say, voting rights) to the new ideals of states without nations etc. In European integration studies, there is an equally growing focus on identity and citizenship. But how often does this rich and enriching literature fully and explicitly link to democratic theory? It is, for the most part, concerned either with understanding the "meaning" of Europe[6] and the possible meaning of European citizenship within the European construct, or with defining and broadening access to citizenship and belonging. It comes closest to our concerns when it links citizenship and identity to legitimacy.[7] As regards democratic theory, the most common feature of European DemDefLit is to write against the authors' national background understanding of democracy and its institutions rather than against an articulated democratic theory. This is the inverse of the democratic theory literature which writes against the background of an existing state.

In this essay I do not and cannot address and redress all these issues of polity and *demos* and democratic discourse. My excuse is not the proverbial lack of space and time but the more mundane lack of gray matter and intellectual ability: I do not know quite how to resolve these problems of translation. But I want to "have a shot" at rethinking polity and democratic theory. Elsewhere in this volume I deal with the vexed question of *demos*.[8]

I will deal first with the polity and then attempt to link that discussion explicitly to democratic theory. By adopting this approach I hope to make a clarifying contribution to European DemDefLit.

THE EUROPEAN POLITY: INTERNATIONAL, SUPRANATIONAL, INFRANATIONAL OR TAKING MACCORMICK SERIOUSLY

A good sign of the complex state of DemDefLit is the difficulty of coming up with a suitable nomenclature to classify the Union. It is not an international organization in the classical sense, but it is surely not a state. So one tries other appellations: confederation, federacy, *Staatenbund*, *Bundesstaat*, *Staatenverbund*, etc. Why the difficulty? For one, the vocabulary and the concepts they represent are simply there. And using an existing vocabulary is always better than resort to the Latin refuge of *sui generis*. But

---

[6] For an exceptionally perceptive study, see Smith, "National Identity and the Idea of European Unity," *International Affairs* (1992), 68.

[7] See, e.g., the two important contributions by G. Soledad (ed.), *European Identity and the Search for Legitimacy* (London, 1993); and E. Meehan, *Citizenship and the European Community* (London, 1993).

[8] See chapter 10.

more profoundly, the vocabulary of *Staat* and *Bund*, of federation and federacy and confederation, is a reflection of a preoccupation, even an obsession, mostly political and ideological, with sovereignty and its location in Europe. The so-called European "federalists" (often Jacobeans in disguise) adore the symbolism in the word "federalism" which obviates the need to talk of a state. And likewise, the shrill voices defending national "identity" and Member State rights will look to a terminology and classification which will patent and trademark the ultimate sovereignty of the Member States. These approaches are also in a paradoxical sense unitarian. They attempt to find an overall framework which would encompass and explain the entire phenomenon. The principal concession to this monolithic approach refers, of course, to the three-pillar structure of the European Union of which the Community is but one pillar. But, the typical (though not uniform) approach taken towards the second and third pillars in the debate about democracy is not that they are not democratic, but that they are a more primitive form of European integration and that the principal strategy in relation to them should be one of eventual "communautarization" or, of course, the contrary view that they represent bulwarks of sovereignty. It is also a discourse which reflects the Schmittian idea that it is exercise of power in the exceptional case which is politically defining.[9]

I do not wish to belittle these preoccupations. I find, however, MacCormick's trilogy on sovereignty[10] – exploring its fragmented, divided and difficult fit to the modern state – far more compelling as a framework for understanding the Union. This is particularly so if, in contrast to Schmitt and his old and new loyal adherents, one looks to the everyday experience, the repetitive and the banal, as the more telling evidence of the nature of the polity and its dysfunctions.

The approach I am commending in this essay leapfrogs the theology of politically classifying the Union and also leaves aside the three-pillar debate. From the perspective of power – its exercise, control and accountability – I prefer to speak not of three pillars but of three modes of governance: international (or intergovernmental), supranational and infranational.

A description and analysis of European governance will depend today in large measure on the literature you choose to study. Three approaches have become prominent: for convenience I have called them international (intergovernmental), supranational, and infranational. There is an inevitable

---

[9] C. Schmitt, *The Concept of the Political* (Rutgers University Press: New Brunswick, NJ, 1976).

[10] N. MacCormick, "Sovereignty, Democracy and Subsidiarity," in Bellamy, Bufacchi and Castiglione, *Democracy and Constitutional Culture*; N. MacCormick, "Beyond the Sovereign State," *Modern Law Review* 56 (1990), 1; and N. MacCormick, "The Maastricht-Urteil: Sovereignty Now," *European Law Journal* 1 (1995), 259.

correlation between the disciplinary background of the literatures and their respective focus on governance. The international approach, typified by the work of, say, Andrew Moravcsik,[11] has its intellectual roots and sensibilities in international relations. The supranational approach, typified, perhaps, by my own work, has its roots and sensibilities in public law and comparative constitutionalism.[12] What I have termed the infranational approach, typified by the work of, say, Giandomenico Majone, Christian Joerges, Renaud Dehousse and their Florence associates,[13] stems from a background in domestic policy studies and the regulatory state. This is not, however, a case of disciplinary entrenchment. All approaches are mindful of the need to weave together the political and social, the legal and the economic. Nor is it yet another simplistic instance of the proverbial blind men and the elephant. The three approaches are aware of the others but choose to "privilege" what, given the disciplinary background, seems most important to explain and understand in Union governance. More importantly the approaches, in our view, reflect a reality. In some crucial spheres Union governance is international; in other spheres it is supranational; in yet others it is infranational. How the Single European Act was negotiated is not simply an example of the international-relations approach; it is an example of the Community at a high international or intergovernmental moment. Instances of supranational decision-making would be, say, the adoption of the big framework harmonization directives such as for banking or video-rental rights or, at a lower level, the tobacco-labeling directive and, no less interestingly, the rejection of the tobacco-advertising directive. The infranational approach is characterized by the relative unimportance of the national element in the decision-making. Technical expertise, economic and social interests, and administrative turf battles shape the process and outcome rather than "national interest." Infranational decision-making is typified by the miasma of, say, health and safety standard-setting, telecommunications-harmonization policy, international trade rules-of-origin.

It is not, then, that the observational standpoint and the sensibility of the observer alone defines the phenomenon. On my reading certain *objective* aspects of the phenomenon attract the attention of different observers.

[11] A. Moravcsik, "Preference and Power in the European Community: A Liberal Intergovernmentalist Approach," in S. Bulmer and A. Scott (eds.), *Economic and Political Integration in Europe: Internal Dynamics and Global Context* (Blackwell: Oxford, Cambridge, MA, 1994).

[12] Weiler, "The Transformation of Europe," *Yale Law Journal* 100 (1991), 2,403.

[13] See, e.g., G. Majone, "The European Community: An 'Independent Fourth Branch of Government'?" (European Union Institute Working Paper SPS No. 93/9); and R. Dehousse, C. Joerges, G. Majone, and F. Snyder, "Europe After 1992: New Regulatory Strategies" (European Union Institute Working Paper Law No. 92/31).

There are three approaches but there are, out there, also three modes of governance. Likewise, it would be facile, based on the above examples, to conclude, *simpliciter*, that intergovernmental deals with "important" issues, supranational with "middle range" issues, and infranational with trivia. The commonsensical wisdom of Parkinson may well apply in this area too: substantial diplomatic effort may be invested in this or that provision of, say, the SEA; enormous resources may be invested in shepherding a harmonization measure through the ever more complex Commission–Council–Parliament procedures; and yet the reality of important aspects of the single market may have a lot more to do with the details of implementation, with the actual standards set by committees and the like. Here, too, I shall resort to a mere summarized version of the three modes.

For the international approach States are the key players and governments the principal actors. As a mode of governance, the Union, on this perspective is seen as an inter-national arena or regime in which governments (primarily the executive branch) are the privileged power holders. The Union is principally a context, a framework within which States/governments interact. In the supranational approach States are privileged players but the Community/Union is not only or primarily a framework but a principal player as well. The privileged actors are State governments and Community institutions. State government here is understood to include the main branches – legislative and judicial – though not necessarily with equal weight. But here, too, the executive branch is the key State player. The Commission, the Council, and increasingly the European Parliament are critical actors and fora of decision-making. The infranational approach downplays both the Community and the Member States as principal players and likewise the role of primary State and community institutions. In that it is distinct from the international and supranational. It is like the international approach in that the Union is primarily a context, a framework within which actors interact. The actors, however, tend to be, both at Union and Member State levels, administrations, departments, private and public associations, and certain, mainly corporate, interest groups.

In the international mode the focus is on negotiation, intergovernmental bargaining, and diplomacy. There is a relatively low level of institutionalization, and a premium on informal and unstructured interaction. Formal sovereign equality (including a formal veto) and the loose reflexes of international law prevail, which, of course, should not be understood as leading to full equalization of power among the actors. The materia is often – though clearly not always – constitutional (in a non-technical sense). The *modus operandi* of the supranational mode is more structured, formal, and rule-bound. Bargaining and negotiation are far more akin to a domestic legislative process of coalition-building, vote-counting, and rule manipulation. The materia is, frequently, primary legislation. Infranationalism is mostly about regulatory governance and management. There is a medium to low level of institutionalization and informal networking between "government" and corporate players abound.

The international mode is characterized typically by high actor visibility and medium to low process visibility. Supranationalism is characterized by medium (aspiring to high!) actor visibility and medium to low process visibility. Infranationalism has both low actor and process visibility.

The inter–supra–infra trichotomy enables us to build a better picture of the disbursement of power and accountability in the Union. Critical in building this picture is to understand not only the different modes of empowerment of, and desert to, various actors according to the mode of governance but also the fluidity and hence dynamics of allocation of issues to the different forms of decision-making. The stakes as to arena, where (in this scheme) issues get decided, is as important as what gets decided – since the where impacts, indeed determines, the what. For the lawyers among readers, the *ERTA* decision, Opinion 1/76, Opinion 1/94, or Opinion 2/94 were not about content but about forum and mode of decision-making: a bid by the Commission to transfer the treaty negotiation from the international to the supranational arena. The Maastricht three-pillar structure is also about arena, and the various positions of the European Parliament in the ongoing Community debate should be partly understood as bids about mode rather than content of policy-making. Since the SEA, which saw the strengthening of both the legal framework of supranational decision-making and the relative empowerment of the Commission and Parliament, we have seen considerable political battles concerning fora rather than outcome. Comitology becomes a live issue in exactly the same period.

The static model already suggested "inbuilt" empowerment of certain actors: State government in the international mode, State government and Community institutions in the supranational mode, administrations (national and Community) and certain corporate actors in the infranational mode. But this, surely, is only a starting point. Examine the three modes from the perspective of non-governmental public and private actors. Actors which have privileged access to national government (e.g., government political parties) could have an interest in international decision-making. An opposition party may, by contrast, presage for supranational decision-making, if the Community balance of power favors its position. A coalition of Member States may presage transfer (or maintenance) of an issue in the supranational arena where majorities have more weight and are more legitimate. A minority of individual Member States may presage for transfer

274

Table 3. *Internationalism, supranationalism, and infranationalism: static (structural) elements*

Arena	International	Supranational	Infranational
Disciplinary background of observers	international relations	law (typically public law)	policy studies; sociology
Typical issues of governance	fundamental system rules; issues with immediate political and electoral resonance; international "high-politics"; issues *dehors* Treaty	the primary legislative agenda of the community; enabling legislation; principal harmonization measures	implementing and executive measures; standard-setting;
Principal players	Member States	Community and Member States	[Community is policy-making context]
Principal actors	governments (cabinets; executive branch)	governments, Community institutions: Commission, Council, Parliament	second-level organs of governance (Commission. directorate, committee, government departments, etc.); certain corporate and social-industrial NGOs
Level of institutionalization	low to medium	high	medium to low
Mode of political process	diplomatic negotiation	legislative process bargaining	administrative process, "networking"
Type/style of intercourse	informal procedures; low level of process rules	formal procedures; high level of process rules	informal procedures; low level of process rules
Visibility/transparency	high actor and event visibility; low transparency of process	medium to low actor and event visibility; medium to low transparency of process	low actor and event visibility; low transparency of process

to the international arena (e.g., France over the Blair House Agreement) where definitionally the specific gravity of each Member State is higher.

Control and accountability are also critical variables in understanding the implication of the three modes. The international mode will favor domestic arenas of accountability (national parliaments, national press). The supranational mode suffers from all the defects which my initial critique highlighted. Infranationalism has an all-round low level of accountability. By contrast, judicial review tends to be more substantive in the supranational arena, procedural in the infranational arena, and scant in the international arena. When judicial review is perceived as a threat we may expect to find arena battles.

Let me now "translate" the model into the politics of Community democracy. Supranationalism, the "authentic" Community process, is well known and hardly needs elaboration. But how do intergovernmentalism and infranationalism play out in the discourse of democracy and especially in the discourse of democratic reform? Note that the political discussion is not to be seen as a blueprint for rectifying the democratic ills of the Community, but as an illustration of the ways in which the model I am proposing can change somewhat both the focus and the substance of the debate.

Intergovernmentalism may be a desirable feature of Community and Union governance or a necessary evil, but, whether one or the other, it is a central feature of the system and will, in all likelihood, stay so for the foreseeable future. It is also self-evident that, given the importance of the decisions adopted in this mode of governance, democratic accountability is as important here as it is elsewhere in the Community. Note that the issue is not only one of the executive branch of the Member States escaping effective parliamentary control both at home and at the European level. Asserting democratic control over intergovernmentalism is to try and ensure transparency of process and, above all, fairness of access to the key intergovernmental players.

Much energy can be expended on trying to eliminate or diminish intergovernmentalism. But if one accepts it as a constant feature of Community governance, certain implications would seem to follow. It is, for example, neither feasible nor desirable that the European Parliament could or should be able to close the intergovernmental democracy deficit. The correct *locus* for such action is within the Member States by, or at the behest of, national parliaments.

Understanding intergovernmentalism and supranationalism as integral parts of Community governance can lead to a more rational division of labor between national parliaments and the European Parliament. At present, following the pioneering Danish model, most national parliaments have in place mechanisms for trying to monitor and control Community activity. While no one would want to curtail such efforts, it must be noted that much of it is conducted in areas where the European Parliament itself is at its strongest and most efficient. By contrast, national parliaments often seem happy to leave to their executive branch a remarkable measure of negotiating freedom and secrecy in the intergovernmental process. The Maastricht process was a clamorous example of this and the Amsterdam IGC is not remarkably different even if much more modest in its outcome. There is truly little domestic control of positions taken within the negotiations and the "take-it-or-leave-it" option given by an *ex post facto* national referendum is an extremely poor substitute for an effective democratic participation in the process. Clearly, in the interest of democracy, rather than silent power tugs, each institution should be focusing on the control to which it can best contribute. Decisional subsidiarity should apply also in the field of democratic control.

The European Parliament is already committed to as full a co-operation with national parliaments in exercises such as the Assizes, in furnishing information and in co-operating with national parliamentary committees. But, in my view, these efforts can be improved if they were conceived as part of a strategy which recognized the intra-Community fault line running not between the Member States and the Community but between the executive branch operating at different levels and "counterposed" by a co-ordinated parliamentary action which sought to maximize and rationalize parliamentary strength – national and European.

Infranationalism poses a different democratic challenge. Comitology is a central arena of infranationalism. The typical comitology debate has become, however, a surrogate for inter-institutional turf battles. Parliament has, by and large, thrown its energy and weight behind the demands to increase the role of the Commission in comitology and to reduce the role of the Council and the Member States. It has been animated in this posture by its "integration" vision according to which the Commission (with appropriate parliamentary control) is the appropriate institution to have primary "comitology responsibility." This may be so even though under the current comitology regime the Commission has become, *de facto*, the dominant institutional voice in comitology and could not care less about its formal lack of control. Its viewpoint prevails in an overwhelming number of instances.

On this view, the Parliament has been expending its energies in the wrong battle and it is time it shifted its focus to what should be its principal concern in relation to comitology. From the perspective of democratic control, of transparency and of a fair and open access – as well as good and efficient administration – this debate about institutional control of comitology is almost irrelevant. For the pathologies and democratic deficiencies will be present in any institutional – Commission–Council – permutation.

The thrust of my argument is as follows:

1. That comitology is an inevitable and, indeed, indispensable feature of administrative governance;
2. that behind the labels, of "Commission" and/or "Council" in the Comitology Regulations, the reality is a cluster of discrete administrative processes of management, the key public official actors of which are European and national mid-level (oft capable and professional) civil servants;
3. that, except in special instances of a rather exceptional political nature, the top echelons of the Commission, the Council, the Parliament and the Member State governments *inevitably* exercise scant effective control of the comitology decisional process and outcome (hence infranationalism);
4. that in many instances, especially in the "technical" harmonization area, comitology is responsible directly for fundamental societal decisions on the allocation of risk and its costs and indirectly for significant decisions on the allocation of resources and redistribution;
5. that no matter what institutional formulation is adopted for formal comitology decision-making, the reality will see the emergence around each discrete process – of which there are hundreds – of a "network" involving public and private interested parties which together will effectively be shaping the normative outcomes of the process; and
6. that these networks, by their nature, tend to privilege certain interests and under-privilege other competing interests.

The principal pathologies of comitology, on this reading, are not to be found in a distortion of power as between, say, Commission to Council and Member States. The pathologies are, instead, to be found in the twin risks of, first, a hugely consequential regulation taking place at a level of public input and accountability which are not commensurate with the importance of such regulation; and, secondly, in a regulatory process which allocates privileges by unequal and hence unfair access.

Addressing this aspect of infranationalism should be a central concern of the European Parliament even if the remedy is not necessarily to be found in an increase of the powers of the European Parliament itself.

MODELS OF DEMOCRACY

Whatever insight the study of the three arenas may eventually yield regarding the disbursement and accountability of power, it will not, in and of itself, point to "democratic" deficiencies or solutions. As mentioned earlier, one key problem is that democratic theory, and democratic sensibilities, have developed almost exclusively in statal contexts. One enterprise would be to fashion a tailor-made democratic theory for the Community. I raise a white flag of defeat as regards that laudable ambition. Instead, I shall do what all those who cannot afford Savile Row do: seek off-the-peg democratic togs. What is needed, however, are different garments for the different arenas and modes of Union governance.

I shall only take a first step in this essay: exploring possible "fits" between various democratic models and Union modes of governance with a view to a better understanding of the problems of democratic governance in the Union. Some important words of caution are in order here. I shall be arguing, for example, that consociational models of democracy offer a good framework for discussing intergovernmentalism or that, by contrast, some of the neo-corporatist models offer a good framework for discussing infranationalism. I have chosen well-worn democratic garments. Not the latest in democratic theory, but the most well known.[14] I am not, thus, claiming that I have found the perfect fit. But my principal objective is to illustrate and induce a discussion of democracy which would acknowledge the differing modes of Union governance and then seek to find a good fit for each mode to an explicit democratic model.

International governance and the consociational model

Consociational theory emerged to fill a gap in traditional democratic theory. One of the principal tasks of democratic theory was to explain the functionality and stability of pluralistic democratic political systems, given that, by definition of pluralist democracy, such systems would be divided by competing political forces. The classical explanation given by democratic theory to this basic paradox of functional stability in a competitive pluralistic society was by reference to the notion of cut-crossing cleavages. Cut-crossing cleavages, for reasons which do not interest us here, have the effect of leading both to stability and to functionality.

By contrast when social cleavages reinforce each other (Catholic–Protestant; poor–rich; urban–agrarian, etc.) when the social policy is deeply fragmented, society becomes conflict-laden which leads (while democracy is preserved) in turn to immobilism in policy-making and erosion of stability.

And yet, historically, several smaller countries in Europe – Holland,

---

[14] See generally P. Schmitter, "Representation and the Euro-Polity," in T. Ellwin, J. J. Hesse, R. Mayntz, and F. W. Scharpf (eds.), *Jahrbuch zur Staats und Verwaltungswissenschaft* 6 (1992/93), 55; and J. Hayward (ed.), *The Crisis of Representation in Europe* (1995).

Austria, Switzerland, and Belgium up to a point – were socially "clea-vaged" in just that way and yet managed to display in certain periods the functionality and stability of the centripetal explanation until the 1960s. Daalder, a Dutchman, and one of the fathers of consociational theory, recalls how he was told by a leading political scientist: "You know, your country theoretically cannot exist." Consociational theory tries to explain the functionality and stability of these countries. Its basic explanatory device has been the behavior of political elites which control or lead the fragmented social segments.

Crucial to consociational theory is the existence of sharply segmented societal sectors. Consociational theory is not interested in the reasons for segmentation (the content of the cleavages), but in their empirical ex-istence. At this level then the model seems to correspond to the interna-tional dimension of Union governance: a transnational polity sharply segmented by its Member States and indeed displaying the expected characteristics of immobilism, and yet somehow creating structures which manage to transcend these immobilistic tendencies.

Of course, the very creation of structures and institutions for the international mode, like the two non-Community Maastricht pillars, like the European Council, may be said to indicate a higher level of common-ality than consociationalism is designed to respond to. I think the common-ality is in the desire to have a common policy but substantive policy fragmentation is acute in relation to several of the contexts in which the international mode operates. Indeed, the very lack of substantive common-ality is what pushed the Member States to insist on this form of governance in this area.

The essential characteristic of consociational democracy is not so much any particular institutional arrangement as the deliberate joint effort by the elites to render the system functional and stable. The key element is what Dahrendorf has termed a cartel of elites.

Consociational theorists seek to show how in all successful consociational democracies, normal traditional political fora were bypassed, and substituted by fora in which the leaders of all social segments participated, and compacts were arrived at, disregarding the principle of majority rule and using instead consensual politics. Competitive features are removed and co-operation sought. Worth noting is that the alternative fora might in themselves become institutionalized and rather formal. Typically consocia-tionalism works on the basis of consensus, package deals, and other features characteristic of elite bargaining. The elites, representing their respective segments, realize that the game is not zero-sum nor is it a winner-take-all.

The two basic requirements for success according to consociational theory would be that elites share a commitment to the maintenance of the system and to the improvement of its cohesion, functionality, and stability; and that elites understand the perils of political fragmentation. Elites must also be able to "deliver" their constituents (and compliance) to deals thus struck.

This of course begs some questions. In traditional consociational theory this commitment will come out of the loyalty of elites to their country and society. Our claim is that the formal extension in Maastricht of Union governance to areas hitherto dealt with informally or, at best, within European political co-operation demonstrates a degree of commitment to the European polity which, however, is not matched by a sufficient degree of trust in supranational governance. Hence consociationalism as a model.

But consociational theorists suggest it is possible in addition to identify several further features which will be conducive to the success of consociationalism. These include the length of time a consociational democracy has been in operation; the existence of external threats to the polity; the existence of a multiple balance of power; and a relatively low total load on the decision-making apparatus. I think all these features are characteristic of the Union international mode of governance too.

So far I have concentrated on the behavior of the elites themselves. Consociational theory stipulates two further conditions for successful functioning: the elites must be able to carry their own segments along; and there should be widespread approval of the principle of government by elite cartel.

In looking at past practice there do seem to be several points of contact between the consociational model and the international practice of the Union: the existence of a structure composed of highly differentiated segments (the Member States) which display a tendency to immobilism (which classical theory would predict) but which manages none the less to score a measure of functionality and stability (which consociational theory tries to explain). The key factor of consociationalism elite behavior (in our case governments) also seems confirmed in the international mode.

The pay-off of consociationalism seems to be the achievement of stability in the face of a high degree of social fragmentation which normal pluralist models cannot achieve. There are, naturally, implications for self-understanding of democracy in the polity. The democratic justification of consociationalism begins from the acceptance of deep and permanent fragmentation in the polity. Even in traditional constitutional pluralist democracies there is an acceptance that certain "high stake" decisions, such as constitutional amendments, require "super-majorities" or other mechanisms which would be more inclusive of minorities. Consociationalism rejects the democratic legitimacy of permanent minorityship which is possible, even likely, for a fragmented polity operating a pluralist, majoritarian electoral and voting system. Consociationalism seems, thus, to enhance legitimacy in its inclusiveness and the broadening of ultimate consent to government. Theoretically, there is a strong case to be made for a consociational type of inclusiveness also in relation to at least certain areas of Union governance. If the international mode is, in fact, consociational, this would be a justification not from an efficiency and stability perspective but from a normative representational one as well.

The democratic problems of consociationalism and hence of the Union when operating in the international mode are no less grave. First, the democratic gaze must shift to the constituent units of the consociational model – in this case to the Member States. It will often be discovered that some elites, within the consociational cartel of elites, have very deficient internal democratic structures of control and accountability. Even a facile comparison among the structures which exist within the various Member States to control their governments is sufficient to illustrate this point. Even more troubling, consociationalism might actually act as a retardant to internal democratization because the "external" context both empowers the representing elite (executive branch of government) and may even create a mobilizing ethos of, say, the "national interest" which justifies sacrificing calls for transparency and accountability. These calls can be, and usually are, presented as "weakening" the ability of the elite to represent effectively in the external context.

Second, consociational power-sharing is favorable to "status" social forces, those whose elites participate in the cartel. It excludes social forces which are not so recognized. "New" minorities are typically disfavored by consociational regimes. The corollary of this in the Union would be "new" minorities within the Member States whose voices are not vindicated by the government and are thus doubly disfavored at both national and Union levels. Consociationalism can be seen as weakening true representative and responsive government.

Finally, consociational politics typically favor the social *status quo* and, whilst mediating the problems of deeply fragmented societies, are also instrumental in maintaining those very fragments. This can be highly problematic for some conceptions of European integration. Given that the consociational fragments in this context are the Member States themselves, the international mode understood in consociational terms is not only about ensuring the inclusion of all Member State voices in certain critical areas but in actually sustaining the Member States and their governments as such and, for example, retarding the formation of transnational coalitions of interests who, in the areas of the international mode, would and could have no impact in a process which privileged States and their governments.

Supranationalism, pluralism, and competitive elitism

The supranational mode of governance is the closest to a State model and thus, paradoxically perhaps, I shall say little about it. It can be analyzed most profitably either with insights from Weberian or Schumpeterian competitive elites model of democracy or, aspirationally at least, with reference to a statal, federal version of pluralist democracy. The critique with which this essay opened captures most of its actual or even would-be shortcomings and I do not plan to recapitulate these here.

Infranationalism and the neo-corporatist model of governance and democracy

It is not my claim that infranationalism is the Union variety of neo-corporatism. But it does share some common features and hence the conjunction of both may help us identify some of the democratic problems with infranationalism.

Classical neo-corporatism identified a privileging of government, industry, and labor in an attempt to avoid a confrontational mode of governance and reach a politics of accommodation which would resolve economic problems in periods both of expansion and stagnation. The focus was on macroeconomic policy as defining the central public choices confronting the polity. Neo-corporatism was, on this view, a technocratic view which believed in management, distrusted to some extent markets, and favored stability and predictability. It is not surprising that its political instincts also favored governance through negotiation with highly organized interests having representational monopoly. In some respect neo-corporatism is a technocratic version of consociationalism. Neo-corporatism does not replace a parliament and other institutions and processes of pluralist democratic government, but simply side-steps them in reaching the fundamental public choices of the polity. Inevitably there is an erosion in the substantive power and status of parliamentary bodies, parties, and the like. The corporatism of pre-World War II was aimed at undermining those aspects of pluralist democracy in the name of efficiency and stability. Its post-war neo-corporatist version did not have that objective but had some similar institutional frameworks.

The infranational arena is no neo-corporatist model. Its reach extends well beyond macroeconomic policy and the concerns of managing the business cycles which dominated the politics of the 1960s and 1970s. It is decidedly not a tripartite relationship between government, business, and labor. But it has some evocatively similar features:

1. The underlying ethos of infranationalism is managerial and technocratic;

the belief that a rational management and regulatory solutions can be found by an employment of technocratic expertise.

2. There is an underlying premise which puts a premium on stability and growth and is suspicious of strongly redistributive policies and, more generally, on ideology and "politics."

3. Infranationalism has a strong push toward representational monopolies and the creation of structures which will channel organized functional interests into the policy-making and management procedures (CEN, CENLEC, and the like).

4. Infranationalism, because of its managerial, functional and technocratic bias, operates outside parliamentary channels, outside party politics. There is nothing sinister or conspiratorial in infranationalism, but its processes typically lack transparency and may have low procedural and legal guarantees. It seeks its legitimation in results rather than process. (I find fanciful recent attempts to describe comitoligical discourse as an expression of an Habermasian dialogue.[15])

As one would expect, in some respects infranationalism overcomes some of the problems of the international mode. It is both an expression of, and instrumental in, the decline of the State and its main organs as the principal vehicle for vindicating interest in the European polity. Infranationalism is about transnational interest groups, governance without (State) government, empowerment beyond national boundaries, and the like. But it suffers too from many of the problems of neo-corporatism and some problems of its own. I would mention in particular the following:

1. The technocratic and managerial solutions often mask ideological choices which are not debated or subjected to public scrutiny beyond the immediate interests related to the regulatory or management area.

2. Participation in the process is limited to those privileged by the process; fragmented and diffuse interests, and other public voices, are often excluded.

3. As in the consociational model, the process itself might distort power relationships and democracy within the groups represented in the process.

4. The process itself not only lacks transparency but is also typically of low procedural formality thus not ensuring real equality of voice of those who actually do take part in the process. Judicial review is scant and tends to insist on a basic right to be heard rather than the fairness of outcome.

---

[15] See generally, C. Joerges, "Social Regulation Through European Committees: Empirical Research, Institutional Politics, Theoretical Concepts and Legal Developments" (Conference at the European University Institute, December 1996, forthcoming).

5. In general, the classical instruments of control and public accountability are ill-suited to the practices of infranationalism. They are little affected by elections, change in government, and the new instruments introduced by, say, Maastricht.

All this would illustrate, if nothing else, that the problems of democracy in relation to infranationalism will not be solved by any of the structural changes in the institutional balances of Community organs. A far more radical approach to transparency would be required.

9

THE AUTONOMY OF THE COMMUNITY LEGAL
ORDER: THROUGH THE LOOKING GLASS*

INTRODUCTION

SURELY ONE of the most embarrassing, and hence endearing moments in the human condition occurs when the proverbial little boy cries out: "The Emperor is Naked!" The embarrassment is not only that of the Emperor whose dignity comes crashing down with his clothes, but more exquisitely that of his subjects whose own gullibility and obsequiousness are fully exposed. Our laughter, that of the spectators, is directed, one hopes, in equal measure at ourselves and at the Emperor. Our civilization cherishes, or ought to cherish, such "little boys."

Theodor Schilling, in his article "The Autonomy of the Community Legal Order – An Analysis of Possible Foundations,"[1] attempts to be such a "little boy" by taking on, to use his own language in the opening phrase of his piece, no less than "[t]he single most far-reaching, and probably most disputed, principle of the European Community . . . its claim to a legal order autonomous from Member State law."[2] In his attempt to explore the foundations of this claim to autonomy, he pricks one of the biggest hot-air balloons of European law[3] – its alleged "new" constitutional garb – and exposes, if not its nakedness, at least its comfortable old togs of international law. Since most of us have been party to the "constitutional" celebration of Community law, we are all invited to join in the merriment. We would like to.

---

* This chapter was originally co-authored with Ulrich Haltern.
[1] Theodor Schilling, "The Autonomy of the Community Legal Order – An Analysis of Possible Foundations," *Harvard International Law Journal* 37 (1996), 389.
[2] *Ibid.*
[3] While Dr. Schilling's article mostly refers to the law of the European Community, we will use the term "European law" to describe either European Community law or European Union law as the case may be. Only when distinctions matter, will we flag them.

But there is one situation which, arguably, is even more embarrassing and, accordingly, more endearing. This happens when the little boy cries out "The Emperor is Naked!" and it turns out instead that it is he who has no clothes on. We fear that Dr. Schilling may have placed himself, unwittingly, in that position.

The bulk of the Schilling article is dedicated to the theoretical exercise of exploring the foundations of the autonomy claim: are these foundations constitutional or international? But fear not: this is not theory merely for the sake of theory. There is a distinct political context to the heavy theorizing. It comes in the very final passages of Schilling's piece, in what he himself describes as "The Decisive Question."[4] Schilling also makes no bones that his article is meant to be instrumental in the battles surrounding this "Decisive Question."[5]

What, then, is the "Decisive Question"? It is the most recent flash point (or "flash-in-the-pan") in the evolving relationship between Community law and Member State law.[6] The supremacy of Community law over, and the direct effect of Community law within, the Member States' legal orders, once all the rage, are now well established. They are accepted by both the constitutional and the international law accounts of the system and confirmed, by and large, in practice. But, as all interpretative communities at least verbally affirm,[7] the Community is a system of "attributed," "enumerated," "limited" competences.[8] The writ of the Community is

---

[4] Schilling, "The Autonomy of the Community Legal Order," 404.   [5] *Ibid.*, 408–9.

[6] J. H. H. Weiler, Ulrich R. Haltern and Franz C. Mayer, "European Democracy and Its Critique," *West European Politics* 18 (1995), 4.

[7] See, e.g., Bengt Beutler *et al.*, *Die Europäische Union: Rechtsordnung und Politik* (4th edn., 1993), 82; Thomas Oppermann, *Europarecht* (1991), 168–9; Philippe Manin, "Les Communautés Européennes," *Droit institutionnel* (1993), 62; Antonio Tizzano, "Les compétences de la Communauté," in *Trente ans de droit communautaire* (European Commission, Perspectives Européennes, 1982), 45; and Roland Bieber, "Artikel 4," in Hans von der Groeben *et al.* (eds.), *Kommentar zum EWG – Vertrag* (4th edn., 1991), para. 38. The virtual disappearance of the principle of enumerated powers, as a constraint on Community material jurisdiction, is analyzed in detail in chapter 2. The diminishing practical significance is also noted by T. C. Hartley, *The Foundations of European Community Law* (3rd edn., 1994), 110–19.

[8] This has been confirmed by the ECJ early on, in, e.g., Case 26/62, *Van Gend and Loos* v. *Nederlandse Administratie der Belastingen* [1963] ECR 1 (the Community constitutes "a new legal order of international law for the benefit of which the states have limited their sovereign rights, *albeit within limited fields*"; emphasis added). For even more striking language (albeit related to the Coal and Steel Community), see Joined Cases 7/56 and 3/57 to 7/57, *Dineke Algera et al.* v. *Common Assembly of the European Coal and Steel Community* [1957] ECR 39, Opinion of Advocate-General Lagrange [1957] ECR 69 at 82 ("The Treaty is based upon delegation, with the consent of the Member States, of sovereignty to supranational institutions *for a strictly defined purpose* ... The legal principle underlying the Treaty is a principle of *limited authority*. The Community is a legal person governed by public law, and as such, it shall enjoy the legal capacity *it requires to perform its functions and attain its objectives*, but only that capacity."). Much of this, today, is mere lip-service. Koen Lenaerts, for instance, concludes, "There simply is no nucleus of

thus supreme only when enacted within its jurisdictional limits. An *ultra vires* Community measure should not be and would not be supreme. The "Decisive Question" is, therefore, as follows: when the legality of a Community measure is challenged on the grounds of *ultra vires* who, in law, gets to make the final determination? Is it the European Court of Justice or the (highest) courts of the individual Member States? Since the jurisdictional limits laid out in the European Treaties are notoriously difficult to identify with precision,[9] the question of who gets to decide is of tremendous political importance for the relationship between the Community and the Member States.

The standard answer to the "Decisive Question," the "imperious answer" if you wish, put forward by most commentators as well as by the ECJ, is that the final determination of this issue, as with any other legal challenge to the legality of a Community measure, rests with the ECJ.[10] The ECJ has the competence, an exclusive competence, to invalidate a Community measure on any ground, including the ground that the measure was *ultra vires*. We may call this *judicial Kompetenz-Kompetenz*: the competence to declare or to determine the limits of the competences of the Community.

This issue, dormant for years,[11] was suddenly thrown into the limelight by the famous (or infamous) 1993 Maastricht Decision of the German Federal Constitutional Court.[12] While conceding that the ECJ had a role to play, the German Court held that from a German constitutional perspective, the ultimate authority to determine this issue rested with domestic law. Indeed, any German court or other emanation of the state had a duty not to apply Community measures which in their eyes were *ultra vires*.[13] In the case of a dispute, the German Federal Constitutional

---

sovereignty that the Member States can invoke, as such, against the Community": Koen Lenaerts, "Constitutionalism and the Many Faces of Federalism," *American Journal of Comparative Law* 38 (1990), 205 at 220; see also chapter 2, pp. 000–00 above.

[9] See chapter 2, pp. 39–59 above.

[10] Case 314/85, *Foto-Frost* v. *Hauptzollamt Lübeck-Ost* [1987] ECR 4,199. (This, it seems, has also been Schilling's first intuition.) See Schilling, "The Autonomy of the Community Legal Order," 405 ("According to the ordinary meaning of this provision, the ECJ is the ultimate umpire of the European system").

[11] Jean Paul Jacqué and J. H. H. Weiler, "On the Road to European Union – A New Judicial Architecture: An Agenda for the Intergovernmental Conference," *Common Market Law Review* 27 (1990), 185; Jean Paul Jacqué and J. H. H. Weiler, "Sur la voie de l'Union européenne, une nouvelle architecture judiciaire," *Revue trimestrielle de droit européen* 26 (1990), 441.

[12] German Constitutional Court, Judgment of October 12, 1993, 89 BVerfGE 155; English translation in ILM 33 (1994), 388 at 422–3.

[13] "If, for example, European institutions or governmental entities were to implement or to develop the Maastricht Treaty in a manner no longer covered by the Treaty in the form of it upon which the German Act of Accession is based, any legal instrument arising from such

Court itself would have the final say.[14] The German Court arrived at this conclusion based on a reasoning of German constitutional law. Though the reasoning has not met with uniform approval, to put it mildly, even among German constitutionalists,[15] we do not plan to take issue with it in this essay.[16] After all, if the German Court understands its authority as flowing from, and its loyalty flowing to, the German Constitution, it could hardly hold otherwise if it came to the conclusion that this is what the German Constitution mandated. Other courts, some with considerably longer traditions of constitutionalism and democracy than their German counterpart, have upheld positions that they thought were mandated by the genesis or function of their constitutions, even if this created or sanctioned a violation of the international obligations of their respective states.[17]

activity would not be binding within German territory. German State institutions would be prevented by reasons of constitutional law from applying such legal instruments in Germany": *ibid.*, 188.

[14] This is the consequence of the German system of centralized judicial review, with the Bundesverfassungsgericht at its core.

[15] See, for instance, Christian Tomuschat, "Die Europäische Union unter Aufsicht des Bundesverfassungsgerichts," *Europäische Grundrechtezeitschrift* 20 (1993), 489 at 494; Jochen A. Frowein, "Das Maastricht-Urteil und die Grenzen der Verfassungsgerichtsbarkeit," *Zeitschrift für ausländisches öffentliches Recht und Völkerrecht* 54 (1994), 1 at 8–10; Meinhard Schröder, "Das Bundesverfassungsgericht als Hüter des Staates im Prozeß der europäischen Integration – Bemerkungen zum Maastricht-Urteil," *Deutsches Verwaltungsblatt* (1994), 316 at 323–4; Jürgen Schwarze, "Europapolitik unter deutschem Verfassungsvorbehalt – Anmerkungen zum Maastricht-Urteil des BVerfG vom 12.10.1993," *Neue Justiz* 48 (1994), 1 at 3; and Karl M. Meessen, "Maastricht nach Karlsruhe," *Neue Juristische Wochenschrift* 9 (1994), 549 at 552–3.

[16] For an extensive discussion, see J. H. H. Weiler, "The State 'Uber Alles': Demos, Telos and the German Maastricht Decision," in Ole Due et al. (eds.), *Festschrift für Ulrich Everling* (1995), 1,651.

[17] For example, English courts have held that English statutory law is binding upon them even if conflicting with international law. See, e.g., *R. v. Chief Immigration Officer, ex parte Salamat Bibi* [1976] 3 All ER 843; *R. v. Secretary of State for the Home Dept., ex parte Thakrar* [1974] 2 All ER 261; and *Woodend (K. V. Ceylon) Rubber and Tea Co. v. Inland Revenue Commissioner* [1970] 2 All ER 801. Under US law, courts have occasionally subordinated treaties to subsequent statutes and held that the US has the prerogative to violate its international commitments. See, above all, references in Louis Henkin, "The Constitution and United States Sovereignty: A Century of Chinese Exclusion and Its Progeny," *Harvard Law Review* 100 (1987), 853 and the response by Peter Westen, "The Place of Foreign Treaties in the Courts of the United States: A Reply to Louis Henkin," *Harvard Law Review* 101 (1987), 511. As to US statutes and international treaties, see, *inter alia*, the *Head Money Cases*, 112 US 580 (1884); *Whitney v. Robertson*, 124 US 190 (1888); and the *Chinese Exclusion Case*, 130 US 581 (1889). As to US statutes and customary international law, see, *inter alia*, the *dictum* in the *Paquete Habana Case*, 175 US 677 at 700 (1900) ("International law is part of our law, and must be ascertained and administered by the courts of justice ... For this purpose, *where there is* no treaty and *no controlling executive or legislative act* or judicial decision, resort must be had to the customs and usages of civilized nations."). Under German law, international treaties do not have a higher status than federal laws, with the consequence that the principle *lex posterior derogat legi posteriori* is applicable and that the treaty must be consistent with the German Constitution, or Grundgesetz. For the obligation to choose

Some German courts, taking their cue from the German Federal Constitutional Court, have already set aside Community law that in their eyes was *ultra vires*.[18] If the German Constitutional Court itself were to do this it would clearly be illegal under Community law. Schilling, however, does not reason ostensibly from a national constitutional law perspective, though he clearly supports the German result. Schilling tries to render this constitutional swine − if that is what it is − kosher by relying on public international law, his preferred foundation for the European Community legal order. His conclusion is uncompromising:

> The international law interpretation of the European Treaties thus leads to the conclusion that the ECJ is not the ultimate umpire of the system . . . Therefore, the Member States, *individually*, must have the final word on questions concerning the scope of the competences they have delegated to the Community.[19]

The stakes for Schilling are high: the "rule of law" itself is at issue. In Schilling's eyes, it is mere rhetoric when, on the "Decisive Question," the ECJ relies on the principle of the rule of law.[20] The "Truth" has been recognized by the German Constitutional Court, which according to Schilling, does not merely constitute, in law, the "final umpire of the system," but is also the clarion of the rule of law itself and has positioned itself, with the help of Schilling, "for eventually holding the ECJ in breach of that rule."[21]

We confess to finding these conclusions, and the reasoning on which they are based, puzzling. They evoke a reaction not unlike that of Alice when she peers into the Looking-Glass House: "that's just the same . . . only the things go the other way."

Whatever the merits, or lack thereof, of a constitutional foundation for European law, the ECJ, in adopting its position on judicial *Kompetenz-*

---

the interpretation of an international treaty that is in accordance with the Constitution, see, *inter alia*, Judgment of May 4, 1955, BVerfG, 4 BVerfGE 157, 168, translated in *Decisions of the Bundesverfassungsgericht − Federal Constitutional Court − Federal Republic of Germany: International Law and Law of the European Communities 1952−1989 Part 1* (1992), vol. I, 70 at 77. Article 25 of the Basic Law, which could be read as an affirmation of the supremacy of international law (although many disagree: see, e.g., Knut Ipsen, *Völkerrecht* (3rd edn., 1990), 1,091−3), does not apply to treaties but only to general customary rules of international law: Grundgesetz, Art. 25 (FRG). For further reference, also relating to other countries, see Sir Robert Jennings and Sir Arthur Watts (eds.), *Oppenheim's International Law*, vol. I, 54−81 (9th edn., 1992). See also Eyal Benvenisti, "Judicial Misgivings Regarding the Application of International Law: An Analysis of Attitudes of National Courts," *European Journal of International Law* 4 (1993), 159.

[18] See Norbert Reich, "Judge-Made 'Europe à la Carte': Some Remarks on Recent Conflicts between European and German Constitutional Law Provoked by the Banana Litigation," *European Journal of International Law* 7 (1996), 103.

[19] Schilling, "The Autonomy of the Community Legal Order," 407 (emphasis added).

[20] *Ibid.*, 408.   [21] *Ibid.*, 409.

Kompetenz, was not following any constitutional foundation but rather an orthodox international law rationale. In other words, even if we agreed with Schilling that international law provided the only basis on which to found the Community legal order, we would argue that this very foundation in international law mandates the opposite conclusions than the ones he reaches: the ECJ does hold the position of "ultimate umpire of the system." Furthermore, international law certainly would not give the states, *individually*, the right to have the final word on questions concerning the competences of an international organization, just as it would not give such decisional finality to a state over any aspect of a Treaty to which it was party. Regardless of whether the position of the German Constitutional Court is justified under German constitutional law, it is not defensible under public international law. At most, all Member States of the Union, acting in unison, usually by following the Treaty-amendment procedure, may determine, amend, and modify the Treaties, including their jurisdictional reach.[22] Ironically, as we argue later in this article, a constitutional law approach to the Community legal order would be more solicitous to an involvement of national jurisdictions in the determination of the jurisdictional limits of the Community legal order.

This, then, is how we plan to proceed. We shall say first a few words on Schilling's "constitutional–international" analysis – a few words only because, for the purposes of this essay, we are happy to remain agnostic on this issue. We agree with much of what Schilling says and our disagreements are mostly unrelated to the so-called "Decisive Question." We will thus be willing to accept, at least arguendo, his international law characterization of the Community legal order as the premise for analyzing his "Decisive Question." On this basis we then proceed to analyze with some

[22] This is, of course, not just a theoretical suggestion. The Member States have altered the Treaties several times, the latest examples being amendments to the framework of Maastricht. The most important example is the Protocol Concerning Article 119 of the Treaty Establishing the European Community, annexed to the EC Treaty which, according to Art. 239 of the EC Treaty, is an "integral part" of it. This Protocol – the so-called "Barber" Protocol – was a reaction to the ECJ judgment in Case C-262/88, *Barber* v. *Royal Guardian Exchange Assurance Group* [1990] ECR 1,889. Being the prototype of a consensus reaction of the Member States to a binding decision of the ECJ, the Barber Protocol is considered by some to be a warning to the ECJ. See, e.g., Deirdre Curtin, "The Constitutional Structure of the Union: A Europe of Bits and Pieces," *Common Market Law Review* 30 (1993), 17 at 51. Another example of the Member States altering the Treaties is the Protocol annexed to the Treaty on European Union and to the Treaties Establishing the European Union (the so-called "Irish Abortion" Protocol). Curtin submits that "the whole purpose of including the Protocol in the first place was to close the door that seemed to be left ajar ... by the [ECJ] ruling in *SPUC* v. *Grogan* [Case C159/90 [1991] ECR I-4,685]": *ibid.*, 49. Further examples – outside the "special case" protocols – include the new provisions on culture (see Arts. 3(p) and 128 of the EC Treaty) and on public health (see Art. 3(o) and Title X of the EC Treaty).

care the reasoning on which Schilling bases his conclusions. Lastly, we shall conclude by addressing, in a somewhat less doctrinal manner, the stand-off between the ECJ and the German Constitutional Court on the issue of judicial *Kompetenz-Kompetenz*.

THE COMMUNITY LEGAL ORDER: CONSTITUTIONAL OR INTERNATIONAL?

Schilling goes to great lengths to debunk the alleged constitutional foundations of the Community legal order. One could, of course – and, in our view, one should – call into question the very dichotomy between "the international" and "the constitutional" implicit in Schilling's argument. The blurring of this dichotomy is precisely one of the special features of the Community legal order and other transnational regimes.[23] But our critique of the Schilling piece does not go, as stated, to his whole argument. We are willing to share with him the constitutional–international distinction and even go further and share with him much of his critique of the constitutional–foundation thesis.

The European legal order was begotten from public international law in the normal way that these things happen: there was a communion among some states – the High Contracting Parties – which negotiated, signed, and subsequently ratified the constituent Treaties which brought into being, first the nascent European Coal and Steel Community and then its twin siblings, the European Economic Community and Euratom. We know their progeny today as the three-pillared European Union. This manner of conception would, in the normal course of international life, determine the genetic – as well as the legal – code of the new infant: an international organization with a separate legal personality but with no measure of independence or power to eradicate its subordination to its states parents and its subjection to the classical laws governing the states' treaty relations. The states, like the Olympian gods, would forever remain ultimate masters of their creation. The Germans have a nice phrase for this: the Member States are called the "Herren der Verträge."[24]

This mastery of the states over their offspring does not prevent, as with other almighties, acts of self-limitation: in the begetting of an international organization through an international treaty, the High Contracting Parties

---

[23] See José de Areilza, "Sovereignty or Management?: The Dual Character of the EC's Supranationalism – Revisited" (Harvard Jean Monnet Working Paper No. 2/95, 1995).

[24] See, e.g., German Constitutional Court, Judgment of October 12, 1993, 89 BVerfGE 155, 190 (FRG). But see Markus Heintzen, "Die 'Herrschaft' über die Europäischen Gemeinschaftsverträge – Bundesverfassungsgericht und Europäischer Gerichtshof auf Konfliktkurs?," *Archiv des öffentlichen Rechts* 119 (1994), 564.

may decide to bestow on their offspring the power to make decisions which will bind them. They may even privilege a few states in the process.[25] But, at any point, as long as the Member States act in unison, they may change the status or the capacities of the organization. The basic principles of the law of treaties would apply to privilege the makers of the treaty at all critical junctures in the life of a treaty – treaty-making, amendment, interpretation, and termination. As masters of the treaty, states are also masters of the organization. Thus, for example, not infrequently will states amend a treaty – including one setting up an international organization – in violation of its specific amendment procedures. As long as the amendment is in accord with the collective will of all parties, it would be considered valid.[26] Likewise, should there be a disagreement over the interpretation of a clause within a treaty, an agreement of all parties will

---

[25] The UN Charter empowers a small number of states in the Security Council to make decisions binding on the international community as a whole: UN Charter Arts. 23–32. The Charter further privileges some states by giving them permanent membership of the Council and a veto power: *ibid.* Other organizations privilege states by according their votes more weight. Henry G. Schermers and Niels M. Blokker give some examples including the International Monetary Fund (IMF, Art. 12, sec. 5(a)); the World Bank (World Bank, Art. 5, sec. 3); the International Fund for Agricultural Development (IFAD, Art. 6(3) and Schedule II); the International Sugar Council (International Sugar Agreement, Art. 25 and Annex); the Multilateral Investment Guarantee Agency (MIGA, Art. 39); the Common Fund for Commodities (UNCTAD, Fundamental Elements of the Common Fund, para. 24); the International Energy Agency (IEA, Art. 62); and the International Maritime Satellite Organization (INMARSAT, Art. 14(3)). Henry G. Schermers and Niels M. Blokker, *International Institutional Law*, §§ 799–812 (3rd edn., 1995).

[26] This so-called "freedom of form" rule seems to be confirmed by Art. 39 of the Vienna Convention on the Law of Treaties, opened for signature May 23, 1969, 1,155 UNTS 331 at 340: "A treaty may be amended by agreement between the parties. The rules laid down in Part II apply to such an agreement except in so far as the treaty may otherwise provide." Part II deals with the conclusion (and entry into force) of treaties. Art. 11, which is in Part II, provides that the consent of a state to be bound can be expressed in any form agreed between the parties. However, Art. 39 subjects this freedom to the condition that the treaty does not provide otherwise. We find an interpretation contrary to the "freedom of form" rule unconvincing. There are two arguments clearly confirming the freedom of form. First, special revision clauses are intended to *facilitate*, not to complicate, the ordinary amendment process. The special amendment procedure, then, bars single states from insisting on amendment by consensus if the treaty provides for a more efficient procedure. There is, however, no reason why in cases in which all parties agree to consensus procedure they should not be able to do so. Second, *argumentum a maiore ad minus ex* Vienna Convention, Art. 54. If treaties can be terminated at any time by the consent of all the parties, then the parties must also be able to employ the less significant measure, the amendment or revision of the treaty by the consent of all the parties. Both arguments are put forward by Wolfram Karl, *Vertrag und spätere Praxis im Völkerrecht* (1983), 341–3; Bruno de Witte, "Rules of Change in International Law: How Special is the European Community?," *Netherlands Yearbook of International Law* 25 (1994), 299 at 313.

normally be the final word as either an authentic interpretation[27] or a *de facto* amendment.[28]

There is a different manner in which disparate states may bring into being a new legal order, by "constitutional" fusion. Birth may take different forms, from constitutional convention[29] to treaty.[30] Arguably each new creature inherits a genetic and legal code altogether different from that of their parents. The constitutive act may explicitly or implicitly extinguish the separate existence of the constituent units,[31] but, in any event, it will subordinate the constituent units to the new creation. Thus, it is sometimes thought that, whereas the subjects of a treaty (or a treaty-based international organization) are the states composing it, the subjects of, say, a federal constitutional order are not only its constituent states, but also its common citizenry. This difference is thought to create a different level of legitimacy for the constitutional order, one where its legitimacy does not come only from the consent of sovereign states but from the broader and more direct consent of the citizens of those constituent units. Typically, the international organization is governed by international law and the constitutional order by its own municipal law.

---

[27] See, e.g., Jennings and Watts, *Oppenheim's International Law*, vol. I, § 630 at 1,268–9; Alfred Verdross and Bruno Simma, *Universelles Völkerrecht: Theorie und Praxis* (3rd edn., 1984), § 775 at 490–1; and Knut Ipsen, *Völkerrecht*, 120–1. See also Art. 31(3)(a) of the Vienna Convention.

[28] It may be difficult to draw a clear line between the two. Authentic interpretation, along the lines of Art. 31(3)(a) of the Vienna Convention, can, substantially, be conceived of as a material amendment to the Treaty. This may have decisive implications, especially in municipal law. While amendments to international treaties generally have to be ratified by a competent body under national law, one could well argue that interpretive declarations do not have to be so ratified. This question arose, for example, under German law when the Bundesverfassungsgericht had to decide upon the constitutionality of the deployment of German armed forces "out of area": judgment of July 12, 1994, BVerfGE, 90 BVerfGE 286; see Wolff Heintschel von Heinegg and Ulrich R. Haltern, "The Decision of the German Federal Constitutional Court of 12 July 1994 in Re Deployment of German Armed Forces 'Out of Area'," *Netherlands International Law Review* 41 (1994), 285 at 305–7.

[29] Consider, for example, the constitutional convention founding the United States. See, e.g., Max Farrand, *The Framing of the Constitution of the United States* (1913); Gordon S. Wood, *The Creation of the American Republic 1776–1787* (1969).

[30] Consider the Einigungsvertrag of August 31, 1990 (FRG–GDR Treaty on the Establishment of German Unity) 1990 Bundesgesetzblatt Teil II [BGBl. II] 889, translated and reprinted in ILM 30 (1991), 457 (leading to German unification). See, e.g., Peter E. Quint, "Constitution-Making by Treaty in German Unification: A Comment on Arato, Elster, Preuss, and Richards," *Cardozo Law Review* 14 (1993), 691. As far as German law is concerned, according to Grundgesetz, Art. 23, unification was implemented by the accession of the German Democratic Republic to the Federal Republic of Germany.

[31] On October 3, 1990, the GDR ceased to exist. Its territory became part of the Federal Republic of Germany. The five states (Länder) that formed the GDR became states of the Federal Republic. See, generally, Jochen Abr. Frowein, "The Reunification of Germany," *American Journal of International Law* 86 (1992), 152.

There is no doubt that the European legal order started its life as an international organization in the traditional sense, even if it had some unique features from its inception.[32] This original internationalism was evident in, for example, the attitude of the institutions of the Communities themselves, including the vaunted ECJ,[33] as well as in the attitude of the Member States receiving expression in, for example, early instances of Treaty amendment.[34] We entirely share, then, Schilling's critique of those who hold that the Community legal order was born as a constitutional order.[35] It should be stated that few would ascribe original constitutionalism to the Community legal order.

Nevertheless, one of the great perceived truisms, or myths, of the European Union legal order is its alleged rupture with, or mutation from, public international law and its transformation into a constitutional legal order.[36] This mutation takes place, allegedly, from 1963 onwards and is reflected in landmark cases of the ECJ – in dialogue with national courts. The ECJ talks first of a "New Legal Order of International Law"[37] and then of a "New Legal Order" *simpliciter*. The "newness" of the legal order is characterized as "constitutional" and the process as "constitutionalization." The subjects of the new order are said to be not only states, but also individuals. Most commentators focus on the legal doctrines of supremacy of European law, the direct effect of European law, implied powers and preemption, and on the evolution of the protection of fundamental human rights as hallmarks of this "constitutionalization."[38]

---

[32] These unique features are so well known as to obviate extensive description. We content ourselves to point to Art. 189 of the EC Treaty, the possibility of binding decision-making and majority voting under EC, and the extraordinary powers of the High Authority under the ECSC.

[33] See, e.g., *Dineke Algera* v. *Common Assembly of the European Coal and Steel Community* [1957] ECR 39.

[34] In 1956 and 1957, the six original Member States of the European Coal and Steel Community twice modified the ECSC Treaty by informal agreement, disrespecting the formal procedure laid down in Art. 36 of the ECSC Treaty. See de Witte, "Rules of Change in International Law" at 316; and Werner Meng, "Artikel 236," in Hans von der Groeben *et al.* (eds.), *Kommentar zum EWG – Vertrag* (4th edn., 1991), para. 31, 5,844. See also J. H. H. Weiler and James Modrall, "Institutional Reform: Consensus or Majority?," *European Law Review* 10 (1985), 316; J. H. H. Weiler and James Modrall, "La création de l'Union européenne et sa relation avec les traités CEE," in *Perspectives européennes – L'Europe de demain* (European Commission, 1985), 173.

[35] Schilling, "The Autonomy of the Community Legal Order," Part II.A at 390–5.

[36] Literature on this subject is endless. For a recent contribution, see Roland Bieber and Pierre Widmer (eds.), *The European Constitutional Area* (1995) and the references therein.

[37] Case 26/62, *Van Gend and Loos* v. *Nederlandse Administratie der Belastingen* [1963] ECR 1.

[38] E.g., G. Federico Mancini, "The Making of a Constitution for Europe," *Common Market Law Review* 26 (1989), 595; and Eric Stein, "Lawyers, Judges, and the Making of a Transnational Constitution," *American Journal of International Law* 75 (1981), 1.

Whether or not, from the perspective of legal theory, these specific legal doctrines constitute real hallmarks of a constitutional order, as distinct from a classical international law order, can be – and has been – open to debate.[39] Assuming the distinction between an international and a constitutional order makes any sense at all – and this too can be doubted! – we would prefer to focus on the following features which distinguish the European legal order from public international law: the different hermeneutics of the European order, its system of compliance which renders European law in effect a transnational form of "higher law"[40] supported by enforceable judicial review, as well as the removal of traditional forms of state responsibility from the system.[41] We shall deal with these issues extensively in a separate article.[42]

However flawed the "constitutionalization" thesis may be from the perspective of legal theory, it has enjoyed huge success in the discourse of European law, and this from all actors concerned. The evidence is everywhere, both sublime and ridiculous – let the reader be the judge of which is which.

For its part, the ECJ did not hesitate to abandon the New Legal Order vocabulary in favor of an explicit constitutional rhetoric.[43] And whatever European law is called elsewhere, it has been treated frequently and consistently by national courts differently from most other treaty law and from the decisions of most other international organizations.[44] Not surprisingly,

---

[39] See Derrick Wyatt, "New Legal Order, or Old?," *European Law Review* 7 (1982), 147; Bruno de Witte, "Retour à 'Costa': La primauté du droit communautaire à la lumière du droit international," *Revue trimestrielle de droit européen* 20 (1984), 425.

[40] Mauro Cappelletti and David Golay, "The Judicial Branch in the Federal and Transnational Union: Its Impact on Integration," in M. Cappelletti, M. Seccombe, and J. H. H. Weiler (eds.), *Integration through Law* (Walter de Gruyter: Berlin, New York, 1985), vol. I, book 2, 261.

[41] See chapter 2, p. 29 above.

[42] We are aware that this issue is disputed. See, e.g., Christian Tomuschat, "Völkerrechtliche Schadensersatzansprüche vor dem EuGH," in Jürgen F. Baur et al. (eds.), *Europarecht – Energierecht – Wirtschaftsrecht, Festschrift für Bodo Börner* (1992), 441; and Bruno Simma, "Self-Contained Regimes," *Netherlands Yearbook of International Law* 16 (1985), 111 at 123–9.

[43] *Parti Ecologiste "Les Verts" v. European Parliament* [1986] ECR 1,339.

[44] This situation becomes most obvious in Member States with a (mitigated) dualist system, above all Germany and Italy. In Germany, the Bundesverfassungsgericht in the German *Handelsgesellschaft Case* held that "[t]his Court – in this respect in agreement with the law developed by the European Court of Justice – adheres to its settled view that Community law is neither a component part of the national legal system *nor international law*, but forms an independent system of law flowing from an autonomous legal source": German Constitutional Court, judgment of May 29, 1974, BVerfGE 37, 271, translated in English in *Decisions of the Bundesverfassungsgericht – Federal Constitutional Court – Federal Republic of Germany: International Law and the Law of the European Communities 1952–1989 (Part I)* (1992), vol. 1, 270 at 274 (emphasis added). The Italian Corte Costituzionale in the Italian *Frontini Case* held: "Fundamental requirements of equality and legal certainty demand that the Community norms, which *cannot be characterised as a source of international law*, nor of foreign law, nor of internal law of the

Community law is often practiced, taught, and studied by different sets of professionals. In what many consider the preeminent English-language international legal journal, the *American Journal of International Law*, you will hardly find articles dealing with European law, ever since Eric Stein published his celebrated article consecrating the European legal order in federal constitutional terms,[45] for the simple reason that the journal does not consider it international law! Even that cheeky upstart rival, the *European Journal of International Law*, treats the European Union as a polity in whose internal law it has little interest, for, again, it is not considered international law. By contrast, this latter journal takes trouble to publish the European Union's "state practice" in international fora for the benefit of its readers, in the way international law journals occasionally publish surveys of the state practice of the nation from which they publish. Furthermore, at most institutions of higher learning, knowledge of international law is not a requisite for the study of European law. It has, in our view, become increasingly artificial to describe the legal structures and processes of the Community with the vocabulary of international law.

Schilling himself is not impressed by the "constitutionalization" thesis. Even if the Community, like a precious metal, has some of the characteristics of a constitutional legal order, it lacks the most fundamental property: legitimation through a popular constituent power which in this case can only be the European people(s). From a purist, Kelsenian perspective, Schilling argues, European constitutionalism is *ersatz* gold. Schilling thus reverts back to the origins of the Community and places his bet on international law.[46]

---

individual States, ought to have full compulsory efficacy and direct application in all the Member States": judgment of December 27, 1973 (No. 183) Corte Cost., translated in [1974] CMLR II-386 at 387 (emphasis added). The different treatment of Community law and other international treaty law is confirmed in the *Granital* v. *Amministrazione delle Finanze dello Stato* decision: judgment of June 8, 1984 (No. 170), Corte Cost., translated in *Common Market Law Review* 21 (1984), 756. See Francesco P. R. Laderchi, "The European Court and National Courts, Doctrine and Jurisprudence: Legal Change in Its Social Context, Report on Italy" (European University Institute Working Paper RSC No. 95/30, 1995). See also Henry G. Schermers and Denis Waelbroeck, *Judicial Protection in the European Communities* (5th edn., 1992), 127–38. However, the issue of *Kompetenz-Kompetenz* has led the German Constitutional Court to seek distance from the rhetoric of an "autonomous legal order" and to retreat to "international law" rhetoric, as in the German Maastricht decision. See, on this development, Juliane Kokott, "The European Court and National Courts, Doctrine and Jurisprudence: Legal Change in Its Social Context, Report on Germany" (European University Institute Working Paper RSC No. 95/25, 1995), 9–13 and 23–5.

45 Stein, "Lawyers, Judges, and the Making of a Transnational Constitution."

46 Schilling, "The Autonomy of the Community Legal Order," 397–8 ("There are, in fact, some indicators that point in the opposite direction, away from constitutionalization. Importantly, the European Treaties continue to be amended by treaties and provide for future amendments. The minor role that Maastricht Treaty Art. N(1)(2) gives the European Parliament in preparing the

But what of the realist perspective? In light of the overwhelming practice of the last three or four decades, if the Community order is treated as constitutional who cares what it "really" is? Schilling does not shy away from the realist perspective, which he calls the Hartian perspective.[47] His critique is more refined. He claims that if one takes the realist approach one buys a European constitutional construct by compromising the legitimacy of the European public sphere.[48]

We cannot accept the purist approach. We do not think that a reversion to public international law is any less artificial than the constitutional characterization. The Community lacks, in our view, some of the fundamental properties of internationalism. We are, however, very sympathetic to Schilling's assessment of the realist perspective. We too have characterized this system as a constitutional order without constitutionalism.[49] We think that the legitimacy gap is for real. The Community has adopted constitutional practices without any underlying legitimizing constitutionalism. Yet, attempts such as those by the German Constitutional Court[50] and by Schilling to try to push the toothpaste back in the tube by asserting that the Community is nothing more than an international organization are self-serving (to that Court) and unhelpful in addressing the real problem of legitimacy. The legitimacy problem that Schilling points out will not go away if we change the theoretical foundation of the legal order from a constitutional one to an international one. Be this as it may, the implication of the internationalist premise on the "Decisive Question" is of greater interest.

JUDICIAL *KOMPETENZ-KOMPETENZ*

How then does Schilling deal with the "Decisive Question" of the ultimate power to invalidate *ultra vires* Community law? And how does he reach the conclusion that an "international law interpretation of the European Treaties thus leads to the conclusion that the ECJ is not the ultimate umpire of the system" from which he believes that it follows that "the

---

craft of amending treaties cannot be an indication that the European people has adopted the treaties as a constitution. In addition, it cannot be claimed that there is, with the European people, a custom supported by a common *opinio juris* that regards the European Treaties as the constitution of an autonomous Europe. While some Europeans take this view, there are as many who do not share it. This is not enough to create a custom.")

[47] E.g., Schilling, "The Autonomy of the Community Legal Order," 398–400.
[48] Ibid., 399–401.
[49] J. H. H. Weiler, "... We Will Do, And Hearken" (Ex. XXIV:7): Reflections on a Common Constitutional Law for the European Union," in Bieber and Widmer, *The European Constitutional Area* at 413.
[50] See Weiler, "The State 'Uber Alles'" at 1,669–70.

Member States, *individually*, must have the final word on questions concerning the scope of the competences they have delegated to the Community"?[51] It is worth following his reasoning with some care.

His first argument, referring to Kelsen's 1952 treatise,[52] is to claim, somewhat surprisingly, that "[g]eneral international law does not provide any guidance on this question because it does not know of international institutions."[53] He then relies on a 1953 essay by Leo Gross[54] to support his thesis that "[t]he accepted method for the interpretation of international treaties, in the absence of treaty institutions, is autointerpretation."[55] We doubt whether either of these statements is an accurate reflection of their authors' intentions[56] or, in any event, of international law in the 1990s. When we offer our alternative construct, we shall return to these points.

First, we think that Schilling mischaracterizes the issue of autointerpretation. Even in treaties without centralized institutions, which is not the case of the European Treaties, autointerpretation, *by each state individually*, is mostly accepted as a practical inevitability with little, if any, normative value. The very article by Leo Gross on which Schilling seems to rely[57] is most eloquent on this issue. Gross explicitly avoids giving any normative

---

[51] Schilling, "The Autonomy of the Community Legal Order," 407 (emphasis added).

[52] Hans Kelsen, *Principles of International Law* (1952).

[53] Schilling, "The Autonomy of the Community Legal Order," 404.

[54] Leo Gross, "States as Organs of International Law and the Problem of Autointerpretation," in *Essays on International Law and Organization* (1993), vol. I, 367 at 382–96.

[55] Schilling, "The Autonomy of the Community Legal Order," 404.

[56] While Schilling's text conveys the impression that "general international law" is to be understood in contrast to "Community law," this is not what Kelsen had in mind. Kelsen was describing the difference between international and national law, characterizing the former as "a relatively decentralized" and the latter as a "relatively centralized" coercive order: Kelsen, *Principles of International Law* at 402–3. For example, Kelsen talks about custom and treaties as "decentralized methods," and mentions that "there are under general international law no special organs for the application of the law and especially no central agencies for the execution of the sanctions," the implication being that national legal orders typically have a special organ to enforce the law. Even more revealing, however, is the fact that Kelsen, writing in 1952, observes that international law is moving towards international institutions. He calls the law of international organizations, which in 1952 was far from being fully developed, "particular international law," as opposed to general international law: "But under particular international law, the creation as well as the application of the law may be – and actually is – centralized; and this process of centralization is steadily increasing by the establishment of international organizations instituting international tribunals and international executive agencies": Kelsen, *Principles of International Law* at 403.

[57] It seems that Schilling draws on the following quote from Gross: "It is generally recognized that the root of the unsatisfactory situation in international law and relations is the absence of an authority generally competent to declare what the law is at any given time, how it applies to a given situation or dispute, and what the appropriate sanction may be. In the absence of such an authority, and failing agreement between the states at variance on these points, each state has a right to interpret the law, the right of autointerpretation, as it might be called." Gross, "States as Organs of International Law" at 386.

spin to autointerpretation and clearly labels it as a *de facto* stand-off when he denies it any binding force. It is useful to quote Gross more extensively.

> This interpretation [of the individual states], however, is not a "decision" and is neither final nor binding upon the other parties ... [We] may never know ... which autointerpretation was correct. A controversy, in other words, may remain unsettled forever or for a long time.[58]

> It can be shown, I believe, that states have the right of autointerpretation but not the right to decide questions of international law, that is, to make binding decisions for others.[59]

> In a dispute regarding the interpretation of a bilateral treaty, the competent authority is the composite organ formed by the two contracting parties, or a tribunal instituted by the parties with the power to settle the dispute. To attribute to one party alone the capacity of an organ, that is, the right to decide the meaning of a treaty, would amount to conferring on it the right to create a norm binding on the other state, that is, juridically speaking, subordinate the other state to the jurisdiction of the former. If no other principle of international law then certainly the principle of equality militates against such an attribution. Obviously, autointerpretation has no binding character. In autodecision, such a character is implied, but without any justification in general international law.[60]

> The same consideration applies in multilateral treaties. Each contracting party has a right of autointerpretation, but not of autodecision. The right of authentic interpretation is vested in the composite organ formed by all the contracting parties. Unless the treaty provides for an alternative procedure, an authoritative interpretation can result from negotiations leading to an agreement, or from arbitration or adjudication.[61]

> It is part of the principle of *pacta sunt servanda* that the right of authentic interpretation belongs to the composite organ which created the treaty and not to any of the states members of that organ.[62]

> Arbitration and adjudication appear to be among the classic methods for seeking and obtaining an authoritative interpretation on questions arising from the autonomous application and interpretation of international law.[63]

Gross warns explicitly against Schilling's mistake:

> Autointerpretation is easily presented, or rather misrepresented, as autodecision for want of a compulsory procedure leading to a heteronomous and binding decision. But appearances are misleading ...'[64]

Presupposing the absence of any mechanism of dispute resolution, we consider autointerpretation as a factual inevitability in a realm of little legal sophistication, and equally little shared goals and co-ordination.[65] It is not

---

[58] *Ibid.*   [59] *Ibid.*   [60] *Ibid.*, 390–1.   [61] *Ibid.*, 391.   [62] *Ibid.*, 392.
[63] *Ibid.*, 393.   [64] *Ibid.*, 394.
[65] Schilling himself acknowledges this: "The accepted method for the interpretation of interna-

by accident that Gross discusses the issue of autointerpretation in reference to Kelsen's theory that states act as organs of the international community,[66] which is closely related to the problem of *bellum justum*.[67] Neither is it by accident that the most notable and recent case on the subject touched upon the unilateral reinterpretation of a Cold War arms-control treaty between the USA and the Soviet Union.[68] Yet even to say that autointerpretation under these conditions would be an "accepted method" proves too much.[69] Both jurisprudential[70] and functional[71] arguments are powerful enough to cast more than a shadow of doubt on a normative claim to autointerpretation.

These difficulties with autointerpretation, both jurisprudential and prag-matic, have increasingly induced states to create a variety of mechanisms to

tional treaties, in the absence of treaty institutions, is autointerpretation by the contracting states": Schilling, "The Autonomy of the Community Legal Order," 404.

[66] Gross' article originally appeared in a volume devoted to Kelsen's theory of international law, *Law and Politics in the World Community: Essays on Hans Kelsen's Pure Theory and Related Problems in International Law* (edited by George A. Lipsky, 1953).

[67] It would be interesting to analyze the theory of autointerpretation as conceived of by Leo Gross and also Hans Kelsen in relation to the claim that the right of self-defense is self-judging. Such an undertaking, however, goes beyond the limits of this article. Cf. Paul W. Kahn, "From Nuremberg to The Hague: The United States' Position in Nicaragua v. United States and the Development of International Law," *Yale Journal of International Law* 12 (1987), 1 (concluding that the claim that, under international law, self-defense is a self-judging function that resists third-party review is incompatible with modern developments in international law).

[68] In 1985, the Reagan administration attempted to reinterpret the Anti-Ballistic Missile Treaty of 1972. See Robert Johnson, "Recent Development, Arms Control: Reinterpretation of the Anti-Ballistic Missile Treaty of 1972," *Harvard International Law Journal* 27 (1986), 659.

[69] Cf. Ebere Osieke, "The Legal Validity of Ultra Vires Decisions of International Organizations," *American Journal of International Law* 77 (1983), 239 at 254 (noting that "[t]he right of member states to reject decisions they consider unconstitutional in the absence of a legal determination by a review body to that effect has not been generally accepted by international lawyers").

[70] A jurisprudential argument would rely on the principle of *pacta sunt servanda*. See, e.g., Abram Chayes and Antonia Handler Chayes, "Testing and Development of 'Exotic' Systems under the ABM Treaty: The Great Reinterpretation Caper," *Harvard Law Review* 99 (1986), 1,956 at 1,970 (stating that treaty provisions cannot be altered unilaterally since they "represent a solemn engagement between nations, binding at international law").

[71] A functional argument would stress the fact that self-interpretation places the very objectives of a treaty in danger. See, e.g., Donald G. Gross, "Negotiated Treaty Amendment: The Solution to the SDI–ABM Treaty Conflict," *Harvard International Law Journal* 28 (1987), 31 at 51–2 ("In an atmosphere where each side felt free to reinterpret treaties to its own advantage, agreement on strategic matters would be exceedingly difficult to attain. Engaging in strained legal interpretation makes a mockery of the negotiating process ... A strained unilateral interpretation dilutes the legal validity of the Treaty and undermines the mutual intention of controlling arms proliferation which lies at the base of the document ... [T]he cost of unilateral reinterpretation would be high. If observed in practice, without the prior acquiescence of the Soviets, reinterpretation could trigger a complete breakdown of arms control. Both parties would be forced to reassess the value of treaties – fragile legal instruments – for controlling nuclear arms in a world where deft manipulations of language can alter previously understood meanings.").

settle disputes – ranging from voluntary arbitration to the creation of international tribunals and a binding commitment to judicial dispute resolution. The extensive experience with international institutions in the last four decades, while it has become part of general international law, has also revealed the intricate problem of *quis judicabit* – who is competent to decide upon measures adopted by international organizations?[72] While we

---

[72] This problem should not be confused with the undisputed proposition that member states of an international organization have the right to challenge the acts and decisions of the organization. Only the competence to decide on these challenges is in question: Osieke, "The Legal Validity of Ultra Vires Decisions" at 240–1. This competence could lie either with the organization that has already acted, or with the challenging member state, or with a different organ, most likely judicial, either part of the organization or independent of it. We must first distinguish between two scenarios, one in which the parties to the treaty or the member states of the organization have not provided for a mechanism to settle disputes arising out of the treaty (scenario 1), and one in which they have (scenario 2). If no dispute-settlement mechanism was created, the problem of *nemo debet esse judex in propria causa* (no person should judge his or her own case) arises. Since there is no (judicial) institution to rule on challenges to the actions of the international organization, the competence to judge those actions must lie either with the organ itself or with the challenging member state. Both would be judging their own case. In addition, surveys of state practice have led to the result that it was always the organ whose act had been challenged that decided the claims of unconstitutionality. For example, in relation to the International Labor Organization, Ebere Osieke concludes: "Some very interesting principles seem to emerge from the foregoing examination of the practice of the International Labor Organization in the determination of claims of illegality or unconstitutionality concerning the acts of its organs ... The fact which emerges from the study is that all the claims of unconstitutionality were decided by the organs whose acts were challenged": Ebere Osieke, "Ultra Vires Acts in International Organizations: The Experience of the International Labor Organization," *British Yearbook of International Law* 48 (1977), 259 at 273–4. The organs whose acts were challenged decided their claims not only when those claims arose in the Governing Body of the International Labor Office but also when they arose at the International Labor Conference: *ibid.*, 262–73. In a different study on the ICAO, Osieke finds that even organizations that have established a review mechanism tend to decide their own case, at least in the first instance. Under Art. 84 of the Chicago Convention, contracting states may appeal to an arbitral tribunal or to the ICJ against a decision of the Council on any disagreement between two or more contracting states relating to the interpretation or application of the Convention. Osieke finds that: "In all the cases examined in the present study, the objects were decided, in the first instance, by the organ whose competence or jurisdiction was challenged": Ebere Osieke, "Unconstitutional Acts in International Organizations": The Law and Practice of the ICAO," *International and Comparative Law Quarterly* 28 (1979), 1 at 23–4. Again, this is true both for objections raised in the Council of the ICAO and for those raised in the Assembly of the ICAO. "This [the result that all claims of unconstitutionality were decided by the organs whose acts were challenged] appears to be the position in international organizations generally": Osieke, "Ultra Vires Acts in International Organizations" at 274. Furthermore: "This principle appears to have been generally accepted in the law of international organizations": Osieke, 'Unconstitutional Acts in International Organizations" at 24. This view is supported by the *Certain Expenses of the United Nations Case* [1962] ICJ 151 at 168: "In the legal systems of States, there is often some procedure for determining the validity of even a legislative of governmental act, but no analogous procedure is to be found in the structure of the United Nations. Proposals made during the drafting of the Charter to place the ultimate authority to interpret the Charter in the International Court of Justice were not accepted; the opinion which the Court is in

expect that the Messiah will have to arrive before total consensus among international lawyers can be reached on any issue, state practice confirms the overwhelming view that when a treaty sets up a procedure for binding dispute resolution, particularly judicial organs, autointerpretation is legally squelched.[73] Tribunals do have jurisdiction to determine their own competence by interpreting their constitutive instruments.[74] Likewise, under

course of rendering is an advisory opinion. As anticipated in 1945, therefore, each organ must, in the first place at least, determine its own jurisdiction." The state practice privileges the organization rather than the individual member states for practical reasons. Denying international organizations the competence to decide claims challenging its authority would "seriously impede the effective attainment of [the] objects and purposes [of those international organizations] because all that a member state would have to do to create an impasse or prevent the adoption of a decision is to challenge the competence of the organ or the organization, or indeed the legal validity of the decision": Osieke, "The Legal Validity of Ultra Vires Decisions" at 242. However, we do not wish to take final sides on this question. Indeed, there also seems to be some state practice to the contrary. See, e.g., Dan Ciobanu, *Preliminary Objections Related to the Jurisdiction of the United Nations Political Organs* (1975), 175–9 (stating that the member states of an international organization have a "right of last resort," because they may claim that their interpretation of the constituent documents is the correct one. He also states that they may refuse to comply with decisions if they think that those decisions are *ultra vires*.). While Ciobanu argues in favor of such a right of last resort for the member states, he also acknowledges that "what might be called the right of autointerpretation of what international law prescribes has not found unanimous, and perhaps [not] even general, support in the doctrine": *ibid.*, 173 note 58. From the realist point of view, this is not satisfactory. The solution, according to the overwhelming majority, is the establishment of legal organs competent to make such decisions. See, e.g., *Legal Consequences for States of the Continued Presence of South Africa in Namibia (South West Africa) Notwithstanding Security Council Resolution 276 (1970)* [1971] ICJ 16 at 2,998 (dissenting opinion of Judge Sir Gerald Fitzmaurice). This is scenario 2. Of course, once such an organ is established, it holds, under general public international law, the competence to decide upon the legality of the acts of the international organization. Even if we acknowledged, arguendo, the right of an alleged member state to determine the validity of the act of the international organization, this right would have been transferred to the judicial organ through the act of establishing it. See Schermers and Blokker, *International Institutional Law* § 600 at 408, who, in this context, assert that this transfer to a judicial organ would bring about "an important restriction on the states' right of autointerpretation which many states do not wish to accept."

[73] See the discussion at note 72 above. It should also be mentioned that, in the rare cases where this right is claimed, a central judicial organ had *not* been established. *Cf. Certain Expenses of the United Nations* [1962] ICJ 151 at 232 (Winiarski, B., dissenting); *Interpretation of the Agreement of 25 March 1951 between the WHO and Egypt* [1980] ICJ 73 at 104 (Gros, A., separate opinion); and Ciobanu, *Preliminary Objections* at 162–79 (distinguishing between "judicial determination" and "political determination," with his examples of autointerpretation illustrating the latter category). Even where non-judicial organs of the international organization have interpreted the constituent document of that organization, their interpretations have been recognized as binding upon the state concerned. See, e.g., Ervin P. Hexner, "Interpretation by Public International Organizations of Their Basic Instruments," *American Journal of International Law* 53 (1959), 341 at 352–6 (providing as early as 1959 telling examples relating to the IMF and the World Bank on the one hand and the Federal Communications Commission on the other). For examples referring to the UN, see note 25 above.

[74] This principle has been long established in international arbitration. See, e.g., *Nottebohm Case (Liechtenstein v. Guatemala)* [1953] ICJ 111 at 119–20 (preliminary objection) ("Since the

general international law, the competence of a tribunal to determine the illegality of the actions of an international organization presumptively includes all grounds of illegality, including, we would submit, this international organization's lack of competence to act.

When the stakes are sufficiently high and states do not want to risk the outcome of a binding resolution, these states can use well-established and widely practiced techniques to preserve their position. Instead of binding judicial resolution, states can, for instance, empower panels or committees to issue recommendations and help in conciliation.[75] But as a general proposition, practically self-evident, it would empty binding judicial dispute resolution of its meaning if states subject to such procedures were then, in law, free to resort to "autointerpretation" and disregard the decision of the international tribunal.

We do not wish to minimize the "hard case" scenario. Arguably, a state is not obligated by an otherwise binding resolution if this resolution was adopted *ultra vires*. But why limit this result to resolutions adopted *ultra vires*? Arguably, a state is not obligated by an otherwise binding resolution if it was illegal for whatever reason, e.g., a procedural failure or a conflict with *jus cogens*. The nature of a mechanism providing for binding judicial resolution is that a state has to live with the risk of an adverse decision.

Under general international law, the state does have certain options. It

---

Alabama case, it has been generally recognized, following the earlier precedents, that, in the absence of any agreement to the contrary, an international tribunal has the right to decide as to its own jurisdiction and has the power to interpret for this purpose the instruments which govern that jurisdiction. This principle was expressly recognized in Articles 48 and 73 of the Hague Conventions of July 29th, 1899, and October 18th, 1907, for the Pacific Settlement of International Disputes ... The Rapporteur of the Convention of 1899 had emphasized the necessity of this principle, presented by him as being 'of the very essence of the arbitral function and one of the inherent requirements for the exercise of this function.' This principle has been frequently applied and at times expressly stated. This principle, which is accepted by general international law in the matter of arbitration, assumes particular force when the international tribunal is no longer an arbitral tribunal constituted by virtue of a special agreement between the parties for the purpose of adjudicating on a particular dispute, but is an institution which has been pre-established by an international instrument defining its jurisdiction and regulating its operation"). See also Ibrahim F. I. Shihata, *The Power of the International Court to Determine Its Own Jurisdiction – Compétence de la Compétence* (1965).

75 Consider, for instance, the dispute settlement mechanism established by the United States–Israel Free Trade Area Agreement, April 22, 1985, ILM 24 (1985), 653 (entered into force August 19, 1985) (the FTAA). Article 19 establishes a hierarchy of intra-FTAA fora: informal consultations, referral to the Joint Committee, and referral by the Joint Committee to a conciliation panel. This panel will then try to get the parties to sign an agreement to resolve the dispute. A report containing the finding of facts will be drawn up and a resolution will be proposed. The report is non-binding: FTAA, Art. 19: *ibid.*, 664–5. It has been uniformly concluded that this dispute settlement mechanism "has the advantages of informality and administrative ease": Nicholas A. Aminoff, "The United States–Israel Free Trade Area Agreement of 1985: In Theory and Practice," *Journal of World Trade* 25 (1991), 5 at 23–4.

can, for example, seek to convince all parties to the treaty to adopt its position. If successful, as masters of the treaty, the member states can jointly modify the treaty provision or the measure in question to remove the alleged illegality. A state can, if allowed, withdraw from the organization.

Of course, it can also decide to follow its own understanding of the law and disregard the tribunal, as states have sometimes done, but by doing so it would be violating international law and incurring state responsibility. While such a violation is a pragmatic option, in that states can, in fact, take this course of action, this option should not be cloaked with the mantle of legality.

Therefore, general international law does give us some guidance, and the guidance it gives us runs counter to Schilling's argument. Be that as it may, Schilling does not stake his claim on general international law, but on an international law interpretation of the Community Treaties. We must therefore turn to these. Do the Community Treaties create some exception to the thrust of general international law?

Faithful to his internationalist approach, Schilling brushes aside the rather particularized hermeneutics, developed and applied for years within the European legal order,[76] and exhorts us to return to Article 31(1) of the Vienna Convention on the Law of Treaties. Interpretation is to follow "the ordinary meaning to be given to the terms of the treaty in their context and in the light of its object and purpose."[77]

The relevant provisions, according to Schilling, are Articles 164 and 169–183 of the EC Treaty. In particular, he focuses on Article 171, which states that: "If the Court of Justice finds that a Member State has failed to fulfill an obligation under this Treaty, [it] . . . shall be required to take the necessary measures to comply with the judgment of the Court of Justice." Schilling finds the ordinary meaning of this provision to indicate that the Court "is the ultimate umpire of the European system."[78] We concur, reading the plain language of the article – which does not restrict the duty of obedience *ratione materiae*. If a Member State were to decide that it did not have to follow a measure it viewed as *ultra vires* but the ECJ thought otherwise, Article 171 would require that the Member State obey the ECJ. But Schilling tries to overturn his own understanding of the ordinary meaning of the words by demonstrating that such a plain meaning would

---

[76] We do not wish to deal, *in extensu*, with the highly complex debate about the different hermeneutics in European law, as opposed to general public international law. When we talk, hereinafter, about "international law interpretation," we mean a hermeneutics that pays great deference to the text and to the presumed intentions of the High Contracting Parties, and that is not informed by the teleology of European integration.

[77] Vienna Convention, Art. 32(b).

[78] Schilling, "The Autonomy of the Community Legal Order," 405.

be inconsistent with the context of the provision and the object and purpose of the European Treaties.

Before we turn to his analysis of context, object and purpose, we must raise a more fundamental question: should Schilling have focused solely (or even principally) on Article 171 of the EC Treaty in his international law interpretation of the European Treaties on the issue of judicial *Kompetenz-Kompetenz*? We think that Articles 173 and 177 are also worthy of special mention.

Taking an internationalist, voluntarist, positivist approach, we recall that the High Contracting Parties to the European Treaties set up a court, the ECJ, to settle disputes arising under the Treaties. In their wisdom, they granted that court wide jurisdiction, including jurisdiction to review the legality and validity of Community measures.[79] They even set out the criteria which the ECJ was to employ when engaging in such review.[80] They could have restricted the competence of the ECJ to review, for example, infringements of procedural requirements. They also could have given wide grounds of review in some fields while excluding others entirely. Schilling claims that a correct internationalist interpretation of the Treaties gives the individual supreme courts of the Member States, acting separately, the final say on the competences of the EC. The Member States could have spelled that out, but they did not. In fact, they appear to have spelled out the opposite. In Article 173, the grounds for review are listed as "*lack of competence*, infringement of an essential procedural requirement, infringement of this Treaty or of any rule of law relating to its application, or misuse of powers."[81]

The first ground for declaring the illegality of an act of a Community institution is lack of competence. This lack of competence might be internal, i.e., if the competence belongs to another institution,[82] or external, i.e., the Community, as such, lacks competence.[83]

But why read Article 173 as making the ECJ the "ultimate" umpire? This is what Schilling would have us believe is a correct international law interpretation of this provision: the High Contracting Parties set up the ECJ and gave it explicit jurisdiction to adjudicate challenges to Community measures by, among others, Member States on the ground of lack of

---

[79] See EC Treaty, Arts. 173–177.   [80] See, e.g., EC Treaty, Art. 173(1).

[81] EC Treaty, Art. 173 (emphasis added).

[82] Of course, that situation would also be illegal because it would be an infringement of the rule of law relating to the application of the Treaty.

[83] See, e.g., Schermers and Waelbroeck, *Judicial Protection in the European Communities* at 194–5; Hans Krück, "Artikel 173," in Hans von der Groeben *et al.* (eds.), *Kommentar zum EWG – Vertrag* (4th edn., 1991), para. 73; and Hartley, *The Foundations of European Community Law* at 428.

competence. That is, a Member State in dispute with a Community institution or with other Member States regarding the observance of Community law, if it believes that it may disregard a Community measure because it was taken *ultra vires*, is given a specific judicial remedy before the ECJ. But according to Schilling, the High Contracting Parties intended with this provision that the state challenging the legality of a Community measure, if it lost in front of the ECJ, could nonetheless disregard the Community measure in question by using its right to "autointerpretation." "Heads I win, tails you lose," is what we used to call that form of adjudication in kindergarten. This, we think, flies against the ordinary meaning and the entire judicial review context of the provision.

It also flies against the purposes of the treaties which include, according to Article 2, harmonious and balanced development, social cohesion, and solidarity among Member States.[84] Consider, as just one example, the pragmatic nightmare that would ensue in a treaty as long, complex, and, by its own terms, open-textured as the EC Treaties if such an interpretation were adopted. State A, in the face of an unfavorable judicial decision, unilaterally abrogates Treaty provision x on the grounds that it is, in its eyes, *ultra vires*. The international law principle of reciprocity would mean that that particular obligation would cease to be operative between A and all the other parties B to Z. So now there would be two co-existing regimes in relation to provision x; x is applied as among parties B to Z, but inapplicable in the relationship of B to Z with A. Now imagine that State B abrogates, on the same grounds, Treaty provision y, and that State C does likewise with Treaty provision z. Some harmonious relations; Gary Kasparov would, we think, have difficulties in sorting out the permutations.

The Vienna Convention, in Article 32(b) suggests that when the ordinary meaning leads to a result manifestly absurd or unreasonable, we may resort to subsidiary means of interpretation, including the *travaux préparatoires*.[85] The *travaux préparatoires* of the EC Treaties have not been published and are not pleaded before the ECJ.[86] Fortunately, we do not need them. In our view, this absurdity does not result from the ordinary meaning of the treaty, but rather from the extraordinary meaning that Schilling's construct would put on this provision.

Is it not more reasonable to imagine that, given the wide economic and social catch of the European Treaties and their unprecedented institutional scope, the delicate compromises which the various substantive obligations must have entailed, and the temptation by states to find excuses to escape

---

[84] TEU Treaty, Art. 2.   [85] Vienna Convention.

[86] Which also throws doubt on the applicability of the Vienna Convention rules of interpretation to the European Treaties.

the results of hard bargains, the High Contracting Parties established such elaborate provisions for centralized judicial review in order to, among other reasons, escape the pragmatic nightmare just mentioned, and not in order to place their multilateral bargains hostage in the hands of oft-partisan national courts?

In addition, the European Treaties, as Schilling himself points out, have been amended frequently and "re-ratified" on each instance of enlargement. For Schilling, this practice is a reminder of the international law character of the Community. So be it. But if the High Contracting Parties disagreed with the ECJ's understanding of its role and powers, would they not have used these repeated occasions to "set the record straight" on what they had in mind?[87] After all, they used these occasions to set the record straight on other issues.[88] Instead, not only did the Member States fail to introduce any clarification in the sense argued by Schilling, they also amended the Treaty in the opposite way. Rather than mentioning the right to disobey the ECJ through autointerpretation of measures taken *ultra vires*, the Member States modified Article 171 to allow for imposing penalties against Member States who disobey the ECJ. And note that we are talking about the very practice which, to Schilling, confirms the international legal character of the Treaties.

Consider next the most celebrated legal provision in the EC Treaty, Article 177.[89] The High Contracting Parties envisaged a role for national courts in the interpretation and application of Community law and in determining questions of its validity — not excluding, one may assume, a challenge to a Community measure alleged to be *ultra vires*. But as hardly needs reminding, when it comes to the highest national courts, against whose decisions there is no judicial remedy (which on any reading of Article 177 would include the highest courts in the land, those courts to which Schilling would give the final say on the jurisdictional limits of the Community), Community law obligates them to make a preliminary

---

[87] J. W. R. Reed, "Political Review of the European Court of Justice and its Jurisprudence" (Harvard Jean Monnet Working Paper No. 13/95, 1995).

[88] As they did in the so-called Barber Protocol: see note 22 above.

[89] Art. 177 provides: "The Court of Justice shall have jurisdiction to give preliminary rulings concerning: (a) the interpretation of the Treaty; (b) the validity and interpretation of acts of the institutions of the Community and of the ECB; (c) the interpretation of the statutes of bodies established by an act of the Council, where those statutes so provide. Where such a question is raised before any court or tribunal of a Member State, that court or tribunal may, if it considers that a decision on the question is necessary to enable it to give judgment, request the Court of Justice to give a ruling thereon. Where any such question is raised in a case pending before a court or tribunal of a Member State against whose decisions there is no judicial remedy under national law, that court or tribunal shall bring the matter before the Court of Justice."

reference to the ECJ.[90] That is the text. Its ordinary meaning is quite clear. Moreover, the purpose of this provision is the same as the purpose of the comparable provisions in domestic constitutional systems such as Germany[91] and Italy,[92] namely to ensure uniform interpretation of treaty provisions throughout the jurisdiction.[93]

Schilling, who champions the rule of law, insists that Article 177 has to be "scrupulously respected."[94] He would, however, have us believe, in accordance with his understanding of the ordinary meaning of this provision and other international legal rules of construction, that Article 177 and the duty to refer are "scrupulously respected" when the highest national Court makes a reference to the ECJ but, once this was done, presumably after saying a polite thank you, "the Member States can use autointerpretation,"[95] meaning the national court can go on to do what it wished to do anyway. Again, "heads I win" (if the Preliminary Ruling finds in my favor), "tails you lose" (if it does not, but then I get to invoke autointerpretation). This, following Schilling, is to be considered a scrupulous observance of Article 177 according to international law? And this is also to be considered the basis from which the German Federal Constitutional Court is to give the ECJ lessons in observing the rule of law?

Schilling's interpretation hardly squares with the ordinary meaning of the words of Article 177. It contradicts the object and purpose of Article 177 without the need to invoke any of the rhetoric, presumptions, or hermeneutics of European constitutionalism. It is, perhaps, not surprising that Schilling decides to stake his claim on Article 171 and to somehow leave Articles 173 and 177 in the shadows.

We now come to one of the most puzzling passages in the entire Schilling argument, the one which uses the object and purpose of the

---

[90] Case 283/81, *CILFIT* v. *Italian Ministry of Health* [1982] ECR 3,415. Further important decisions on the obligation to ask for a preliminary ruling are Case 6/64, *Flaminio Costa* v. *ENEL* [1964] ECR 585; and Joined Cases 28/62 to 30/62, *Da Costa en Schaake et al.* v. *Nederlandse Belastingadministratie* [1963] ECR 31.

[91] *Cf.* Grundgesetz, Arts. 93–94 and 99–100.

[92] *Cf.* Costituzione, Art. 134–137. For an exposition of the different conceptions of centralized and decentralized judicial review, see Mauro Cappelletti, *The Judicial Process in Comparative Perspective* (1989), 117–49.

[93] See, e.g., Schermers and Waelbroeck, *Judicial Protection in the European Communities* at 393–4; and Hans Krück, "Artikel 173" at paras. 10–14. The ECJ, in the second *Rheinmühlen* case, held: "Article 177 is essential for the preservation of the Community character of the law established by the Treaty and has the object of ensuring that in all circumstances this law is the same in all States of the Community ... [I]t thus aims to avoid divergences in the interpretation of Community law which the national courts have to apply": Case 166/73, *Rheinmühlen-Düsseldorf* v. *Einfuhr- und Vorratsstelle für Getreide und Futtermittel* [1974] ECR 33 at 38.

[94] Schilling, "The Autonomy of the Community Legal Order," 408.   [95] *Ibid.*, 408.

European Treaties as a way to negate the ordinary meaning of Article 171. It is worth citing *in extensu*.

> The purposes of the EC Treaty, as stated in article 2, relate to the activities of an economic community and, therefore, are arguably restricted to these activities. It follows that the European Treaties should not be interpreted as granting the Community unrestricted powers, in particular *Kompetenz-Kompetenz*. But such a conclusion is at odds with a *Kompetenz-Kompetenz* of the ECJ over questions of the respective competences of the Community and the Member States.[96]

In part, we believe the problem comes from the language, in particular from a possible conflation of the term *Kompetenz-Kompetenz*, which means two different things when applied to the Community and the ECJ. In part, the statement is simply misconceived.

Let us take the argument step by step.

First, it should be noted that the object and purpose of the European Treaties, even of the rather narrow Treaty of Paris establishing the European Coal and Steel Community, are by no means economic only. While preambles do not create positive legal obligations, they can help in understanding the purpose of a treaty, as expressly provided for in Article 31 of the Vienna Convention on the Law of Treaties.[97] Entire chunks of the politically charged and visionary Schuman Declaration are written into the Preamble of the Treaty of Paris.[98] And the Treaty of Rome commences with that highly

---

[96] *Ibid.*, 406 (footnotes omitted).

[97] Vienna Convention, Art. 31 provides: "1. A treaty shall be interpreted in good faith in accordance with the ordinary meaning to be given to the terms of the treaty in their context and in the light of its object and purpose. 2. The context for the purpose of the interpretation of a treaty shall comprise, in addition to the text, *including its preamble* and annexes . . ." (emphasis added). See also *Case Concerning the Rights of Nationals of the United States of America in Morocco* [1952] ICJ 176 at 196, where the ICJ had regarded the preamble of certain treaties as showing their object and purpose. The principle that preambles can be used for the contextual and purposive interpretation of treaties is not only a principle of general international law but is also part of the hermeneutics of Community law. The ECJ has referred to the Preamble of the EC Treaty for the interpretation of that Treaty several times; e.g., Case 26/62, *Van Gend and Loos* v. *Nederlandse Administratie der Belastingen* [1963] ECR 1; *Italy* v. *Council and Commission* [1966] ECR 389 at 408. See also Stefan Schepers, "The Legal Force of the Preamble to the EEC Treaty," *European Law Review* 6 (1981), 356 (arguing that parts of the preamble to the EC Treaty enjoy the same legal force as specific articles of the Treaty); and Manfred Zuleeg, "Präambel," in Hans von der Groeben *et al.* (eds.), *Kommentar zum EWG – Vertrag* (4th edn., 1991), para. 3 (arguing that the commitment to democracy and the fundamental rights and freedoms laid down in the Preamble to the Single European Act form part of the Community law as unwritten principles).

[98] The Preamble to the ECSC Treaty provides: "The Heads of Government and State . . . Considering that world peace can be safeguarded only by creative efforts commensurate with the dangers that threaten it, Convinced that the contribution which an organized and vital Europe can make to civilization is indispensable to the maintenance of peaceful relations, Recognizing that Europe can be built only through practical achievements which will first of all

economic objective of laying the foundations "of an ever closer union among the peoples of Europe."[99] Do these texts have no hermeneutic significance in international law? We have always believed that the genius of the Treaties was to have political ends achieved by economic means.

Even in Article 2 of the EC Treaty, which Schilling privileges in his view as to where one should look to determine the object and purpose of the EC Treaties, he glosses over the explicit task of creating closer relations among the states of the Community which takes place alongside the more economic tasks.[100] Maastricht rejects any claim that the Treaties are aiming, "basically" or otherwise, purely at economic goals. As one example undermining the claim of a "basic" economic community, it is sufficient to note that the Maastricht Treaty introduces a European citizenship.[101] The alleged "basic" economic nature of the EC Treaties is a tired old horse that should be let out to graze.

None the less, let us assume, *quod non*, that the objects and purposes of the European Treaties were basically economic. Independently of that assumption, we can agree that the EC Treaty should not be interpreted in such a way as to give the Community organs unrestricted powers, in particular *Kompetenz-Kompetenz*. This would be true regardless of whether the purposes of the Treaties were broad or narrow. For let us be clear: in this context, *Kompetenz-Kompetenz* takes its meaning from its traditional usage in German constitutional law. This is the power of the Community to determine (or enlarge) its own competences.[102] We agree that the

---

create real solidarity, and through the establishment of common bases for economic development, Anxious to help, by expanding their basic production, to raise the standard of living and further the works of peace, Resolved to substitute for age-old rivalries the merging of their essential interests; to create, by establishing an economic community, the basis for a broader and deeper community among peoples long divided by bloody conflicts, and to lay the foundations for institutions which will give direction to a destiny henceforward shared, Have decided to create a European Coal and Steel Community ..."

[99] Preamble to the EC Treaty.

[100] Also, most people would consider the more explicit economic objectives part of a political-economic vocabulary. For example, Art. 2 of the EC Treaty reads as follows: "The Community shall have as its task, by establishing a common market and an economic and monetary union and by implementing the common policies or activities referred to in Articles 3 and 3A, to promote throughout the Community a harmonious and balanced development of economic activities, sustainable and non-inflationary growth respecting the environment, a high degree of convergence of economic performance, a high level of employment and of social protection, the raising of the standard of living and quality of life, and economic and social cohesion and solidarity among Member States."

[101] Art. 8 of the TEU provides: "1. Citizenship of the Union is hereby established. Every person holding the nationality of a Member State shall be a citizen of the Union. 2. Citizens of the Union shall enjoy the rights conferred by this Treaty and shall be subject to the duties imposed thereby."

[102] This is the meaning the German Constitutional Court gave to *Kompetenz-Kompetenz* in the

competences of the Community, however broadly or narrowly defined, should remain attributed – i.e., limited by the explicit or implicit grants in the Treaty, as interpreted by the rules of international law.[103]

The crunch comes at this point in the Schilling text. Even if all the above is true, why does this imply that the ECJ, charged with adjudicating disputes arising from the Treaties and seeing that in the interpretation and application of the Treaty "the law is observed,"[104] cannot also decide disputes over the jurisdictional reach of the Community between the various actors? And why can it not be the ultimate umpire of such disputes? Why does it follow that if one of the purposes of the Treaties was to create an international organization with limited powers, the Community, and with no *legislative Kompetenz-Kompetenz* (i.e., without the power to extend its own jurisdiction), the Treaties cannot establish a court, the ECJ, with *judicial Kompetenz-Kompetenz* (i.e., the power to be the ultimate arbiter of disputes concerning the extent of those limited competences), giving one decisive answer, valid for everyone, which would ensure that the same measure of Community law is not considered legal in one jurisdiction and illegal in another?

The assumption that a Community without legislative *Kompetenz-Kompetenz* cannot contain a court with judicial *Kompetenz-Kompetenz* is at the core of Schilling's argument. It is not self-evident. In fact, we think it is false. Because Schilling assumes it without proof, Schilling's reasoning is, in our view, a classical *non-sequitur*, presuming that which he needs to prove and resting on assertion rather than reason.

Imagine a far narrower treaty than the European Treaties, for instance, a treaty setting up among several states a transnational regime with law-making institutions empowered to regulate all matters affecting, say, migratory birds. Inevitably, by the very nature of language and law, there will be a "twilight zone" where the precise jurisdictional limit of which

---

Maastricht Decision in relation to Art. F(3) of the TEU: 89 BVerfGE 155 at 194–9; English translation in ILM 33 (1994), 395 at 428–32. (We believe that the English translation of this part of the decision is misleading because the Court's notion of *Kompetenz-Kompetenz* has been transformed into "exclusive competence for jurisdictional conflicts" and this is exactly what it does not mean, as used by the Bundesverfassungsgericht.) On the history of *Kompetenz-Kompetenz*, see Peter Lerche, "'Kompetenz-Kompetenz' und das Maastricht-Urteil des Bundesverfassungsgerichts," in Jörn Ipsen *et al.* (eds.), *Verfassungsrecht im Wandel* (1995), 409.

103 International law accepts that powers of an organization can be implied. In its Advisory Opinion of April 11, 1949, *Reparations for Injuries Suffered in the Service of the United Nations* [1949] ICJ 182, the ICJ held that: "Under international law, the Organization must be deemed to have those powers which, though not expressly provided in the Charter, are conferred upon it by necessary implication as being essential to the performance of its duties." For writings on the implied powers doctrine in relation to international organizations, see the references in Schermers and Blokker, *International Institutional Law* at §§ 232–6.

104 EC Treaty, Art. 164.

matters affect migratory birds will be disputed. Imagine further that the High Contracting Parties of this hypothetical organization set up a court with judicial review provisions identical to those of the ECJ. Schilling himself admits that the ordinary meaning of the EC Treaty provisions clearly points to that court being the ultimate umpire on the jurisdictional limit of the organization. Why does the fact that the purpose of this hypothetical organization is rather narrowly defined necessarily lead one to the conclusion that the ordinary meaning is to be overturned? Given that any jurisdictional limit is going to have a gray zone, why not, in the interest of avoiding otherwise insoluble disputes, empower a centralized court to be the ultimate umpire? This question is even more legitimate in the light of the fact that the law-making institutions envisioned by the Treaty legislate by majority voting, and that the Treaty has notoriously open-textured provisions such as Article 100 and its progeny, and Article 235.

Once again, the specter of Alice hovers. If at all, it is just the other way around: the narrower the purposes and jurisdiction, the more willing the parties will be to entrust adjudication to judicial organs because the stakes, even if the court were to err, would not be so high. By contrast, if the organization was given broader powers, states may hesitate to entrust to a transnational court such power. Proof of this may be found in the EC Treaties. The Maastricht Treaty expanded the reach of the Union in a few notable areas.[105] The Member States were quick to seek to disenfranchise the ECJ when engaging in foreign policy, security, and their immigration policies.[106] Likewise, in drafting the UN Charter with its extremely broad objectives and jurisdiction, the Member States were careful not to enfranchise the International Court of Justice.[107]

---

[105] See, e.g., TEU, Arts. J to J.11 (providing for a common foreign and security policy); and TEU, Arts. K to K.9 (providing for co-operation "in the fields of justice and home affairs").

[106] According to TEU, Art. L, the common policy in foreign affairs and security matters is not subject to the jurisdiction of the ECJ. Although Neuwahl argues that the ECJ's jurisdiction is not as restricted as it may seem at first sight, it is fair to say that judicial review of Community acts in the field of the CFSP is limited: Nanette Neuwahl, "Foreign and Security Policy and the Implementation of the Requirement of 'Consistency' under the Treaty on European Union," in David O'Keeffe and Patrick M. Twomey (eds.), *Legal Issues of the Maastricht Treaty* (1994), 227 (arguing that the ECJ's jurisdiction also covers, *inter alia*, questions as to the compatibility with Community law of the CFSP acts of the Council). Also, Article L of the TEU excludes the jurisdiction of the ECJ over justice and home affairs (with the exception of conventions concluded under Article K.3(2)(c) of the TEU), leaving the third-pillar structure essentially without judicial review. For reform proposals, see, e.g., David O'Keeffe, "Recasting the Third Pillar," *Common Market Law Review* 32 (1995), 893, 909–11. See also J. H. H. Weiler, "Neither Unity Nor Three Pillars – The Trinity Structure of the Treaty on European Union," in Jörg Monar *et al.* (eds.), *The Maastricht Treaty on European Union: Legal Complexity and Political Dynamic* (1993), 49.

[107] During the UN Conference on International Organization in 1945, Belgium repeatedly suggested that the World Court should play a significant role in the peaceful settlement of

Schilling raises one last argument to "buttress" the presumptive will of the Member States in entering into the European Treaties. He cites Advocate-General Warner in the *ICRA* case:

> No Member State can . . . be held to have included, in [the partial] transfer [of sovereignty to the Community] power for the Community to legislate in infringement of rights protected by its own constitution.[108]

Warner was writing in the context of European Community protection of fundamental human rights. He also makes clear the consequences of his statement:

> a fundamental right recognized and protected by the Constitution of any Member State must be recognized and protected also in Community law.[109]

disputes and proposed that the World Court be given the power of judicial review. The Conference rejected these proposals and, instead, adopted the report of the Legal Committee IV/2. With this report, it renounced the idea of setting up a specific mechanism for interpreting the Charter provisions, and recognized that each organ would inevitably interpret from day to day those provisions of the Charter which concerned its activities. It also invited the Organization and states to consider themselves legally bound by any "generally accepted" interpretation, pragmatically leaving the question of an authoritative interpretation of the Charter open for the time being. In addition, a "committee of experts" was entitled to make suggestions for the creation of a special organ for giving official interpretations of the Charter: Geoffrey R. Watson, "Constitutionalism, Judicial Review and the World Court," *Harvard International Law Journal* 34 (1993), 1, 1–14. The Lockerbie decision, the *Case Concerning Questions of Interpretation and Application of the 1971 Montreal Convention Arising From the Aerial Incident at Lockerbie* [1992] ICJ 114, has stirred up the debate over whether or not the ICJ has the power of judicial review within the UN legal system. See, e.g., Michael Reisman, "The Constitutional Crisis in the United Nations," *American Journal of International Law* 87 (1993), 83; Thomas Franck, "The 'Powers of Appreciation': Who is the Ultimate Guardian of UN Legality?," *American Journal of International Law* 86 (1992), 519; Christian Tomuschat, "The Lockerbie Case before the International Court of Justice," *International Commission of Jurists Review* 48 (1992), 38; José Alvarez, "Theoretical Perspectives on Judicial Review by the World Court," in *Proceedings of the 89th Annual Meeting* (American Society of International Law, 1995), 85; and Vera Gowlland-Debbas, "The Relationship Between the International Court of Justice and the Security Council in Light of the Lockerbie Case," *American Journal of International Law* 88 (1994), 643. Even though the focal point of the discussion was the relationship between the ICJ and the Council, no one suggested that the Member States had the power to make the final decision on the legality of a Council measure.

[108] Case 7/76, *Industria Romana Carni e Affini SpA* v. *Amministrazione delle Finanze dello Strato* [1976] ECR 1,213 at 1,230 (Opinion of Advocate-General Warner of June 22, 1976 on the preliminary ruling requested by the Ufficio di Conciliazione). Schilling refers to a critique of that statement in Michael Akehurst, "The Application of General Principles of Law by the Court of Justice of the European Communities," *British Yearbook of International Law* 52 (1981), 29 at 44. Schilling cites Advocate-General Warner: Schilling, "The Autonomy of the Community Legal Order," 407.

[109] Case 7/76, *Industria Romana Carni e Affini SpA* v. *Amministrazione delle Finanze dello Strato* [1976] ECR 1,213 at 1,237 (Opinion of Advocate-General Warner).

If not, it would indeed mean that a Member State would have transferred to the Community the power to violate its constitution.

A seductive proposition but, alas, not good law. With all respect to former Advocate-General Warner, his construct has been flatly rejected by the ECJ, and for good reasons. In *Hauer*, decided after *ICRA*, the ECJ forcefully states:

> [T]he question of a possible infringement of fundamental rights by a measure of the Community institutions can only be judged *in the light of Community law itself*. The introduction of special criteria for assessment stemming from the legislation *or constitutional law of a particular Member State* would, by damaging the substantive unity and efficacy of Community law, lead inevitably to the destruction of the unity of the Common Market and the jeopardizing of the cohesion of the Community.[110]

Schilling may argue that he finds the Advocate General more persuasive than the ECJ. Advocate-Generals often are! But not here. *Grogan*,[111] the celebrated abortion rights case, provides a classic illustration of why the approach of Warner was rejected and why it cannot, as a matter both of policy and logic, be accepted in most instances. What if the constitution in one Member State guaranteed the near absolute right of the fetus to life, yet in another Member State, the "opposing" right of a woman to autonomy over her body was constitutionally guaranteed, including the right to abort a fetus in certain circumstances? Which of the two rights would Warner have the ECJ choose to recognize as a Community right? In the case of abortion, how can the ECJ recognize the near absolute right of the unborn in the Irish constitution[112] and at the same time uphold a woman's right to self-determination?[113] Even for a court guilty of constitutionalism run amok, this would be one twist too far.[114]

---

[110] Case 44/79, *Hauer* v. *Land Rheinland-Pfalz* [1979] ECR 3,727 at 3,744 (emphasis added).

[111] Case C-159/90, *Society for the Protection of Unborn Children Ireland Ltd* v. *Stephen Grogan et al.* [1991] ECR I-4,685, reported in Dena T. Sacco and Alexia Brown, "Recent Developments, Regulation of Abortion in the European Community: Society for the Protection of Unborn Children Ireland Ltd v. Grogan, Judgment of the European Court of Justice of 4 October 1991 in Case C-159/90 (1991)," *Harvard International Law Journal* 33 (1992), 291.

[112] Irish Constitution, Art. 40, §3(3). See also Caroline Forder, "Abortion: A Constitutional Problem in European Perspective," *Maastricht Journal of European and Comparative Law* 1 (1994), 56 (discussing the restrictive interpretation of this Article by the Irish Supreme Court and the other constitutional problems of Ireland).

[113] J. H. H. Weiler and Nicolas J. S. Lockhart, "'Taking Rights Seriously' Seriously: The European Court and its Fundamental Rights Jurisprudence," *Common Market Law Review* 32 (1995), 51 at Part 2, 579 at 598.

[114] For a full discussion, see J. H. H. Weiler, "Fundamental Rights and Fundamental Boundaries: On Standards and Values in the Protection of Human Rights," in Nanette Neuwahl and Allan Rosas (eds.), *The European Union and Human Rights* (1995), 51; and Weiler and Lockhart, "'Taking Rights Seriously'."

Two further things ought to be mentioned in this context. First, it seems that Schilling is moving beyond the limited proposition that the final say on issues of competences and *ultra vires* rests with the highest jurisdictions of the Member States, and is expanding the proposition to any rule or principle of national constitutional law. That conclusion would logically follow from his reasoning. If the proposition is that the Member States could not delegate to the Community matters reserved to them by their respective constitutions, surely this could not be limited to issues of jurisdiction but would extend to all material conflicts with a national constitution. The practical nightmare would be considerable.

But most surprising, and most telling, is that Schilling endorses the view of Warner from an international law point of view. The general rule of international law does not allow, except in the narrowest of circumstances which do not prevail here,[115] for a state to use its own domestic law, including its own domestic constitutional law, as an excuse for non-performance of a treaty. That is part of the "abc" of international law and is reflected in the same Vienna Convention on which Schilling relies.[116] The authoritative treatise, *Oppenheim's International Law*, is clear:

> It is firmly established that a state when charged with a breach of its international obligations cannot in international law validly plead as a defense that it was unable to fulfill them because its internal law . . . contained rules in conflict with international law; this applies equally to a state's assertion of its inability to secure the necessary changes in its law by virtue of some legal or constitutional requirement.[117]

In the PCIJ decision on the treatment of Polish nationals in Danzig,[118] the World Court held explicitly that a state cannot adduce its own constitution in order to evade obligations incumbent upon it under international law.

---

[115] One cannot rely on Art. 46 of the Vienna Convention for this proposition. First, a minor violation of the constitutional law of each Member State concerning the jurisdictional reach of the Community could hardly be said to be manifest and objectively evident. The fracas following the Maastricht Decision of the German Constitutional Court within the public law community in Germany itself would testify to that. See also the analysis of Mendelson as to the non-applicability of the decision in the Community context: M. H. Mendelson, "The European Court of Justice and Human Rights," *Yearbook of European* Law 1 (1981), 125 at 155. But more importantly, Art. 46 can be invoked when a state claims that its very consent to be bound was given in violation of its constitution. Schilling is arguing for a far more comfortable position: he affirms the consent to be bound, but allows the state to pick and choose what it consented to in relation to specific EC provisions.

[116] Vienna Convention, Art. 27. See also, e.g., Louis Henkin *et al.*, *International Law: Cases and Materials* (3rd edn., 1993), 149–53.

[117] Jennings and Watts, *Oppenheim's International Law*, 84–5.

[118] *Treatment of Polish Nationals and Other Persons of Polish Origin or Speech in the Danzig Territories* [1932] PCIJ (Ser. A/B), No. 44 at 24 (advisory opinion).

International law, thus, turns out to be a broken reed for the propositions advanced by Schilling. Indeed, after all his advocacy of an international law approach, at the end of the day, it is national constitutional authority which seems to animate him.

REDEFINING THE DECISIVE QUESTION

This analysis is telling because, we think, it leads us to identify what we believe is the real concern of Schilling and the German Federal Constitutional Court to whose support he runs. The real concern is not with the integrity of the Treaty under international law, nor even with the rule of law. On the one hand, there seems to be an unhappiness with the erosion of state sovereignty in a classical sense in a materially and legally interdependent world.[119] It is really state rights which concern Schilling, albeit cloaked in a would-be mantle of international law.

But there probably is yet another concern for which we have greater sympathy. Imagine the unlikely scenario that Schilling were persuaded by our arguments. Would he really be happy to see the ECJ remain in its pivotal position as ultimate umpire on questions of competences? We doubt it. His other concern, we think, is not with the *idea* of a centralized court that states may create to police their transnational legal undertakings

---

[119] Schilling also asserted classical state sovereignty in his 1990 article in the German public law journal, *Der Staat*: Theodor Schilling, "Artikel 24 Absatz 1 des Grundgesetzes, Artikel 177 des EWG-Vertrags und die Einheit der Rechtsordnung," *Der Staat* 29 (1990), 161. In that article, he used, as he does here, an interpretation reconciling two allegedly incompatible legal provisions (German constitutional legal doctrine calls this concept "praktische Konkordanz") in relation to Art. of the 177 EC Treaty and the former Art. 24 of the German Basic Law. The outcome was exactly the same: the interpretation of Art. 177 of the EC Treaty along the lines of Art. 24(1) of the Grundgesetz demanded that ECJ decisions had only persuasive power, i.e., that of an advisory opinion, if (a) the legal question touched upon the issue of competences, and (b) the ECJ's interlocutor was the German Federal Constitutional Court. Schilling, in the article that we are responding to, "internationalizes" this conclusion by undertaking a similar interpretation of Art. 171 of the EC Treaty in relation to Art. 2 of the EC Treaty. Even more revealing is Schilling's recent article on the "Sovereignty of the Members of the United Nations": Theodor Schilling, "Die 'neue Weltordnung' und die Souveränität der Mitglieder der Vereinten Nationen," *Archiv des Völkerrechts* 33 (1995), 67. There, Schilling turns against another international institution that, in the name of international integration, fetters national sovereignty, namely the Security Council, using its right to make decisions that are legally binding upon the member states of the UN: *ibid.*, 92–103. He argues that the member states are bound only by *legal* decisions of the Security Council: *ibid.* Since the ICJ can only review Council acts *incidenter*, he asserts that the state in question has the power to judge for itself whether or not a measure of the Council is legal. Yet that state is, according to Schilling, not necessarily the judge of its own cause because its decision can be reviewed by a "decentral decision of the state community" ("dezentrale Entscheidung der Staatengemeinschaft"): *ibid.*, 101–3. Schilling dismantles the UN mechanism of dealing with breaches of peace and brushes away "certain doubts" in the name of state sovereignty: *ibid.*, 101.

(which from an international law perspective is legitimate and unexceptional), but with the *performance of this particular Court*, especially on the issue of competences.

The decisive question that truly underlies Schilling's engagement with international law is quite different from the one he poses. The question is not, do the European Treaties make the ECJ the final umpire over Community competences?; but rather, can we trust and have confidence in the ECJ to perform the task of ultimate umpire of the jurisdictional limits? The issue, then, is not one of formal definition of task, but of trust in the performance.

The history of the Community jurisdictional powers explains Schilling's concerns. He is not alone in developing that sensitivity. During the debate accompanying the Maastricht Treaty, there erupted the dormant question of Community "competences and powers."[120] This question and the accompanying debate found their code in, for example, the deliciously vague concept of "subsidiarity." This question has been inevitably connected to the continued preoccupation with governance structures and processes, with the balance between Community and Member States, and with the questions of democracy and legitimacy of the Community to which the Maastricht debate gave a new and welcome charge.

What accounts for this eruption?[121]

First, a bit of history. The student of comparative federalism discovers a constant feature in practically all federal experiences: a tendency towards concentrations of legislative and executive powers in the center or general power at the expense of constituent units.[122] This concentration apparently occurs independently of the mechanism allocating jurisdiction/competences/powers between the center and the "periphery." Differences, where they occur, depend more on the ethos and political culture of polities than on legal and constitutional devices.[123] The Community has both shared and differed from this general experience.[124]

It has *shared* it in that the Community, especially in the 1970s, had seen a weakening of any workable and enforceable mechanism for the allocation of jurisdiction/competences/powers between the Community and its Member States.

---

[120] See generally chapter 2, pp. 83–6 above.
[121] In this part of the article, we are relying on Weiler, Haltern, and Mayer, "European Democracy and Its Critique."
[122] See generally Renaud Dehousse (ed.), *Europe After Maastricht: An Even Closer Union?* (1994).
[123] See J. H. H. Weiler, "Limits To Growth? On the Law and Politics of the European Union's Jurisdictional Limits, in State and Nation – Current Legal and Political Problems Before the 1996 Intergovernmental Conference," (IUSEF No. 15, 1995), 1–32.
[124] We are relying here on Jacqué and Weiler, "On the Road to European Union."

How has this occurred? It has occurred by a combination of two factors:

1. profligate legislative practices especially in, for example, the usage of Article 235; and
2. a bifurcated jurisprudence of the Court which on the one hand extensively interpreted the reach of the jurisdiction/competences/powers granted the Community and on the other hand had taken a self-limiting approach towards the expansion of Community jurisdiction/competence/powers when exercised by the political organs.[125]

To make the above statement is not tantamount to criticizing the Community, its political organs and the ECJ. The question is one of values. It is possible to argue that this process was beneficial overall to the evolution and well-being of the Community as well as beneficial to the Member States, its citizens and residents. But this process was also a ticking constitutional time bomb which one day could threaten the evolution and stability of the Community. Sooner or later, "supreme" courts in the Member States would realize that the "socio-legal contract" announced by the ECJ in its major constitutionalizing decisions – namely, that "the Community constitutes a new legal order ... for the benefit of which the states have limited their sovereign rights, *albeit within limited fields*"[126] – had been shattered. Although these "supreme" courts had accepted the principles of the new legal order, supremacy and direct effect, the fields seemed no longer limited. In the absence of Community legal checks, they would realize, it would fall upon them to draw the jurisdictional lines of the Community and its Member States.

Interestingly enough, the Community experience differs from the experience of other federal polities, in that, despite the massive legislative expansion of Community jurisdiction/competences/powers, there had not been any political challenge of this issue from the Member States.

How so? The answer is simple and obvious, and it resides in the decision-making process as it stood before the Single European Act (SEA). Unlike the state governments of most federal states, the governments of the Member States, jointly and severally, could control the legislative expansion of Community jurisdiction/competences/powers. Nothing that was done could be done without the assent of all states. This diffused any sense of threat and crisis on the part of governments. Indeed, if we want to seek "offenders" who have disrespected the principle of limited competence, the governments of the Member States, in the form of the Council of Ministers, conniving with the Commission and the Parliament, would be

---

[125] See chapter 2, pp. 39–59 above.
[126] Case 26/62, *Van Gend and Loos* v. *Nederlandse Administratie der Belastingen* [1963] ECR 1 at 2 (emphasis added).

the main ones. How convenient to be able to do in Brussels what would often be politically more difficult back home, and then exquisitely blame the Community! The ECJ's role has been historically not one of activism, but one of, at most, active passivism. Nonetheless, it did not build up a repository of credibility as a body which effectively patrols the jurisdictional boundaries between the Community and Member States.

This era passed with the shift to majority voting after the entry into force of the SEA and the seeds – indeed, the buds – of crisis became visible.[127] It became a matter of time before one of the national courts would defy the ECJ on this issue. Member States would become aware that, in a process that gives them neither *de jure* nor *de facto* veto power, the question of jurisdictional lines has become crucial. The Maastricht Decision of the German Federal Constitutional Court fulfilled this prediction, albeit later than anticipated.

Of course, the German decision is an egregious violation of the Treaty – ironically, especially if understood in classical international legal terms. But this view is grounded in the classical, hierarchical, centrist view of the European legal order. How should one evaluate this development given the questions concerning the normative authority of European constitutionalism and a more horizontal, conversation-based view of that very same constitutionalism?

Somewhat inappropriately, given the conversation metaphor, we want to use some of the dynamics of the Cold War as a device for evaluating the judicial *Kompetenz-Kompetenz* aspect of the Maastricht Decision of the German Federal Constitutional Court.

According to this analogy, the German decision is not an official declaration of war, but the commencement of a cold war with its paradoxical guarantee of co-existence following the infamous MAD (Mutual Assured Destruction) logic. For the German Court actually to declare a Community norm unconstitutional, rather than simply threaten to do so, would be an extremely hazardous move so as to make its usage unlikely. The use of tactical nuclear weapons was always considered to carry the risk of creating a nuclear domino effect. If other Member State courts followed the German lead, or if other Member State legislatures or governments were to suspend implementation of the norm on some reciprocity rationale, a real constitutional crisis would arise in the Community – the legal equivalent of the "empty chair" political stand-off in the 1960s.[128] It would be hard for the German government to remedy the situation, especially if the German Court decision enjoyed general public

---

[127] See chapter 2, pp. 66–74 above.

[128] Weiler, Haltern and Mayer, "European Democracy and Its Critique."

popularity. Would the German Federal Constitutional Court be willing to face the responsibility of dealing such a blow to European integration, rather than just threatening to do so?

Maybe not, but the logic of the Cold War is that each side has to assume the worst and to arm as if the other side would actually deal the first blow. The ECJ would then have to watch over its shoulder the whole time, trying to anticipate any potential move by the German Federal Constitutional Court.

If we now abandon the belligerent metaphor, it could be argued that this situation is not *per se* unhealthy. The German move is an insistence on a more polycentered view of constitutional adjudication and will eventually force a more even conversation between the European Court and its national constitutional counterparts. We would suggest that, in some ways, the German move of the 1990s in relation to competences resembles their prior move in relation to human rights.[129] It was only that move which forced the ECJ to take human rights seriously.[130] The current move could also force the ECJ to take competences seriously.

This view is not without its functional problems.

1. There is no "non-proliferation treaty" in the Community structure. MAD works well, perhaps, in a situation of two superpowers. But there must be a real fear that other Member State Courts will follow the German lead in rejecting the exclusive *Kompetenz-Kompetenz* of the ECJ. The more courts adopt the weapon, the greater the chances that it will be used. Once that happens, it will become difficult to push the paste back into the tube.

2. Courts are not the principal Community players. But this square-off will have negative effects on the decision-making process of the Community. The German government and governments whose courts will follow the German lead, will surely be tempted to play that card in negotiation ("We really cannot compromise on this point, since our Court will strike it down").

Here, too, we find an interesting paradox. The consistent position of the ECJ, as part of its constitutional architecture, has been that it alone has judicial *Kompetenz-Kompetenz* because the jurisdictional limits of the Community are a matter of interpretation of the Treaty. The German Federal Constitutional Court, as part of its reassertion of national sovereignty and insistence of legitimization of the European construct through states' instrumentalities and the logic of public international law, has defied the

---

[129] See German Federal Constitutional Court, judgment of May 29, 1974, 37 BVerfGE 271 ("Solange I"); judgment of October 22, 1986, 73 BVerfGE 339 ("Solange II").

[130] *Cf.*, *in extensu*, Weiler and Lockhart, " 'Taking Rights Seriously.' "

ECJ. As we argued throughout this article, the internationalist logic claimed by the German Court negates its own conclusions. Surely, the reach of an international treaty is a matter of international law and depends on the proper interpretation of that treaty. Therefore, from the internationalist perspective, the ECJ must be the final umpire of that system.

If, however, the European polity constitutes a constitutional order as claimed by the ECJ, then this issue is far more nuanced. There has been no constitutional convention in Europe. European constitutionalism must depend on a common-law type rationale, one which draws on and integrates the national constitutional orders. The constitutional discourse in Europe must be conceived as a conversation of many actors in a constitutional interpretative community, rather than a hierarchical structure with the ECJ at the top. It is this constitutional perspective that, paradoxically, gives credibility to the claim of the German Court. A feature of neo-constitutionalism in this case would be that the jurisdictional line (or lines) should be a matter of constitutional conversation, not a constitutional *diktat*.

And yet, the solution offered by the German Federal Constitutional Court and endorsed by Schilling is no conversation either. Although the German Court mentions that these decisions have to be taken in co-operation with the ECJ, it reserves the last word to itself. A European *diktat* is simply replaced by a national one. And the national *diktat* is far more destructive to the Community, if one contemplates the possibility of fifteen different interpretations.

How, then, can one square this circle?

One possible solution is institutional and we would like to outline only its essential structure. We have proposed the creation of a Constitutional Council for the Community, modeled in some ways after its French namesake. The Constitutional Council would have jurisdiction only over issues of competences (including subsidiarity) and would decide cases submitted to it after a law was adopted but before coming into force. It could be seized by any Community institution, by any Member State or by the European Parliament acting on a majority of its Members. Its president would be the President of the ECJ, and its members would be sitting members of the constitutional courts or their equivalents in the Member States. Within the Constitutional Council, no single Member State would have a veto power. The composition would also underscore that the question of competences is fundamentally also one of national constitutional norms, but still subject to a Union solution by a Union institution.

We will not elaborate in this Article some of the technical aspects of the proposal. The principal merit of this proposal is that it addresses the concern over fundamental jurisdictional boundaries without compromising the constitutional integrity of the Community, as did the Maastricht Decision of the German Federal Constitutional Court. Since, from a material point of view, the question of boundaries has a built-in indeterminacy, the critical issue is not what the boundaries are, but who gets to decide. On the one hand, the composition of the proposed Constitutional Council removes the issue from the purely political arena; on the other hand, it creates a body which would, we expect, enjoy a far greater measure of public confidence than the ECJ itself.

10

TO BE A EUROPEAN CITIZEN: EROS AND CIVILIZATION

INTRODUCTION

THE CHALLENGING tensions between national consciousness and multi-cultural sensibility take place not only *within* the classical state but also at the transnational level, of which the European Union is one of the most developed. A focal point is the recent discussion concerning European citizenship. The 1992 Treaty of European Union (the Maastricht Treaty) introduced the concept. Its citizenship clause provided:

> Citizenship of the Union is hereby established. Every person holding the nationality of a Member State shall be a citizen of the Union.

The recent 1997 draft Amsterdam Treaty modified the Maastricht citizenship clause by adding the phrase:

> [c]itizenship of the Union shall complement and not replace national citizenship.

This is a trite, banal phrase. But it reflects a profound anxiety and offers a semantic device with which to address, analytically and normatively, some of the deepest dilemmas in constructing the ends and means of transnational integration within the framework of the European Union. One way of describing this essay is to say that in it I want to explore that anxiety and offer a normative interpretation of this provision: not what the provision means, but what it ought to mean.

But there is more to European citizenship (and to this essay). The ever-growing discussion on the politics of European citizenship has an exquisite Janus-like quality. For many, the concept is considered one of the least successful aspects of Maastricht, trivial and empty, and hence irrelevant. From this perspective, those who believe in it are engaged in wishful thinking and those who fear it suffer from paranoid delusion. On this view, the recent modification was another unnecessary and empty gesture placating dreamers and loonies. For others, European citizenship is an important symbol with far-reaching potential and dangers. The story of European integration is, after all, replete with ideas and policies which, at inception, seemed trivial and empty, but which later attained a life of their own. From this perspective the powers-that-be made a Pascal-like wager. Empty and irrelevant maybe. But why take risks?

The two views are not altogether contradictory and I wish to track and explain elements of both. I have no interest in making predictions about the future of the concept and its attendant policies. But to the extent that ideas and symbols shape attitudes and, maybe, even policy options, the discourse of European citizenship is important not only to the theory of European integration but also to its praxis. In this essay I build on work I have done in this field since 1995 though, in one fundamental respect – the articulation of the relationship between Member State nationality and Community citizenship – I have modified my earlier position significantly.

EUROPEAN CITIZENSHIP: DILEMMAS AND CONTRADICTIONS

With inimitable acerbity, Perry Anderson begins his essay, "Under the Sign of the Interim," as follows:

> Mathematically, the European Union today represents the largest single unit in the world economy. It has a nominal GNP of about $6 trillion compared with $5 trillion for the US and $3 trillion for Japan. Its total population, now over 360 million, approaches that of the United States and Japan combined. Yet in political terms such magnitudes continue to be virtual reality. Beside Washington or Tokyo, Brussels remains a cipher. The Union is no equivalent to either the United States or Japan, since it is not a sovereign state. But what kind of formation is it? Most Europeans themselves are at a loss for an answer. The Union remains a more or less unfathomable mystery to all but a handful of those who, to their bemusement, have recently become its citizens. It is well-nigh entirely arcane to ordinary voters; a film of mist covers it even in the mirror of scholars.[1]

And bemused they should be. It was Maastricht which bestowed the august title of "European citizen" on Member State nationals. Even the handful for whom the Union is, perhaps, less than an unfathomable mystery would have to admit to some perplexity at this new innovation. Citizens of the Union were to enjoy the rights conferred by the TEU and be subject to the duties imposed thereby. But the citizenship chapter itself seemed to bestow precious few rights, hardly any that were new, and some

---

[1] P. Anderson, "Under the Sign of the Interim," in P. Gowan and P. Anderson (eds.), *The Question of Europe* (Verso: London, New York, 1997).

explicitly directed at all residents and not confined to citizens. Even if we were to take the entire gamut of rights (duties are usually forgotten in most accounts of European citizenship) granted under the treaties to European citizens, we would be struck by the poverty of provisions normally considered as political and associated with citizenship. Thus, we find (unrealized) promises of true free movement and residence throughout the European Union situated uncomfortably with relatively trivial guarantees of political participation in local and European Parliament elections for those Community citizens taking advantage of those very partial freedoms. And whereas the discipline of a European Common Marketplace in which goods would circulate freely was long understood (even if resisted in practice) as necessitating a European Common External Tariff towards the rest of the world, the same logic – internal free movement and residence requiring a common European "membership" policy – has been rejected. European citizenship emphatically does not mean what it has come to mean in all federal states: a "communitarization" of the actual grant of citizenship or even a harmonization of Member State conditions for such grant. The exclusive gate-keepers remain the Member States.

The question of "added value" cannot but be raised: with very few exceptions, the rights (and duties) associated with European citizenship predated Maastricht. In the past they attached to nationals of the Member States. Given the way this saga has evolved, what if anything, we may ask, has been gained by adding a new concept, citizenship, to a pre-existing package of rights and duties rather than, as one may (or might) have expected adding new rights and duties to a concept? And the "What?" leads to a rather big "Why?" If the powers-that-be had, as is evident, no intention of substantially enlarging those rights and duties already attaching to nationals of their respective Member States, if they had no intention of making in relation to humans that critical move that was made in relation to goods, why do anything at all?

There are even deeper dilemmas than this political riddle. Citizenship and nationality are more than an element in the mechanics of political organization. We live in an era – perhaps the entire century – obsessed with questions of individual and collective identity. The treatment of the celebrated "other," the other in our selves, in our midst, and the other clamoring at our doors or shores is an issue extremely high on the public agenda in most European societies.

Interestingly, as we slouch towards a new *fin-de-siècle*, after close to fifty years of European integration, the captivating idea of nation and people have retained a surprising amount of their astonishing allure and grip on our collective psyches. And I do not only refer to the new found nationalisms in the "Alt-Neu" Europe of the East. Is the European debate in Great Britain really moved by economic differences on the desirability of EMU or, instead, by political differences concerning identity and control of national destiny? Was the debate over Maastricht in France (which split the electorate straight down the middle) or Denmark (who voted against) not about the same thing? And is it mere teasing to suggest that *fin-de-siècle* Vienna – *première edition, circa* 1900 – boasted a far more cosmopolitan *Geist* than its current miserable shadow 100 years later?

The fault lines of this debate are usually not about differences in the self-understanding of the nation and the state. Typically in these debates many of the integrationists proclaim, usually in good faith, to be deeply concerned with, and committed to, national identity and national welfare and all the rest. They simply argue that the European Union will enhance these goals and values rather than threaten them.

Despite this attachment, the *vocabulary* of citizenship/nationality/peoplehood, the classical concepts from the armory of statecraft and political theory which address these issues, the only ones we have, seem to provoke complicated reactions. The words – nation, people, citizenry – often strike us as cynical when uttered by our political masters ('The British people do not want ... ') pernicious when employed by the far right of Le Pen or Haider, and embarrassing when discussed in good society other than to denounce them. Who will admit to being a nationalist? The very word is pejorative. And in an environment which worships at the altar of multiculturalism, who will own up to a thick concept of peoplehood or even citizenship? And if one does own up it is only to imagine a society of "others." (How greedy and cruel of some – usually comfortably positioned – to rob the real "others" of their "otherness" by claiming that we are all "others.")

This ambivalence may explain why the introduction in the Treaty of Maastricht of a European citizenship has struck so many not simply as bemusing but as problematic. At one level and to some, it symbolized yet another bold encroachment on the national by its worst antagonist the supranational. At a deeper level, it seemed to be tinkering with one of the very foundations of European integration.

If, indeed, the traditional, classical vocabulary of citizenship is the vocabulary of the state, the nation and peoplehood, its very introduction into the discourse of European integration is problematic, for it conflicts with one of Europe's articles of faith, encapsulated for decades in the preamble to the Treaty of Rome. Mystery, mist and mirrors notwithstanding, one thing has always seemed clear: that the Community and Union were about "lay[ing] the foundations of an ever closer union among the *peoples* of Europe." Not the creation of one people, but the union of many. In that, Europe was always different from all federal states which, whether in the USA, Germany, Australia, and elsewhere, whilst purporting to preserve all manner of diversity, real and imaginary, always insisted on the existence of a single people at the federal level. The introduction of citizenship understood in its classical vocabulary could mean, then, a change in the very *telos* of European integration from a union among the peoples of Europe to a people of Europe. With the change of the *telos* would commence – some would hope, others fear – a process which would eventually result in people thinking of themselves of European in the same way they think of themselves today as French or Italian. Citizens of Europe would become, not only formally, but in their consciousness, European citizens.

The introduction of European citizenship to the discourse of European integration could, however, mean not that the *telos* of European integration has changed, but that our understanding of national membership has changed, is changing, or ought to change – possibilities that have been discussed widely at the national and European level, most recently in a comprehensive work by the British scholar, Jo Shaw.[2] It would be changing because of a change in our understanding of the state and the nation as well as a change in our self-understanding and our understanding of the self. If citizenship classically postulates a sovereign state, is it not anachronistic to introduce it in an age in which, as MacCormick has shown so lucidly, sovereignty itself has become fragmented and states constitutionally cannot even pretend to have control over their most classical functions: the provision of material welfare and personal and collective security?

Think, too, of the linguistic trio – "identity," "identical," "identify." Surely no self is identical to another. It is trite to recall that identity – in an age where for long "choice" has replaced "fate" as the foundation for self-understanding – is, to a large extent, a political and social construct which privileges one (or one set of) characteristics over all other, calls on the self to identify with that, and is then posited as identity. It is equally trite to recall that the modern self has considerable problems with the move from identical to identity to identify. I may be German, or Italian or French. But is that my identity? What about being male or female? Or a Stones lover or Beatles lover (Verdi or Mozart, if you wish)? As the referents of identity grow, would it not be more accurate, in relation to the self today, to talk of my *differentity*?

This construct should not be confused with multiculturalism; in some ways it is its opposite. Whether in the USA or Hungary the labeling of people as black, or white male, or Jew etc. as a basis for group political

---

[2] J. Shaw, "Citizenship of the Union – Towards Post-National Membership?" (Harvard Jean Monnet Working Paper 6/97, http://www.law.harvard.edu/Programs/JeanMonnet, 1997).

entitlement is the celebration of a bureaucratically sanctioned polity of "multicultural" groups composed of mono-culturally identified individuals – the antithesis of individual *differentity*.

Constructing, then, a new concept of citizenship around the fragmented sovereignty of the porous state and the fractured self of the individuals who comprise those "states" – citizenship as a hallmark of *differentity* – could have been and could still be a fitting project for Union architects. That would be the major challenge to the conceptualization of European citizenship. Especially, since accepting and celebrating the *differentity* of individuals offers a new lease of life to the nation – nationality becoming a legitimate rather than oppressive bond among the individuals comprising the nation.

Such an architecture will have to explore both the shape of the construct and the technologies to sustain it. In the remainder of this lecture I will explore some of the available approaches and will offer my own variant too.

THE AFFECTIVE CRISIS OF EUROPEAN CITIZENSHIP

As we shall see, the introduction of European citizenship was brought about by a deep sense of malaise and public disaffection with the European construct which threatened to undermine its political legitimacy. Understanding this disaffection is an important background to the subsequent unfolding saga of constitutional engineering.

The expressions of the disaffection were manifest in the reaction to the Treaty of European Union – a public reaction which ranged from the hostile through the bewildered to the indifferent. The discontent was not with the Treaty itself – it was with the condition of Europe itself. What accounts for this attitude, for this change in fortune towards the idea of European integration?

There is, first, what one could term the paradox of success. In its foundational period, the European construct was perceived as part of a moral imperative in dealing with the heritage of World War II. Governments and states may have been happily pursuing their national interest but the European construct could be cloaked with a noble mantle of a new-found idealism. Rendering war as neither possible nor thinkable and restoring economic prosperity in a framework of transnational social solidarity were key elements of that idealism. But once achieved, once you remove the moral imperative, it's politics as usual with the frustrating twist that in Europe you cannot throw the scoundrels out at election time. So you try and throw the whole construct out.

Arguably, public attitudes go even deeper than that. We come here to a more sobering consideration in this regard, whereby the European Union may be seen not simply as having suffered a loss of its earlier spiritual values, but as an actual source of social *ressentiment*. Here are the highlights of what surely deserves much more than this superficial summary. In his pre-choleric days, Ernst Nolte wrote a fascinating study on the origins of fascism in its various European modes. Consider, chillingly, the turn to fascism in Italy, France and Germany at the beginning of the twentieth century. In his profound comparative analysis of the cultural–political roots of the phenomenon, the common source was identified as a reaction to some of the manifestations of modernity.

At a pragmatic level, the principal manifestations of modernity were the increased bureaucratization of life, public and private; the depersonalization of the market (through mass consumerism, brand names and the like) and the commodification of values; the "abstractism" of social life, especially through competitive structures of mobility; rapid urbanization; and the centralization of power.

At an epistemological level, modernity was premised on, and experienced in, an attempt to group the world into intelligible concepts which had to be understood through reason and science – abstract and universal categories. On this reading, fascism was a response to, and an exploitation of, the angst generated by these practical and cognitive challenges. So far this is a fairly well-known story.

Eerily, at the end of the twentieth century, the European Union can be seen as replicating, in reality or in the subjective perception of individuals and societies, some of these very same features: it has come to symbolize, unjustly perhaps, the epitome of bureaucratization and, likewise, the epitome of centralization. One of its most visible policies, the Common Agricultural Policy, has had historically the purpose of "rationalizing" farm holdings which, in effect, meant urbanization. The single market, with its emphasis on competitiveness and the transnational movement of goods, can be perceived as a latter-day thrust at the increased commodification of values (consider how the logic of the Community forces a topic such as abortion to be treated as a "service") and depersonalization of, this time round, the entire national market. Not only have local products come under pressure, even national products have lost their distinctiveness. The very transnationalism of the Community, which earlier on was celebrated as a reinvention of Enlightenment idealism, is just that: universal, rational, transcendent, and wholly modernist.

To this sustained and never resolved angst of modernity we have new, *fin-de-siècle* phenomena as illuminated brilliantly by Brian Fitzgerald. To capture these phenomena, we can resort to what Jose Ortega y Gasset called *creencias* – the certainties of life which needed no proof – both in the physical and social world: water falls downward, there is a difference between machines and humans, higher forms of life differentiate by gender, etc. To the sustained challenge of modernity is added a profound shattering of the most fundamental *creencias* – deeper still, a shattering of the ability to believe in anything. It is worth tracing some of the manifestations of this process.

There is first, or was, for a sustained period in this century, the assault of the reductive social sciences. Not only are things not what they seem to be, but their reality always has a cynical malevolence. Public life and its codes mask power and exploitation; private life with its codes masks domination. By an inevitable logic this assault turned on itself, whereby the illumination brought by these insights was not a vehicle for liberation but in itself for manipulation. The epistemic challenge of post–modernism deepens the shattering. For, in the old, modernist perspectives, there was at least a truth to be explored, vindicated – even if that truth was one of power, exploitation and domination. One can find distasteful the post–modernist self–centered, ironic, sneering posturing. But, without adjudicating the philosophical validity of its epistemic claim, there is no doubt that the notion that all observations are relative to the perception of the observer, that what we have are just competing narratives, has moved from being a philosophic position to a social reality. It is part of political discourse: multiculturalism is premised on it as are the breakdown of authority (political, scientific, social) and the ascendant culture of extreme individualism and subjectivity. Indeed, objectivity itself is considered a constraint on freedom – a strange freedom, to be sure, empty of content. Finally, the shattering of so many *creencias* (of the notion of *creencia* itself) has found a powerful manifestation in the public forum: it is dominated by television which distrusts and, by its pandering, non–judgmental transmission or cheap moralization, itself undermines *creencias*. This occurs in a vertical forum in which each viewer is isolated and addressed alone, unable to hear and join the objections of other viewers. To the angst of modernity is added the end–of–century fragmentation of information, and the disappearance of a coherent worldview, belief in belief and belief in the ability to know, let alone control.

There are many social responses to these phenomena. One of them has been a turn, by many, to any force which seems to offer "meaning." Almost paradoxically, but perhaps not, the continued pull of the nation–state, and the success in many societies of extreme forms of nationalism (measured not only in votes and members but in the ability of those extreme forms to shift the center of the public debate) are, in part of course, due to the fact that the nation and state are such powerful vehicles in responding to the existential craving for meaning and purpose which modernity and post–modernity seem to deny. The nation and state, with their organizing myths of fate and destiny, provide a captivating and reassuring answer to many.

Here too the failure of Europe is colossal. Just as Europe fuels the angst of modernity it also feeds the angst of post-modernity: giant and fragmented at the same time, built as much on image as on substance, it is incomprehensible and challenges increasingly the *creencias* of national daily life. This is not to suggest that Europe is about to see a return to fascism, nor most certainly should this analysis, if it has any merit, give joy to *fin-de-siècle* chauvinists, whose wares today are as odious as they were at the start of the century. But it does suggest a profound change in its positioning in public life not, as in its founding period, as a response to a crisis of confidence, but fifty years later as one of the causes of that crisis.

In the realm of the symbolic, citizenship should reflect the ethos of the polity. If European citizenship should serve as an icon of identification, if this is what Europe has become – what is one identifying with? On this reading, the collective enterprise of constructing or redefining a European citizenship is part and parcel of constructing and redefining a European ethos. How disappointing to observe the response of the powers-that-be.

TO BE A EUROPEAN CITIZEN: THE OFFICIAL, BREAD-AND-CIRCUS VISION

There is a legend about the genesis of Article 8 according to which the issue of citizenship was far from the mind of the drafters of the TEU until the very last minutes when one prime minister (Felipe Gonzalez according to this legend), unhappy with the non-EMU parts of the Treaty, and conscious of the brewing legitimacy crisis in the European street, suggested that something be done about citizenship. A skeptical Intergovernmental Conference (IGC) quickly cobbled the citizenship "Chapter" in response. It is of course, a legend. IGCs do not happen in that way as pointed out in O'Leary's admirable new book.[3] But it *could* be true to judge from the content of Article 8.

As already mentioned, as is a commonplace, the treatment of European citizenship both in the TEU itself and, subsequently, by the institutions and the Member States of the Union, is an embarrassment. The seriousness of this notion – after all the cornerstone of our democratic polities – and its fundamental importance to the self-understanding and legitimacy of the Union are only matched by its trivialization at the hands of the powers-that-be. One has to believe that the High Contracting Parties understood

---

[3] S. O'Leary, *The Evolving Concept of Community Citizenship* (Kluwer: The Hague, Boston, London, 1996).

the fundamental nature of citizenship in redefining the nature of the Union – and it is this understanding, rather than misunderstanding, which led them to the desultory Article 8 and its aftermath. Which returns us to the "Why" question. Why, indeed, open Pandora's box at all?

The recently concluded IGC offers us two clear clues. In the Commission's input to the Reflection Group we find that, in the eyes of the Commission, the two key values which make Union citizenship most worthy and, thus, worth developing to the full are, first, that citizenship reinforces and renders more tangible the individual's sentiment of belonging to the Union; and, secondly, that citizenship confers on the individual citizen rights which tie him to the Union. It is endearing and telling that the Commission describes the relationship between Union and citizens using the terminology of ownership, and that it is the citizen which belongs to the Union. When the Irish Presidency put out its mid-term report on the IGC this Freudian *glissage* was corrected. It is Europe which belongs to citizens, we were assured this time in the very opening statement of the document. And this was followed by: "The Treaties establishing the Union should address their most direct concerns." These were then listed as respect for fundamental rights, full employment etc. This approach is followed through in the new Amsterdam Treaty. There is, on my reading, only a semantic difference in these two official statements which is echoed in similar statements from the Council and even the Parliament.

What is the political culture and ethos which explain a concept of citizenship which, for example, speaks of duties but lists none? Which speaks of the rights of citizens but not of empowering them politically? Which, in a dispiriting kind of Euro NewSpeak denies to all and sundry the nation-building aspect of European citizenship whilst, at the same time, appeals to a national understandings of citizenship expecting it to provide *emotional* and *psychological* attachments which are typical of those very constructs which are denied?

Is it the discourse of civic responsibility and consequent political attachment at all? Or is it not closer to a market culture and the ethos of consumerism? Is it an unacceptable caricature to think of this discourse as giving expression to an ethos according to which the Union has become a product for which the managers, alarmed by customer dissatisfaction, are engaged in brand development. Citizenship and the "rights" associated with it are meant to give the product a new image (since it adds very little in substance) and make the product ever more attractive to its consumers, to reestablish their attachment to their favorite brand. The Union may belong to its citizens but no more, say, than a multinational corporation belongs to its shareholders. The introduction of citizenship on this reading

333

is little more than a decision of the board voting for an increased dividend as a way of placating restless shareholders.

A word should be said about fundamental human rights and European citizenship. I myself will be arguing that human rights have an important place in the construction of a meaningful concept of European citizenship. But all too frequently in this discourse even human rights are commodified and represent just another goodie with which to placate a disaffected consumer of European integration. A first typical feature of most official discourse is the conflation of citizenship with (human) rights. This has become so natural that it seems both right and inevitable. I consider this conflation as part of the problem. If the problem is defined as alienation and disaffection towards the European construct by individuals and the medicine is European citizenship, an essential ingredient of this medicine becomes human rights, more rights, better rights, all in the hope of bringing the citizen "closer to the Union." Critically, the discussion is not about rights as, say, representing a cultural undertaking, as imposing a cost on a society which is committed to their respect, even as a duty and burden at the individual level, but as a need which has to be satisfied. Even more interesting, rights on this view are something that the Union grants and that individuals receive – a brutally honest image of the extant power relationship.

The official view is not only problematic in the way rights are conceived but also in the impact they are expected to have on individuals. On what basis is the claim made, again and again, that rights will make people closer to the Union? Even if there is some truth to that, the picture is, at a minimum, far more complex in the current European context.

I think rights do have that effect in transformative situations from, say, tyranny to emancipation. But that has long ceased to be the western European condition. Somewhat polemically, let me make three points to illustrate that the nexus rights–closeness is not nearly as simple as the IGC literature suggests.

1. Take, say, an Austrian or Italian national. Their human rights are protected by their constitution and by their constitutional courts. As an additional safety net they are protected by the European Convention on Human Rights and the Strasbourg organs. In the Community, they receive judicial protection from the ECJ using as its source the same Convention and the constitutional traditions common to the Member States. Many of the proposed European rights are similar to those which our citizen already enjoys in his or her national space. Even if we imagine that there is a lacuna of protection in the Community space, that would surely justify closing that lacuna – but why would anyone imagine in a culture of rights saturation, not rights deprivation, that this

334

would make the citizen any closer to the Community? Make no mistake: I do think the European human rights patrimony, national and transnational, has contributed to a sense of shared identity. But I think one has reached the point of diminishing returns. Simply adding new rights to the list, or adding lists of new rights, has little effect. Rights are taken for granted; if you managed to penetrate the general indifference towards the European construct by waving some new catalog or by broadcasting imminent accession to the ECHR, the likely reaction would be to wonder why those new rights or accession were not there in the first place.

2. For the most part rights set "walls of liberty" around the individual against the exercise of power by public authority. The rights culture, which I share, tends to think of this as positive. But, at least in part, at least psychologically, it might have the opposite effect to making the individual closer to "his" or "her" Union. After all, every time you clamor for more rights, which in this context are typically opposable against Community authorities, you are claiming that those rights are needed, in other words that the Union or Community pose a threat. You might be crying "wolf" to score some political point, or you may be right. Either way, if you are signaling to the individual that he or she needs the rights since they are threatened, it is not exactly the stuff which will make them closer to "their" Union or Community.

3. Finally, there is very little discussion of the divisive nature of rights, their "disintegration effect." Deciding on rights is often about deciding on some of the deepest values of society. Even though we blithely talk about the common constitutional traditions, there are sharp differences within that common tradition. Some of the rights highest on the Christmas list of, say, the European Parliament, noble and justified as they may be, could if adopted for the Community be celebrated by the political culture in some Member States and regarded with suspicion and worse in other Member States. Remembering the *Grogan* v. *SPUC* abortion saga, which the ECJ inelegantly, but perhaps wisely, ducked, will drive home this point.

Mine is not an anti-market view, the importance of which to European prosperity is acknowledged. But it is a view which is concerned with the degradation of the political process, of image trumping substance, of deliberative governance being replaced by a commodification of the political process, of consumer replacing the citizen, of a Saatchi and Saatchi European citizenship. To conceptualize European citizenship around needs (even needs as important as employment) and rights is an end-of-millennium version of bread-and-circus politics.

335

TOWARDS THE RECONSTRUCTION OF A EUROPEAN ETHOS

Do we need a European citizenship at all? The importance of European citizenship is a lot more than a device for placating an alienated populace. It goes to the very foundations of political legitimacy.

The European Union enjoys powers unparalleled by any other transnational entity. It is not a state but in its powers it is pretty close. It has, *inter alia*, the capacity

1. to enact norms which create rights and obligations both for its Member States and their nationals, norms which are often directly effective and which are constitutionally supreme;
2. to take decisions with major impact on the social and economic orientation of public life within the Member States and within Europe as a whole;
3. to engage the Community and, consequently, the Member States by international agreements with third countries and international organizations; and
4. to spend significant amounts of public funds.

Europe has exercised these capacities to a very considerable degree.

Whence the authority to do all this and what is the nature of a polity which has these powers? One place to look for the answer would be in international law: let us discard this as artificial and formalistic. International Law can neither explain nor legitimate the reality of Community life. If not that, then what?

In Western liberal democracies public authority requires legitimation through one principal source: the citizens of the polity. The deepest, most clearly engraved hallmark of citizenship in our democracies is that in citizens vests the power, by majority, to create binding norms, to shape the socio-economic direction of the polity, in fact, all those powers and capacities which, I suggested, the Union now has. More realistically, in citizens vests the power to enable and habilitate representative institutions which will exercise governance on behalf of, and for, the citizens.

Under our constitutional understanding of the Treaty, was that not what was achieved? I know that some believe this. Individuals as subjects? Lawyers recite dutifully that the:

> Community constitutes a new legal order . . . for the benefit of which the states have limited their sovereign rights, albeit within limited fields, and the subjects of which comprise not only Member States but also their nationals.

But note: individuals are subjects only in the *effect* of the law; very important to bringing cases before court. In this sense alone is it a new legal order. But you could create rights and afford judicial remedies to slaves.

336

The ability to go to court to enjoy a right bestowed on you by pleasure of others does not emancipate you, does not make you a citizen. Long before women or Jews were made citizens, they enjoyed direct effect.

Citizenship is not only about the politics of public authority. It is also about the social reality of peoplehood and the identity of the polity. Citizens constitute the *demos* of the polity – citizenship is frequently, though not necessarily, conflated with nationality. This, then, is the other, collective side of the citizenship coin. *Demos* provides another way of expressing the link between citizenship and democracy. Democracy does not exist in a vacuum. It is premised on the existence of a polity with members – the *demos* – by whom and for whom democratic discourse with its many variants takes place. The authority and legitimacy of a majority to compel a minority exists only within political boundaries defined by a *demos*. Simply put, if there is no *demos*, there can be no democracy.

But this, in turn, raises the other big dilemma of citizenship: who are to be the citizens of the European polity? How are we to define the relationships among them? A *demos*, a people, cannot after all be a bunch of strangers. Are we not back then to the changed *telos*, to nation-building and all that? How should we understand, then, and define the peoplehood of the European *demos* if we insist that the task remains the "ever closer union among the peoples of Europe"?

Are we then faced with a crucial choice: reject European citizenship and content yourself to living in a polity which may provide you with bread and circus a-plenty but which lacks the core of individual political dignity and public legitimation? Adopt European citizenship and fundamentally change the very *telos* of European integration from its unique concept of Community to, frankly, a more banal notion of nation-building? This is an unappealing choice.

In offering a resolution I want to bring together three elements:

1. I first want to re-articulate my understanding of the special nature – and identity! – of the European polity as encapsulated in the term "supranationalism." It is the central concept for understanding the ethos of Europe, a key in the understanding of citizenship. Mine, as will appear, is a politically conservative view since it insists not simply on the inevitability of the nation-state but on its virtues.
2. I will then restate the move of de-coupling nationality from citizenship, a key idea which Closa, O'Leary, Ingram, and others have helped explore in the context of European integration.
3. Finally I shall re-couple them but in a specific European geometry. This geometry reflects – as citizenship should – the unique supranational values of the polity.

In trying to explain the ways in which the Community is, or has become, supranational, most discussion over the years has tended, interestingly, to focus on its relation to the "state" rather than the "nation." This conflation of nation and state is not always helpful. Supranationalism relates in specific and discrete ways to nationhood and to statehood. To see the relationship between supranationalism, nationhood and statehood, I propose to focus in turn on nationhood and statehood and try and explore their promise and their dangers.

First, then, nationhood. I have culled here, without doing any justice to the originals, from some of the old and new masters, Herder and Mazzini, Berlin, Arendt and Gelner, A. D. Smith and Tamir. It seems to me that, at least in its nineteenth-century liberal conception, two deep human values are said to find expression in nationhood: belongingness and originality. (It should immediately be stated that nationhood is not the only social form in which these values may find expression.) Belongingness is inherent in nationhood; nationhood is a form of belonging. Nationhood is not an instrument to obtain belongingness, it *is* it.

What are the values embedded in belonging, in national belonging, beyond the widely shared view that belonging is pleasant, is good? We can readily understand a certain basic appeal to our human species which is, arguably, inherently social: the appeal that family and tribe have, too. Part of the appeal is, simply, the provision of a framework for social interaction. But surely one has to go beyond that: after all, much looser social constructs than nationhood, let alone tribe and family, could provide that framework. Belonging means, of course, more than that. It means a place, a social home.

The belonging of nationhood is both like and unlike the bonds of blood in family and tribe and in both this likeness and unlikeness we may find a clue to some of its underlying values.

It is like the "bonds of blood" in family and tribe in that those who are of the nation have their place, are accepted, belong, independently of their achievements — by just being — and herein lies the powerful appeal (and terrible danger) of belonging of this type — it is a shield against existential aloneness. The power of this belongingness may be understood by the drama and awesomeness of its opposites: isolation, seclusion, excommunication.

But nationhood transcends the family and tribe, and maybe here lurks an even more tantalizing value: nationhood not only offers a place to the familyless, to the tribeless, but in transcending family and tribe it calls for loyalty — the largest coin in the realm of national feeling — towards others which go beyond the immediate "natural" (blood) or self-interested social unit. And, indeed, belongingness of this type is a two-way street. It is not only a passive value: to be accepted. It is also active: to accept. Loyalty is one of those virtues which, if not abused, benefits those on both the giving and receiving ends.

Ironically, the artificial belonging of nationality, once it sheds its ethnic and culturally repressive baggage, has an altogether more poignant meaning in the age of multiculturalism – its artificiality gives it its bridging potential.

This is the place to acknowledge, too, the virtues of autochthony – the nexus to place and land, the much maligned soil. Blood and soil have, of course, horrific associations which need no exploring here. But not only must we acknowledge the hold which the spatial has in conditioning perception, sensibility and, hence, identity. One must also realize the appeal and virtue of autochthony as an antidote to the fragmentation of the post-modern condition.

The other core value of nationhood, in some ways also an instrument for national demarcation, is the claim about originality. On this reading, the Tower of Babel was not a sin against God but a sin against human potentiality; and the dispersal that came in its aftermath, not punishment, but divine blessing. In shorthand, the nation, with its endlessly rich specificities, co-existing alongside other nations, is, in this view, the vehicle for realizing human potentialities in original ways, ways which humanity as a whole would be the poorer for not cultivating.

It is here that one may turn from the nation to the modern state. It is worth remembering at the outset that national existence and even national vibrancy do not in and of themselves require statehood, though statehood can offer the nation both intrinsic advantages, as well as advantages resulting from the current organization of international life which gives such huge benefits to statehood.

I would argue that in the modern notion of the European organiz-national nation-state, the state is to be seen principally as an instrument, the organizational framework within which the nation is to realize its potenti-alities. It is within the statal framework that governance, with its most important functions of securing welfare and security, is situated. The well being and integrity of the state must, thus, be secured so that these functions may be attained. That is not a meager value in itself. But to the extent that the state may claim, say, a loyalty which is more than pragmatic, it is because it is at the service of the nation with its values of belongingness and originality. (This conceptualization underscores, perhaps exaggerates, the difference with the American truly radical alternative liberal project of the non-ethno-national polity, and of a state, the republic, the organization of which, and the norms of citizenship behavior within, were central to its value system.)

It is evident, however, that in the European project, boundaries become a very central feature of the nation-state. There are, obviously, boundaries in the legal-geographical sense of separating one nation-state from another. But there are also internal, cognitive boundaries by which society (the nation) and individuals come to think of themselves in the world.

At a societal level, nationhood involves the drawing of boundaries by which the nation will be defined and separated from others. The categories of boundary-drawing are myriad: linguistic, ethnic, geographic, religious etc. The *drawing* of the boundaries is exactly that: a constitutive act, which decides that certain boundaries are meaningful both for the sense of belonging and for the original contribution of the nation. This constitutive element is particularly apparent at the moment of "nation-building" when histories are rewritten, languages revived etc. Of course, with time, the boundaries, especially the non-geographical ones, write themselves on collective and individual consciousness with such intensity that they appear as natural: consider the virtual interchangeability of the word international with universal and global; it is hard not to think, in the social sphere, of the world as a whole without the category of nation (as in international).

Finally, at an individual level, belonging implies a boundary: you belong because others do not.

As evident as the notion of boundaries is to the nation-state enterprise, so is the high potential for abuse of boundaries.

The abuse may take place in relation to the three principal boundaries: the external boundary of the state, the boundary between nation and state and the internal consciousness boundary of those making up the nation.

1. The most egregious form of abuse of the external boundary of the state would be physical or other forms of aggression towards other states.

2. The abuse of the boundary between nation and state is most egregious when the state comes to be seen not as instrumental for individuals and society to realize their potentials but as an end in itself. Less egregiously, the state might induce a "laziness" in the nation – banal statal symbols and instrumentalities becoming a substitute for truly original national expression. This may also have consequences for the sense of belonging-ness whereby the apparatus of the state becomes a substitute for a meaningful sense of belonging. An allegiance to the state can replace human affinity, empathy, loyalty, and sense of shared fate with the people of the state.

3 There can be, too, an abuse of the internal boundary which defines belongingness. The most typical abuse here is to move from a boundary which defines a sense of belonging to one which induces a sense of superiority and a concomitant sense of condescension or contempt for the other. A sense of collective national identity implies an other. It should not imply an inferior other.

340

The manifestations of these abuses are a living part of the history of the European nation–state which are so well known as to obviate discussion.

A central plank of the project of European integration may be seen, then, as an attempt to control the excesses of the modern nation–state in Europe, especially, but not only, its propensity to violent conflict and the inability of the international system to constrain that propensity. The European Community was to be an antidote to the negative features of the state and statal intercourse; its establishment in 1951 was seen as the beginning of a process that would bring about the elimination of these excesses.

Historically, there have always been those two competing visions of European integration. While no one has seriously envisioned a Jacobean-type centralized Europe, it is clear that one vision, to which I have referred as the unity vision, the United States of Europe vision, has really posited as its ideal type, as its aspiration, a statal Europe, albeit of a federal kind. Tomorrow's Europe in this form would indeed constitute the final demise of Member State nationalism replacing or placing the hitherto warring Member States within a political union of federal governance.

It is easy to see some of the faults of this vision: it would be more than ironic if a polity set up as a means to counter the excesses of statism ended up coming round full circle and transforming itself into a (super) state. It would be equally ironic if the ethos which rejected the boundary abuse of the nation–state gave birth to a polity with the same potential for abuse. The problem with this unity vision is that its very realization entails its negation.

The alternative vision, the one that historically has prevailed, is the supranational vision, the community vision. At one level aspirations here are both modest compared to the unity model and reactionary: supranationalism, the notion of community rather than unity, is about affirming the values of the liberal nation–state by policing the boundaries against abuse. Another way of saying this would be that supranationalism aspires to keep the values of the nation–state pure and uncorrupted by the abuses I described above.

But it is still a conservative modernist vision since it does not reject boundaries: it guards them but it also guards against them.

At another level the supranational community project is far more ambitious than the unity one and far more radical. It is more ambitious since, unlike the unity project which simply wishes to redraw the actual political boundaries of the polity within the existing nation–state conceptual framework, albeit federal, the supranational project seeks to redefine the very notion of boundaries of the state, between the nation and state, and within the nation itself. It is more radical since, as I shall seek to show, it involves more complex demands and greater constraints on the actors.

How, then, does supranationalism, expressed in the community project of European integration, affect the excesses of the nation-state, the abuse of boundaries discussed above? At the pure statal level, supranationalism replaces the "liberal" premise of international society with a community one. The classical model of international law is a replication at the international level of a liberal theory of the state. The state is implicitly treated as the analogue, on the international level, to the individual within a domestic situation. In this conception, international legal notions such as self-determination, sovereignty, independence, and consent have their obvious analogy in theories of the individual within the state. In the supranational vision, the community as a transnational regime will not simply be a neutral arena in which states will seek to pursue the national interest and maximize their benefits but will create a tension between the state and the community of states. Crucially, the community idea is not meant to eliminate the national state but to create a regime which seeks to tame the national interest with a new discipline. The challenge is to control at the societal level the uncontrolled reflexes of national interest in the international sphere.

Turning to the boundary between nation and state, supranationalism is meant to prevent abuses here, too. The supranational project recognizes that at an inter-group level nationalism is an expression of cultural (political and/or other) specificity underscoring differentiation, the uniqueness of a group as positioned *vis-à-vis* other groups, calling for respect and justifying the maintenance of intergroup boundaries. At an intragroup level nationalism is an expression of cultural (political and/or other) specificity underscoring commonality, the "sharedness" of the group *vis-à-vis* itself, calling for loyalty and justifying elimination of intragroup boundaries.

But, crucially, nationality is not the thing itself − it is its expression, an artifact. It is a highly stylized artifact, with an entire apparatus of norms and habits; above all it is not a spontaneous expression of that which it signifies but a code of what it is meant to give expression to, frequently even translated into legal constructs. Nationality is inextricably linked to citizenship, citizenship not simply as the code for group identity, but also as a package of legal rights and duties, and of social attitudes.

Supranationalism does not seek to negate as such the interplay of differentiation and commonality, of inclusion and exclusion and their potential value. But it is a challenge to the codified expressions in nationality. Since, in the supranational construct with its free-movement provisions which do not allow exclusion through statal means of other national cultural influences and with its strict prohibition on nationality/citizenship-based discrimination, national differentiation cannot rest so easily on the artificial boundaries provided by the state. At intergroup level, then, it pushes for cultural differences to express themselves in their authentic, spontaneous form, rather than the codified statal legal forms. At the intragroup level, it attempts to strip the false consciousness which nationalism may create instead of belongingness derived from a non-formal sense of sharedness. This, perhaps, is the first Kantian strand in this conceptualization of supranationalism. Kantian moral philosophy grounds moral obligation on the ability of humans not simply to follow ethical norms, but, as rational creatures, to determine for themselves the laws of their own acting and to act out of internal choice according to these norms. Supranationalism on our view favors national culture when, indeed, it is authentic, internalized, a true part of identity.

There is another, Enlightenment, Kantian idea in this discourse. Supranationalism at the societal and individual, rather than the statal level, embodies an ideal which diminishes the importance of the statal aspects of nationality – probably the most powerful contemporary expression of groupness – as the principal referent for transnational human intercourse. That is the value side of non-discrimination on grounds of nationality, of free-movement provisions and the like. Hermann Cohen, the great neo-Kantian, in his *Religion der Vernunft aus den Quellen des Judentums*, tries to explain the meaning of the Mosaic law which calls for non-oppression of the stranger. In his vision, the alien is to be protected, not because he was a member of one's family, clan, religious community or people, but because he is a human being. In the alien, therefore, man discovered the idea of humanity.

We see through this exquisite exegesis that in the curtailment of the totalistic claim of the nation-state and the reduction of nationality as the principal referent for transnational human intercourse, the Community ideal of supranationalism is evocative of, and resonates with, Enlightenment ideas, with the privileging of the individual, with a different aspect of liberalism which has as its current progeny our modern notions of human rights. In this respect the Community ideal is heir to Enlightenment liberalism. Supranationalism assumes a new, additional meaning which refers not to the relations among nations but to the ability of the individual to rise above his or her national closet.

And yet, at the same moment we understand one of the profound paradoxes of European integration. These very values, which find their legal and practical expression in, e.g., enhanced mobility, the breakdown of local markets, and the insertion of universal norms into domestic culture, are also part of the deep modern and post-modern anxiety of European belongingness and part of the roots of European angst and alienation. A meaningful concept of European citizenship must address this paradox.

TOWARDS A RECONSTRUCTION OF EUROPEAN
CITIZENSHIP: THREE VIEWS OF MULTIPLE *DEMOI*

How does the understanding of the paradox help us in the construction of
European citizenship and in the resolution of that tragic choice of preserving the European *telos* which opposes European peoplehood, without
comprising the necessity of a *demos* for a legitimate democracy? It is here
that I will try and give normative meaning to the citizenship clause in
Maastricht and Amsterdam:

> Citizenship of the Union is hereby established. Every person holding the
> nationality of a Member State shall be a citizen of the Union [Maastricht].
> Citizenship of the Union shall complement and not replace national citizenship
> [Amsterdam].

As mentioned, the introduction of citizenship to the conceptual world of
the Union could be seen as just another step in the drive towards a statal,
unity vision of Europe, especially if citizenship is understood as being
premised on a statal understanding of nationality. But there is another more
tantalizing and radical way of understanding the provision, namely as the
very conceptual decoupling of nationality from citizenship and as the
conception of a polity the *demos* of which, its membership, is understood in
the first place in civic and political rather than ethno-cultural terms. On
this view, the Union belongs to, is composed of, citizens who *by definition*
do not share the same nationality. The substance of membership (and thus
of the *demos*) is in a commitment to the shared values of the Union as
expressed in its constituent documents, a commitment, *inter alia*, to the
duties and rights of a civic society covering discrete areas of public life, a
commitment to membership in a polity which privileges exactly the
opposites of nationalism – those human features which transcend the
differences of organic ethno-culturalism. On this reading, the conceptualization of a European *demos* should not be based on real or imaginary trans-
European cultural affinities or shared histories nor on the construction of a
European "national" myth of the type which constitutes the identity of the
organic nation. European citizenship should not be thought of either as
intended to create the type of emotional attachments associated with
nationality-based citizenship. The decoupling of nationality and citizenship
opens the possibility, instead, of thinking of co-existing multiple *demoi*.

One view of multiple *demoi* may consist in what may be called the
"concentric circles" approach. On this approach one feels simultaneously as
belonging to, and being part of, say, Germany and Europe; or, even,
Scotland, Britain and Europe. What characterizes this view is that the sense
of identity and identification derives from the same sources of human

attachment albeit at different levels of intensity. Presumably the most intense (which the nation, and state, always claims to be) would and should trump in normative conflict.

The problem with this view is that it invites us to regard European citizenship in the same way that we understand our national citizenship. This was precisely the fallacy of the German Constitutional Court in its Maastricht decision: conceptualizing the European *demos* in the way that the German *demos* is conceptualized.

One alternative view of multiple *demoi* invites individuals to see themselves as belonging simultaneously to two *demoi*, based, critically, on different subjective factors of identification, in the way someone may regard himself or herself as being Irish and Catholic. I may be an Irish national in the in-reaching strong sense of organic-cultural identification and sense of belongingness. I am simultaneously a European citizen in terms of my European transnational affinities to shared values which transcend the ethno-national diversity.

On this view, the Union *demos* turns away from its antecedents and understanding in the European nation-state. But equally, it should be noted that I am suggesting here something that is different than simple American republicanism transferred to Europe. The values one is discussing may be seen to have a special European specificity, a specificity I have explored elsewhere, but one dimension of which, by simple way of example, could most certainly be that strand of mutual social responsibility embodied in the ethos of the welfare state adopted by all European societies and by all political forces. Human rights as embodied in the European Convention on Human Rights would constitute another strand in this matrix of values as would, say, the ban on discrimination on grounds of nationality and all the rest.

But this view, too, has its problems. In the first place, it is not clear how this matrix of values would be qualitatively different from the normal artifacts of constitutional democracy practiced in most European nation-states. After all, all of them are signatories to the European Convention on Human Rights, all of them, to varying degrees share in those "European values." Secondly, a community of values expressed in these terms provides a rather thin, even if laudable, content to the notion of citizenship.[4] And as A. N. Smith convincingly argues, without resonant fiction of relatedness through memory, and myth and history and/or real kinship, a real sense of membership is hard to come by.[5] It is noticeable that even national polities

---

[4] *Cf.* Ladeur, "Towards a Legal Theory of Supranationality – The Viability of the Network Concept," *European Law Journal* 3 (1997), 33.

[5] Smith, "National Identity and the Idea of European Unity," *International Affairs* 68 (1992), 55.

who supposedly understand themselves as communities of values, such as France or the United States, cannot avoid in their evolution, self-understanding and even self-definition many of the features of communities of fate.

I want to offer a third version of the multiple *demoi*, one of true variable geometry. It is like the second version in one crucial respect: it too invites individuals to see themselves as belonging simultaneously to two *demoi*, based, critically, on different subjective factors of identification. And in this version too the invitation is to embrace the national in the in-reaching strong sense of organic-cultural identification and belongingness and to embrace the European in terms of European transnational affinities to shared values which transcend the ethno-national diversity.

But there are, too, critical differences. One can be Irish without being Catholic. One can be Catholic without being Irish. In this model of European citizenship, the concepts of Member State nationality and European citizenship are totally interdependent. One cannot, conceptually and psychologically (let alone legally), be a European citizen without being a Member State national. It is in this respect the mirror of my analysis of supranationalism itself, which, as I was at pains to argue, had no ontological independence but was part and parcel of the national project, in some way its gate-keeper.

There is a second critical difference to this model of multiple *demoi*: its matrix of values is not simply the material commitment to social solidarity, to human rights and other such values which, as I argued, would hardly differentiate it from the modern constitutional, western European liberal state. It has a second important civilizatory dimension. It is the acceptance by its members that in a range of areas of public life, one will accept the legitimacy and authority of decisions adopted by fellow European citizens in the realization that in these areas preference is given to choices made by the out-reaching, non-organic *demos*, rather than by the in-reaching one. The treaties on this reading would have to be seen not only as an agreement among states (a union of states) but as a "social contract" among the nationals of those states – ratified in accordance with the constitutional requirements in all Member States – that they will in the areas covered by the treaty regard themselves as associating as citizens in a broader society. But crucially, this view preserves the boundaries, preserves the Self and preserves the Other. But it attempts to educate the I to reach to that Other. We can go even further. In this polity, and to this *demos*, one cardinal value is precisely that there will not be a drive towards, or an acceptance of, an overarching organic-cultural national identity displacing those of the Member States. Nationals of the Member States are European citizens, not the other way around. Europe is "not yet" a *demos* in the organic national-

346

cultural sense and should never become one. The value matrix has, thus, two civilizing strands: material and processual. The first subordinates the individual and the national society to certain substantive values. The second subordinates them to the discipline of decisional procedures representing a range of interests and sensibilities going beyond the national polity. Naturally, the two are connected. We are willing to submit aspects of our social ordering to a polity composed of "others" precisely because we are convinced that in some material sense they share our basic values. It is a construct which is designed to encourage certain virtues of tolerance and humanity.

One should not get carried away with this construct. Note first that the Maastricht formula does not imply a full decoupling: Member States are free to define their own conditions of membership and these may continue to be defined in national terms. But one should not read this construct as embracing an unreconstructed notion of nationalism within each Member State. As I have already argued, a nationalism which seeks to overwhelm the self has been a major source of bigotry and prejudice. A nationalism which acknowledges the multicultural self can be a positive unifying concept. On this reading European citizenship as a reflection of supranationalism can be regarded as part of the liberal nation project. That, in my view, is the greatest promise of introducing supranational citizenship into a construct the major components of which continue to be states and nations. The national and the supranational encapsulate on this reading two of the most elemental, alluring and frightening social and psychological poles of our cultural heritage. The national is Eros: reaching back to the pre-modern, appealing to the heart with a grasp on our emotions, and evocative of the romantic vision of creative social organization as well as responding to our existential yearning for a meaning located in time and space. The nation, through its myths, provides a past and a future. And it is always a history and a destiny in a place, in a territory, a narrative that is fluid and fixed at the same time. The dangers are self-evident. The supranational is civilization: confidently modernist, appealing to the rational within us and to Enlightenment neo-classical humanism, taming that Eros. Importantly, the relationship is circular – for its very modernism and rationalism is what, as I sought to show earlier, is alienating, and would have but an ambivalent appeal if it were to represent alone the content of European identity.

Martin Heidegger is an unwitting ironic metaphor for the difficulty of negotiating between these poles earlier in this century. His rational, impersonal critique of totalistic rationality and of modernity remain a powerful lesson to this day; but equally powerful is the lesson from his fall: an irrational, personal embracing of an irrational, romantic pre-modern nationalism run amok.

For some, European citizenship is an icon signifying the hope of transcending state and national society altogether. For others it is no more than a symbol for the demise of the classical European nation-state in the bureaucratic, globalized market. For others still it is the icon of a shrewd, Machiavelli-like scheme of self-preservation of the same statal structure which has dominated Europe for a century and more. Finally, it could be regarded as emblematic of that new liberal effort which seeks to retain the Eros of the national, its demonic aspects under civilizatory constraints.

DEMOCRACY AND EUROPEAN CITIZENSHIP: THE SECOND IMPERATIVE

The discourse of democracy, too, takes an additional significance in this context. The primary imperative of democracy in Europe is in bestowing legitimacy on a "formation" – the Union – which, want it or not, exercises manifold state functions. It was this imperative from which the search for *demos* and European citizenship emerged. But now we have seen that our construct of European citizenship was also seen as having a particular supranational, educational, civilizing function, by submitting certain aspects of our national autonomy to a community which in significant aspects is a community of "others." But the civilizing impulse would, surely, be lost if in the Community decisional process, the individual became totally lost, and instead of a deliberative engagement across differences we had bureaucratic subordination.

The question remains then, what, if anything, can be done to operationalize and particularly empower individuals in Europe in their capacity as citizens. This is not the place to rehearse the full litany of the European democratic deficit. But clearly, on any reading, as the Community has grown in size, in scope, in reach and despite a high rhetoric including the very creation of "European citizenship," there has been a distinct disempowerment of the individual European citizen, the specific gravity of whom continues to decline as the Union grows. The roots of disempowerment are many but three stand out.

1. First is surely the inability of the Community and Union to develop structures and processes which adequately replicate at the Community level the habits of governmental control, parliamentary accountability and administrative responsibility which are practiced with different modalities in the various Member States. Further, as more and more functions move to Brussels, the democratic balances within the Member States have been disrupted by a strengthening of the ministerial and executive branches of government. The value of each individual in the

political process has inevitably declined including the ability to play a meaningful civic role in European governance.

2. The second root goes even deeper and concerns the ever-increasing remoteness, opaqueness, and inaccessibility of European governance. An apocryphal statement usually attributed to Jacques Delors predicts that by the end of the decade 80 percent of social regulation will issue from Brussels. We are on target. The drama lies in the fact that no accountable public authority has a handle on these regulatory processes. Not the European Parliament, not the Commission, not even the governments. The press and other media, a vital estate in our democracies, are equally hampered. Consider that it is even impossible to get from any of the Community institutions an authoritative and mutually agreed statement of the mere number of committees which inhabit that world of comitology. Once there were those who worried about the supranational features of European integration. It is time to worry about infranationalism – a complex network of middle-level national administrators, Community administrators and an array of private bodies with unequal and unfair access to a process with huge social and economic consequences to everyday life – in matters of public safety, health, and all other dimensions of socio-economic regulation. Transparency and access to documents are often invoked as a possible remedy to this issue. But if you do not know what is going on, which documents will you ask to see? Neither strengthening the European Parliament nor national parliaments will do much to address this problem of post-modern governance which itself is but one manifestation of a general sense of political alienation in most Western democracies.

3. Another issue relates to the competences of the Union and Community. In one of its most celebrated cases in the early 1960s the European Court of Justice described the Community as a "new legal order for the benefit of which the States have limited their sovereign rights, albeit in limited fields." There is a widespread anxiety that these fields are limited no more. Indeed, not long ago a prominent European scholar and judge has written that there "simply is no nucleus of sovereignty that the Member States can invoke, as such, against the Community."

We should not, thus, be surprised by a continuing sense of alienation from the Union and its institutions.

ENHANCING TRANSNATIONAL DEMOCRACY

I want to conclude by discussing some proposals concerning the technology of transnational democracy. It is not, of course, my contention that such proposals would actually solve the vexed problems of the European democracy deficit. They are intended as illustrations, taken from a wide-ranging study on European governance submitted to the European Parliament,[6] of the type of mechanisms which focus specifically on the transnational dimension of democratic governance. In my view, each one of them means a great deal more than, say, the extension of co-decision in the Amsterdam Treaty hailed by some as a major achievement for democracy in Europe.

Proposal 1: The European legislative ballot

The democratic tradition in most Member States is one of representative democracy. Our elected representatives legislate and govern in our name. If we are unsatisfied we can replace them at election time. Recourse to forms of direct democracy – such as referenda – are exceptional. Given the size of the Union referenda are considered particularly inappropriate.

However, the basic condition of representative democracy is, indeed, that at election time the citizens "can throw the scoundrels out," that is replace the government. This basic feature of representative democracy does not exist in the Community and Union. The form of European governance is – and will remain for a considerable time – such that there is no "government" to throw out. Even dismissing the Commission by Parliament (or approving the appointment of the Commission President) is not the equivalent of throwing the government out. There is no civic act of the European citizen whereby he or she can influence directly the outcome of any policy choice facing the Community and Union as citizens can when choosing between parties which offer sharply distinct programs. Neither elections to the European Parliament nor elections to national parliaments fulfill this function in Europe. This is among the reasons why turn-out to European Parliamentary elections has been traditionally low and why these elections are most commonly seen as a mid-term judgment of the Member State governments rather than a choice on European governance.

The proposal is to introduce some form of direct democracy at least until such time as one could speak of meaningful representative democracy at the European level. My proposal is for a form of a Legislative Ballot Initiative coinciding with elections to the European Parliament. My proposal is allow the possibility, when enough signatures are collected in, say, more than five Member States, to introduce legislative initiatives to be voted on by citizens

---

[6] J. H. H. Weiler, Alexander Ballmann, Ulrich Haltern, Herwig Hofmann, Franz Mayer, and Sieglinde Schreiner-Linford, "Certain Rectangular Problems of European Integration" (Project IV/95/02, Directorate General for Research, European Parliament, http://www.iue.it/AEL/EP/pp.html, 1996).

when European elections take place (and, after a period of experimentation, possibly at other intervals too). In addition to voting for their MEPs, the electorate will be able to vote on these legislative initiatives. Results would be binding on the Community institutions and on Member States. Initiatives would be, naturally, confined to the sphere of application of Community law i.e., in areas where the Community institutions could have legislated themselves. Such legislation could be overturned by a similar procedure or by a particularly onerous legislative Community process. The Commission, the Council, the Parliament or a national parliament could refer a proposed initiative to the European Court of Justice to determine – in an expedited procedure – whether the proposed ballot initiative is within the competences of the Community or is in any other way contrary to the Treaty. In areas where the Treaty provides for majority voting the ballot initiative will be considered as adopted when it wins a majority of votes in the Union as a whole as well as within a majority of Member States (other formulae could be explored). Where the Treaty provides for unanimity a majority of voters in the Union would be required as well as winning in all Member States.

Apart from enhancing symbolically and tangibly the voice of individuals *qua* citizens, this proposal would encourage the formation of true European parties as well as the transnational mobilization of political forces. It would give a much higher European political significance to elections to the European Parliament. It would represent a first important step, practical and symbolic, to the notion of European citizenship and civic responsibility.

Proposal 2: Lexcalibur – The European Public Square

This would be the single most important and far-reaching proposal which would have the most dramatic impact on European governance. It does not require a Treaty amendment and can be adopted by an Inter-Institutional Agreement among the Commission, the Council and the Parliament. It could be put in place in phases after a short period of study and experimentation and be fully operational within, I estimate, two to three years. I believe that if adopted and implemented it will, in the medium and long term, have a greater impact on the democratization and transparency of European governance than any other single proposal currently under discussion.

I am proposing that, with few exceptions, the entire decision-making process of the Community, especially but not only comitology, be placed on the internet. For convenience I have baptized the proposal: *Lexcalibur –* The European Public Square.

I should immediately emphasize that what I have in mind is a lot more than simply making certain laws or documents such as the *Official Journal* more accessible through electronic databases. I should equally emphasize that this proposal is without prejudice to the question of confidentiality of process and secrecy of documents. As shall transpire, under my proposal documents or deliberations which are considered too sensitive to be made public at any given time could be shielded behind "fire-walls" and made inaccessible to the general public. Whatever policy of access to documentation is adopted, it could be implemented on *Lexcalibur*.

The key organizational principle would be that each Community decision-making project intended to result in the eventual adoption of a Community norms would have a "decisional web site" on the Internet within the general *Lexcalibur* home page which would identify the scope and purpose of the legislative or regulatory measures; identify the Community and Member States persons or administrative departments or divisions responsible for the process; specify the proposed and actual timetable of the decisional process so that one would know at any given moment the progress of the process; permit access to all non-confidential documents which are part of the process; and under carefully designed procedures directly submit input into the specific decisional process. But it is important to emphasize that my vision is *not* one of "virtual government" which will henceforth proceed electronically. The *primary locus* and mode of governance would and should remain intact: political institutions, meetings of elected representative and officials, Parliamentary debates, media reporting – as vigorous and active a Public Square as it is possible to maintain, and a European civic society of real human beings. The huge potential importance of *Lexcalibur* would be in its *secondary effect*: it would enhance the potential of all actors to play a much more informed, critical and involved role in the primary Public Square. The most immediate direct beneficiaries of Euro-governance on the internet would in fact be the media, interested pressure groups, NGOs and the like. Of course "ordinary citizens" would also have a much more direct mode to interact with the process of government. Providing a greatly improved system of information would, however, only be a first step of a larger project. It would serve as the basis for a system that allows widespread participation in policy-making processes so that European democracy becomes altogether more accessible through the posting of comments and the opening of a dialogue between the Community institutions and interested private actors. The Commission already now sometimes invites e-mail comments on its initiatives. Such a system obviously needs a clear structure in order to allow a meaningful and effective processing of incoming information for Community institutions. Conceivable would be, for example, a two-tier system, consisting of a forum with limited access for an interactive exchange between Community institutions and certain private actors and an open forum where all interested actors can participate and discuss Community policies with each other. This would open the unique opportunity for deliberations of citizens and interest groups beyond the traditional frontiers of the nation-state, without the burden of high entry costs for the individual actor.

Hugely important, in my view, will be the medium and long term impact on the young generation, our children. For this generation, the internet will be – in many cases already is – as natural a medium as to older generations were radio, television and the press. European governance on the net will enable them to experience government at school and at home in ways which are barely imaginable to an older generation for whom this New Age "stuff" is often threatening or, in itself, alien.

The idea of using the internet for improving the legitimacy of the European Union may seem to some revolutionary and in some respects it is. Therefore its introduction should be organic through a piecemeal process of experiment and reevaluation but within an overall commitment towards more open and accessible government. There are dimensions of the new Information Age which have all the scary aspects of a "Brave New World" in which individual and group autonomy and privacy are lost, in which humanity is replaced by "machinaty" and in which government seems ever more remote and beyond comprehension and grasp – the perfect setting for alienation captured most visibly by atomized individuals sitting in front of their screens and "surfing the net."

Mine is a vision which tries to enhance human sovereignty, demystify technology and place it firmly as servant and not master. The internet in my vision is to serve as the true starting point for the emergence of a functioning deliberative political community, in other words a European polity-cum-civic-society.[7]

Proposal 3: The European Constitutional Council

The problem of competences is, in my view, mostly one of perception. The perception has set in that the boundaries which were meant to circumscribe the areas in which the Community could operate have been irretrievably breached. Few perceptions have been more detrimental to the legitimacy of the Community in the eyes of its citizens. And not only its citizens. Governments and even courts, for example the German Constitutional Court, have rebelled against the Community constitutional order

---

[7] For those who wish to see what this might look, a simulation of *Lexcalibur* can be found on the internet at http://www.iue.it/AEL/EP/Lex/index.html.

because, in part, of a profound dissatisfaction on this very issue. One cannot afford to sweep this issue under the carpet. The crisis is already there. The main problem, then, is not one of moving the boundary lines but of restoring faith in the inviolability of the boundaries between Community and Member State competences.

Any proposal which envisages the creation of a new institution is doomed in the eyes of some. And yet I propose the creation of a Constitutional Council for the Community, modeled in some ways on its French namesake. The Constitutional Council would have jurisdiction only over issues of competences (including subsidiarity) and would, like its French cousin, decide cases submitted to it after a law was adopted but before coming into force. It could be seized by the Commission, the Council, any Member State or by the European Parliament acting on a majority of its members. I think that serious consideration should be given to allowing Member State parliaments to bring cases before the Constitutional Council.

The composition of the Council is the key to its legitimacy. Its President would be the President of the European Court of Justice and its members would be sitting members of the constitutional courts or their equivalents in the Member States. Within the European Constitutional Council no single Member State would have a veto power. All its decisions would be by majority.

The composition of the European Constitutional Council would, I believe, help restore confidence in the ability to have effective policing of the boundaries as well as underscore that the question of competences is fundamentally also one of national constitutional norms but still subject to a binding and uniform solution by a Union institution. It would underscore the interlocking variable geometry of the supranational construct.

I know that this proposal might be taken as an assault on the integrity of the European Court of Justice. That attitude would, in my view, be mistaken. The question of competences has become so politicized that the European Court of Justice should welcome having this hot potato removed from its plate by an *ex ante* decision of that other body with a jurisdiction limited to that preliminary issue. Yes, there is potential for conflict of jurisprudence and all the rest – nothing that competent drafting cannot deal with.

Proposal 4: Taxation and horizontal human rights

To raise the specter of direct European taxation is to feed the worst fears of the final collapse of national sovereignty. But from the perspective of citizenship the problem of the Union is, in some respect, one of representation (flawed, to be sure) with no taxation. The subjecthood of individuals as non-citizens is no more evident in the financing of the Union. Revenues derive from levies on imports and exports and, principally, from state transfers from VAT receipts. So, like the political process itself, though it is the money of individuals which the state collects, it is the money of the state which is transferred to the Union. One speaks of the British contribution or the Danish contribution to the European Union, even if, ultimately, it is money of individuals. What if Community financing or a portion of it derived directly from income tax and that portion would be designated as such – like social security contributions? This is a proposal which will be rejected by all concerned: the states because of the empowerment of the Union to levy direct taxation; the Union because it will fear the wrath of the taxpayers who might suddenly take an interest in the finances of the beast; the individual because they will, directly, have to shell out. But taxation, although levied on residents too, is a classical and meaningful artifact of citizenship: it instills accountability, it provokes citizen interest, it becomes an electoral issue, *par excellence*. It also established a duty – even an unpleasant one – towards the polity. Choosing between MEPs and parties will no longer be just an extension of local politics and national preferences.

Finally, there is one dimension where rights, in their positive law dimension, may be directly relevant to the discourse of citizenship. In the run-up to the IGC practically all institutions and parties interested in the IGC put on their Christmas lists, their pet rights. Parliament's resolution, for example, requested in tantalizingly non-committal language: "inclusion of an explicit reference in the Treaty to the principle of equal treatment irrespective of race, sex, age, handicap or religion, including mentioning the fundamental social rights of workers set out in the Charter, enlarging upon them and extending them to all citizens of the Union" etc. or, in equally ambiguous language, "the Treaty should contain a clear rejection of racism, xenophobia, sexism, discrimination on grounds of a person's sexual orientation, anti-Semitism, revisionism and all forms of discrimination and guarantee adequate protection against discrimination for all individuals resident within the EU."

The Treaty of Amsterdam, in extremely guarded language, allows the Council, acting unanimously and only within the powers conferred on the Community, to adopt measures designed to combat various forms of discrimination. The unmentioned default position of classic non-discrimination provisions is that they give guarantees against actions of Community authorities and, in some restricted circumstances elaborated by the ECJ, against Member State acts when the Member States are acting on behalf of the Community or acting in derogation of one of the four fundamental economic freedoms. Typically, the human rights apparatus does not apply horizontally as among individuals. Rights conceived in this way give but do not take from individual citizens. But the problems of racism, xeno-phobia and the like do not, on the whole, derive from acts of public authorities. The proposal I am suggesting is for the Council to target some of these rights, and model them on Article 119 by introducing legislation which would prohibit certain conduct among individuals in, say, the workplace, or other zones of commercial activities such as housing or employment. In this way, the right of the individual against public authority is converted into a duty towards other human beings. This would enrich the notion of a human right as part of citizenship (even if the duty extends to non-citizens as well) by asking something tangible of European citizens as part of that status.

It is no more appropriate to end this reflection on European citizenship with the grandiose concept than with the programmatic proposal. In some respects they are equally "unrealistic," equally bombastic. To its credit, I think, in the modern evolution of European integration ideas of both types have mattered. These are mine, for what they are worth.

FURTHER READING

I acknowledge a deep debt to the following works which contributed to the shaping of the thoughts expressed in this essay.

Arendt, H., *The Origins of Totalitarianism* (George Allen & Unwin: London, revised edition, 1967)

Bauböck, R., *Transnational Citizenship: Membership and Rights in International Migration* (Edward Elgar: Aldershot, 1994)

Boeckenfoerde, E. W., "Die Nation: Identität in Differenz," *Politische Wissenschaft* (1995), 974

Cartabia, *Cittadinanza Europea, Enciclopedia Giuridica* (Istituto della Enciclopedia Italiana: Rome, 1995)

Closa, "The Concept of Citizenship in the Treaty on European Union," *Common Market Law Review* 29 (1992), 1,137
  "Citizenship of the Union and Nationality of the Member States," *Common Market Law Review* 32 (1995), 487

Curtin, D., "The Constitutional Structure of the Union: A Europe of Bits and Pieces," *Common Market Law Review* 30 (1993), 17

D'Olivera, J. H. U., "European Citizenship: Its Meaning, Its Potential" in J. Monar, W. Ungerer and W. Wessels (eds.), *The Maastricht Treaty on European Union* (European Interuniversity Press: Brussels, 1993)

de Witte, "Community Law and National Constitutional Values," *Legal Issues of European Integration* (1991), 1

Evans, "Union Citizenship and the Equality Principle," in E. Antola and A. Rosas (eds.), *A Citizens' Europe: In Search of a New Legal Order* (Sage: London, 1995)

Fitzgerald, B., "The Future of Belief," *First Things* 63 (1996), 23

Gellner, E., *Nations and Nationalism* (Blackwell: Oxford, 1983)

Grimm, "Does Europe Need a Constitution?," *European Law Journal* 1 (1995), 282

Habermas, J., "Citizenship and National Identity," *Praxis International* 12 (1992), 1

"Comment on the Paper by Dieter Grimm: Does Europe Need a Constitution?," *European Law Journal* 1 (1995), 303

Ingram, "Separating State and Nation, State and Nation" (IUSEF No, 15. 1995), 33

Koessler, "Subject, Citizen, National, and Permanent Allegiance," *Yale Law Journal* 56 (1946), 58

Kymlicka, W., *Multicultural Citizenship* (Oxford University Press: Oxford, 1995)

MacCormick, N., "Sovereignty, Democracy and Subsidiarity," in Bellamy, R., Bufacchi, V., and Castiglione, D. (eds.), *Democracy and Constitutional Culture in the Union of Europe* (Lothian Foundation: London, 1995)

"Beyond the Sovereign State," *Modern Law Review* 56 (1990), 1

"The Maastricht-Urteil: Sovereignty Now" *European Law Journal* 1 (1995), 259

Meehan, E., *Citizenship and the European Community* (Sage: London, 1993)

O'Keeffe, D., "Union Citizenship," in O'Keeffe, D. and Twomey, P. (eds.), *Legal Issues of the Maastricht Treaty* (Chancery Press: London, 1993)

O'Leary, S., "Nationality and Citizenship: A Tale of Two Unhappy Bedfellows," *Yearbook of European Law* 12 (1984), 353

The Evolving Concept of European Citizenship (Kluwer: The Hague, London, Boston, 1996)

Preuss, U. K., "Problems of a Concept of European Citizenship," *European Law Journal* 1 (1995), 267

Shaw, "Citizenship of the Union – Towards Post-National Membership?" (Harvard Jean Monnet Working Paper 6/97, http://www.law.harvard.edu/Programs/Jean-Monnet)

Smith, "National Identity and the Idea of European Unity," *International Affairs* 68 (1992), 55

Soledad, G. (ed.), *European Identity and the Search for Legitimacy* (London, 1993)

Tamir, Y., *Liberal Nationalism* (Princeton University Press: Princeton, NJ, 1993)

INDEX

Index